THE FUTURE OF CONTRACT LAW IN LATIN AMERICA

This book presents, analyses and evaluates the Principles of Latin American Contract Law (PLACL), a recent set of provisions aiming at the harmonisation of contract law at a regional level. As such, the PLACL are the most recent exponent of the many proposals for transnational sets of 'principles of contract law' that were drafted or published over the past 20 years, either at the global or the regional level. These include the UNIDROIT Principles of International Commercial Contracts, the Principles of European Contract Law, the (European) Draft Common Frame of Reference and the Principles of Asian Contract Law.

The PLACL are the product of a working group comprising legal academics from Argentina, Brazil, Colombia, Chile, Paraguay, Uruguay and Venezuela. The 111 articles of the instrument deal with problems of general contract law, such as formation, interpretation and performance of contracts, as well as remedies for breach.

The book aims to introduce the PLACL to an international audience by putting them in their historical and comparative context, including other transnational harmonisation measures and initiatives. The contributions are authored by drafters of the PLACL and contract law experts from Europe and Latin America.

Volume 24: Studies of the Oxford Institute of European and Comparative Law

Studies of the Oxford Institute of European and Comparative Law

Recent titles in this Series

Volume 16: The Involvement of EU Law in Private Law Relationships
Edited by Dorota Leczykiewicz and Stephen Weatherill

Volume 17: Current Problems in the Protection of Human Rights: Perspectives from Germany and the UK
Edited by Katja S Ziegler and Peter M Huber

Volume 18: Legal Challenges in the Global Financial Crisis: Bail-outs, the Euro and Regulation
Edited by Wolf-Georg Ringe and Peter M Huber

Volume 19: The Unitary EU Patent System
Edited by Justine Pila and Christopher Wadlow

Volume 20: The EU Charter of Fundamental Rights as a Binding Instrument: Five Years Old and Growing
Edited by Sybe de Vries, Ulf Bernitz and Stephen Weatherill

Volume 21: The Images of the Consumer in EU Law: Legislation, Free Movement and Competition Law
Edited by Dorota Leczykiewicz and Stephen Weatherill

Volume 22: Passing Wealth on Death: Will-Substitutes in Comparative Perspective
Edited by Alexandra Braun and Anne Röthel

Volume 23: General Principles of Law: European and Comparative Perspectives
Edited by Stefan Vogenauer and Stephen Weatherill

The Future of Contract Law in Latin America

The Principles of Latin American Contract Law

Edited by
Rodrigo Momberg and Stefan Vogenauer

•HART•
PUBLISHING
OXFORD AND PORTLAND, OREGON
2017

Hart Publishing
An imprint of Bloomsbury Publishing Plc

Hart Publishing Ltd
Kemp House
Chawley Park
Cumnor Hill
Oxford OX2 9PH
UK

Bloomsbury Publishing Plc
50 Bedford Square
London
WC1B 3DP
UK

www.hartpub.co.uk
www.bloomsbury.com

Published in North America (US and Canada) by
Hart Publishing
c/o International Specialized Book Services
920 NE 58th Avenue, Suite 300
Portland, OR 97213-3786
USA

www.isbs.com

First published 2017

British Library Cataloguing-in-Publication Data
A catalogue record for this book is available from the British Library.

ISBN: HB: 978-1-50991-427-2
ePDF: 978-1-50991-426-5
ePub: 978-1-50991-429-6

Library of Congress Cataloging-in-Publication Data

Names: Momberg Uribe, R. A. (Rodrigo Andres), editor. | Vogenauer, Stefan, 1968-, editor.

Title: The future of contract law in Latin America : the principles of Latin American contract law / Edited by Rodrigo Momberg and Stefan Vogenauer.

Description: Portland, Oregon : Hart Publishing, 2017. | Series: Studies of the Oxford Institute of European and Comparative Law ; volume 24 | Includes bibliographical references and index. | Description based on print version record and CIP data provided by publisher; resource not viewed.

Identifiers: LCCN 2017018591 (print) | LCCN 2017020856 (ebook) | ISBN 9781509914296 (Epub) | ISBN 9781509914272 (hardback : alk. paper)

Subjects: LCSH: Contracts—Latin America.

Classification: LCC KG202 (ebook) | LCC KG202 .F88 2017 (print) | DDC 346.802/2—dc23

LC record available at https://lccn.loc.gov/2017018591

Typeset by Compuscript Ltd, Shannon
Printed and bound in Great Britain by TJ International Ltd, Padstow, Cornwall

To find out more about our authors and books visit www.hartpublishing.co.uk. Here you will find extracts, author information, details of forthcoming events and the option to sign up for our newsletters.

PREFACE

The harmonisation of contract law has long been discussed by private lawyers in Europe. The Oxford Institute of European and Comparative Law has been an active participant in this debate. The very first volume of its book series, the *Studies*, was a collection of essays on *The Harmonisation of European Contract Law*, published more than a decade ago. In recent years, the idea of regional harmonisation of contract law has spread to other parts of the world. The most prominent example in the southern hemisphere is a set of rules with the title *Principios Latinoamericanos de Derecho de los Contratos* (*Principles of Latin American Contract Law*, or 'PLACL').

The PLACL are the product of a working group of legal academics from Argentina, Brazil, Colombia, Chile, Paraguay, Uruguay and Venezuela. The 111 articles of the instrument deal with problems of general contract law, such as formation, interpretation and performance of contracts and remedies for breach. Like other instruments of their kind—the Principles of European Contract Law ('PECL') and the UNIDROIT Principles of International Commercial Contracts ('PICC') spring to mind—the PLACL are intended to be a non-binding set of 'soft law' rules. Work on the PLACL is still in progress; the most recent draft dates from 2014 and still awaits minor amendments. It is expected that a final version will be approved by the Drafting Group later this year.

To the comparative lawyer, the draft naturally invites comparative analysis. We therefore felt that the PLACL would be an excellent topic for one of the conferences that were held in the summer of 2015 in order to mark the twentieth anniversary of the Oxford Institute where we were both affiliated at the time. As a result, a sizeable group of private lawyers from Europe and Latin America met in the beautiful surroundings of Keble College on 25 June 2015 in order to examine and evaluate the draft provisions of the instrument. For those who wish to read a first-hand account of the proceedings, we refer to the conference reports by María Elisa Morales, (2015) 2 *Revista de Derecho Civil*, no 3, 221–25; Beatriz Gregoraci, (2015) LXVIII *Anuario de Derecho Civil* 1083–90; Pedro Rubim Borges Fortes, (2016) 24 *European Review of Private Law* 287–96 and Christina Ramberg, [2016] *Uniform Law Review* 129–36.

In collecting most of the conference papers, this volume aims to provide a comprehensive introduction to the PLACL and present them to an international—or, rather, non-Spanish speaking—audience for the first time. The text of the draft instrument is reproduced in an Appendix, both in the Spanish original and in an English translation. The first part of the book aims to situate the PLACL in the specific environment of Latin America and Latin American law. This not only calls for a look at the more recent process of harmonisation of private law in Latin America and the more than 25 years of experience with the Convention on Contracts for the International Sale of Goods ('CISG'), another instrument aiming at the harmonisation of contract law. It also requires us to go back further, mapping out the development of private law in the continent during the nineteenth and twentieth centuries more broadly. This might come as a bit of a surprise to some of our readers, given the explicit reference in the title of this book to the 'Future of Latin American Contract Law'. However, we are not able to fully understand the present, let alone predict the future, without knowing where we come from.

The second part of this volume then proceeds to a comparative analysis of particularly relevant issues of contract law, as dealt with in the PLACL: the general conception of contracts underlying the instrument and its rules on formation, defects of contract, performance and non-performance. The volume concludes with an overall assessment of one of the leading figures involved in the drafting of the first instrument to map out the harmonisation of contract law at a regional level—the PECL.

This book does not merely provide information on the PLACL. It also invites the reader to pause and reflect on the merits and demerits of harmonisation of contract law more broadly, and beyond the much-discussed European context. We hope, therefore, that it will not only be of interest to contract lawyers in Latin America but will also find an audience among all those who are concerned with the harmonisation of private law, in the European context and beyond, and comparative lawyers in general.

We are extremely grateful to the authors who contributed to this volume. This was a challenging project, not least for reasons of legal language and terminology. We are indebted to the John Fell Fund of the University of Oxford and the Max Planck Institute for European Legal History for their generous funding of the conference and the editorial work. Jenny Dix, the administrator of the Oxford Institute, steered us through the preparations for the conference in her usual calm and competent manner. The New York office of Linklaters LLP generously supported the translation of the PLACL into English: our thanks go to Adriana Maestas and Manuel Alcalde for providing an extremely fine piece of work and to Charles Clark and Conrado Tenaglia for making this possible in the first place. Patricia Nissing and Insa Jarass made considerable improvements to the manuscripts during the editorial process; John Cartwright, series editor of the *Studies*, and Sinead Moloney, Editorial Director and General Manager at Hart Publishing, supported this book project from the start—we are very grateful to all of them.

Rodrigo Momberg Uribe
Stefan Vogenauer
Valparaiso and Frankfurt
31 January 2017

CONTENTS

CONTRIBUTORS

Hugh Beale QC FBA is Professor of Law at the University of Warwick, Senior Research Fellow of Harris Manchester College and Visiting Professor at the University of Oxford, UK.

Jean-Sébastien Borghetti is Professor of Private Law at the Université Panthéon-Assas, Paris, France.

Gerardo Caffera is Assistant Professor of Private Law of the Universidad de la República, Montevideo, Uruguay.

John Cartwright is Professor of the Law of Contract at the University of Oxford and Tutor in Law at Christ Church, Oxford, UK; and Professor of Anglo-American Private Law at the University of Leiden, the Netherlands.

Sabrina Lanni is Professor of Comparative Private Law at the Department of Legal, Historical, Economic and Social Studies, University 'Magna Graecia', Catanzaro, Italy.

Iñigo de la Maza Gazmuri is Professor of Civil Law at Universidad Diego Portales, Santiago, Chile.

Rodrigo Momberg is Professor of Private Law at the Faculty of Law of the Catholic University of Valparaíso, Chile.

Agustín Parise is Assistant Professor of Law at the Faculty of Law of Maastricht University, the Netherlands.

Pilar Perales Viscasillas is Professor of Commercial Law at University Carlos III of Madrid, Spain.

Carlos Pizarro Wilson is Professor of Civil Law at Universidad Diego Portales, Santiago, Chile.

Jan Peter Schmidt is a Senior Research Fellow at the Max Planck Institute for Comparative and International Private Law, Hamburg, Germany.

Stefan Vogenauer is Director of the Max Planck Institute for European Legal History, Frankfurt, Germany.

CONTRIBUTORS

TABLE OF CASES

United States

TABLE OF LEGISLATION AND RELATED INSTRUMENTS

Argentina

Austria

Bolivia

Brazil

Chile

Costa Rica

Cuba

Dominican Republic

Ecuador

El Salvador

European

International

Italy

Louisiana

Mexico

Netherlands

Nicaragua

Panama

Paraguay

Peru

Portugal

Prussia

Puerto Rico

Spain

Venezuela

Part I

The Principles of Latin American Contract Law: History and Context

1

The Process of Harmonisation of Private Law in Latin America: An Overview

RODRIGO MOMBERG*

I. Introduction

Since the late twentieth century, the harmonisation of private law, in particular contract law, has been an issue both in academia and on the institutional agenda of different international organisations. The most salient examples at a global level have been the work developed by the United Nations Commission on International Trade Law (UNCITRAL) and the International Institute for the Unification of Private Law (UNIDROIT), with the United Nations Convention on Contracts for the International Sale of Goods (CISG) and the Unidroit Principles of International Commercial Contracts (PICC) as the most visible and influential outcomes. At a regional level, the process of harmonisation of private law in the European Union is by far the most relevant example.[1]

Following the European trend, harmonisation initiatives have been launched in other regions of the world. Thus, in Africa, the Organisation pour l'Harmonisation en Afrique du Droit des Affaires (OHADA), with 17 Member States, has adopted 10 Uniform Acts in different subjects of private law and is working on the drafting of a Uniform Act in the law of contract. More recently, a group of East-Asian academics have established a research team for the drafting of the Principles of Asian Contract Law.[2]

* This chapter is a revised and updated version of the paper 'Harmonization of Contract Law in Latin America: Past and Present Initiatives', published in [2014] *Uniform Law Review* 411–28.

[1] The last initiatives are the Proposal for a Directive on certain aspects concerning contracts for the supply of digital content, COM (20015) 634, and the Proposal for a Directive on certain aspects concerning contracts for the online and other distance sales of goods, COM (2015) 635.

[2] See S Han, 'Principles of Asian Contract Law: An Endeavor of Regional Harmonization of Contract Law in East Asia' (2013) 58 *Villanova Law Review* 589.

Until recently, Latin America has been absent from this trend. In this sense, one curious feature of Latin American law is that, despite the countries of the region admittedly sharing a common legal heritage, the degree of (formal) harmonisation between Latin American legal systems, especially in private law, is markedly low.[3]

This chapter intends to describe the past and current initiatives and efforts on the harmonisation of contract law in Latin America. A general overview of the Latin American system of private law is provided, with historical remarks about the codification process and later developments. Following this overview, the private international law initiatives of unification are described, providing also a brief summary of the regional Latin American integration efforts and their impact on the harmonisation of private law. An analysis of the most recent academic initiative of harmonisation is provided. Finally, some remarks about the future of harmonisation of private law in Latin America are expressed.

II. The Latin American Legal Family: Codification and Later Developments

Latin American law is without any doubt part of Western law. Moreover, Latin American jurisdictions are, to a great extent, civil law systems. Traditional comparative law places Latin America within the Romano-Germanic legal family, attached to the French group of influence.[4] Similarly, Zweigert and Kötz categorise Latin America in the Romanistic legal family, ie, those legal systems which adopted the French Civil Code as a main source of inspiration.[5]

However, the particularities of Latin American law have also been stressed, stating the existence of a Latin American law subsystem or even of a Latin American legal family.[6] Thus, the distinctive character of Latin American law has been recognised ever since the works of René David, who states that 'on est obligé de reconnaitre que, tout en appartenant au groupe du droit français, les droits de l'Amérique latine présentent certaines caractéristiques et particularités qui le sont propres', concluding that the Latin American legal system constitutes an original

[3] See A Garro, 'Unification and Harmonization of Private Law in Latin America' (1992) 40 *American Journal of Comparative Law* 587, stating that 'the civil and commercial codes of the Latin American countries share a general framework from which general principles on commercial contracts may be derived. Despite such favourable conditions, the Latin American experience in the unification of private law to date has not been very significant'.

[4] See R David, *Traité élémentaire du droit civil comparé: introduction à l'étude des droits étrangers et à la méthode comparative* (Paris, Librairie Générale de Droit, 1950).

[5] K Zweigert and H Kötz, *An Introduction to Comparative Law*, 3rd edn (trans T Weir, Oxford, Clarendon Press, 1998) 73.

[6] A Guzmán Brito, *Historia de la codificación civil en Iberoamérica* (Cizur Menor, Thomson Aranzadi, 2006) 187; D Fernández Arroyo, *La codificación del derecho internacional privado en América Latina* (Madrid, Beramar, 1994) 52–55.

category of the French legal family.[7] Similarly, Schipani recognises the existence of a Latin American legal system, different from the European legal families but inserted in the Roman law tradition.[8]

In this sense, as a general statement, it can be acknowledged that historically Latin American law is a product of comparative law. The codification process, broadly described in the following paragraphs, demonstrates the considerable use of comparative legal sources by the drafters of the codes.[9] Thus, the development of Latin American law has always been a mixture between multiple foreign influences and domestic idiosyncrasy, which has led to the configuration of a legal system with particular characteristics. This mixture has been described as the 'polycentric nature' of Latin American law, implying that Latin American legal culture has been influenced and shaped by a notable number of sources as well as by the mutual circulation of ideas between the countries of the region.[10] As a consequence, this openness has allowed the reception of legal ideas both from the major continental traditions and from the common law, in particular the United States. Therefore, the most influential Latin American codifications of the nineteenth century, namely the Civil Codes of Chile and Argentina, as well as the Brazilian Civil Code of 1916, can properly be considered as original works, like their European counterparts.

In any case, it cannot be denied that the French *Code civil* was the main source of inspiration for the drafters of Latin American codes. First, from a legal perspective, and because of its strong links with Roman law, it does not represent a complete break with the previous colonial sources such as *Las Siete Partidas* or the *Fueros*; and it was the only available model of a national and unified Code at that time.[11] Secondly, from a philosophical perspective, it was considered a reflection of the ideals of the French Revolution as individual freedom, equality under the law, private property and the separation of powers.[12] Finally in practical terms,

[7] David (n 4) 259 and 267.

[8] S Schipani, 'Armonización y unificación del derecho: derecho común en materia de obligaciones y contratos en América Latina' in D Fabio Esborraz (ed), *Cuadernos del curso de master en Sistema jurídico romanista y unificación del derecho en América Latina, Sistema Jurídico Latinoamericano y unificación del derecho* (Mexico, Ed. Porrua, 2006) 226.

[9] See J Kleinheisterkamp, 'Development of Comparative Law in Latin America', in M Reimann and R Zimmermann (eds), *The Oxford Handbook of Comparative Law* (Oxford, Oxford University Press, 2008) 274, describing the drafters of the Latin American Civil Codes as '*de facto* comparative scholars'.

[10] D López-Medina, 'The Latin American and Caribbean Legal Traditions' in M Bussani and U Mattei (eds), *The Cambridge Companion to Comparative Law* (Cambridge, Cambridge University Press, 2012) 360–61.

[11] Zweigert and Kötz (n 5) 113. The Prussian General Land Law of 1794 and the Austrian Civil Code of 1811 were also available at that time, but both were linked to absolute and monarchical regimes and had a level of conceptualism and abstraction which was not familiar to Latin American jurists. Further factors to exclude them as main sources of inspiration included their structure, with both instruments containing not only private law, but also public law provisions, and the volume of the Prussian General Land Law (almost 20,000 articles). See A Guzmán Brito, 'L'influence du code civil francais sur les codifications américaines' www.senat.fr/colloques/colloque_codification/colloque_codification.pdf.

[12] M Murillo, 'The Evolution of Codification in the Civil Law Legal Systems: Towards Decodification and Recodification' (2001) 11 *Journal of Transnational Law Policy* 1, 5.

it was easily accessible for Latin American jurists and for the elites who were at that time highly competent in French.[13] In this sense, it has been stated that 'the Napoleonic form of codification moreover provides common structures and common vocabulary throughout much of civil law America'.[14]

Nevertheless, the influence of the *Code civil* in the text of the Latin American codes of the nineteenth century was far from uniform. A group of early codifications can be considered as mere translations of the *Code civil*: Haiti (1825), Bolivia (1830 and 1845), Peru (1836), Costa Rica (1842) and the Dominican Republic (1845).

By contrast, in a second group of codifications, led by the Chilean Civil Code (1855), even when the *Code civil* and its comments were the main source of inspiration (especially with regard to the law of obligations), these codifications were far from being simple copies of the French model. In turn, they became original and modern instruments. Thus, Andrés Bello, the drafter of the Chilean Civil Code, substantially based his work not only on French law and doctrine, but also on Roman law (mainly the *Corpus Iuris Civilis* and the Spanish compilation *Las Siete Partidas*), German Pandectism (particularly Savigny) and the review of contemporary codifications mainly via the *Concordance entre les Codes Civils Étrangers et le Code Napoléon* of Anthoine de Saint-Joseph.[15]

Finally, the *Code civil* turned out to be only one of a large number of sources in the last influential code of the nineteenth century, ie the Argentinean Civil Code of 1869.[16] These sources included Texeira de Freita's *Esboço* (sketch) for a Brazilian Civil Code, the *Corpus Iuris Civilis*, the German Pandectists, the works of Aubry and Rau, the Spanish draft of García Goyena, the Chilean Civil Code and the French *Code civil*, among others.[17]

As a result of the common sources (mainly the *Code civil* and Roman law), mutual influence between the new Latin American civil codes contributed to the harmonisation of the law, in a form of 'spontaneous harmonisation'. For example, the Chilean Civil Code was adopted in El Salvador (1859), Ecuador (1860),[18]

[13] M Mirow, 'Individual Experience in Legal Change: Exploring a Neglected Factor in Nineteenth-Century Latin American Codification' (2005) 11 *Southwestern Journal of Law and Trade in the Americas* 301, 305, adding that 'France served as a model in mid-nineteenth century Latin America not only in politics and legislation, but also in culture, fashion, language and intellectual outlook'.

[14] HP Glenn, 'Harmony of Laws in the Americas' (2003) 34 *University of Miami Inter-American Law Review* 229, citations omitted.

[15] See Kleinheisterkamp (n 9) 275 and Guzmán Brito (n 6) 373.

[16] Guzmán Brito (n 6).

[17] Kleinheisterkamp (n 9) 281.

[18] The case of Ecuador is the best example of the influence of Bello's Code. The Supreme Court discarded its own project once it learned about the Chilean Code: 'The Supreme Court, being free of pride or vanity, believes that there is no harm in adopting what has been already been done. Therefore, it has not hesitated to step back, leave its own work aside and examine the (Chilean) code. From its examination we concluded that its plan is preferable to that of the Court, and that its doctrines and even style can be adopted by us …': Statement of the Supreme Court of Ecuador, 21 February 1857, cited by I Jaksic, *Andrés Bello: Scholarship and Nation-Building in Nineteenth-Century Latin America* (Cambridge, Cambridge University Press, 2006) 175.

Venezuela (1863), Nicaragua (1871), Colombia (1873) and Honduras (1880);[19] and influenced a number of other domestic Latin American codifications: Uruguay (1869), Mexico (1871 and 1884), Guatemala (1877), Costa Rica (1888) and Paraguay (1876).[20] Finally, as stated above, the Chilean Code was taken into consideration by the drafters of the Civil Codes of Argentina and Brazil.[21] Therefore, the Chilean Civil Code has been referred to as the most influential codification in the development of Latin American private law and as a remarkably novel and original work.[22]

Another source for spontaneous harmonisation was the Argentinean Civil Code. Its eclectic nature made it an interesting model for other Latin American countries: Paraguay adopted it in 1876, and it influenced the Codes of Nicaragua (1904) and Panama (1916).[23]

The classic period of Latin American codification ended with the enactment of the Brazilian Civil Code (also in 1916). After that, during the twentieth century, a new generation of codes was adopted. Thus, in 1936 Peru enacted a new Civil Code, replaced again in 1984. The Argentinean Civil Code was reformed in 1968. Bolivia adopted a new Civil Code in 1975, preceded by a Family Law Code in 1973, and Paraguay also adopted a new Civil Code in 1985. Colombia enacted a new Commercial Code in 1971. Finally, Brazil adopted the first Latin American Civil Code of the twenty-first century in 2002, followed by the recent Argentinean Civil and Commercial Code, enacted in 2014 and in force since 1 August 2015.

The twentieth-century domestic reforms and developments in private law took place with little or no attention to the law of neighbouring countries, so despite the existing legal common core the informal harmonisation of the nineteenth century was lost. For instance, the Italian Civil Code of 1942 was the main source of inspiration for the reform of the Argentinian Civil Code of 1968 and for the new Civil Code of Paraguay, adopted in 1985. In the same way, the new Brazilian Civil Code of 2002 drew inspiration from the Italian Civil Code and the German BGB.[24]

Similarly, the influence of the *Code civil* diminished to a great extent with regard to the reform or enactment of the new civil codes. In the case of commercial law, influence shifted from Europe to the United States. Thus, in the banking, financing and corporate sectors, legislation has been enacted following the models and rules

[19] The Chilean Code is still in force (with amendments and modifications) in Ecuador, El Salvador, Colombia and Honduras.

[20] See M Mirow, 'Borrowing Private Law in Latin America: Andres Bello's Use of the Code Napoleon in Drafting the Chilean Civil Code' (2001) 61 *Louisiana Law Review* 291, 292; Guzmán Brito (n 6).

[21] Bello's Code is recognisable as the direct source of 170 articles of the Argentinian Civil Code. See M Mirow, *Latin American Law: A History of Private Law and Institutions in Spanish America* (Austin, TX, University of Texas Press, 2004) 140.

[22] Mirow (n 20), and Zweigert and Kötz (n 5) 114, adding that 'In its structure (the Chilean code) … is superior to the Code civil, and in its language it is equally clear and forceful'.

[23] See A Guzmán Brito, 'La influencia del Código Civil de Vélez Sarsfield en la codificación de Iberoamérica hasta principios del siglo XX' (2000) 18 *Revista Chilena de Historia del Derecho* 235, 254.

[24] But see Parise, Ch 3 in this book, stating that the *exposé de motifs* of the new Argentinean Civil and Commercial Code stresses the Latin American cultural identity of the Code.

of US statutes and regulations.[25] However, again these have not been simple legal transplants but have been adapted and transformed by its incorporation into the European legal background of Latin America.[26]

In any case, the relevant point is that the law of other Latin American countries has played no role in the domestic private law reforms of the twentieth century in Latin America. As stated above, they were mainly influenced by the European codifications and doctrine of the twentieth century, with no reference to the law or doctrine of neighbouring jurisdictions, neglecting the spontaneous harmonisation that could still be observed in the nineteenth century. Interestingly, it has been stated that, while the codification process as such was a unifying factor between the new independent republics, at the same time, the enactment of the codes reflected the need for differentiation and the reaffirmation of national sovereignty. Arguably, this distinction would be one of the reasons for the later failure of regional legal integration of the new Latin American republics.[27]

III. International Private Law and Regional Integration as Sources of Harmonisation

Alongside the (failed) process of spontaneous harmonisation described above, formal harmonisation of private law in Latin America has been attempted in two ways, either in association with the enactment of private international law instruments or in the context of Latin American integration initiatives. With regard to international private law as a mechanism for harmonisation, two stages can be differentiated: first, the attempt to achieve the unification of the rules of international private law through a common codification; and secondly, the shift towards specialised international Conventions.

A. Harmonisation (Unification) Through Private International Law Treaties

The first tool by which Latin American countries intended to achieve the harmonisation of private law was through codification of the rules of private international

[25] For a detailed discussion of the growing influence of the United States in Latin American commercial law, see Kleinheisterkamp (n 9) 285–88. See also E Hondius, 'The Impact of American Law and American Legal Theory: Threat or Incentive?' in Société de législation comparé (ed), *De tous horizons: Mélanges Xavier Blanc-Jouvan* (Paris, Librairie Générale de Droit, 2005) 271–80.

[26] López-Medina (n 10) 337–38, stating that 'In this way, Latin America soon proved that the apparently irreducible distance that existed between the common and the civil law families was not real'.

[27] D Fernández Arroyo, 'Integración y derecho en América Latina: doscientos años de indiferencia mutua' in A Oropeza (ed), *Latinoamérica frente al espejo de su integración 1810–2010*, https://archivos.juridicas.unam.mx/www/bjv/libros/6/2923/18.pdf.

law. More precisely, the original aim was to unify the application of private law by the use of a single body of private international rules, common to all Latin American countries. With hindsight, this process can also be considered as a consequence of the political individualism and fragmentation of the new Latin American countries which were unable to develop common political or legal institutions.[28]

This codification process started in the nineteenth century with the so-called Congress of Lima (1877–78), where a treaty on conflict of laws rules was signed by seven Latin American countries. However, the War of the Pacific (1879–83) between Peru and Bolivia on the one hand and Chile on the other caused the failure of the treaty, which was finally only ratified by Peru and thus never came into force.[29] Along similar lines, although more successful, was a conference held in Montevideo (1888), which laid the foundations for the drafting of eight treaties on private and procedural international law.[30]

However, the most comprehensive and ambitious effort was the drafting of the Pan-American Code of Private International law in 1928, widely known as the Bustamante Code in honour of its drafter, the Cuban legal scholar Antonio Sánchez de Bustamante. The merits and quality of the Code have been widely recognised by Latin American and European legal doctrine, and it is still cited in international private law treatises and textbooks.[31]

The Bustamante Code was, however, only an apparent success: the text contained excessive concessions to the internal law of the contracting states, and in addition, it was not signed by Argentina, Colombia, Mexico, Paraguay, the United States and Uruguay. Moreover, five of the ratifying countries entered reservations excluding the application of the Code with regard to all the provisions contradicting the local law.[32] Therefore, the application of the Code by national courts remained exceptional, and the Code cannot be considered as an effective tool of harmonisation of private law in Latin America.[33]

Finally, the failure of private international law treaties as a source of unification is confirmed by the fact that the Inter-American Convention on the Law Applicable to International Contracts (Mexico, 1994), has only been ratified by Mexico and Venezuela.[34]

[28] See Fernández Arroyo (n 27).

[29] Garro (n 3) 589–590.

[30] Most of the treaties were only ratified by Argentina, Bolivia, Colombia and Peru. See Garro (n 3) 590. The low adherence to the treaties led to a second conference in 1939–40, but the practical result was even more disappointing. See A Pérez, 'The Inter-American Juridical Committee and Private Law in the Americas (or a Roadmap for making the Best the Enemy of the Good)' *Columbus School of Law, Legal Studies Series*, http://papers.ssrn.com/sol3/papers.cfm?abstract_id=%201019297.

[31] Fernández Arroyo (n 6) 155–58.

[32] See Garro (n 3) 591–92.

[33] For a more optimistic view, see Fernández Arroyo (n 6) 155–58.

[34] Inter-American Convention on the Law Applicable to International Contracts 33 ILM 732 (1994).

B. The Inter-American Specialised Conferences on Private International Law

As explained above, the initiatives mentioned earlier in this chapter failed as a result of the small number of ratifications or because of the reservations entered by the ratifying countries which prevented real unification or even harmonisation. During the twentieth century, these complete codification projects were replaced with the sectorial and specialised approach of the Inter-American Specialized Conferences on Private International Law (CIDIPs, because of their acronym in Spanish).[35]

The CIDIPs have been promoted by the Organization of American States (OAS), the oldest regional body (established in 1948) that includes all the independent countries of the North and South American continents.[36] Within the OAS structure, the basic attributes of the Inter-American Juridical Committee are

> to serve the Organization as an advisory body on juridical matters; to promote the progressive development and the codification of international law; and to study juridical problems related to the integration of the developing countries of the Hemisphere and, insofar as may appear desirable, the possibility of attaining uniformity in their legislation.[37]

Therefore, the Committee aims to contribute to the progressive development and the codification of international law, as well as uniformity in domestic legislation.

In the field of private law, the leading initiative of the Committee has been the organisation of the CIDIPs. The failure of a common codification of private international law for the Americas has led to a specialised approach to relevant subjects of procedural and substantive law, through the drafting of international Conventions to be ratified by the OAS contracting states.

Since 1975, seven CIDIPs have taken place. In general, the Conferences have been related to private international law and can be divided into three categories: international commercial law, international procedural law and international civil law.[38] Within the CIDIP process, 26 Inter-American instruments have been drafted: 20 Conventions, three Protocols, two Uniform Documents and one Model Law. Some examples of those instruments are the Inter-American Conventions on

[35] The Charter of the OAS describes, in general, the Specialized Conferences as 'intergovernmental meetings to deal with special technical matters or to develop specific aspects of Inter-American cooperation'.

[36] Cuba was suspended as member of the OAS from 1962 to 2009 and has, to date, refused to rejoin the organisation.

[37] Charter of the Organization of American States, Art 99.

[38] It should be mentioned that this approach took place after the failure of the adoption of an International Private Law Code drafted by the Committee. See Pérez (n 30).

Conflict of Laws concerning Bills of Exchange, Promissory Notes, and Invoices; on International Commercial Arbitration; on Extraterritorial Validity of Foreign Judgments and Arbitral Awards; and on Conflict of Laws Concerning the Adoption of Minors.[39]

After a promising start, the ratification rate of the Conventions drafted in the context of the CIDIP process has diminished considerably. For instance, the Inter-American Convention on International Commercial Arbitration (1975) has received 18 ratifications, the Inter-American Convention on Letters Rogatory (1975) 17 ratifications;[40] the Inter-American Convention on Jurisdiction in the International Sphere for the Extraterritorial Validity of Foreign Judgments (1984) and the Inter-American Convention on Contracts for the International Carriage of Goods by Road (1989), one and no ratifications, respectively.[41] In addition to the steadily dwindling number of ratifications, another difficulty faced by the CIDIP approach to harmonisation has been the absence of a formal process for the CIDIPs, as well as the lack of commitment (and resources) of the contracting states with regard to the Conferences.[42] Because of these problems the latest CIDIP (VII), initially scheduled for 2005, was postponed on a number of occasions and is as yet still not complete.[43]

The absence of an independent institutional structure for the CIDIPs has been stressed as one of the main reasons for the lack of continuity of the conferences.[44] In addition, most Latin American countries are also members of other global organisations aimed at the harmonisation or unification of private law, such as the Hague Conference on Private International Law or UNIDROIT. The CISG has also been ratified by a sizeable number of Latin American countries. The gradual involvement of Latin American countries with these initiatives could explain their increasing lack of interest in the continuity of the CIDIPs.

However, the indirect influence of the CIDIP Conventions on domestic legislation has also been highlighted. It has been stated that the modernisation of

[39] Inter-American Convention on Conflict of Laws Concerning Bills of Exchange, Promissory Notes, and Invoices 1438 UNTS 211; Inter-American Convention on International Commercial Arbitration 1438 UNTS 245; Inter-American Convention on Extraterritorial Validity of Foreign Judgments and Arbitral Awards 1439 UNTS 87; and Inter-American Convention on Conflict of Laws Concerning the Adoption of Minors 24 ILM 460 (1985).

[40] Inter-American Convention on Letters Rogatory 1438 UNTS 288.

[41] Inter-American Convention on Contracts for the International Carriage of Goods by Road 29 ILM 81 (1990). For detailed information see the OAS website, http://www.oas.org/dil/privateintlaw_studytopics.htm.

[42] CM Vásquez and J Grandino, Report to the OAS, 'CIDIP VII and Beyond', http://www.oas.org/dil/PrivateIntLaw-introduction-Eng.htm.

[43] The first part of CIDIP VII took place in October 2009. The second part of CIDIP VII, devoted to consumer protection, has no certain date yet.

[44] Fernández Arroyo (n 6) 184–86.

the national private international law systems has relied to a great extent on these Conventions.[45] Thus,

> some of the instruments adopted at the CIDIP enjoy wide hemispheric acceptance and a few of them have been quite successful in coordinating policies for transnational litigation between the United States and the countries of Latin America. Moreover, some of the Conventions have served as vehicles for law reform.[46]

In an attempt to revitalise the CIDIP process, the methodology of the Conferences has changed from codification (ie the drafting of international treaties or Conventions) to more flexible instruments, such as model laws.[47] Furthermore, the focus of the works is increasingly being directed from procedural to substantial matters, such as consumer protection. However, 'substantial private law has remained essentially untouched by any such supranational or international measures'.[48]

In addition, the active intervention of the United States in the latest CIDIPs has been considered by some Latin American countries as an effort to introduce American-style common law concepts, in order to benefit US economic interests in the region. This may have led to resistance towards the legal instruments adopted in recent Conferences.[49]

C. Latin American Integration as a Source for Harmonisation

Another (failed) source of harmonisation have been the Latin American integration initiatives. To date, there are a significant number of regional integration initiatives in Latin America, most of them originally established with economic purposes, particularly the promotion of trade between contracting states. A non-exhaustive list of these organisations includes the following:

(a) The Andean Community (formerly the Andean Pact), founded in 1969 by Bolivia, Chile, Colombia, Ecuador and Peru (Cartagena Agreement). Chile withdrew from the Pact in 1976, and Venezuela was a member from

[45] D Fernández Arroyo, 'What's New in Latin American Private International Law' (2005) 7 *Yearbook of Private International Law* 87; N González Martin, 'Private International Law in Latin America: From Hard to Soft Law' (2011) XI *Anuario Mexicano de Derecho Internacional* 393.

[46] Garro (n 3) at 595, citations omitted.

[47] See N González Martin, 'La conferencia especializada interamericana de derecho internacional privado y la modernización del derecho internacional privado latinoamericano ¿Un cambio en el íter convencional hacia la ley modelo?' [2008] *Boletín Mexicano de Derecho Comparado, número conmemorativo, sexagésimo aniversario* 511–44.

[48] Glenn (n 14) 232.

[49] See Kleinheisterkamp (n 9) 291 stressing the remarks made by a number of CIDIP VI Latin American delegates concerning the Inter-American Model Law in Secured Transactions, in order that 'no Latin American parliament would enact such a solution.' But see A Garro, 'The OAS-sponsored Model Law on Secured Transactions: Gestation and Implementation' [2010] *Uniform Law Review* 391, 396, stating that the Model Law has been adopted or implemented to some extent in Mexico, Peru, Guatemala and Honduras; however, with no unitary concept of security interest. See also JM Wilson, 'Financial Leasing and its Unification by UNIDROIT: The Role of the Organization of American States' [2011] *Uniform Law Review* 469.

1973 to 2006. Regarding the purposes of the Community, Article 1 of the Cartagena Agreement states that 'The objectives of this Agreement are to promote the balanced and harmonious development of the Member Countries under equitable conditions, through integration and economic and social cooperation; to accelerate their growth and the rate of creation of employment; and to facilitate their participation in the regional integration process, looking ahead toward the gradual formation of a Latin American Common Market'.

(b) The Mercosur (Mercado Común del Sur, or the Southern Common Market) was established in 1991 by the Treaty of Asunción and later amended by the Treaty of Ouro Preto (1994). The founding members were Argentina, Brazil, Paraguay and Uruguay. Venezuela became a full member in July 2012, and Bolivia signed the incorporation protocol in December of the same year.[50] Chile, Colombia, Ecuador and Peru are associated members, which means that they are not members of the customs union and have no participation in the Mercosur directive bodies, but they do have preferential trade access to the common market.

Mercosur's main purpose is to create a common market. This common market includes the free movement of goods and services, the establishment of a common external tariff, the adoption of a common trade policy and the commitment of the Member States to harmonise their legislation in the relevant areas to achieve a strong integration process (Article 1 of the Treaty of Asunción).

(c) The ALADI (Asociación Latinoamericana de Integración, or the Latin American Integration Association), established in 1980 by the Montevideo Treaty, has the objective to promote the development of an economic area within the region, in order to gradually implement a Latin American common market. ALADI also aims to serve as an institutional and normative platform for other regional or sub-regional integration initiatives. To date, ALADI has 13 member countries: Argentina, Bolivia, Brazil, Chile, Colombia, Cuba, Ecuador, Mexico, Paraguay, Panama, Peru, Uruguay and Venezuela.

(d) The ALBA (Alianza Bolivariana para los Pueblos de América, or the Bolivarian Alliance for the Americas) is an initiative with a limited and incomplete institutional structure, inspired by the Bolivarian ideals of Latin American political unity, solidarity and endogenous development, with a pre-eminence of the political over the economic.[51] Antigua and Barbuda, Bolivia, Cuba, Dominica, Ecuador, Nicaragua, St Vincent and the Grenadines, and Venezuela are full members of ALBA.

[50] The membership of Venezuela has been suspended because of breach of its community obligations.

[51] GL Gardini, 'MERCOSUR: What You See Is Not (Always) What You Get' (2011) 17 *European Law Journal* 697.

(e) UNASUR (Unión de Naciones Sudamericanas, or the Union of South American Nations) was established in 2008 and is composed of the 12 South American nations. The general objective of UNASUR is 'to set up, in a participatory, agreed manner, a space for integration and union among its peoples in the cultural, economic and political fields' (Article 1 of the constitutive treaty).

By its own nature, any integration initiative requires some degree of legal unification or harmonisation between the internal legislation of its Member States. In the case of Latin America, the success of harmonisation efforts in the context of regional integration has been relatively limited, with the exception of very specific and technical topics such as transport, customs and tariffs. Even in cases where a proper organisational structure is present, as in the Andean Community, it has been stated that 'the Andean legal system remains vulnerable to Member State decisions that compromise community rules in favour of national political objectives'.[52] Additionally, another curious feature of the integration initiatives in Latin America is that, in most cases, they compete for the same geographical space and have overlapping memberships.

Thus, it can be stated that harmonisation of private law through Latin American regional bodies has failed, mostly because of the lack of an adequate political and legal structure. For instance, in the structure of Mercosur, there are no supranational bodies as in the case of the European Union (eg, the European Commission or the European Court of Justice), but simply intergovernmental bodies, with strong dependence of the internal political orientation of the contracting states. Therefore, the whole process of integration has been subject in practice to the will of the contracting states and their domestic administrations.[53] The position of secondary Mercosur legislation is also weak. It has no direct effect, since it is not automatically incorporated into domestic law and therefore is not a source of rights and duties for legal subjects. In addition to unanimity for its adoption, secondary legislation requires incorporation through the internal legal procedures of each Member State, entering into force only after the approval by all of them.[54]

[52] KJ Alter and LR Helfer 'Legal Integration in the Andes: Law-Making by the Andean Tribunal of Justice' (2011) 17 *European Law Journal* 715.

[53] See Gardini (n 51) 687, stating that Mercosur '… was characterised from the beginning by the primacy of economics over politics, a weak institutional structure, the strong role of the big two [Argentina and Brazil] and a high degree of control by the executives over the integration process'.

[54] See J Vervaele, 'MERCOSUR and Regional Integration in South America' (2005) 54 *International and Comparative Law Quarterly* 408; and J Kleinheisterkamp, 'Legal Certainty in the Mercosur: The Uniform Interpretation of Community Law' [2000] *NAFTA: Law and Business Review of the Americas* 1–34. However, some limited harmonisation on matters of private international law and judicial cooperation has been reached. See JP Schmidt, 'MERCOSUR' in R Wolfrum (ed), *Max Planck Encyclopaedia of Public International Law* (Oxford, Oxford University Press, 2012) 110–17.

IV. Academic Initiatives: The Principles of Latin American Contract Law

A. Recent Developments

As has been stated earlier, the main tools for unification or harmonisation of Latin American private law have been associated with the enactment of private international law instruments or Latin American integration initiatives. By contrast, the harmonisation of substantive private law has not been a priority for Latin American legal academia.

Nevertheless, in the last few years, apparently motivated by the massive number of European projects in the field, some academic initiatives have been launched. Thus, in November 2010, the First Latin American Congress of Private Law (*Primera convención latinoamericana de derecho civil*) took place in Lima to analyse the 'Foundations for a Latin American Code of Contract Law' (*Bases para un código latinoamericano de contratos*). It was agreed that in the next meeting, scheduled for 2011, the draft of the Code would be examined.[55] Similarly, the Argentinean XXIIIrd National Conference of Private Law (XXIII *Jornadas Nacionales de Derecho Civil*, Tucumán, 2011) adopted a recommendation to create a research network with the aim of studying the 'normative integration of private law in Ibero-America'.[56]

A most fruitful initiative has been the 'Group for the Harmonization of Latin American Private Law', founded in 2008 by a group of South American academics, with the purpose of 'develop[ing] a Latin American juridical model' and 'lay[ing] the foundations for a Code on the law of obligations'.[57] Its last meeting was held in 2011,[58] and its work was collected in the book *De las obligaciones en general*, which contains a series of papers delivered at the 2011 meeting, dealing with key issues in the law of obligations.[59] The book also includes the first draft of a Proposal for a Latin American Model Code of Obligations (*Propuesta de articulado para un código tipo de obligaciones para América Latina*). The Proposal contains

[55] L Leiva Fernández, 'Bases para un Código Iberoamericano de Contratos', www.unisob.na.it/universita/facolta/giurisprudenza/age/leiva2.pdf.

[56] S Diaz Alabert, 'La armonización del derecho de contratos en la UE y en el continente sudamericano' [2012] *Revista de Derecho Privado* 115–16.

[57] The Constitutive Declaration of the group can be found at https://drive.google.com/file/d/0B4pfm-dmuycMWi16eXNRMkcwMnc/view.

[58] See Roma e America Diritto Romano Comune, 31-32/2011.

[59] R Morales and G Priori (eds), *De las obligaciones en general—Coloquio de iusprivatistas de Roma y América. Cuarta reunión de trabajo* (Lima, Fondo Editorial, Pontificia Universidad Católica del Perú, 2012). See also F Hinestrosa, S Schipani and F Navia (eds), *Obligaciones, Contratos, Responsabilidad—Grupo para la armonización del derecho privado latinoamericano* (Bogotà, Universidad del Externado de Colombia, 2011).

rules intended to be applicable to obligations in general, not limited to contractual obligations but arising from any legal source (particularly torts). However, the text of the Model Code is only a collection of the individual proposals of the reporters on each subject. Thus, it is expressly stated by the drafters that substantial issues are still to be discussed and agreed in subsequent meetings of the group.[60]

The work of the aforementioned group was continued by the 'Group for the Harmonization of Latin American Law' (*Grupo para la armonización del derecho en América Latina—GADAL*) which was founded in 2013. GADAL has the aim of drafting normative instruments (model codes or statutes) for the harmonisation or unification of the law of obligations which reflect the Romanist tradition and the peculiarities of the region, which they have identified as the *Subsistema jurídico latinoamericano* (the Latin American juridical subsystem). The group includes academics from Argentina, Brazil, Colombia, Chile, Mexico, Peru and Venezuela, and has had six meetings to date, with the last held in November 2016.[61]

B. The Principles of Latin American Contract Law (*Principios Latinoamericanos de Derecho de los Contratos*)

The Principles of Latin American Contract Law (PLACL—*Principios latinoamericanos de derecho de los contratos*) is an academic initiative. The idea emerged in 2010 when a group of legal academics from Argentina, Colombia and Chile gathered in France to participate in a conference about the evolution of French and Latin American contract laws. The project attracted the support of the French *Fondation pour le droit continental* and the Chilean *Fundación Fernando Fueyo*, attached to Diego Portales University. At present, in addition to the original group, academics from Brazil, Guatemala, Paraguay, Uruguay and Venezuela have joined the project.

C. Purposes of the Principles

The main purpose of the PLACL is to provide a source of inspiration for the reform and modernisation of contract law in Latin America. This is particularly true in the cases of Chile and Colombia, where no substantial reform in the law of contract has taken place since the enactment of Bello's Civil Code in the mid-nineteenth century.[62] Because the reform of civil and commercial codes can be a difficult and lengthy process,[63] the purpose of the PLACL implicitly also entails the idea that national or international courts might use the Principles to

[60] See the footnote accompanying the text of the Proposal in Morales and Priori (n 39).
[61] Information about GADAL can be accessed at http://gadal.uexternado.edu.co/.
[62] However, as mentioned before, Colombia enacted a Commercial Code in 1971.
[63] The Argentinean case is a good example. Since 1926, three civil code projects failed at some stage of the legislative process, until finally the new Civil and Commercial Code was enacted in 2014.

interpret and supplement domestic and uniform law, considering the PLACL as the 'Latin American *lex mercatoria*'.

In this sense, it has been stated that 'the applicability of non-state law to contracts is widely accepted in the [Latin American] region through a vast array of legal and conventional enactments'.[64] As a consequence, Latin American courts and arbitral tribunals have increasingly resorted to uniform law instruments such as the CISG or the PICC to support their decisions.[65] The availability of a Latin American set of principles could be an incentive for the courts and arbitrators to use a more 'familiar' instrument of contract law in their decisions.

The proposed Article 1 PLACL (Scope of Application) reflects the aims of the drafters, stating that the Principles will apply not only when the parties have expressly agreed to this effect, but also when the parties have agreed that their contract be governed by general principles of law, *lex mercatoria* or the like (Article 1(4)(a)). The same provision stipulates that the PLACL will apply to interpret and supplement the domestic law governing the contract and as a model for national and international legislators (Article 1(4)(d) and (f)).

A further and more difficult stage is the acceptance of the PLACL by private parties either as guidelines for negotiations and drafting or as the governing law of the contract. This would require the consolidation of a relevant body of doctrine and case law in order to transform the PLACL into a familiar set of rules for practising lawyers. The (formal or informal) inclusion of the PLACL in law degrees, at both undergraduate and postgraduate level, could raise awareness about the Principles in national legal communities.

D. Methodology

Perhaps the greater challenge for the PLACL is to demonstrate their originality, in the sense that they are not just a copy or sub-product of the CISG, the PICC or European initiatives, such as the Principles of European Contract Law (PECL) or the Draft Common Frame of Reference (DCFR). This has been an issue since the early stages of the project. Therefore, in order to ensure the 'Latin American juridical identity' of the project, a questionnaire with key aspects of contract law was designed. The purpose of the questionnaire was that national reporters might provide a description of the current status of contract law in the countries of the region, with special reference to domestic legal doctrine and the development of the case law in each jurisdiction. The questionnaire was structured to comprise most of the relevant subjects of the law of contract, including the general principles of contract law (good faith, freedom of contract, the binding force of contracts and privity) and individual topics ranging from pre-contractual liability to remedies for breach.

[64] JA Moreno, 'Contracts and Non-State Law in Latin America' [2011] *Uniform Law Review* 877.

[65] For a detailed survey of the decisions, see ibid.

The national reports were published in the book *El derecho de los contratos en Latinoamérica. Bases para unos principios de derecho de los contratos.*[66] The book is arguably the most up-to-date work on comparative contract law in Latin America. The questionnaire method allows the reader to easily explore core subjects in contract law and to identify the similarities and differences of the national jurisdictions included in the survey.[67] The volume is therefore a useful source of information for both academics and practitioners.

With the material provided by the national reports, different reporting and drafting teams were appointed. Basically, the subjects assigned to each team were formation, effects, and performance and non-performance of contract. The teams produced reports with comparative notes, comments and the preliminary drafts of the provisions. These were analysed in general meetings, organised by commissions that examined and approved a draft of the black letter rules.

The last meeting of the drafting group took place in August 2016. It was agreed that the final text of the PLACL should be published in 2017. That text will include the black letter rules, with the comments and comparative notes to be added in the near future. The current draft text of the PLACL, as of October 2014, is reproduced in a bilingual version in the Appendix to this book.[68]

E. Nature of the PLACL: Restatement, Innovation or Both?

As stated above, the contract laws of Latin American countries share a common basis. Nevertheless, differences are present not only at the level of detail, but also with regard to some substantive issues. This necessarily entails that the drafters have to make some normative and policy decisions, and, as in the case of the PECL and the PICC, this will eventually require the adoption of some innovative solutions.[69]

The national reports are illustrative of some major differences between two groups of jurisdictions. There are, on the one hand, what can be considered as 'conservative jurisdictions' (Chile, Colombia, Venezuela,[70] Uruguay), that is, those

[66] C Pizarro Wilson (ed), *El derecho de los contratos en Latinoamérica. Bases para unos principios de derecho de los contratos* (Bogotà, Universidad Externado de Colombia, 2012).

[67] For general criticisms of the 'questionnaire method' see M Schultz, 'The Questionable Questionnaire: Reflections on Comparative Law Method in Light of Principles of European Tort Law' in A Bakardjieva and J Nergelius (eds), *New Directions in Comparative Law* (Cheltenham, Edward Elgar Publishing, 2009) 173–84.

[68] This is the last official text available. It has been subject to minor additions and modifications in subsequent meetings, but these have not been subject to final approval by the drafting group.

[69] See R Zimmermann, 'The Present State of European Private Law' (2009) 57 *American Journal of Comparative Law* 479, 483 describing the same situation in the case of the PECL. The Introduction to the PICC also stresses that the Principles 'also embody what are perceived to be the best solutions, even if still not yet generally adopted'.

[70] Although the Civil Code of Venezuela has been reformed and amended on several occasions, the last one in 1982, the rules concerning obligations and contracts are substantially the same as in the Code of 1873. See Guzmán Brito (n 6) 343.

whose contract law has remained mainly untouched since the nineteenth century, preserving the principle of freedom of contract to a great extent and rejecting the revision of the contract by the courts. On the other hand, there are 'progressive jurisdictions' (Argentina, Brazil, Paraguay) where contract law has been reformed and modernised during the twentieth or even in the twenty-first century, as in the case of Brazil and Argentina.[71] These jurisdictions have adopted more socially oriented legislation, providing protection to weaker parties and allowing revision of the contract in cases of major imbalance between the counter-obligations.

A few examples may illustrate these divergences. The Civil Codes of Argentina, Brazil and Paraguay expressly provide for the termination or revision of the contract in cases of *laesio enormis* and *imprévision* (change of circumstances); whereas *laesio* is accepted only in restricted cases in Chile, Colombia and Uruguay; and *imprévision* is rejected in Chile and Venezuela, being exceptionally accepted by the case law in Colombia and Uruguay.[72] In addition, the Brazilian Civil Code expressly recognises as a limit of freedom of contract the so-called 'social function of the contract', an open concept that relates the contract not only to the private interests of the parties, but also to the interests of society at large.[73] Finally, the concept of *causa* as a necessary element for the existence of a contract is still maintained in many jurisdictions but was abolished by the Brazilian and Paraguayan Civil Codes. Certainly, these are all core issues on which policy decisions are necessary. Depending on the options, the final outcome could result in a more (or less) market-oriented or a more (or less) socially oriented set of principles.[74]

F. Difficulties

It must be recognised that the PLACL, even when labelled as 'Latin American', are, at most, South American. Thus, only recently a country of Middle America has been included (Guatemala). Important jurisdictions such as Mexico and Panama are absent. Furthermore, not all the South American nations are represented in the drafting teams (eg, Peru is missing). This could raise questions as to the legitimacy of the PLACL in the future, and these could prevent the parties and, more importantly the courts from referring to the Principles.

Additionally, the private nature of the initiative could have some negative consequences. The lack of political support can be considered as an advantage in terms of intellectual independence, but it could also constitute a great difficulty

[71] However, it must be noted that most of the drafting of the Brazilian Civil Code took place in the early 1970s.

[72] *Imprévision* is also recognised by the Colombian Commercial Code of 1971.

[73] Art 421 of the Brazilian Civil Code provides that 'Freedom of contract has to be performed in function and within the limits of the social function of the contract'. The provision has been subject to extensive analysis by Brazilian legal doctrine, but its real relevance and influence remain unclear.

[74] See M Hesselink, 'Common Frame of Reference and Social Justice' (2008) Working Paper Series 4/2008, Centre for the Study of European Contract Law.

for the consolidation of the Principles. For instance, the role of the European Commission has been relevant for the development of harmonisation initiatives in Europe. In the same sense, OHADA asked for the official support of UNIDROIT in elaborating its Uniform Act on the Law of Contracts. Therefore, the support of international organisations such as the OAS or Mercosur may be fundamental to establish a permanent network of academics, judges, public officers and practising lawyers for the dissemination of the PLACL as well as for the development of further comparative studies and research on Latin American private law.

V. Conclusions

Overall the efforts and initiatives of harmonisation or unification of private law in Latin America have not been successful, with a low level of involvement of the countries of the region that of late is limited to particular and technical subjects of substantive private law.

Nevertheless, some current developments seem to indicate that a new trend towards harmonisation is emerging in Latin America. Thus, the CIDIP conferences are moving from hard to soft law in an effort to convince rather than impose. For instance, in the VIIth CIDIP of 2009, a model law on secure transactions was approved, and it has been implemented to a different extent in some Latin American countries.[75] However, as stated above, the second part of this Conference, which is meant to analyse subjects on consumer protection, has not been held to date.

With regard to integration initiatives, there are some recent developments that may lead to strengthening of regional integration and, therefore, to increasing the necessity for more and better harmonisation of private law. For instance, in the case of Mercosur, in 2006 the Parliament of Mercosur (Parlasur) was established with the aims of strengthening integration, harmonising national legislation and promoting societal participation and legitimacy within a regional framework.[76] However, to date, Parlasur 'exists but has virtually no power, its composition has not been fully decided, and its functioning is at best incomplete'.[77] In the same sense, the Permanent Review Court of Mercosur has issued some Consultative Opinions stating the primacy of community legislation over domestic law, but in all cases only after they had been incorporated by Member States.[78] As stated above, the implementation of Mercosur's norms remains within the domestic

[75] See B Kozolchyk, 'Implementation of the OAS Model Law in Latin America: Current Status' (2011) 28 *Arizona Journal of International and Comparative* Law 1.

[76] Common Market Council Decision 23/05, preamble.

[77] Gardini (n 51) 693.

[78] However, Consultative Opinions are neither obligatory nor binding.

competence of each Member State, which in practice is essentially the same process designed for the ratification of international treaties.

The most recent harmonisation initiative, the drafting of the PLACL, should contribute to changing the status described earlier. Most probably, the publication of the PLACL will give a new impetus to comparative law studies in Latin America and, therefore, increase the interest in further harmonisation measures. In this regard, the PLACL will most probably not be the final outcome of Latin American private law harmonisation, but just the starting point for the development of a new Latin American *ius commune*.[79]

[79] See Zimmermann (n 69) 510, stating that in Europe, 'The Principles of European Contract Law have played a pioneering role'.

2

The Principles of Latin American Contract Law: A General Introduction

CARLOS PIZARRO WILSON

Working on the Principles of Latin American Contract Law (PLACL) has been a real challenge, and rightfully so. It has been a complex and rocky process, and it is not yet finished. I am confident that this conference will prove a source of enrichment that will enable us to perfect the PLACL. I therefore invite you to be critical, so as to create a better set of Principles for the Latin American region.

The project originated in Brittany, in the French city of Rennes. It was the brainchild of a group of Latin American professors, most of whom had studied in France, under the wing of Professor Christian Larroumet. At the Rennes conference, we discussed the state of South American contract law as compared to that of contract law in France. At that time, in October 2009, Professor Michel Grimaldi was just beginning his work on the *Fondation pour le Droit Continental*, after the critical report *Doing Business* issued by the World Bank, which had denounced the contract law of the continental legal family and lauded the virtues of the common law. This provided an incentive for us Latin Americans to look at our own laws and analyse whether the criticism about lack of efficiency was apt. It was also an invaluable opportunity to work with the institutional support of our universities.

The process of putting together the Principles has been rocky, harsh and at times even bitter. Yet our determination to carry on in hopes of achieving valuable results for our countries has remained. A main issue was the search for identity, which is at times constructed from the traditional or legal culture of each specific country, and which can impede ready consensus. There is also a wide range of educational and professional experience among the members of the group, some of them having studied the French tradition, others the Italian and Spanish, which are more open to a uniform global contract law.

The permanent question debated by the group was to determine which legal culture represents our region: whether one may be said to exist, or whether we should advance toward a kind of 'uniform thinking', a global contract law that is the same for the entire continent.

This conflict is obvious in the wording of the rules that compose the Principles. The debate was particularly arduous with reference to the inclusion of *cause* as an element of the contract, which the French have renounced, and also in regard to non-performance and its effects. The latter issue is, of course, a passionate, technical, ideological and even political theme—the sharp stone in the system of contractual liability.

In our quest for an original work that is not just a copy of the Principles of European Contract Law (PECL), this conflict was tangible all along. We have sought to move forward with an authentic text that respects our tradition while addressing those aspects that we deemed it necessary to improve. We were inspired by various models, ranging from the Spanish proposal for a reform of the law of obligations to the proposal for contract reform headed by Professor François Terré, the codes of our own region and, of course, instruments of soft law such as the PECL and the UNIDROIT Principles of International Commercial Contracts.

At the end of the day, our Principles feature both confluences that deserve the name of consensus, and dissent. These two poles explain the tensions in the text we are proposing.

I. The Vocation or Finality of the Principles

The laws on contracts in South America vary widely within the region. Some legal systems, such as that of Chile, have experienced almost no reform, their laws remaining untouched since they were first codified. Although the Colombian situation is similar, modification and evaluation have had an impact on the Code of Commerce, for example, in the introduction of *imprévision* or change of circumstances, and have also resulted in a more active jurisprudence, both in the civil courts and in the Constitutional Court, which has had a major influence on civil law. In other cases—Argentina, for example—the rules put forth in contract law are fresh and only took effect with the new Code in August 2015. In the case of Venezuela, we see a twentieth-century code, strongly influenced by the Italian Civil Code of 1942, which itself is now undergoing changes by means of a jurisprudence that is revising contract law from the perspective of the weaker party, evidence of an important political and ideological influence.

The diversity not only of sources, but also of the eras that have shaped national laws is self-evident. Because of this, our objective could never have been to create a model code or an idea of uniformity in contract law. The objective therefore was that the Principles would serve as a model for reform in those countries that needed it, such as Chile and Colombia, and that in other cases, it could provide inspiration for better solutions for courts and judges in the name of *lex mercatoria*.

II. The Identity and Innovation of the Principles

As I have already mentioned, this is not about creating an iteration of other principles or processes of contractual harmonisation. Some innovations may be found in the following areas, which I should like to highlight: formation, non-performance and remedies.

One such area is the decision to include in the requirements of the contract particular conditions the absence of which signifies the ineffectiveness of the contract. The introduction of such elements is the result of a consensus among the diverse Latin American systems that recognise as such consent, subject-matter, *cause* and, in some cases, formalities.

The inclusion or exclusion of *cause*, in particular, generated much attention and discussion. But since this is a subject that will be addressed by Professor Iñigo de la Maza I shall leave it aside and direct your attention to some of the issues related to breach of contract and remedies.

First of all, the group rejected the expression 'remedies', which we have seen is being introduced in continental law, deeming 'means of relief' (Article 84) more appropriate. The reason for doing so was ideological, since the notion is foreign to the continental civil law tradition, even though the doctrine, like the jurisprudence of some of the participating countries, is accepted and employed habitually; and, secondly, because in Anglo-American law, where we find the origin of the term, its reach extends beyond the contractual, a fact which may at some time or other lead to undesired errors.

With respect to 'non-performance', this notion underpins the entire structure of contractual liability. After long debate, the group opted for a neutral notion that does not allude to the imputability of the conduct of the debtor, but rather to the lack of conformity between that which was agreed and that which was performed. In general, the Latin American codes do not contemplate a definition of non-performance, and in many cases, non-performance is still considered a matter of fault, a failure to perform that, in every case, leads to a sanction of the debtor's conduct.

Two ideas were discussed to arrive at this definition.

The first was that any non-conformity in the performance, regardless of its cause, should be considered as equivalent to non-performance. This position is based on an understanding that original or initial impossibility of performance due to force majeure, that is to say, without fault, is also equivalent to non-performance. The Colombian group fiercely resisted this notion since their tradition, like that of Chile, understands non-performance as the consequence of fault by the debtor. And, in the case of original impossibility, it is treated as a case of nullity for lack of subject-matter.

This debate was marked by the inclusion or exclusion of fault as an element of non-performance, and the relationship between non-performance and force majeure. If we consider that force majeure is an excuse and at the same time a means of extinction of the obligation, excluding the 'non-performance' of the obligation, we should agree that it will not be a hypothesis for termination of the contract.

Instead, if we consider, on the contrary, that force majeure does not impede the categorisation of the creditor's dissatisfaction as 'non-performance', the creditor could terminate the contract and in this way exercise the appropriate means of relief. It is a critical subject for organising the effects of non-performance.

In both cases, it is true that there will be no place for damages, since this would indeed require fault in the non-performance.

This reluctance to accept the notion of non-performance even in the case of force majeure was not confined to the Colombian participants, but was also evident in the Argentinean camp. In the end, however, the notion of non-performance remained neutral but was regulated in a form such as to express the total or partial impossibility of compliance due to force majeure.

Article 83, in case of total impossibility, opted for the extinction of the obligation of the debtor, and granted the creditor the option of terminating the contract, with restorative effects or by requiring the assignment of the rights and actions that, due to the impossibility, the obligor held against a third party.

On the other hand, in the case of partial or temporary impossibility, the creditor can suspend or reduce the performance. In this way, fault in relation to non-performance was eliminated.

Does this mean that fault disappears?

Not at all. As I have just indicated, fault constitutes an unavoidable element in the case of compensation of damages. This is stipulated in the final part.

After clarifying the notion of non-performance and its relation to impossibility, we must take into account a substantive aspect regarding the binding force of the contract. Here, it is important to highlight the differences between legal systems, although not as such in the Latin American region. We understand that, in the face of non-performance, the common law privileges damages, which allows for the construction of a contractual environment that marginalises specific performance to exceptional cases and allows for the minimisation of adverse effects for the creditor as a general rule.

However, in the Latin American countries, specific performance is prioritised as a remedy, or, at least, the creditor has this option in all cases except in the case of impossibility.

Until now, no system in the region has promoted the limits of irrational costs or other formulae of economic analysis that leave the door open to effective non-performance. This is the subject of heated debate and, so far, although it is not defined, a rule is maintained that mitigates specific performance through the formula 'Even though it is possible, specific performance may not be demanded when it is extremely burdensome for the obligor, taking into consideration that the obligee may satisfy its interest by choosing another means of relief' (Article 86(2)(b) PLACL).

The relevant question is, what place should be given to the word of the promisor or to the agreement of the parties? In countries such as ours, it seems more relevant to affirm performance as it was agreed than to establish an escape for the debtor for pragmatic or economic reasons. It is more appropriate, given the culture and practice of the region, to introduce limits beginning with notions that are already known and applied, such as abuse of rights, which allows for the establishment of a sanction on any party that misuses a rule to thwart its purpose, rather than turn the matter into a question of arithmetic or a simple cost-benefit operation. This debate, I believe, is still open.

With regard to the resolution of the contract, the model imposed by the international instruments has been spreading in the form of termination by notification of an extrajudicial character, which allows the creditor to steer clear of the courts, which, at least in our countries, are always at the ready, waiting for the chance to intervene so as to model the conditions and effects of the resolution. The possibility of conventional termination has also been proposed, which is quite relevant to Chilean and Colombian law, given their defective regulation of termination clauses (*pacto comisorio*) with a fully fledged legal decisional effect.

The inclusion or total exclusion of judicial termination also gave rise to some debate. What is clear is that judicial termination is alive, well and maintaining a strong presence. Its critics certainly have a point, but its permanence in our legal practice is inescapable. That is not to say that extrajudicial termination was seen as a panacea, especially when in the majority of cases legal proceedings are the result of claims for restitution or demands of penalty clauses for the restorative effects of the resolution to take effect.

With regard to the latter, inspired by the reforms proposed in Spain, we crafted a text that was more prolific than a version covering simple payment of what was not owed, or the rules on the consecutive restitutions of nullity or the actions in the 'recovery' domain. There, the effort is distinct from the other international instruments.

Articles 91, 92 and 93 PLACL deal with the effects of resolution, in particular restorative effects in kind or, in the case of impossibility of restitution, its substitution for the value of performance at the moment of impossibility.

With regard to resolution, we propose an express solution to the usual courtroom game between resolution and *exceptio non adimpleti contractus* (defence of the unperformed contract: Article 95 PLACL). In general, the problem is frequent in respect of reciprocal non-performance in bilateral contracts. The termination proceeds even in the case of reciprocal non-performance, distancing its origin from the necessity of fault and achieving satisfactory effects from the restitution point of view.

With regard to the remedy of price reduction, even though it is included and recognised in the laws of the region, specifically in sales contracts in the case of defective goods, the group did argue about its advantage in respect of compensation of damages. Its relevance is determined by the moment at which the court sets the compensation. In relation to damages, it is anticipated that this will proceed if the non-performance causes harm or loss and the debtor is not exonerated from liability, establishing that the constitutive circumstances of unforeseeable events or force majeure are the cause of exoneration.

It is provided that compensation includes both monetary and non-monetary damages. Rules that determine the extension of the restitution are also included:

(a) the regulation of the foreseeability of damage at the time of the contract, except for fraud or gross negligence, in which case the limit is determined by causality—this follows the tradition of Latin American regulations;
(b) the regulation of the contribution of the creditor to its own harm, subjecting the compensation to a reduction if the creditor, by its action or omission, contributed to the non-performance; and
(c) the regulation of mitigation of losses. The creditor is charged with responsibility for minimising loss, subjecting the compensation to reduction if the creditor failed to take those steps that, in accordance with good faith, were reasonable for the purpose of mitigating loss. The reduction will correspond to the level to which the creditor could have mitigated the damage. What is missing in this rule is a clarification that refers to cases in which such mitigating measures were adopted but were unsuccessful, and another allowing for the use of restitution to cover the costs of the adoption of the measures or incidental damages.

III. Conclusion

I hope that the foregoing will have provided a panorama of some of the most significant problems and debates that faced our group.

The task has been an arduous one, mainly because it is difficult to secure a space for the cultural identity of the countries in the region, which have always taken their cue from the European, primarily continental experience.

Speaking for myself, I am sceptical of the possibility of a global contract law—one that is the same everywhere, a homogeneous system without the differences that represent the culture of each region or country. I am even more sceptical of the understanding that the regulations that govern contracts should only be subject to economic precepts.

The debate remains open, and we still have time to put the final touches to these Principles. I remain confident that this effort will serve to perfect our legislation and contribute to a contract law that is well adapted to the social needs of our countries.

3

Harmonisation of Private Law in Latin America and the Emergence of Third-generation Codes

AGUSTÍN PARISE*

I. Introduction

Each generation has its own traits, and generations of civil codes are no exception. This chapter claims that three subsequent generations of civil codes emerged in Latin America. Looking at a specific area of the law within a code may assist in identifying traits. Contract law occupies a pre-eminent position within private law,[1] and a look into the harmonisation of that important part of private law in Latin America may help to identify the traits of the third generation of codes. It should be further noticed that the Principles of Latin American Contract Law (PLACL), a joint effort of the Fundación Fernando Fueyo Laneri[2] and the Fondation pour le Droit Continental,[3] may be approached from the perspective of third-generation codes.

* This contribution benefited from comments by participants and attendees at the conference on *The Future of Contract Law in Latin America*, organised by the Oxford Institute of European and Comparative Law on 25 June 2015, mainly Jan P Schmidt—who also commented on earlier drafts of this paper—and Hugh Beale, Diego Fernández Arroyo, Alejandro Garro, and Roger Halson. The author is indebted to Julieta Marotta de Parise for her research assistance, and for her suggestions and constructive criticisms. Unless otherwise indicated, translations are provided by the author. When citing journal articles, the numbers in square brackets at the end of the citation indicate pin-points in the online version of the respective journal.

[1] RA Etcheverry, 'Contratos asociativos' y la nueva legislación' [2012] *Revista Jurídica Argentina La Ley* 645 [1].

[2] On the harmonisation efforts of Fernando Fueyo Laneri in Chile and the Americas at large, see A Ferrante, '¿Es correcta la elección del método de cálculo de la reducción del precio en los principios latinoamericanos de contratos?' (2014) 22 *Revista Chilena de Derecho Privado* 9, 20 at n 44.

[3] C Eyzaguirre Baeza and J Rodríguez Diez, 'Expansión y límites de la buena fe objetiva—A propósito del "Proyecto de Principios Latinoamericanos de Derecho de los Contratos"' (2013) 21 *Revista Chilena de Derecho Privado* 137, 138–39.

Participating in a globalised economy indeed requires great sacrifices and significant changes.[4] Globalisation has spread from the economy to culture, politics, science, technology, ideology and the law.[5] Globalisation affects the law and motivates harmonisation efforts.[6] Harmonisation requires policy coordination among different jurisdictions: it requires cooperation.[7] Harmonisation succeeds when a degree of common ground is achieved among the provisions of different jurisdictions.[8] Codes serve as prime examples of provision-containers, where harmonisation could be sought. It has been claimed—for quite some time now—that the world is turning into a global village, as defended by the Canadian philosopher Marshall McLuhan.[9] This scenario requires new solutions,[10] and hence, new codes: it requires a new generation of codes. These new texts should provide a lingua franca for juridical relations.[11]

This chapter is divided into three sections. First, it will introduce the theoretical framework behind the different generations of codes and their shifts. This section will also depict the traits of the first two generations of codes. Secondly, this chapter will show how private law harmonisation efforts in Latin America have generated a developing third generation of codes. Attention will be devoted to elements that are common to the region, to earlier harmonisation efforts and to the PLACL. Thirdly, this chapter will focus on an ongoing shift in generations of codes. Accordingly, it will define the characteristics of third-generation codes, and see the interaction of new codes and harmonising principles. A look into the Argentine Civil and Commercial Code (ACCC) will offer an example of that new generation of codes. The entire chapter will aim to provide a broader context for the understanding of third-generation codes in Latin America.

II. Generations of Codes

Three generations of civil codes have developed in Latin America. Dalmacio Vélez Sarsfield—drafter of the influential Civil Code of Argentina 1871—claimed back

[4] AA Menicocci, 'Los contratos internacionales ante el concurso local' [2007] *Revista Jurídica Argentina La Ley* 1096 [6].

[5] AA Alterini, '¿Hacia un geoderecho?' [2005] *Revista Jurídica Argentina La Ley* 1258 [1].

[6] M Pereña Vicente, 'Unificación del derecho contractual: convergencia de los principios UNIDROIT y de los principios del derecho europeo de contratos' (2005) 8 *Revista de Responsabilidad Civil y Seguros* 115 [1].

[7] A Dreyzin de Klor, 'Hacia el ordenamiento jurídico del Mercosur' [1996] *Revista Jurídica Argentina La Ley* 1189 [6].

[8] AA Alterini, 'Derecho internacional de los contratos' [2009] *Revista Jurídica Argentina La Ley* 671 [1].

[9] See generally M McLuhan, *The Gutenberg Galaxy: The Making of Typographic Man* (Toronto, University of Toronto Press, 1962). See also JP Pampillo Baliño, 'La integración jurídica americana. Génesis, desenvolvimiento y futuro' [2014] *Revista Jurídica Argentina La Ley—Suplemento Actualidad*, 25 September 2014, 1 [1].

[10] ER Hooft, 'El Mercosur y el derecho privado' [1992] *Revista Jurídica Argentina La Ley* 870 [2].

[11] Alterini (n 8) [1].

in the 1870s that codes were meant to be modified by new generations, and that the future could not be chained to an unchangeable provision.[12] Codes further serve the function of unifying and centralising the framework of legal sources, while they also provide a certain vision of individuals as part of society, serving as pedagogical and disciplinary instruments.[13] These statements apply to all generations of codes.

Carlos Ramos Núñez correctly indicated that codification could be seen as a legal paradigm.[14] Each generation of codes can be seen as a different paradigm, while shifts in generations imply shifts in paradigms. Paradigms and generations of codes can therefore be assimilated. The conceptualisation of generation of codes used in this chapter derives from the more generic understanding of scientific paradigms used by philosophers of science and of legal paradigms used by jurists. A paradigm, as defined by *The Oxford English Dictionary*, is 'a conceptual or methodological model underlying the theories and practices of a science or discipline at a particular time; (hence) a generally accepted world view'.[15]

Thomas S Kuhn offered ground-breaking, and currently seminal, ideas on scientific paradigms in his work *The Structure of Scientific Revolutions* (1962).[16] According to Kuhn, a scientific paradigm—referred to by part of the literature as model, *Leitbild*, or archetype[17]—is an achievement that is 'sufficiently unprecedented to attract an enduring group of adherents away from competing modes of scientific activity'[18] and 'sufficiently open-ended to leave all sorts of problems for the redefined group of practitioners to resolve'.[19] A scientific revolution results in the generation of a consensual model that modifies the historical perspective of a certain scientific community;[20] and acquiring scientific paradigm status indeed reflects maturity in the development of a scientific field.[21] The American philosopher of science understood that scientific paradigms are 'universally recognised

[12] The statement in Spanish reads: 'La codificación no puede ser jamás la última palabra de la perfección legislativa ni el término de un progreso. La prudencia humana tiene sus límites y los códigos de una generación serán siempre reformados por los mejores de una generación nueva y porque el porvenir no puede encadenarse a una letra inmutable'. *Cuaderno de Vélez Sarsfield, 1800–1875*, cited in JC Rivera, 'El Proyecto de Código Civil para la República Argentina' (2001) 35 *Revista Jurídica Universidad Interamericana de Puerto Rico* 381, 381.

[13] E Zuleta Puceiro, 'Apuntes para una teoría de las fuentes en la Codificación Civil Hispanoamericana' [1979] *Revista Jurídica Argentina La Ley* 855 [3].

[14] C Ramos Núñez, *Codificación, Tecnología y Postmodernidad* (Lima, Ara Editores, 1996) 23.

[15] 'paradigm, n' OED Online. March 2015. Oxford University Press. www.oed.com/view/Entry/137329?redirectedFrom=paradigm.

[16] TS Kuhn, *The Structure of Scientific Revolutions*, 2nd edn, enlarged (Chicago, IL, The University of Chicago Press, 1970). Kuhn introduced several modifications and clarifications to his 1962 work, mainly in his *Postscript-1969*. See EP Haba, 'Ciencias del derecho, La controversia de paradigmas en la Teoría del Derecho contemporánea' in M Ossorio y Florit et al (eds), *Enciclopedia Jurídica Omeba*, Appendix Volume VII (Buenos Aires, Driskill, 1996) 122; and Ramos Núñez (n 14) 23.

[17] Ramos Núñez (n 14) 23.

[18] Kuhn (n 16) 10.

[19] ibid.

[20] Ramos Núñez (n 14) 23.

[21] Kuhn (n 16) 11.

scientific achievements that for a time provide model problems and solutions to a community of practitioners'.[22] A scientific paradigm invites consensus on a certain assumption that enables the devising of a problem and of arguments and solutions to deal with that problem.[23] These scientific paradigms provide tools for the observation of a body of knowledge,[24] being informative of the type of research questions that must be posed and on how answers should be interpreted.[25]

Legal paradigms are welcomed by the legal narrative. Some scholars used the work of Kuhn as a means to understand legal disciplines,[26] while others claimed that the Kuhnian model did not apply to social sciences, such as law.[27] Looking at paradigms within the realm of law, however, requires the study of *how*, at a certain time and place, legal orderings are affected by social interaction.[28] Paradigms, in the legal realm, can deal with an overarching legal doctrine or dogma, as combined with the prevailing ideologies in a certain society.[29] In a narrower sense, legal paradigms can consist of, among other things, laws, customs, court decisions and doctrinal writings that provide solutions to specific problems at specific times and places, and that have gained recognition among jurists.[30] Accordingly, a legal paradigm can be defined as a value or concept that is shared by a legal community at a certain time and place.[31] Jean L Cohen further stated that legal paradigms are 'an integrated set of cognitive and normative background assumptions about the relationship the law should establish between the state and society, and the form legal regulation must take'.[32] Other literature highlighted that legal paradigms are useful tools to assess the conditions of certain matters that are subject to regulation.[33] Legal paradigms, indeed, can refer to the implicit images that actors might have of their own societies and that guide the law-making and application processes.[34]

Generations of codes consist of the abstract understanding of what are the scope, purpose and effects of civil codes in a certain society at a certain time. This abstract understanding finds consensus among jurists, provides model problems and solutions, and changes according to time and space. Generations should, therefore, be considered tools to assess the conditions of the codes. All three Latin

[22] ibid at viii. See also Haba (n 16) 122.

[23] U de Vries, 'Kuhn and Legal Research: A Reflexive Paradigmatic View on Legal Research' (2013) 3 *Recht en Methode in onderzoek en onderwijs* 7, 8.

[24] ibid, 9.

[25] ibid.

[26] T Schultz, *Transnational Legality: Stateless Law and International Arbitration* (Oxford, Oxford University Press, 2014) 64.

[27] See the examples mentioned in de Vries (n 23) 11.

[28] ibid, 12.

[29] Haba (n 16) 122.

[30] ibid, 123.

[31] R Boulot, 'A New Legal Paradigm: Towards a Jurisprudence Based on Ecological Sovereignty' (2012) 8 *Macquarie Journal of International and Comparative Environmental Law* 1, 10.

[32] JL Cohen, *Regulating Intimacy: A New Legal Paradigm* (Princeton, NJ, Princeton University Press, 2002) 143.

[33] de Vries (n 23) 7.

[34] J Habermas, 'Paradigms of Law' (1996) 17 *Cardozo Law Review* 771, 771.

American generations of codes are distinguishable because of their contents, time of enactment and motivation.

Legal institutions are subject to mutation[35] and—being human creations—are transformed together with societies, with political structures and with mentalities.[36] Legal institutions are in constant evolution and transformation, either at a slow or a fast pace.[37] Generations of codes never fade overnight, yet the main points of inflection can be spotted.[38] A shift or scientific revolution will break with a previous generation and set in place a new one that will be likewise accepted.[39] Therefore, an established assumption will be replaced when a generational shift occurs.[40] These revolutions and shifts evolve around the idea of reaching equilibrium. The normativity and social condition of legal institutions may attain equilibrium, yet if they dissociate due to the emergence of anomalies, mutation will take place and society will interpret or apply the legal institution in a different way. Ultimately, if the dissociation continues, a reform will take place, and the legal institution will need to be reformed.[41] As societies and mentalities evolve, anomalies evolve. These anomalies sometimes may not be explained by prevailing generations, showing weaknesses that will ultimately demand new generations to emerge.[42]

A. First Generation: Secessionist[43]

The first generation of codes may be deemed secessionist. Independence from European domination in Latin American jurisdictions was followed by the enactment of local private law provisions. Those enactments took place in the region mainly by the promulgation of first-generation civil codes during the period 1826–1917,[44] from Haiti to Brazil. Comprehensive attempts at codification were

[35] A Levaggi, *Manual de Historia del Derecho Argentino (Castellano-Indiano/Nacional)*, 2nd edn, vol I (Buenos Aires, Depalma, 1996) 6; and R Congost, *Tierras, leyes, historia: estudios sobre 'la gran obra de la propiedad'* (Barcelona, Crítica, 2007) 40.

[36] JL Halpérin, *Histoire du droit des biens* (Paris, Économica, DL, 2008) 2.

[37] Levaggi (n 35) 3.

[38] See, for example, the reference to the paradigm shift in Germany from codification to constitution in KW Nörr, 'From Codification to Constitution: On the Changes of Paradigm in German Legal History of the Twentieth Century' (1992) 60 *Tijdschrift voor Rechtsgeschiedenis* 145, especially 149.

[39] Ramos Núñez (n 14) 23.

[40] de Vries (n 23) 7.

[41] Levaggi (n 35) 3.

[42] Schultz (n 26) 63–64.

[43] This section draws, often verbatim, on A Parise, 'Civil Law Codification in Latin America: Understanding First and Second Generation Codes' in JM Milo, JHA Lokin and JM Smits (eds), *Tradition, Codification and Unification: Comparative-Historical Essays on Developments in Civil Law* (Cambridge, Intersentia, 2014).

[44] The list of Latin American jurisdictions and the years of effect of their first-generation civil codes reads as follows: Haiti, 1826; Bolivia, 1831; Peru, 1836; Costa Rica, 1841; Dominican Republic, 1844; Chile, 1857; El Salvador, 1860; Panama, 1860; Ecuador, 1861; Venezuela, 1862; Uruguay, 1868; Argentina, 1871; Mexico, 1871; Nicaragua, 1871; Colombia, 1873; Guatemala, 1877; Paraguay, 1877; Honduras, 1880; Cuba, 1889; Puerto Rico, 1889; and Brazil, 1917.

made in the Americas.[45] There was interest in the region in grasping the panorama of civil law legislation in a succinct and comprehensive way. There was also a demand for examination of the ideas circulating in other civilised states that had achieved codification.[46] By replicating European events, many American jurisdictions started to replace their versions of *ius commune* with codified systems of national laws,[47] a process that would be completed with the second-generation civil codes.

The structure and content of first-generation civil codes in Latin American jurisdictions reflected a clear harmony among the different codes. The structure of most codes followed the model provided by the *Code Napoléon*. At the turn of the century, the German Civil Code (BGB) and other European civil codes also had a considerable impact on first-generation codes, though the impact was mainly recognised later in second-generation texts.

First-generation codification, however, was not limited to the impact of the French and German texts. Studies on comparative legislation also motivated an interest in codification. Two main works of legislative concordances helped in spreading first-generation codification across the Americas. A work of concordances by Fortuné Anthoine de Saint-Joseph included a synoptic chart that helped compare the texts of the *Code Napoléon* with the texts of several nineteenth-century codes.[48] A work by Florencio García Goyena directed readers through the text of a Spanish civil code project of 1851 which included scholarly analysis for each of its articles.[49] Those comparative works were essential tools for the drafters of civil codes around the world.[50] The works of Saint-Joseph and García Goyena indeed had a significant impact on the codification efforts that emerged across the Americas. The Spanish Concordance was very well circulated in Spain and in the Americas,[51] and it was an inspiration for codifiers in the Americas such as Vélez Sarsfield in Argentina and Andrés Bello in Chile. Vélez Sarsfield made express references to the Spanish Concordance, for example, in the notes to the different Articles of the Civil Code of Argentina of 1871.[52] The Civil Code of Chile of 1857 also found inspiration in the Spanish Concordance, where the Venezuelan

[45] A Parise, 'The Place of the Louisiana Civil Code in the Hispanic Civil Codifications: Inclusion in the Comments to the Spanish Civil Code Project of 1851' (2008) 68 *Louisiana Law Review* 823, 831.

[46] F Stone, 'A Primer on Codification' (1955) 29 *Tulane Law Review* 303, 307; cited also in JW Cairns, *The 1808 Digest of Orleans and 1866 Civil Code of Lower Canada: An Historical Study of Legal Change*, vols I–II, unpublished PhD thesis (Edinburgh, University of Edinburgh, 1980) 19.

[47] B Bravo Lira, *Derecho Común y Derecho Propio en el Nuevo Mundo* (Santiago, Editorial Jurídica de Chile, 1989) 54.

[48] A de Saint-Joseph, *Concordance entre les codes civils étrangers et le Code Napoléon* (Paris, Charles Hingray, 1840).

[49] F García Goyena, *Concordancias, motivos y comentarios del código civil español*, vols I–IV (Madrid, Sociedad Tipográfico-Editorial, 1852).

[50] See generally R Knütel, 'Influences of the Louisiana Civil Code in Latin America' (1996) 70 *Tulane Law Review* 1445.

[51] See generally Parise (n 45).

[52] See the note to Art 186 of the Argentine Civil Code. See 'Ley 340 Código Civil' in *Anales de Legislación Argentina*, vol 1852–1880 (Buenos Aires, La Ley, 1954) 526.

jurist Bello closely followed the provisions of the Spanish Concordance in his drafting.[53]

First-generation codes, therefore, found sources of inspiration on the American continent. The civil codes of Argentina and Chile served as ways to spread codification in the region. The 1871 Argentine text found inspiration, among many others, in the *Code Napoléon* and the two works of legislative concordance. The Argentine text was adopted by Paraguay (1877) and was influential in the drafting of several other Latin American jurisdictions. The 1857 Chilean text also found inspiration in similar sources to those of Argentina. The influence of the Code of Chile was, however, much more significant than that of its sister state: many Latin American civil codes adopted the text in full or subject to certain changes.[54]

The motivation for the first generation of texts connected many of the resulting codes. One motivation may be found in the intention to break with the past and with the Spanish presence. The recently independent jurisdictions aimed at ending the normative subjugation that had existed during the previous period. Another motivation for civil codes, which relates to the previous one, may be found in regarding the codes as a constitutive element of the new republics and states. Jurisdictions included within their legislative agendas the need to promulgate codes as a kind of constitutive element, some including references to codification even in their Constitutions.[55] First-generation codes aimed to project a sense of differentiation between the Old and the New World, between former dependence and empire. These codes were indeed an expression of a secessionist movement.

Some jurisdictions enacted a multiplicity of civil codes that preserved a first-generation status.[56] First-generation codes, therefore, are not necessarily associated with the first enacted code. They may include a series of civil codes that never reach second-generation status, even though they amend the text of the original enactments. Accordingly, the adoption of two or more intermediate codes may be needed to achieve a complete mutation to the second generation.

B. Second Generation: Differentialist[57]

The second generation of codes may be deemed differentialist. As with the secessionist codes, this second generation is distinguishable because of its content,

[53] V Pescio Vargas, *Manual de Derecho Civil*, 2nd edn, vol I (Santiago, Editorial Jurídica de Chile, 1978) 115.

[54] eg, Colombia, Ecuador, El Salvador, Honduras, Nicaragua and Venezuela.

[55] The Argentine Constitution of 1853 stated in Art 64(11) that the National Congress had to enact, among other things, a national civil code. See 'Constitución de la Confederación Argentina' in *Anales de Legislación Argentina*, vol 1852–1880 (Buenos Aires, La Ley, 1954).

[56] Venezuela may serve as an illustration. This country adopted its first-generation code in 1862. The second-generation code was adopted in Venezuela only in 1942, after a multiplicity of codes had been enforced in the country during those 80 years. For more information on codification in Venezuela, see O Moréteau and A Parise, 'Recodification in Louisiana and Latin America' (2009) 83 *Tulane Law Review* 1103, 1140–41.

[57] This section draws, often verbatim, on Parise (n 43).

the time of enactment and its motivation. Codification went on evolving throughout the twentieth century,[58] and jurisdictions kept amending and replacing the texts of their existing codes, adapting them to their particular societies. A number of Latin American jurisdictions replaced their first-generation codes.[59] Since societies mature at different times, second-generation codes emerged in the period 1888–2003, from Costa Rica to Brazil. The resulting second-generation codes were adopted during the twentieth century,[60] although some were enacted already during the nineteenth century[61] and still others during the twenty-first century.[62] Some replacements took place shortly after the first-generation codes were enacted,[63] while others took several decades to complete.[64]

The structure and content of second-generation codes in Latin American jurisdictions also reflected a harmony among the different texts. That identity was also shaped by the new social aspects of legislation, which had developed especially since the adoption of the Mexican (1917) and Weimar (1919) Constitutions. Second-generation codes, however, were more eclectic than their predecessors. When looking for sources, the drafters of second-generation codes did not ignore the developments of the law in Europe[65] and in the Americas.[66] Nor did they ignore their own court judgments, legislation and doctrine; thus providing the texts with a more distinctive national identity. Second-generation codes were able to incorporate elements of local law that the different jurisdictions had been developing since their first codes had been enacted. The typifying characteristic of these codes is that they were able to incorporate local elements that distinguished them from the codes of other American jurisdictions, while also differentiating them from the texts of their previous-generation codes. As mentioned earlier, second-generation codes were able to highlight their own identity.

Second-generation codes found more mature societies seeking their own identities. Latin American jurisdictions found that they could use their codes to differentiate themselves. Accordingly, second-generation codes gave identity to jurisdictions that had adopted texts borrowed from other Latin American codes

[58] See, in general, the complete study by A Guzmán Brito, *La codificación civil en Iberoamérica. Siglos XIX y XX* (Santiago, Editorial Jurídica de Chile, 2000). See also the survey and references in ML Murillo, 'The Evolution of Codification in the Civil Law Legal Systems: Towards Decodification and Recodification' (2001) 11 *Journal of Transnational Law and Policy* 163; and R Pérez-Perdomo, *Latin American Lawyers: A Historical Introduction* (Stanford, CA, Stanford University Press, 2006) 61–67.

[59] The list of Latin American jurisdictions and the years of effect of their second-generation civil codes reads as follows: Costa Rica, 1888; Puerto Rico, 1902; Nicaragua, 1904; Honduras, 1906; Panama, 1917; Mexico, 1932; Peru, 1936; Venezuela, 1942; Guatemala, 1963; Bolivia, 1976; Cuba, 1987; Paraguay, 1987; and Brazil, 2003.

[60] eg, Mexico, 1932.

[61] eg, Costa Rica, 1888.

[62] eg, Brazil, 2003.

[63] eg, Puerto Rico adopted its first-generation code in 1889, and replaced that code for one of second generation in 1902.

[64] eg, Paraguay adopted its first-generation code in 1877, and replaced that code—borrowed from that of Argentina—with one of the second generation in 1987.

[65] eg, Civil Code of Switzerland, 1912; and Civil Code of Italy, 1942.

[66] eg, Civil Code of Peru, 1936; and Civil Code of Venezuela, 1942.

(predominantly from the text of the Chilean Code) and to jurisdictions that aimed to renovate texts that no longer reflected the local *ethos*. Alongside these developments, these new codes aimed to project a sense of differentiation between American jurisdictions, between the different parts of the New World. These codes were indeed an expression of a differentialist movement.

III. Private Law Harmonisation in Latin America

Harmonisation efforts in the field of private law in Latin America may help to explain the ongoing generation shift. Some common elements indeed favour harmonisation in Latin America. This is a region with a certain degree of homogeneity, based on the historical, cultural and religious continuity it experienced.[67] Harmonisation efforts have taken place in the region, and can be traced to the nineteenth century. A recent harmonisation effort may result from the drafting and reception of the PLACL.

A. Common Elements

A combination of elements indicate that the harmonisation of law in Latin America could be undertaken successfully. Those common deemed elements relate to culture and history, and can be linked to language and legal traditions.[68] Likewise, they call for further harmonisation efforts in Latin America.

A degree of linguistic uniformity and the prevailing legal tradition are a significant advantage for harmonisation in Latin America.[69] Romance languages prevail in the region, where Spanish crosses through all jurisdictions, with a few exceptions, such as Portuguese in Brazil and French in Haiti. Linguistic uniformity in Latin America favours daily life and commerce, and facilitates research by simplifying cooperative work and access to output by scholars in other jurisdictions that share the same language. The civil law legal tradition prevails in Latin America. That tradition is a result of, among other things, the common Romanisation that took place in Latin America,[70] and which was highlighted in a number of studies, by among many others, Agustín Díaz Bialet[71]

[67] Pampillo Baliño (n 9) [4].

[68] For information on the alleged Latin American legal family, see generally DP Fernández Arroyo, 'Sobre la existencia de una familia jurídica latinoamericana' [1995] *Jurisprudencia Argentina* 913.

[69] Ferrante (n 2) 13.

[70] S Schipani, 'Armonización y unificación del derecho: derecho común en materia de obligaciones y contratos en América Latina' in J Adame Goddard (ed), *Derecho privado. Memoria del congreso internacional de culturas y sistemas jurídicos comparados* (Mexico, UNAM, 2005) 684–85.

[71] eg, A Díaz Bialet, *El derecho romano en la obra de Vélez Sarsfield*, vols I–III (Córdoba, Imprenta de la Universidad, 1949–1952).

and Sandro Schipani.[72] The Romanist conception clearly prevails in the two pillars of the economy: property law and contract law.[73] Latin American legislation has been poured into a cast provided by Roman law.[74] Bello in Chile, Vélez Sarsfield in Argentina and Augusto Teixeira de Freitas in Brazil were the main codifiers in the region and were renowned Romanists who incorporated Roman elements in their drafting activities.[75] It should be acknowledged that the Romanist background that was implemented in the nineteenth century could now offer a new recompense and help overcome potential obstacles in the harmonisation of private law.[76]

Other common elements have been highlighted by scholars. Alejandro Garro—as early as 1992—pointed out that the legal systems in Latin America to some extent shared 'a similar socioeconomic structure, political culture and a common legal heritage'.[77] It has been noticed, for example, that the region's institutional framework is a liberal one, and that it was modelled to some extent after the constitutional example of the United States.[78] Furthermore, there is a strong inter-American commitment to the protection of human rights.[79] Legislation shares a similar 'legal expression' for private law that is present in a 'stylistic expression, legal phraseology, and terminology'.[80] In addition, contract law principles may be extracted from the common ground that is shared among civil and commercial codes of Latin America.[81]

Despite such common elements, the harmonising efforts in the field of substantive private law have not gained momentum in Latin America.[82] A return to an American *ius commune* should be promoted,[83] since the essential human bases

[72] eg, S Schipani (ed), *Dalmacio Vélez Sarsfield e il diritto latinoamericano* (Padua, CEDAM, 1991); and S Schipani (ed), *Augusto Teixeira de Freitas e il diritto latinoamericano* (Padua, CEDAM, 1988).

[73] MU Salerno, 'Treinta años de integración latinoamericana: perspectiva jurídica y empresaria' [1991] *Revista Jurídica Argentina La Ley* 1104 [2].

[74] AA Alterini, 'La contratación en el Mercosur' [1992] *Revista Jurídica Argentina La Ley* 735 [8].

[75] AA Alterini, 'La responsabilidad extracontractual en los Códigos Civiles del Mercosur' [1997] *Doctrina Judicial* 133 [3]; Ferrante (n 2) 14; and S Schipani, 'Unità e specificità del sistema giuridico latinoamericano e "principi di Unidroit": Cenni per un programma di lavoro' in MJ Bonell and S Schipani (eds), *'Principi per i contratti commerciali internazionali' e il sistema giuridico latinoamericano* (Padua, CEDAM, 1996) 315–16.

[76] E O'Farrell, 'La armonización del derecho en los países del Mercosur' [1993] *Revista Jurídica Argentina La Ley* 1069 [2].

[77] AM Garro, 'Unification and Harmonization of Private Law in Latin America' (1992) 40 *American Journal of Comparative Law* 587, 587.

[78] JC Rivera, 'El derecho privado en los grandes espacios económicos (Unión Europea, Mercosur, Área de Libre Comercio de las Américas)' (2005) 2(3) *Revista Latinoamericana de Derecho* 243, 269.

[79] ibid.

[80] Garro (n 77) 608.

[81] ibid, 587.

[82] ibid; and R Momberg, 'Harmonization of Contract Law in Latin America: Past and Present Initiatives' [2011] *Uniform Law Review* 111, 112.

[83] J Oviedo Albán, 'Los Principios UNIDROIT para los Contratos Internacionales' (2002) 11 *Díkaion* 96, 125; Momberg (n 82) 28; and AM Garro, 'Contract Law in Latin America: Building of a "Latin American" Ius Commune', Paper presented at the conference *35 Years CISG and Beyond* (30 January 2015), at Universität Basel available at www.cisgbasel2015.com/index_htm_files/24_

are compatible.[84] As Alejandro Guzmán Brito claimed, a *mos Latinoamericanus iura legendi*[85] should be designed, a Latin American 'way to understand, create, apply and teach the law'.[86] Latin Americans need to know more about each other.[87] In that respect, disciplinary studies by legal historians, comparatists and philosophers of law would be beneficial.[88] In addition, the teaching of Latin American Comparative law in law schools on both sides of the Atlantic should be promoted.[89]

B. Earlier Experiences

Efforts to harmonise private law are not new in Latin America,[90] since they can be traced back to the early days of independence.[91] Harmonisation is helpful in attaining more international legal certainty,[92] and to achieve certainty in international and domestic contracts.[93] Harmonisation of laws should ideally be accompanied by economic, social, cultural and political integration.[94] It requires a shift from the exclusive interests of the nation state to those of a broader entity.[95] Therefore, a shift from the national to the regional level would be desirable. This shift could be motivated by commercial needs, by the export of goods and by economic growth.[96] Finally, harmonisation benefits from horizontal networks of collaboration.[97]

paper_Alejandro%20Garro_Harmonization%20of%20Contract%20Law%20in%20Latin%20America;%20Efforts%20and%20Purposes.pdf at 2.

[84] C Suárez Anzorena, 'Notas sobre el "Mercado Común del Cono Sur"' [1991] *Revista Jurídica Argentina La Ley* 942 [3].

[85] See generally, A Guzmán Brito, 'Mos latinoamericanus iura legendi' (1996) 1 *Roma e America* 15. The claim by Guzmán Brito related to the special way of studying the *Corpus iuris civilis* by the Romanists and the jurists of Latin America (ibid, 15).

[86] JP Pampillo Baliño, 'The Legal Integration of the American Continent: An Invitation to Legal Science to Build a New Ius Commune' (2011) 17 *ILSA Journal of International and Comparative Law* 517, 544.

[87] H Alegría, 'El Derecho Privado hoy y la innovación jurídica' [2013] *Revista Jurídica Argentina La Ley* 1020 [9].

[88] Pampillo Baliño (n 86) 547–48. Comparative law was also mentioned in Alegría (n 87) [9].

[89] Alegría (n 87) [9]; and HP Glenn, 'Harmony of Laws in the Americas' (2003) 34 *University of Miami Inter-American Law Review* 223, 235–38.

[90] For an overview, see A Tomasello, 'El proceso de integración en el Mercosur' [1999] *Doctrina Judicial* 647 [1–2]; and JC Smith, 'De la comunidad jurídica de Savigny a las comunidades económicas contemporáneas' [1997] *Revista Jurídica Argentina La Ley* 933 [3].

[91] Pampillo Baliño (n 9) [2].

[92] La Ley, 'Temas de derecho privado' [2001] *Revista Jurídica Argentina La Ley* 1096 [1].

[93] A Besalú Parkinson, 'Los principios del derecho europeo de los contratos' [2001] *Revista de Responsabilidad Civil y Seguros* 343 [1].

[94] Pampillo Baliño (n 9) [2].

[95] MC Dartayete, 'Armonización de normas en el Mercosur' (1999) 1 *Revista de Derecho del Mercosur* 63 [1].

[96] RA Etcheverry, 'El arbitraje en el Mercosur. El nuevo parlamento' [2007] *Revista Jurídica Argentina La Ley* 1239 [1].

[97] Pampillo Baliño (n 9) [1].

A selection of mainly Latin American-born efforts deserve to be highlighted.[98] These efforts can be divided—as Rodrigo Momberg has stated—into two groups: on the one hand, the emergence of integration initiatives; and on the other hand, the adoption of private international law instruments.[99] The latter instruments were first attempted through codification and subsequently by means of specialised international Conventions.[100] The 1878[101] Congress of 'American Jurists' held in Lima argued that uniform codes of substantive law should wait.[102] The harmonising efforts undertaken in Lima resulted in the first worldwide treaty on private international law.[103]

Harmonisation efforts continued in the region during the twentieth century. For example, the Montevideo treaties, eight in all, were adopted in 1889 and 1940.[104] These treaties, however, were not fully geared to harmonisation since they gave pride of place to the nation state.[105] They gave a fundamental role to the place of performance in international contracts.[106] In addition, they did not include all Latin American jurisdictions. Another example of harmonisation was the Bustamante Code: a landmark in the region. That 1928 text again dealt with conflict of laws and was adopted in Havana,[107] during the Sixth Pan-American conference.[108] However, countries such as Argentina, Mexico and Colombia did not sign the code.[109] A third harmonisation attempt was encapsulated in the proceedings of the Seventh Pan-American Conference, held in Montevideo in 1933, which recommended that jurists should work towards the drafting of a unified civil code for the Americas.[110] That claim was indeed avant-garde for the Western hemisphere.

The Organization of American States (OAS) also engaged in harmonisation activities.[111] It sponsored the Specialized Conferences on Private International Law (CIDIP is the Spanish acronym),[112] first held in Panama in 1975,[113] which bring together experts on conflict of laws, aiming to find common ground.[114]

[98] There were academic efforts in the US, also. See www.natlaw.com; and Glenn (n 89) 235.

[99] Momberg (n 82) 416.

[100] ibid; and Rivera (n 78) 269.

[101] Tomasello (n 90) [1]–[2]; and Smith (n 90) [3].

[102] Alterini (n 8) [2]; and Garro (n 77) 589.

[103] Alterini (n 8) [2]; and Garro (n 77) 589.

[104] Garro (n 77) 590.

[105] MA Ciuro Caldani, *El derecho internacional privado ante los procesos de integración* (Rosario, Fundación para las Investigaciones Jurídicas, 1998) 72.

[106] L Da Gama E Souza, 'The Unidroit Principles of International Commercial Contracts and their Applicability in the Mercosur Countries' (2002) 36 *Revue juridique Thémis* 375, 387.

[107] Garro (n 77) 591; and Tomasello (n 90) [1]–[2].

[108] W Goldschmidt, 'El derecho internacional privado en Latinoamérica. El Código Bustamante en la Teoría y en la práctica' [1981] *Revista Jurídica Argentina La Ley* 938 [1].

[109] Garro (n 77) 591.

[110] Ferrante (n 2) 15.

[111] Garro (n 77) 593.

[112] See www.oas.org/dil/private_international_law.htm.

[113] Alterini (n 8) [2].

[114] Garro (n 77) 593.

These specialised conferences[115] focus on the drafting of Model Laws (*Leyes Modelo*) for the Americas.[116] The conferences invite countries to adapt their regulations to those models through a mechanism resembling—*mutatis mutandis*—that of the EU directives.[117] Contract law, as the most common institution of international law, could not be absent in the CIDIPs.[118] CIDIP V, therefore, gave a paramount position to contract law.[119] Held in Mexico City in 1994, it resulted in the adoption of the Inter-American Convention on the Law Applicable to International Contracts.[120]

Some American integration projects overlap, competing for geographical space,[121] and suffer from structural and operational complexity, hence have limited success in improving the quality of life in Latin America.[122] There are over 80 sectoral agreements and more than 40 treaties and protocols,[123] some being short-lived, as stated correctly by Schipani.[124] For example, the efforts of the Economic Commission for Latin America and the Caribbean resulted in the establishment of the Latin American Free Trade Association in 1960,[125] which was ultimately replaced in 1980 by the Latin American Integration Association, aiming to integrate markets and following the worldwide trend towards mega-markets.[126]

Mercosur[127] deserves special attention as a means to achieve harmonisation of the law in Latin America. Mercosur was established by the Asunción Treaty of 1991,[128] which states in its Article 1 the agreement to harmonise the laws of its Member States.[129] Therefore, the treaty calls upon the Mercosur Member States to work on harmonising their laws.[130] Special enactments of Mercosur also

[115] For more information on the conferences, see Momberg (n 82) at 18–20.

[116] Pereña Vicente (n 6) 2.

[117] ibid.

[118] JC Arcagni, 'La Convención Interamericana sobre derecho aplicable a los contratos internacionales' [1996] *Revista Jurídica Argentina La Ley* 1434 [1].

[119] Ciuro Caldani (n 105) 73.

[120] See www.oas.org/dil/CIDIPV_home.htm. For more information on the CIDIPs see, Garro (n 83) 5.

[121] Momberg (n 82) 413.

[122] Pampillo Baliño (n 86) 545.

[123] ibid, 535.

[124] Schipani (n 70) 682.

[125] Smith (n 90) 6.

[126] CR Brizzio, 'Códigos únicos y "restatements" para unificar la regulación internacional del contrato' [2001] *Revista de Responsabilidad Civil y Seguros* 123 [2]; Etcheverry (n 96) [1]; and Alterini (n 5) [4].

[127] For the path to Mercosur, see RA Etcheverry and GM Etcheverry, *Mercosur: negocios y empresas: Historias y futuro de la integración americana* (Buenos Aires, Ciudad Argentina, 2001).

[128] See www.mercosur.int/innovaportal/file/719/1/CMC_1991_TRATADO_ES_Asuncion.pdf.

[129] ibid; and Dreyzin de Klor (n 7) [1].

[130] H Masnatta, 'Bases constitucionales del proceso de integración. La cuestión de las asimetrías entre los ordenamientos' [1996] *Revista Jurídica Argentina La Ley* 1129 [4]; C Harrington and JE Montoya De Filippi, 'Los principios del Derecho Comunitario Europeo: ¿Una esperanza para el Mercosur?' (2001) 5 *Revista de Derecho del Mercosur* 43 [10]; and H Alegría, 'El Mercosur hoy: la realidad, pragmatismo e ideales' [1995] *Revista Jurídica Argentina La Ley* 838 [3].

welcomed the harmonisation of contract law, as reflected in the 1994 Buenos Aires Protocol on International Jurisdiction for Contracts,[131] which placed freedom of will in a paramount position.[132] It should be noted, however, that Mercosur is still a long way from achieving a harmonised codification of private law provisions.[133]

Purely academic efforts were also undertaken to harmonise contract law in Latin America.[134] For example, in the late 1990s, a group led by Fernando Hinestrosa Forero, referred to as the *El Externado* Group, which took its name from the University of the Externado of Bogotá (Colombia), worked on the harmonisation of contract law in the region.[135] In addition, in 2000, the Alfa Group presented the first part of a project for a Latin American code of contract law,[136] and offered courses, with financial support from the EU.[137]

All these harmonisation efforts had an eroding impact on the first- and second-generation codes. They challenged the secessionist and differentialist movements that accompanied the first two generations of codes, since they advocated a globalist movement.

[131] See www.mercosur.int/msweb/Normas/normas_web/Decisiones/ES/CMC_DEC_1994-001_ES_Protocolo%20JurisdicInternaContractual.PDF. See also A Kemelmajer de Carlucci, 'Armonización y codificación regional. Las debilidades del Mercosur' in A Guzmán Brito et al (eds), *De la codificación a la descodificación. Code Civil (1804–2004) Código de Bello (1855–2005)* (Santiago, Ediciones Universidad Diego Portales Escuela de Derecho, 2005) 234; Ciuro Caldani (n 105) 91; and A Uriondo de Martinoli, 'Aspectos contractuales. Prórroga de la competencia. La función de la jurisprudencia de los Estados Parte' in M Pérez González et al (eds), *Desafíos del Mercosur* (Buenos Aires, Ciudad Argentina, 1997) 191.

[132] DP Fernández Arroyo, 'La nueva configuración del Derecho Internacional Privado del Mercosur: Ocho respuestas contra la incertidumbre' (1999) 4 *Revista de Derecho del Mercosur* 38 [4].

[133] Kemelmajer de Carlucci (n 131) 250. For approaches to the harmonisation of obligations and contracts in Mercosur, see M Fresneda Saieg, SA Frustagli, DF Esborraz and CA Hernández, 'Hacia la unificación del derecho de las obligaciones y de los contratos en el Mercosur' in MA Ciuro Caldani (ed), *Del Mercosur. Aduana—Jurisdicción—Informática—Relaciones intercomunitarias* (Buenos Aires, Ciudad Argentina, 1996) 253; and N Nicolau, MA Araujo, A Ariza, J Baldarenas, D Esborraz, S Frustagli, C Guglielmett, C Hernández, C Melo, M Ramonda, ME Vitale and C Galano, 'Necesidad y posibilidad de unificar la teoría general del contrato en el Mercosur' in M Pérez González et al (eds), *Desafíos del Mercosur* (Buenos Aires, Ciudad Argentina, 1997) 209.

[134] For example, Mario Rotondi suggested the region should adopt the 1927 French-Italian project of a code of obligations and contracts; while the work led by Giuseppe Gandolfi in Pavia was followed by scholars interested in the harmonisation of laws in Latin America and was addressed in, for example, the Argentine Conference of Private Law, held in Tucumán in 2011, where the foundations for a South American code of contract law were explored. See S Schipani, 'Treinta años de diálogo con los juristas latinoamericanos' [2004] *Revista Jurídica Argentina La Ley* 1499 [11]; Ferrante (n 2) 18; and S Díaz Alabart, 'La armonización del derecho de contratos en la Unión Europea y en el continente sudamericano' (2012) 4 *Revista de Derecho Privado* 115–16.

[135] For example, members of that group published A Guzmán Brito et al, *El contrato en el sistema jurídico latinoamericano. Bases para un código latinoamericano tipo* (Bogota, Universidad Externado de Colombia, 1998). See also Rivera (n 70) 269, and Ferrante (n 2) 18.

[136] JC Rivera, 'The Scope and Structure of Civil Codes. Relations with Commercial Law, Family Law, Consumer Law and Private International Law. A Comparative Approach' in JC Rivera (ed), *The Scope and Structure of Civil Codes* (Dordrecht, Springer, 2013) 37.

[137] Ferrante (n 2) 18.

C. PLACL

The PLACL may be added to the efforts towards the harmonisation of private law in Latin America. The origins of these Principles can be traced to the message conveyed in the *Doing Business Reports*[138] published by the World Bank indicating that the common law system was more efficient from an economic point of view than the civil law system.[139] Michel Grimaldi immediately took up the gauntlet that was thrown down by that report.[140] As part of the reaction, the Fondation pour le Droit Continental sponsored the creation of chairs and projects in traditional civil law jurisdictions, with a view to enhancing the merits of the civil law.[141] Others soon joined the efforts led by Grimaldi. Accordingly, in 2009, Bruno Caprile, Fabricio Mantilla, Sebastián Picasso and Carlos Pizarro Wilson participated in a conference in Rennes (France) on the transformations in contract law;[142] and while attending that conference laid the grounds for the PLACL project.[143]

The PLACL aim to identify the juridical identity of the region.[144] The project can be divided into three stages. A first stage was undertaken in the period 2009–10 and set out to identify the state of the art for contract law in the different jurisdictions.[145] A second stage followed in the period 2010–11 and consisted of a comparative study of American jurisdictions, however including also some European systems.[146] A third stage began in 2012, and consists of the drafting of the Principles.[147] A set of 40 questions was sent to scholars from different jurisdictions,[148] for the purposes of identifying the regional identity[149] and to highlight differences and similarities in the contract law of the relevant jurisdictions.[150] The questionnaire

[138] See the Reports available at www.doingbusiness.org/reports/global-reports/doing-business-2015.

[139] ibid; and GA Cavalier and T Straub, 'Mergers and Acquisitions. Comparative Economic Analysis of Laws: France vs. USA' (2009) 2 *Journal of Civil Law Studies* 147, 149 (especially references at n 1).

[140] C Pizarro Wilson, 'Presentación' in C Pizarro Wilson (ed), *El derecho de los contratos en Latinoamérica (Bases para unos principios de Derecho de los Contratos)* (Bogota, Universidad del Rosario and Universidad del Externado de Colombia, 2012) 15; and AM Morales Moreno, 'Los Principios latinoamericanos de derecho de los contratos. Un debate abierto sobre las grandes cuestiones jurídicas de la contratación' (2014) 67 *Anuario de Derecho Civil* 227, 229.

[141] Pizarro Wilson (n 140) 15; and Morales Moreno (n 140) 229.

[142] See www.cda.univ-rennes1.fr/themes/cooperation-internationale/Am%C3%A9rique+latine/. See also Pizarro Wilson (n 140) 15–16; Momberg (n 82) 425; and Garro (n 83) 8–9.

[143] Pizarro Wilson (n 140) 16.

[144] ibid, 16–17.

[145] C Madrid Martínez and J Annicchiarico, 'Reporte de evento: Hacia los Principios Latinoamericanos de Derecho de los Contratos' at Cartas Blogatorias, 13 October 2014, available at cartasblogatorias.com/2014/10/13/reporte-de-evento-hacia-los-principios-latinoamericanos-de-derecho-de-los-contratos/#more-234.

[146] ibid.

[147] ibid.

[148] A similar approach was suggested by N Nicolau, 'Un "Código de los contratos" para el Mercosur' [1996] *Revista Jurídica Argentina La Ley* 941 [3].

[149] Pizarro Wilson (n 140) 16–17; Momberg (n 82) 426; and Morales Moreno (n 140) 229.

[150] Madrid Martínez and Annicchiarico (n 145).

invited the addressees to pay special attention also to other sources of law, such as local doctrine and jurisprudence.[151] The replies to the questionnaire were published in book form in 2012[152] and included perspectives from Argentina, Brazil, Chile, Colombia, Paraguay, Uruguay and Venezuela.[153] Meetings were also held by the members of the PLACL project. A first such meeting took place in Colombia in 2010,[154] a more recent one in Chile in 2014.[155]

These Principles, as correctly stated by Garro, may provide the common core of contract law that is typically Latin American.[156] The PLACL may also provide a Latin American approach to private law.[157] Similarly to other instruments (inter alia, the UNIDROIT Principles for International Commercial Contracts or the United Nations Convention on Contracts for the International Sale of Goods), the PLACL may inspire reform and modernisation of contract law in the region.[158] They may help bridge the gap between domestic legal systems and the *lex mercatoria*.[159] This ongoing effort may provide innovative solutions that are better adapted to international trade.[160] Above all, the Principles could be considered an effort towards the harmonisation of laws,[161] and they may serve as a guide to harmonise contract law practices.[162] A 'typical' Latin American flavour or sound[163] should be sought when analysing the contract law of the different jurisdictions. It should be acknowledged that the PLACL may provide the common core of contract law that is typically Latin American: it may provide a 'typical' Latin American flavour, and a Latin American approach, a *mos Latinoamericanus iura legendi*.

IV. Generation Shift

A shift in the generation of codes is currently being perceived in Latin America. That shift heralds a third generation of codes that may be deemed globalist.

[151] Pizarro Wilson (n 140) 16; and Garro (n 83) 11.

[152] C Pizarro Wilson (ed), *El derecho de los contratos en Latinoamérica (Bases para unos principios de Derecho de los Contratos)* (Bogota, Universidad del Rosario and Universidad del Externado de Colombia, 2012).

[153] Momberg (n 82) 426; and Garro (n 83) 10–11.

[154] Pizarro Wilson (n 140) 16.

[155] Madrid Martínez and Annicchiarico (n 145).

[156] Garro (n 83) 10.

[157] ibid at 14.

[158] See www.law.ox.ac.uk/event=13672.

[159] Alterini (n 8) [7].

[160] Oviedo Albán (n 83) 100, 108.

[161] Ferrante (n 2) 20.

[162] Alterini (n 8) [6].

[163] The idea of a typical *flavour* or *sound* has been borrowed, *mutatis mutandis*, from the writings of Olivier Moréteau and Nicholas Kasirer. See O Moréteau, 'The Louisiana Civil Code Translation Project: An Introduction' (2012) 5 *Journal of Civil Law Studies* 97, 102.

There is an ongoing interaction of new codes and harmonising principles, and texts in the making now attend to both vernacular and foreign needs. The ACCC of 2015 offers a recent example of the new generation of codes that is emerging in the region. The drafters of that Argentine code responded in their provisions both to the vernacular and international needs of society.

A. Third Generation: Globalist

Reforms of civil codes are currently taking place in the region.[164] A series of new codes, or changes to existing codes, are needed in order to speak of a third generation, since generations of codes are distinguishable by their content, the time of enactment, and their motivation. That said, it should be borne in mind that the unification of civil and commercial codes is not necessarily a manifestation of a shift in generation. Early in the twentieth century voices were already being raised against the separation of private law codes into civil and commercial parts.[165] Unified private law texts were adopted in, among other jurisdictions, Switzerland (1881), Tunisia (1906), Poland (1934), Italy (1942), the USSR (1964) and Portugal (1967).[166] In the Americas, there were also calls for unification of private law texts. For example, the proceedings of the conferences of the Inter-American Bar Association advocated such unity in Rio de Janeiro (1943), Mexico (1944), Santiago de Chile (1945), Lima (1947) and Detroit (1949).[167] The Americas also offered examples of unified civil and commercial codes. Paraguay adopted a unified code in 1987 to replace the previous civil and commercial codes that had been borrowed from Argentina since 1877 and 1904, respectively.[168] A new code took effect in Brazil in 2003,[169] and unified civil and commercial provisions.[170]

The structure and content of third-generation codes in Latin American jurisdictions should reflect a harmony among the different texts. Third-generation codes need to attend to the Latin American regional context and the new cultural, social and economic settings.[171] They will be characterised by their efforts

[164] HA Acciarri, 'Los criterios de eficiencia como fundamento para la reforma del derecho privado en Latinoamérica' [2001] *Revista de Responsabilidad Civil y Seguros* 26.

[165] O Camisar, 'A 20 años del Proyecto de Unificación de nuestra legislación civil y comercial' [2007] *Revista Jurídica Argentina La Ley—Suplemento Actualidad*, 17 July 2007, 1 [3].

[166] ibid; and RM López Cabana, 'El proyecto de unificación legislativa civil y comercial (Su coordinación con recomendaciones de congresos jurídicos y soluciones del derecho comparado)' [1987] *Revista Jurídica Argentina La Ley* 845 [2].

[167] López Cabana (n 166) [1].

[168] See L Rienzi, 'Unidad del derecho privado. El problema de la autonomía del derecho comercial y la unificación de la legislación Civil y Comercial' [2014] *Doctrina Judicial*, 26 November 2014, 6 [5].

[169] On the Brazilian Code see, for example, R Momberg, 'Código Civil brasilero de 2002: nuevos principios para el derecho de contratos' (2014) 13 *Opinión Jurídica* 159.

[170] See Rienzi (n 168) [5].

[171] See the reference to the context and settings in AA Alterini, 'El futuro de la codificación en Francia y en América Latina: ¿Por qué es necesario un nuevo código?' [2004] *Revista Jurídica Argentina La Ley* 1337 [5].

to harmonise internal private law with that of other Latin American jurisdictions. Third-generation codes need to find an equilibrium between what is good for the individual and what is good for society at large, even beyond national borders.[172] The new generation of codes will build on the transfer of the nation state's law-making monopoly: codes will therefore welcome supranational content resulting from harmonisation.[173] New codes will have to encapsulate the common core of what is 'typically' Latin American, for the different areas of private law. For example, in contract law—and following the expression coined by Garro—they will have to include provisions that encapsulate the common core of contract law that is typically Latin American.[174]

Third-generation codes will be also characterised by their time of enactment. As mentioned above, first-generation codes are generally associated with the nineteenth century, while second-generation codes are generally regarded as typically twentieth-century products. This new generation is already taking shape, and even where the harmonising ideas can be traced to the previous century, their effects will be felt in the years to come. The twenty-first century will be the century of harmonised, dynamic and interrelated laws.[175] The globalist movement results in a lingua franca that is developing for juridical relations between jurisdictions; this lingua offers legal certainty.[176]

The motivation for third-generation codes will connect many of the resulting texts. Technological developments and the increase in the circulation of goods are associated with globalisation[177] and require changes in the wording of codes. Another motivation could be the harmonisation of private laws at a regional level.[178] Patrick Glenn has stated that the 'laws of the Americas are subject to a presumption of harmony rather than a presumption of conflict'.[179] Harmonisation efforts may inspire changes in codes, and motivate a third generation.[180] Harmonisation currently aims at a private law that will bridge national and regional scopes;[181] and few, if any, Latin American jurisdictions would currently consider

[172] See the reference to the above-mentioned equilibrium in AA Alterini, 'Tendencias en la contratación moderna' [1999] *Revista Jurídica Argentina La Ley* 1229 [8].

[173] Alterini (n 74) [7].

[174] It should be noted that a number of Latin American Constitutions already incorporated elements of private law, and regulated, for example, consumer law and environmental law. See Alegría (n 87) [4].

[175] LMR Garrido Cordobera, 'Código Europeo de contratos' [2007] *Revista Jurídica Argentina La Ley* 1353 [2].

[176] JM Prevot, 'El Código Civil y su función en la era del consumo' [2008] *Revista Jurídica Argentina La Ley* 421 [4].

[177] AI Piaggi and JR Vanossi, 'Integración, regionalización: idea y realidad' [1999] *Revista Jurídica Argentina La Ley* 1037 [1]. The trend of jurisdictions to group into economic blocks is seen as a means to deal with potential financial crises. See LK Vieira, 'La reforma de las constituciones de los Estados partes del Mercosur' [2012] *Revista Jurídica Argentina La Ley* 1112 [1].

[178] See the different perspectives of Glenn (n 89); Schipani (n 104), and Parise (n 43) 192.

[179] Glenn (n 89) 232.

[180] Parise (n 43) 185.

[181] ibid, 184.

harmonisation a threat to national sovereignty.[182] Jurisdictions now seem to seek participation in the international community by joining regional agreements.[183] Secession and differentiation now lie behind, and a degree of globalisation is welcomed in Latin America.

B. Interaction of Codes and Harmonising Principles

First- and second-generation codes were not designed to deal with the contract law requirements of a globalised economy.[184] A general theory of contract law should therefore be projected for Latin America,[185] and efforts such as the PLACL could serve to achieve that 'typical' Latin American flavour. Changes may be made to first- and second-generation codes through revision, benefiting from harmonising efforts that will evolve into a third-generation code. A one-lump shift into third-generation status may be difficult: piecemeal shifts or shifts in instalments should be preferred. The harmonisation of different areas of private law may be the way forward, since a fully globalist text represents a significant challenge to drafters. Some provisions will need to be added to or removed from existing codes in order to achieve third-generation status. This, however, should be less complicated than the shifts required to move from first to second generation. After all, the drafters will be working with existing realities and experiences, while looking for inspiration beyond national and regional borders.[186]

A shift in generation has to start from within the different jurisdictions, yet pay attention to harmonising efforts that may help to incorporate the 'typical' Latin American flavour into the resulting codes. A Latin American civil code hardly seems a feasible objective and changes will have to spring from within the different jurisdictions. Changes have to be made to national codes, since national private law ultimately needs to establish the guidelines by which the local society will engage with the globalised world.[187]

Codes were enacted during the past decades in Latin America. Some may have paved the way for a generation shift, while others may have missed that opportunity. Again, a one-lump shift into third-generation status may be difficult, and piecemeal changes should be welcomed. On the one hand, the 1984 Peruvian Code, a second-generation text, took a first step towards the identification of the

[182] Garro (n 77) 616.

[183] ibid.

[184] AL Calvo Caravaca and J Carrascosa González, 'Los contratos internacionales y el mito de la "nueva lex mercatoria"' (2005) 6 *Revista de Derecho del Mercosur* 103 [1].

[185] Nicolau (n 148) [3]. Academic discussion should be based on current law, as reflected in the questionnaire of the PLACL, to avoid abstract constructions that may turn out not to be applicable. See Schipani (n 134) [12].

[186] Nicolau (n 148) [1].

[187] JC Rivera, 'Globalización y derecho. Las fuentes del derecho de los contratos comerciales' [2005] *Revista Jurídica Argentina La Ley* 1005 [15].

'typical' Latin American flavour.[188] On the other hand, the 2003 Brazilian Code was enacted without heeding previous harmonisation efforts, despite the invitation to do so in the Mercosur treaties.[189]

C. Emergence in the Argentine Civil and Commercial Code[190]

The adoption of national commercial and civil codes was delayed in Argentina until the 1860s. Eduardo Acevedo and Vélez Sarsfield worked together in drafting a commercial code for the province of Buenos Aires.[191] That text, drafted mainly by Acevedo in consultation with Vélez Sarsfield, was approved without parliamentary debate by the Buenos Aires Congress in 1859.[192] The National Congress finally extended the application of that code to all of Argentina in 1862, taking effect as the *Código de Comercio para la Nación Argentina*.[193] In 1864, Vélez Sarsfield was appointed to draft a project,[194] this time of a civil code. His resulting work was approved without parliamentary debate by the National Congress,[195] taking effect in 1871 as the *Código Civil de la República Argentina*.[196]

The Argentine Commercial and Civil Codes were only replaced in 2015, although the texts went through many alterations that were introduced mainly by means of revisions.[197] Decodification had a significant impact on the Commercial Code, eroding most of the original text of 1862, as modified in 1889.[198] For example, bankruptcy was soon removed from the code, together with the enactment of special legislation on, among many others, bills of exchange, insurance, warrants and agricultural pledges.[199] The Civil Code was also subject to significant changes.

[188] Schipani (n 75) 316, at n 4.

[189] Alterini (n 5) [5]; and Alterini (n 8) [5].

[190] This section draws, often verbatim, on J Marotta and A Parise, 'On Codes, Marriage, and Access to Justice: Recent Developments in the Law of Argentina' (2014) 7 *Journal of Civil Law Studies* 237.

[191] A Levaggi, *Manual de Historia del Derecho Argentino (Castellano-Indiano/Nacional)*, 3rd edn, vol III (Buenos Aires, Abeledo Perrot, 2013) 183.

[192] ibid.

[193] *Código de Comercio para la Nación Argentina. Sancionado por el Honorable Congreso Nacional. El 10 de Setiembre de 1862* (Buenos Aires, Imprenta Argentina de 'El Nacional', 1863).

[194] A Levaggi, *Manual de Historia del Derecho Argentino (Castellano-Indiano/Nacional)*, vol II (Buenos Aires, Depalma, 1987) 266.

[195] ibid, 269. See also the study by J Cabral Texo, *Historia del Código Civil argentino* (Buenos Aires, Jesús Menéndez, 1920) 156–78.

[196] Ley 340 Código Civil (n 52). See also Moréteau and Parise (n 56) 1143–45; and Levaggi (n 194) 266.

[197] JJ Llambías, *Tratado de Derecho Civil—Parte General*, 6th edn, vol I (Buenos Aires, Editorial Perrot, 1975) 199–203.

[198] G Medina, 'Argentina on the Eve of a New Civil and Commercial Code' in JC Rivera (ed), *The Scope and Structure of Civil Codes* (Dordrecht, Springer, 2013) 54. For more information on the 1889 reform see H Cámara, 'Código de Comercio de la República Argentina y reformas o tentativas hasta la actualidad' in Instituto de Investigaciones Jurídicas, *Centenario del Código de Comercio* (Mexico, UNAM, 1991) 116–17.

[199] Medina (n 198) 54.

For example, *secular laws* were enacted in the 1880s in Argentina. Accordingly, a law on civil marriage was adopted in 1888, together with laws on civil registry that were adopted in 1884 and 1898.[200] Reforms extended throughout the twentieth century and the first years of the twenty-first century, until the texts were replaced by the ACCC. Most partial reforms, however, dealt with specific areas of the Commercial and Civil Codes[201] and lacked a comprehensive approach.

The revision and recodification efforts of the Civil Code deserve special mention. They were undertaken in Argentina from the turn of the twentieth century. Three of those efforts were undertaken in 1936, 1954 and 1968 and they were instrumental in leaving behind the liberal conception that had characterised the first-generation code. At the break of the twentieth century, scholarly writings indicated a need to harmonise the Civil Code with the new context.[202] Accordingly, a first recodification effort was started in 1926 with the appointment of a codifying commission[203] which entrusted the drafting of a pre-project to one of its members—Juan A Bibiloni.[204] The pre-project was then revised by the commission, and Héctor Lafaille and Gastón Tobal undertook the final drafting of a text[205] that was completed in 1936, was notably brief and was ultimately never adopted by the legislature.[206] In the 1950s, scholars claimed that there was a need to change civil code provisions to make them reflect current standards.[207] Within that scenario, a second recodification effort was undertaken in 1950 by the Civil Law Institute of the Ministry of Justice, under the leadership of Jorge J Llambías.[208] The work resulted in a preliminary draft that welcomed the developments of the national jurisprudence.[209] This text was also brief, was completed in 1954 and, again, was never adopted by the legislature.[210] A third major revision effort was

[200] See A Cháneton, *Historia de Vélez Sársfield*, vol II (Buenos Aires, Editorial 'La Facultad', 1937) 335–36.

[201] Levaggi (n 194) 271. That claim by Abelardo Levaggi related mainly to the Civil Code.

[202] See generally A Parise, 'La comisión de reformas al Código Civil (1926). Aproximación histórico-jurídica a su proyección' (2006) 3 *Iushistoria Revista Electrónica* 1, available at www.ijeditores.com.ar/articulos.php?idarticulo=62005&print=2.

[203] See ER Aftalión and F García Olano, *Introducción al Derecho*, 4th edn (Buenos Aires, sn, 1939) 454; and JC Rébora, 'Nota e informe presentados por el profesor Dr. Juan Carlos RÉBORA al Honorable Consejo Académico de la Facultad de Ciencias Jurídicas y Sociales de la Universidad de La Plata, con motivo de su actuación dentro de la Comisión de Reformas del Código Civil' (1937) 5 *Revista Jurídica Argentina La Ley* 66, 69.

[204] Aftalión and García Olano (n 203) 454. See generally JA Bibiloni, *Anteproyecto de Reformas al Código Civil Argentino: presentado a la comisión encargada de redactarlo*, vols I–VII (Buenos Aires, Valerio Abeledo, 1929–32).

[205] See GA Borda, *Tratado de Derecho Civil—Parte General*, 9th edn, vol I (Buenos Aires, Editorial Perrot, 1987) 148; and Moréteau and Parise (n 56) 1145.

[206] See Aftalión and García Olano (n 203) 454; and Levaggi (n 194) 272.

[207] ST Ramella, 'Propiedad en función social en la constitución de 1949. Una "mentalidad" del Antiguo Régimen representada en el constitucionalismo social de la época' (2007) 35 *Revista de Historia del Derecho* 297, 308.

[208] *Anteproyecto de Código Civil de 1954 para la República Argentina* (Tucumán, Universidad Nacional de Tucumán, 1968) 7; and Levaggi (n 194) 272.

[209] Levaggi (n 194) 272; and Moréteau and Parise (n 56) 1145.

[210] Levaggi (n 194) 272.

completed in 1968. That effort, however, did not aim to achieve recodification, and was limited to the revision of 204 articles.[211] The new texts were adopted by Law 17.711 of 1968,[212] and drafted by José F Bidau, Abel M Fleitas and Roberto Martínez Ruiz, with the decisive participation of Guillermo A Borda.[213] Their revisions introduced principles of social solidarity in a code that had been known as individualistic.[214]

More recent major revision and recodification efforts have been undertaken in Argentina since the 1980s. Drafts of new codes were completed in 1987, 1992, 1993 and 1998, though none ever achieved the force of law.[215] These efforts aimed at the unification of civil and commercial provisions in a single text.[216] The drafting of the 1987 text was led by, among others, Héctor Alegría and Sergio Le Pera, and was approved by the National Congress, only to be rejected by the Executive in 1991.[217] The 1992 draft, referred to also as that of the Federal Commission (*Comisión Federal*) of the House of Representatives, was led by, among others, Alegría, Alberto Bueres, Jorge Mosset Iturraspe, and Ana I Piaggi,[218] and ultimately only received the approval of the House in 1993.[219] The 1993 draft was the result of the work of a commission appointed by Executive decree and led by, among others, Augusto C Belluscio, Aída R Kemelmajer de Carlucci, Le Pera, Julio C Rivera and Eduardo A Zannoni.[220] It was submitted to the National Senate in 1993 but not approved.[221] Finally, the 1998 draft was elaborated by a commission led by, among others, Alegría, Atilio A Alterini, Jorge H Alterini, and Rivera[222] and, following the fate of the previous drafts, was ultimately not adopted.[223] Some of these recent attempts valued harmonising instruments. For example, the 1987 draft incorporated provisions of the UN Convention on Contracts for the International Sale of Goods (CISG) on formation of contracts.[224] The 1998 draft, likewise, incorporated modern principles of contract law, and aimed to internationalise contract law. The drafters also looked at early European harmonisation efforts,

211 Borda (n 205) 143. See also LM Valiente Noailles, *Comentarios a las reformas al código civil (Ley 17.711): Legislación, doctrina, jurisprudencia* (Buenos Aires, Ediciones Depalma, 1968) 7–9; and GA Borda, *La reforma de 1968 al código civil* (Buenos Aires, Editorial Perrot, 1971).

212 See the text of Law 17.711, available at www.infojus.gob.ar/documentDisplay.jsp?guid=123456789-0abc-defg-g31-11000scanyel&title=reformas-al-codigo-civil-.

213 Levaggi (n 194) 271.

214 ibid; and Moréteau and Parise (n 56) 1145.

215 Medina (n 198) 58. On some of those drafts, see R Brebbia (ed), *Estudios sobre el Proyecto de Código Unificado de 1998* (Buenos Aires, Zavalía, 2001) and Rivera (n 12).

216 Rienzi (n 168) [5]–[6].

217 ibid.

218 *El Proyecto de Unificación de Código Civil y su Historia*, Cámara de Diputados de la Nación, Comisión de Legislación General, available at www1.hcdn.gov.ar/dependencias/clgeneral/historia.html.

219 Rienzi (n 168) [5]–[6].

220 *El Proyecto de Unificación de Código Civil y su Historia* (n 218).

221 Rienzi (n 168) [5]–[6].

222 Moreteau and Parise (n 56) 1146.

223 Rienzi (n 168) [5]–[6].

224 Garro (n 77) 607.

especially the European civil code project of the Pavia Group, the McGregor code and the first part of the Principles of European Contract Law (PECL).[225] That draft also looked at the UNIDROIT Principles[226] and the CISG.[227] The 1998 draft, however, failed to bring the Argentine provisions clearly into line with those of other Latin American jurisdictions, notably Mercosur members.[228]

The ACCC draft[229] was submitted to the Executive on 27 March 2012[230] and took effect as the *Código Civil y Comercial de la Nación* on 1 August 2015.[231] Parts of the proposed text encountered opposition from different groups and members of society[232] and generated copious literature commenting on their virtues and weaknesses.[233] The codifying commission was led by Elena Highton de Nolasco and Kemelmajer de Carlucci, under the presidency of Ricardo Lorenzetti.[234] That recodification effort unified the Civil and Commercial Codes into a single body, and introduced numerous alterations to the previous provisions. According to Lorenzetti,[235] the codifying commission respected the Roman, Spanish and French traditions that had had an impact on Argentine legal history, yet they also aimed to provide a text immersed in a Latin American cultural identity.[236] The codifying commission also benefited from an analysis of all the previous major revisions and recodification efforts that had taken place in Argentina.[237] Alterations

[225] CR Brizzio, 'Teoría general del contrato y contratos predispuestos en el anteproyecto de Código Europeo de Contratos y en el proyecto de Código Civil argentino de 1998' [1999] *Doctrina Judicial* 839 [2]; and CR Brizzio, 'Anteproyecto de Código Europeo de Contratos—Estudio Preliminar' [1999] *Revista Jurídica Argentina La Ley* 985 [2].

[226] Brizzio (n 126) [6].

[227] Alterini (n 171) [4]; EL Gregorini Clusellas, 'Proyección del contrato en el Siglo XXI' [2004] *Revista Jurídica Argentina La Ley* 847 [5]; and Da Gama E Souza (n 106) at 416.

[228] Brizzio (n 126) [7].

[229] Relevant information regarding the draft and the adopted ACCC is available at www.nuevocodigocivil.com.

[230] RL Lorenzetti, 'Presentación del Código Civil y Comercial de la Nación' [2014] *Revista Jurídica Argentina La Ley* 1243 [1]. Another document from the codifying commission indicated that the document was presented on 24 February 2012. See 'Modificaciones del poder ejecutivo nacional al anteproyecto de reforma del código civil elaborado por la comisión de reformas decreto 191/2011' available at www.nuevocodigocivil.com/pdf/Fundamentos-de-los-cambios-introducidos-por-el-PEN.pdf at 1.

[231] *Código Civil y Comercial de la Nación* (Buenos Aires, Infojus, 2014). On 1 October 2014, the National Congress adopted Law 26.994, which approved the text of the ACCC. The Argentine President, Cristina Fernández de Kirchner, promulgated the above-mentioned law on 7 October of that same year. According to Article 7 of the law, the new code would have taken effect on 1 January 2016. However, Law 27.077 moved the effective date of the ACCC to 1 August 2015. See Marotta and Parise (n 190) 269; and Law 27.077, available at www.infoleg.gob.ar/infolegInternet/anexos/235000-239999/239773/norma.htm.

[232] See, eg, 'Debate por la reforma del Código Civil' in *La Nación* (7 March 2012) 15.

[233] For a comprehensive study on the draft of the ACCC, see JC Rivera (ed), *Comentarios al Proyecto de Código Civil y Comercial de la Nación 2012* (Buenos Aires, Abeledo Perrot, 2012).

[234] See the text of Decree 191/2011 available at www.infojus.gob.ar/documentDisplay.jsp?guid=123456789-0abc-191-0000-1102soterced.

[235] See *Fundamentos del Anteproyecto de Código Civil y Comercial de la Nación* available at www.nuevocodigocivil.com/wp-content/uploads/2015/02/5-Fundamentos-del-Proyecto.pdf.

[236] ibid, 4.

[237] ibid, 6.

were proposed in almost all areas of private law, yet it is relevant to highlight the following: (i) incorporation of a title dealing with private international law,[238] along the lines of modern codes; (ii) incorporation of protection of inalienable personal rights (*derechos personalísimos*), which had already found their way into Argentine domestic legislation by means of the adoption of international Conventions, but which had not yet been expressly addressed in the Argentine Civil Code;[239] (iii) incorporation of prenuptial agreements, which were not included in the Argentine Civil Code;[240] (iv) incorporation of several changes in the field of divorce, inter alia, the elimination of the impossibility to file for divorce within the first three years of the celebration of the marriage;[241] and (v) incorporation of provisions on assisted reproductive technologies.[242]

The ACCC recognised the impact of globalisation, not only in commerce but also in daily life.[243] That recognition required a proper framework to protect juridical relations, aiming to coordinate and harmonise different national provisions.[244] Argentina seems to have moved from first generation to third generation in one go.[245] Argentina had no need for a second-generation code, since the 1871 text separated Argentina from Spain and was distinctive in the region: secessionist and differentialist at the same time. Argentine jurists and society at large seemed to sense a need for a generation shift. The first-generation Civil Code needed a refurbishment that could no longer be achieved by simple revision or decodification.

The ACCC helps visualise the emergence of the new generation. The *exposé des motifs* of the ACCC frequently refers indirectly to the 'typical' Latin American flavour. For example, the members of the codifying commission, represented by Lorenzetti, stated clearly that their code had a 'Latin American cultural identity'.[246] They further stated that the code had 'a conception oriented towards integration with the Latin American cultural block [and] that [that] is a relevant change'.[247] The codifiers also stated that they had 'incorporated notions that were

[238] Book VI, Title IV, Arts 2594–2671 (*Código Civil y Comercial de la Nación* (n 231) at 450–465).

[239] Inalienable personal rights are addressed, inter alia, in Arts 646, para (c), and 1738 of the ACCC (*Código Civil y Comercial de la Nación* (n 231) at 130 and 304).

[240] See Book II, Title II, Section 1, Arts 446–450 and Art 2625 (*Código Civil y Comercial de la Nación* (n 231) at 91–92 and 455–56).

[241] See Book II, Title I, Chapter 8, Section 2, Arts 436–438 (*Código Civil y Comercial de la Nación* (n 231) at 89).

[242] The general rules dealing with that type of filiation are included in Book II, Title V, Chapter 2, Arts 560–564 (*Código Civil y Comercial de la Nación* (n 231) at 112).

[243] ME Uzal, 'Lineamientos de la reforma del Derecho Internacional Privado en el Código Civil y Comercial de la Nación' [2014] *Suplemento Especial Nuevo Código Civil y Comercial 2014—Revista Jurídica Argentina La Ley*, 17 November 2014, 247 [2].

[244] ibid.

[245] It was claimed on previous occasions, however, that Argentina could shift to a second-generation code. See Parise (n 43) 189–90; and Marotta and Parise (n 190) 208.

[246] The text in Spanish reads: 'Código con identidad cultural latinoamericana'. *Fundamentos del Anteproyecto de Código Civil y Comercial de la Nación* (n 235) 4.

[247] The text in Spanish reads: 'Existe una concepción orientada a integrar el bloque cultural latinoamericano. Este es un cambio relevante …' ibid, 4.

peculiar to the Latin American culture, together with a series of criteria that are considered common to the region'.[248] That same *exposé* stated that the codifying commission asked Argentine and Latin American experts who were already involved in the activities of a number of working groups to participate.[249] The codifying commission indicated in the *exposé* whenever a proposal differed clearly from the Latin American tradition. Accordingly, the *exposé* on punitive damages stated that these damages were culturally distant from continental Europe and Latin America.[250] Graciela Medina naturally (and correctly) noted that the ACCC aimed to adapt provisions to the implications deriving from Argentina's membership of Mercosur.[251]

Contract law aimed to incorporate that 'typical' Latin American flavour within the ACCC. Accordingly, the *exposé* comments that 'the different options [in contract law] were extensively debated in the Commission amongst the jurists that contributed and that they adopted the method they considered most adequate for the Argentine and Latin American legal tradition'.[252] In its part on consumer contracts, the *exposé* provided a good example of the harmonisation efforts made. There, the drafters referred to, among others, the consumer laws in Argentina, Bolivia, Brazil, Chile, Colombia, Ecuador, Paraguay, Peru, Uruguay and Venezuela, and other references were made to the UNIDROIT Principles and to the more recent codes of Quebec and the Netherlands.[253] In its part on agency, the *exposé* referred to principles such as the UNIDROIT Principles, and to the texts of the Pavia Group and the PECL.[254] Article 2651[255] reveals the interest in a globalist

[248] The text in Spanish reads: '... hemos incorporado nociones propias de la cultura latinoamericana así como una serie de criterios que se consideran comunes a la región.' ibid, 4.

[249] ibid, 7; and Lorenzetti (n 230) [3].

[250] The text in Spanish reads: 'El instituto que referimos proviene de un campo ajeno a la responsabilidad civil, tradicionalmente enfocada en la reparación. Es culturalmente distante, porque su desarrollo se ha producido en Estados Unidos de América, y no en el área latinoamericana o europea que han sido las tradicionales influencias en nuestro derecho'. *Fundamentos del Anteproyecto de Código Civil y Comercial de la Nación* (n 235) 178.

[251] Medina (n 198) 58.

[252] The text in Spanish reads: 'Las diferentes opciones fueron ampliamente discutidas en la Comisión y entre los juristas que han colaborado y se ha adoptado un método que se considera adecuado a la tradición jurídica argentina y latinoamericana.' *Fundamentos del Anteproyecto de Código Civil y Comercial de la Nación* (n 235) 100.

[253] ibid, 115–16.

[254] ibid, 53.

[255] The text in Spanish reads:

> Los contratos se rigen por el derecho elegido por las partes en cuanto a su validez intrínseca, naturaleza, efectos, derechos y obligaciones. La elección debe ser expresa o resultar de manera cierta y evidente de los términos del contrato o de las circunstancias del caso. Dicha elección puede referirse a la totalidad o a partes del contrato.
>
> El ejercicio de este derecho está sujeto a las siguientes reglas:
>
> ...
>
> d) los usos y prácticas comerciales generalmente aceptados, las costumbres y los principios del derecho comercial internacional, resultan aplicables cuando las partes los han incorporado al contrato;

code; it addresses freedom of contract, and its paragraph (d) states that 'generally accepted commercial practices, custom and principles of commercial international law are applicable when parties refer to them in their contracts'.[256] Therefore, instruments such as the PLACL will now fulfil an important updating function in Argentina.[257] Paragraphs (e) and (f) of that same article seek to eliminate the difficulties of applying international public order and imperative norms of international and domestic contract law.[258] The ACCC is, therefore, placed within a global context.

It is worth noting a final aspect that deals with the circularity of harmonisation efforts. Pollination of these efforts is not rare, and ideas are transferred across jurisdictions, even across continents. For example, the ACCC draft was a source of inspiration for the PLACL in the area of contract law, as stated by Pizarro.[259] This should come as no surprise, since both texts share a common aim: *a conception oriented towards the integration of the Latin American cultural block.*

V. Closing Remarks

Generations of civil codes have shifted in Latin America. Three generations are recognised in Latin America (ie, secessionist, differentialist, globalist), each one distinct from the other because of its content, the time of enactment, and its motivation. This chapter first introduced the theoretical framework behind the different generations of codes and their shifts, and made manifest that generations should be considered as tools to assess the conditions of the different codes. It then went on to describe the traits of the first two generations of codes. First-generation codes aimed at projecting a sense of differentiation between the Old and the New World, between former dependence and empire. These codes were the expression of a secessionist movement. Second-generation codes aimed at projecting a sense of differentiation between American jurisdictions, between the different parts of the New World. These codes were the expression of a differentialist movement.

e) los principios de orden público y las normas internacionalmente imperativas del derecho argentino se aplican a la relación jurídica, cualquiera sea la ley que rija el contrato; también se imponen al contrato, en principio, las normas internacionalmente imperativas de aquellos Estados que presenten vínculos económicos preponderantes con el caso;

f) los contratos hechos en la República para violar normas internacionalmente imperativas de una nación extranjera de necesaria aplicación al caso no tienen efecto alguno;

...

Código Civil y Comercial de la Nación (n 231) 461.

[256] ibid.

[257] SJ Batello Calderón, *El orden público en el derecho internacional privado del Mercosur* (Córdoba, Advocatus Ediciones, 2012) 167.

[258] ibid, 159.

[259] Morales Moreno (n 140) 230.

Several efforts to harmonise private law in Latin America were addressed in this chapter. Common elements were highlighted, showing that there are some elements that may facilitate harmonisation in the region. Those common elements relate to culture and history, and can be linked to language and legal traditions. This chapter also addressed a number of specific harmonisation efforts. These efforts were undertaken as part of treaties and international agreements, though also within academic circles, as illustrated by the endeavours of the drafters of the PLACL. These efforts helped to develop a globalist movement that impacted on the generations of codes, triggering the momentum for a shift in generation.

Finally, this chapter focused on the third generation of codes. That generation may be deemed globalist, since secession and differentiation have been left behind, and a degree of globalisation is welcomed in Latin America. The chapter defined the characteristics of third-generation codes and stressed how the new-generation codes will need to find an equilibrium between what is good for the individual and what is good for society at large, even beyond national borders. This chapter then addressed the interaction of new codes and harmonising principles, and made manifest that shifts in generations have to start from within the different jurisdictions, yet heed the harmonising efforts that may help to incorporate the 'typical' Latin American flavour into the resulting codes. Finally, a look at the ACCC offered an example of that new generation of codes because harmonisation efforts and the search for a 'typical' Latin American flavour were reflected in the *exposé des motifs* and articles of that new South American text.

The interaction of harmonisation efforts and generations of codes—as studied in this chapter—have generated an awareness of a number of code-related aspects. First, the interaction revealed that harmonisation efforts must start in areas that share common ground, and then go on, if needed, in specialised areas of private law.[260] Contract law could indeed provide a first path to reach the 'typical' Latin American flavour, to reach that third-generation status.[261] Secondly, the interaction made manifest that harmonisation efforts such as the PLACL must aim at a degree of universality that respects particularities.[262] Private law must certainly protect particularities and individualities, while seeking harmonisation.[263] Finally, the interaction showed that—as Glenn correctly highlighted—harmonisation efforts should stay politically neutral and a-national, and allow for jurisdictions to advance at their own pace.[264] This will assure an optimal environment for the emergence of third-generation codes and the harmonisation of private law in Latin America.

[260] LM Boffi Boggero, 'Las obligaciones en el proyecto franco-italiano y en el derecho argentino' (2005) 11 *Revista de Responsabilidad Civil y Seguros* 169 [1] and Glenn (n 89) 241.

[261] Other areas should follow, inter alia, abuse of rights and good faith. See RL Lorenzetti, 'Sistema jurídico del Mercosur' [1998] *Revista Jurídica Argentina La Ley* 1258 [9].

[262] As correctly claimed by Miguel Ángel Ciuro Caldani, cited in Batello Calderón (n 257) 87.

[263] G Alpa, 'Las tareas actuales del derecho privado' [2008] *Revista Jurídica Argentina La Ley* 1208 [5].

[264] Glenn (n 89) 241.

4

The 'Principles of Latin American Contract Law' Against the Background of Latin American Legal Culture: A European Perspective

JAN PETER SCHMIDT*

I. Introduction

In assessing the Principles of Latin American Contract Law (PLACL)[1] as to their content and purposes, we also need to look at the background against which they were drafted, ie the private law of the Latin American countries. This seems to be especially true when the PLACL are discussed in a forum that brings together scholars from both Latin America and Continental Europe. For although the representatives from either side of the Atlantic may rightfully assume that they share a common legal tradition and, language notwithstanding, a common legal vocabulary, there is a risk that other parallels are unjustifiably taken for granted. As is well known, such unspoken assumptions can easily create serious obstacles to communication, or worse, a false sense of agreement when in fact each side has a different understanding of the matter in question.

For these reasons, this chapter aims to sketch some general aspects of Latin American private law culture in order to lay a common basis for future discussions and, especially, to dispel some of the preconceptions and stereotypes that are still quite widespread among European scholars. Having said that, I will have to be very careful not to create any misconceptions myself. To begin with, it is by no means clear whether there is such a thing as 'the' Latin American private law culture, just

* This is an extended version of the paper I presented at the conference *The Future of Contract Law in Latin America*, which was held on 25 June 2015 at Keble College, Oxford. I am very grateful to Alexandra Braun, Francisco Medina, Agustín Parise and Jürgen Samtleben for their valuable comments on an earlier draft.

[1] For an introduction, see Pizarro Wilson, Ch 2 in this book. An interim draft of the PLACL was published in (2014) 47 *Anuario de Derecho Civil* 241–53.

as one should be careful in referring to 'the' European private law culture. On both continents, there is a huge variety of individual legal systems that have a lot in common, but which also differ in many respects. At the cost of some inevitable oversimplification, I will nevertheless try to pinpoint some characteristics of the Latin American legal orders that seem relevant to me in the present context. As an external observer, I hopefully enjoy the advantages of an unbiased and unobstructed view, but of course I also run the risk of overlooking or misunderstanding decisive factors.

I will first discuss the picture of Latin American private law in mainstream comparative legal literature (Section II). I will then give a brief outline of its historical development (Section III), followed by an analysis of some features of Latin American contract law (Section IV). Subsequently, important differences between Europe and Latin America in matters of legal methodology will be discussed (Section V), while the final section will draw conclusions for the aims and purposes of the PLACL.

II. The Forgotten Continent: Latin America's Neglect in Mainstream Comparative Law

It is no secret that Latin American private law has never received much attention in mainstream comparative law.[2] The two classical and possibly still leading[3] treatises on comparative law, namely those by René David, and Zweigert and Kötz, dedicate no more than two pages each to the Latin American legal orders.[4] It is not hard to think of plenty of reasons for this neglect. Some are of an external nature. In pre-Internet times, the Latin American legal orders were not easy to access; even for scholars from within the region it could be difficult to get hold of the relevant legal materials, such as legislation, textbooks and case law.[5] Besides, a

[2] See also J Kleinheisterkamp, 'Development of Comparative Law in Latin America' in M Reimann and R Zimmermann (eds), *The Oxford Handbook of Comparative Law* (Oxford, Oxford University Press, 2006) 261, 262; M Reimann 'The Progress and Failure of Comparative Law in the Second Half of the Twentieth Century' (2002) 50 *American Journal of Comparative Law* 671, 674 ('Latin America continues to be understudied').

[3] In 2002, Reimann (n 2) 685 still regarded them as leading worldwide.

[4] R David and JEC Brierley, *Major Legal Systems in World Today*, 3rd edn (London, Stevens & Sons, 1985) 75–76. A slightly more detailed account is given by K Zweigert and H Kötz, *An Introduction to Comparative Law*, 3rd edn (Oxford, Clarendon Press, 1998) 113–15. As Kleinheisterkamp (n 2) 263 points out, even less attention is paid to Latin America in JH Merryman's *The Civil Law Tradition—An Introduction to the Legal Systems of Western Europe and Latin America*, 2nd edn (Stanford, CA, Stanford University Press, 1985), despite the promising title (the situation is basically unchanged in the 3rd edition of 2007, co-authored by R Pérez-Perdomo).

[5] However, even in 1953 René David regarded this excuse as no longer acceptable for the lack of interest in Latin America: 'L'originalité des droits de l'Amérique latine' (Paris, Institut des Hautes Etudes de l'Amerique latine, 1953; reprinted in id, *Le Droit Comparé: Droits d'hier, Droits de demain*

desire to know more about the law of a certain country or region is usually sparked not just by academic curiosity, but often by practical demands, and compared to the United States, Europe, Japan and (more recently) China, Latin America never seems to have been 'relevant' enough from an economic point of view. Cynics might add that a region which in the last century mostly became famous for the 'magical realism' of its literature, the technical skills of its football players and constant military coups is a fascinating object of study in many respects, but certainly not as to a supposedly rational discipline such as law.

However, the main reason why Latin American private law has received such scant attention in mainstream comparative law is probably that its study was simply not regarded as rewarding, or even necessary (very much unlike, for example, the common–civil law dichotomy, one of the discipline's 'obsessions'[6]). As the Latin American civil codes were considered to be but 'des imitations ou des répliques, parfois même la copie exacte du code Napoléon',[7] the whole region could be safely tucked away in the big box of the 'French'[8] or 'Romanistic' legal family.[9] Even if the corresponding comparative treatises often showed, in evident contradiction to their classification, that the French *Code civil* had actually been only one among many influences, or that some Latin American civil codes must even be regarded as 'original'.[10] It seems that it was only the general taxonomy which stuck in the minds of lawyers, who, as personal experience has shown time and time again, happily continue to map the world according to it.[11]

(Paris, Economica, 1982) 161–73) 17–18. It is certainly no longer valid in the Internet era, as most Latin American countries have seized the opportunity and provide very good, and usually free, online access to legal materials, especially legislation and case law.

[6] Reimann (n 2) 685.

[7] The traditional perception as described (and criticised) by René David in 1953 (n 5) 1. This 'gross oversimplification' (MC Mirow, 'The Code Napoleón, Buried but Ruling in Latin America' (2005) 33 *Denver Journal of International Law & Policy* 179) has survived until today; see also Kleinheisterkamp (n 2) 262, and D López-Medina, 'The Latin American and Caribbean Legal Traditions: Repositioning Latin America and the Caribbean on the Contemporary Maps of Comparative Law' in M Bussani and U Mattei (eds), *The Cambridge Companion to Comparative Law* (Cambridge, Cambridge University Press, 2012) 344, 347–48, 359–60.

[8] P Arminjon, BB Nolde and M Wolff, *Traité de droit comparé*, vol I (Paris, Librairie générale de Droit et de Jurisprudence, 1950) 117ff, 162–76. For other early works, see Kleinheisterkamp (n 2) 262, n 3. Somewhat misleading is the classification offered by René David. In his *Traité élémentaire de droit civil comparé* (Paris, Librairie générale de Droit et de Jurisprudence, 1950) 258, he puts the Latin American countries into the 'groupe français' of Western law, but one must be aware that David uses this category in a wide sense and includes, somewhat surprisingly, all legal orders from the European continent in it. Therefore, this 'groupe français' seems to be basically the same category which David in his later work called the 'Romano-Germanic family'. Hence, he actually did not regard Latin America as being part of a particular French legal family, but simply as being part of the continental tradition in a wider sense.

[9] Zweigert and Kötz (n 4) 74ff, 113–5, who by their own admission (73) closely followed the classification of Arminjon, Nolde and Wolff (n 8).

[10] See, eg, Arminjon, Nolde and Wolff (n 8) 163: 'Le Code civil du Chili … est original'.

[11] Also one of the speakers at the conference from which this contribution originates admitted that he had taken for granted that all Latin American contract regimes were built on the *Code civil*.

There has certainly been no lack of attempts, both by European and Latin American scholars, to overcome this Eurocentric, or rather Francocentric, perspective and to argue for the existence of a 'Latin American' or 'Iberoamerican' legal family (usually as an independent subsection within the civil law tradition).[12] The starting point of these efforts even goes back to the nineteenth century.[13] However, for the purposes of this chapter it does not seem necessary to discuss these alternative taxonomies in detail.[14] One reason is that they have been unsuccessful in shaping, or at least differentiating, the picture of Latin America in mainstream comparative law. The other, and more important, reason is that the search for the 'correct' taxonomy seems to be a questionable endeavour in itself. Not only is every classification necessarily arbitrary[15] as it depends on the chosen criteria and on the aims that are pursued with it, but more importantly, comparative law has rightly come to regard the 'doctrine of legal families' as such with considerable suspicion, or even as a methodological tool that had better be abandoned altogether.[16] As its focus tends to be both too narrow and too static, it reveals as much as it conceals (or even distorts). The taxonomies that were offered for Latin American private law exemplify this problem very clearly. They all have their virtues when it comes to highlighting certain characteristics, but they also suffer from serious limitations:[17]

— they all take for granted that the Latin American legal systems form a homogeneous unit, and that the only question is in which 'box' that unit belongs (or whether it forms a box of its own). What the laws of the Latin American

[12] See, eg, P Catalano, 'Sistema y ordenamientos: El ejemplo de América Latina' and S Schipani, 'Armonización y unificación del Derecho: Derecho común en materia de obligaciones y contratos en América Latina' in DF Esborraz (ed), *Sistema Jurídico Latinoamericano y Unificación del Derecho* (México, Porrúa, 2006) 51–74 and 209–36.

[13] See the Brazilian C Bevilaqua (who later drafted the Brazilian Civil Code of 1916), *Resumo das Licções de Legislação Comparada sobre o Direito Privado*, 2nd edn (Bahia, Magalhães, 1897) 73–79, 101–05. Bevilaqua's classification had been strongly influenced by the French comparatist E Glasson, for whom the central criterion of distinction had been the role of Roman law, see M Pargendler, 'The Rise and Decline of Legal Families' (2012) 60 *American Journal of Comparative Law* 1043, 1047ff. On Bevilaqua's classification, see also Esborraz (n 12) 25–32.

[14] For a good overview, see T Scholl, *Die Rezeption des kontinental-europäischen Privatrechts in Lateinamerika am Beispiel der allgemeinen Vertragslehre in Costa Rica* (Berlin, Duncker & Humblot, 1999) 27.

[15] As was freely admitted by René David himself (n 8) 222.

[16] For a detailed assessment, see HP Glenn, 'Comparative Legal Families and Comparative Legal Traditions' in M Reimann and R Zimmermann (eds), *The Oxford Handbook of Comparative Law* (Oxford, Oxford University Press, 2006) 421–40; H Kötz, 'Abschied von der Rechtskreislehre?' in H Kötz, *Undogmatisches: Rechtsvergleichende und rechtsökonomische Studien aus dreißig Jahren* (Tübingen, Mohr Siebeck, 2005) 91, 93 (also in [1998] *Zeitschrift für Europäisches Privatrecht* 495–505). See also H Kötz 'Legal Families' in J Basedow, KJ Hopt and R Zimmermann (eds), *The Max Planck Encyclopedia of European Private Law*, vol II (Oxford, Oxford University Press, 2012) 1063–64; Reimann (n 2) 676–78.

[17] For a similar criticism, DP Fernández Arroyo, 'Sobre la existencia de una familia jurídica latinoamericana' [1995-II] *Jurisprudencia Argentina* 913ff. Most of the shortcomings mentioned characterise the doctrine of legal families as such, see n 16 above.

states actually have in common with *one another*, besides their common past as Iberian colonies, is hardly ever discussed.[18]

— They focus predominantly on the nineteenth century, when the Latin American states were founded, and seldom look at later developments. This takes on a comical (or rather tragic) dimension when their 'democratic character' is regarded as a distinctive feature of the Latin American legal orders.[19]
— Their approach is distinctly positivistic, ie, they tend to look only at statutory law and hardly at case law or social customs. But even blackletter law is not taken into account comprehensively; instead, the focus is on the respective civil codes, and perhaps also the commercial codes. Ancillary legislation, in contrast, which may be obscure but extremely relevant for practical purposes, is happily ignored.
— Among various influences, they tend to overemphasise one in particular. A Francophile lawyer will highlight the role of the *Code civil*, his colleague from Spain will stress the Iberian legacy,[20] a Romanist the role of Roman law,[21] etc.
— Their assessments of Latin American private law in general are mainly based on the law of obligations, whereas a look at family law and the law of succession would often lead to different conclusions.

Finally, and this point seems especially relevant in the present context, the doctrine of legal families can never be more than a didactic device[22] and does not allow for any kind of deductive reasoning. The assumption that a certain legal order belongs to a certain legal family never permits the conclusion that in a particular matter of, say, contract law, its rules are identical to those of the supposed 'parent system'.[23] Instead, one would always have to look at the provisions themselves.[24] Only in a

[18] cf also E Hernández-Bretón, 'Sueño o pesadilla de un comparatista: El Derecho en Suramérica' (1998) 109 *Revista de la Facultad de Ciencias Jurídicas y Políticas de la Universidad Central de Venezuela* 33.

[19] J Castan Tobeñas, *Los sistemas jurídicos contemporáneos del mundo occidental* (Madrid, Reus, 1957) 62, with reference to the ideas of Bevilaqua (n 13), which were formulated at the end of the nineteenth century and thus in a totally different global political scenario.

[20] See, eg, JM Castán Vásquez, 'El Sistema Jurídico Iberoamericano', in DF Esborraz (ed), *Sistema Jurídico Latinoamericano y Unificación del Derecho* (México, Porrúa, 2006) 143, 149ff.

[21] See, eg, Schipani (n 12) 222.

[22] See David and Brierley (n 4) 21.

[23] However, this is exactly the approach underlying the so-called 'legal origins thesis'. For a convincing criticism, see R Michaels, 'Comparative Law by Numbers? Legal Origins Thesis', *Doing Business Reports*, and The Silence of Traditional Comparative Law' (2009) 57 *American Journal of Comparative Law* 765, 780ff. Ironically, it was mostly the modest performance of the Latin American economies which ended up ruining the reputation of French law in terms of its efficiency, see M Siems, 'Legal Origins: Reconciling Law & Finance and Comparative Law' (2007) 52 *McGill Law Journal* 55, 68, and also JL Esquirol, 'The Latin American Tradition of Legal Failure' (2011) 2 *Comparative Law Review* 1, 14. Incidentally, the 'Doing Business Reports' of the World Bank were the trigger for the elaboration of the PLACL, see C Pizarro Wilson, 'Presentación' in C Pizarro Wilson (ed), *El derecho de los contratos en Latinoamérica (Bases para unos principios de Derecho de los Contratos)* (Bogota, Universidad del Rosario and Universidad del Externado de Colombia, 2012) 15.

[24] See also Fernández Arroyo (n 17) 929–30.

second step could one affirm, by way of inductive reasoning, the existence of a certain group.

For these reasons, the analysis in the following sections is not intended as a contribution to the doctrine of legal families, but rather seeks to point out some aspects of Latin American private law that most European scholars do not seem to be aware of. Hopefully, this will not only help to improve the understanding of, but also the interest in, Latin American private law.

III. Origins and Later Development of the Latin American Legal Orders

A. Nineteenth- and Twentieth-century Codification

It cannot be denied that the *Code civil* did indeed, both directly and indirectly,[25] exert strong influence in Latin America, especially in the first half of the nineteenth century. The newly independent countries were looking for a way to substitute the inherited Spanish law, which in many respects was chaotic and outdated,[26] and the *Code civil* offered them exactly what they were looking for, by stating the law in a clear and concise manner and reflecting the values of a bourgeois society.[27] One may add that the Latin American elites, who after their break from their former rulers were in search of a new cultural identity, were generally very much drawn towards the French lifestyle at the time.[28]

[25] Important 'intermediaries' of the *Code civil* were the Louisiana Civil Code of 1825 and García Goyena's draft for a Spanish Civil Code of 1851, which he complemented a year later with an impressive comparative commentary: F García Goyena, *Concordancias, motivos y comentarios del código civil español* (1852, reprint Zaragoza, Cometa, 1974). For the influence of the mentioned texts in Latin America, see A Parise, 'The Place of the Louisiana Civil Code in the Hispanic Civil Codifications: Inclusion in the Comments to the Spanish Civil Code Project of 1851' (2008) 68 *Louisiana Law Review* 823, 839ff. A curious detail is that the drafters of the Louisiana Digest of 1808, the predecessor of the Louisiana Civil Code of 1825 (see Parise, ibid, 831–33), apparently did not have access to the final version of the French *Code civil*, but only to its preceding drafts. As a result, there are provisions of French origin which did not enter the *Code civil*, but the legislation of Louisiana, from where they travelled south to Latin America, see J Samtleben, 'Territorialität der Gesetze' in J Samtleben, *Rechtspraxis und Rechtskultur in Lateinamerika* (Aachen, Shaker, 2010) 344, 348–49.

[26] A Garro, 'Unification and Harmonization of Private Law in Latin America' (1992) 40 *American Journal of Comparative Law* 587, 605, who also points out that the European codifications often fulfilled the purpose of legal unification within the national territory. However, the aim of systematising the law was a driving factor of at least equal importance, see JP Schmidt, 'Codification' in J Basedow, KJ Hopt and R Zimmermann (eds), *The Max Planck Encyclopedia of European Private Law*, vol I (Oxford, Oxford University Press, 2012) 221, 222.

[27] See also López-Medina (n 7) 349; R Momberg, 'Harmonization of Contract Law in Latin America: Past and Present Initiatives' [2014] *Uniform Law Review* 411, 413–14; MC Mirow, 'Individual Experience in Legal Change: Exploring a Neglected Factor in Nineteenth Century Latin American Codification' (2005) 11 *Southwestern Journal of Law and Trade* 301, 304.

[28] Mirow (n 27) 305.

However, it should be stressed that only the very first Latin American civil codes, eg, the 1825 Code of Haiti (which is still in force) or the first Bolivian Code of 1830, were more or less carbon copies of the *Code civil*.[29] In contrast, the second generation[30] of Latin American civil codes was already much more sophisticated and independent.[31] The most famous and important of these codes is the Chilean Code of 1855 (still in force today), drafted by Andrés Bello (1781–1865). In what has been labelled as 'spontaneous harmonisation',[32] Bello's Code was soon taken over more or less wholesale by a number of other Latin American states, such as Colombia and Ecuador, and was generally very influential in the region.[33]

For his draft, Bello had made use of all existing codifications of his time, including, for example, the General Code of Prussia of 1794 or the Austrian General Civil Code of 1811. Of course, the French *Code civil* was also a source of inspiration for Bello, and arguably even the primary one, at least where the law of obligations was concerned.[34] However, two aspects need to be emphasised: first, Bello did not slavishly copy French law, but in several respects sought to improve or at least to adapt it to Chilean circumstances.[35] Secondly, Bello also went to great pains to continue and carefully modernise the inherited Spanish legal tradition, which for its part was firmly rooted in the Roman-Canon *ius commune*.[36] As a result, one may say that the most important source of the Chilean Code was actually the *Corpus Iuris Civilis*, also because those provisions that Bello did take directly from the *Code civil* were mainly those which, in his view, aptly formulated a Roman law rule.[37]

In the second half of the nineteenth century, another important influence made itself felt in Latin America, and it is one that is often overlooked, because it was not transported via a code, but via legal writing:[38] the influence of 'Pandectism', ie nineteenth-century German scholarship on Roman law. Especially Savigny, whose eight volumes on the *System des heutigen Römischen Rechts* (1840–49) were also

[29] Kleinheisterkamp (n 2) 271–72.

[30] The concept is used here purely in a chronological sense. For a distinction between different generations of Latin American civil codes on the basis of certain general characteristics, see Parise, Ch 3 in this book.

[31] For a detailed account of the codification of private law in Latin America see A Guzmán Brito, *La Codificación Civil en Iberoamérica: Siglos XIX y XX* (Santiago, Editorial Jurídica de Chile, 2000) 289ff.

[32] Momberg (n 27) 415.

[33] See Guzmán Brito (n 31) 374ff.

[34] Momberg (n 27) 414.

[35] For a detailed analysis, see D Nelle, *Entstehung und Ausstrahlungswirkung des chilenischen Zivilgesetzbuches von Andrés Bello* (Frankfurt am Main, Metzner, 1988) 111ff and 217ff. Illustrative examples are the numerous provisions that deal with the coast and the sea and thus reflect Chile's unique geography (240–43).

[36] This was especially the case of the *Siete Partidas* of 1265. See Esborraz (n 12) 27–28, Kleinheisterkamp (n 2) 264–65, both with further references.

[37] Guzmán Brito (n 31) 264ff, 373; Kleinheisterkamp (n 2) 273–76.

[38] Contrary to López-Medina (n 7) 354, it was not only towards the end of the 19th century that foreign legal writing became prestigious and widely used in Latin America.

available in a French translation,[39] was revered throughout the Latin American continent. Another popular German writer was Karl Salomo Zachariä, whose *Handbuch des französischen Civilrechts* (first published in 1808) presented French law according to Pandectist methods. After it had been translated into French by Aubry and Rau in 1839 (who went on to continue it), Zachariä's work rapidly became very influential in France[40] and, as a consequence, also in Latin America.[41]

The systematic and conceptual rigour of the Pandectists did not fail to 'seduce'[42] their Latin American readers, who realised that legal scholarship had been taken to a new level. The influence of German legal thinking was very visible, for example, in the Argentinean Code of 1869[43] (substituted in 2014) and especially in the Brazilian Code of 1916[44] (substituted in 2002). The latter rested to a large extent on an earlier draft by Augusto Teixeira de Freitas (1816–83), the founding father of Brazilian legal scholarship, who deeply admired Savigny and at the same time was highly critical of the *Code civil*.[45] However, it must also be stressed that, just like its Chilean or Argentinean counterpart, the Brazilian Code sought to avoid a radical break with the past, to the effect that it continued the (again heavily Romanised) Portuguese legal tradition more faithfully than did Portugal itself, which from the 1820s onwards had come under strong influence from French law.[46]

In the twentieth century, yet another source of influence came into play and even became predominant, namely Italian law.[47] While initially strongly shaped by French law, at the beginning of the twentieth century, Italian law not only opened itself to other foreign influences, especially from Germany, but also started to

[39] FC von Savigny, *Traité de Droit Romain*, translated by MCh Guenoux. The first volume appeared back in 1840 (Paris, Firmin Didot Frères). In 1878–79, a Spanish translation of the French version was published, but it seems to have been much less influential (if only for the reason that it did not arrive until after most Latin American codifications had been enacted).

[40] See AB Schwarz, 'Einflüsse deutscher Zivilistik im Auslande' in H Thieme and F Wieacker (eds), *Rechtsgeschichte und Gegenwart. Gesammelte Schriften zur Neueren Privatrechtsgeschichte und Rechtsvergleichung von Andreas B. Schwarz* (Karlsruhe, Müller, 1960) 40–41.

[41] On Zachariä's influence in Costa Rica, see Scholl (n 14) 103–04, 183. Also the Argentinean Code of 1869 showed considerable influence of Zachariä, see Kleinheisterkamp (n 2) 281.

[42] Thus, for the Brazilian context, R David, 'Le droit brésilien jusqu'en 1950' (*Cours de droit civil comparé*, Doctorat, 1949–1950, 210–394) in A Wald and C Jauffret-Spinosi (eds), *Le Droit Brésilien d'hier, d'aujord'hui et de demain* (Paris, Société de Législation Comparée, 2005) 25, 164.

[43] Its drafter, Dalmacio Vélez Sarsfield, had been in close contact with the Brazilian Augusto Teixeira de Freitas (see text accompanying n 45) and was strongly influenced by him, and thus, indirectly, by the German *Pandektenwissenschaft*. See Kleinheisterkamp (n 2) 280–81, with further references.

[44] The clearest expression of this influence is the structure of the Code of 1916, which followed the so-called *Pandektensystem*, thus consisting of a 'General Part' and four books on Family, Property, Obligations and Succession. For a detailed account, see JP Schmidt, *Zivilrechtskodifikation in Brasilien: Strukturfragen und Regelungsprobleme in historisch-vergleichender Perspektive* (Tübingen, Mohr Siebeck, 2009) 23ff.

[45] Schmidt (n 44) 36–41.

[46] G Braga da Cruz, 'A formação histórica do moderno direito privado português e brasileiro (I)' (1955) 50 *Revista da Faculdade de Direito da Universidade de São Paulo* 32, 65ff. For examples, see A dos Santos Justo, 'O Direito Brasileiro: Raízes Históricas' (2002) 20 *Revista Brasileira de Direito Comparado* 131, 150–54.

[47] Garro (n 26) 605.

develop in an original fashion.[48] Thus, the second Italian Code of 1942 could in many ways claim to be the most modern codification of its time, and it is not surprising that it left a strong imprint on several subsequent Latin American codes, such as the Peruvian Code of 1984,[49] the Paraguayan Code of 1985[50] or the Brazilian Code of 2002.[51]

B. Conclusions as to Some General Features of Latin American Private Law

i. Codification

The first conclusion we can draw from the brief outline just presented is that the idea of civil codification was extremely successful in Latin America. This should come as no surprise, since the adoption of a code allowed the newly founded states to kill several birds with one stone: to systematise their law, to modernise it and to stress their national sovereignty.[52] An interesting question concerns the role of Jeremy Bentham in this process, one of the most forceful advocates of the idea of codification. Bentham had been in direct contact with many Latin American political leaders of the time, offering them his ideas for legislative reform in all areas of the law. Chilean codifier Andrés Bello had even earned his living from copying Bentham's (barely legible) manuscripts while residing in London.[53] However, compared to his great 'missionary' efforts, Bentham's influence on Latin American law seems to have remained rather limited after all, as most of his ideas proved to be too abstract and unsuitable for the Latin American reality.[54]

The second half of the twentieth century saw the importance of the Latin American civil codes substantially diminished, due to the phenomenon of

[48] See Zweigert and Kötz (n 4) 104–07.

[49] See Guzmán Brito (n 31) 526.

[50] See Guzmán Brito (n 31) 529.

[51] The most illustrative example of the Italian influence is the inclusion of commercial law into the Civil Code (see Book II of the 'Special Part') and its re-conceptualisation as the 'law of the enterprise' (*direito da empresa*), as opposed to the older theories of commercial law as the law of 'merchants' or of 'commercial acts', which are still present in Germany and France; see Schmidt (n 44) 163ff.

[52] On the 'secessionist' element in the first Latin American codes, see also Parise (n 30). The idea of codification as an expression of national identity was very powerful also in Europe, see N Jansen, *Binnenmarkt, Privatrecht und europäische Identität* (Tübingen, Mohr Siebeck, 2004) 19.

[53] See ML Amunátegui, *Vida de Don Andrés Bello* (Santiago de Chile, Ramirez, 1882) 144–45; A de Avila Martel, *Andrés Bello: A Short Essay on his Life and Work* (Santiago de Chile, Universitaria, 1981) 23ff.

[54] For a detailed analysis with abundant references, see J Samtleben, 'Menschheitsglück und Gesetzgebungsexport—Zu Jeremy Benthams Wirkung in Lateinamerika' in J Samtleben, *Rechtspraxis und Rechtskultur in Brasilien und Lateinamerika* (Aachen, Shaker, 2010) 321–43 (first published in (1986) 50 *Rabels Zeitschrift für ausländisches und internationales Privatrecht* 451–480). On the influence Bentham had on Andrés Bello, see A de Avila Martel, 'La filosofía jurídica de Andrés Bello' in *Congreso Internacional: Andrés Bello y el Derecho* (Santiago de Chile, Jurídica, 1982) 41, 47–49, 56–62. For an example of Bentham's influence, see Caffera, Ch 5 in this book.

'decodification' and the advent of modern Constitutions. However, just as in Europe, this development has not led to the idea of codification being abandoned altogether.[55] On the contrary, the adoption of recent codes such as the Brazilian Code of 2002 or the Argentinean Code of 2014 can be seen as proof that the Latin American legal orders continue to believe that private law is best organised in a central source, which not only contains the bulk of its rules, but also provides its conceptual and systematic framework.[56]

ii. Continuity

The second conclusion is that the rules, concepts and institutions of Latin American private law are firmly rooted in Roman-Canon *ius commune*, which came to the New World as part of Spanish and Portuguese law, and was later continued in a modernised version.[57] In other words, the independence of Latin America resulted only in a cutting of its political ties with Europe, not in a radical break with the inherited legal tradition. The secession from the Iberian metropolis had not entailed a social revolution; rather, the local elites had remained the same. They were content with the abolition of certain feudal institutions (eg, privileges of the nobility or entailed estates)[58] and not interested in fundamental private law reforms.[59] Just like the French *Code civil*,[60] the Latin American codifications were more concerned with restating private law than with revolutionising it, and their general spirit was rather conservative, in the sense that they primarily reflected the values and the interests of the ruling classes.[61] Family law is probably the area where this was most visible.[62]

In later decades, influences from the common law also made themselves felt, and in view of the geographical proximity to the United States, it would have been surprising if they had not.[63] However, unlike in constitutional law[64] or procedural law,[65]

[55] See Schmidt (n 26).

[56] However, as will be discussed in Section V.C below, the aims of codification are frequently undermined by Latin American legal methodology.

[57] However, the affirmation of López-Medina (n 7) 352–53, namely that the Portuguese and Spanish tradition were *only* continued in a modernised version, does not seem to be valid for private law, as in the law of succession, for example, many institutions from colonial times survive even today.

[58] See Kleinheisterkamp (n 2) 271.

[59] David (n 5) 11; FW von Rauchhaupt, 'Vergleich- und Angleichbarkeit der Rechte Süd- und Mittelamerikas, (1955) 20 *Rabels Zeitschrift für ausländisches und internationales Privatrecht* 121, 128; PH Eder, 'Law and Justice in Latin America' in A Reppy (ed), *Law—A Century of Progress 1835–1935* (New York, New York University Press, 1937) 50–51; Samtleben (n 54) 341.

[60] See J Gordley, 'Myths of the French Civil Code' (1994) 42 *American Journal of Comparative Law* 459ff.

[61] See also Section IV below.

[62] Eder (n 59) 53. On the patriarchal nature of the Brazilian Code from 1916, see Schmidt (n 44) 52.

[63] See Mirow (n 7) 185ff, especially on the 'Law and Development Movement' of the 1960s and 1970s.

[64] See David (n 5) 8.

[65] On the admission of collective suits, especially in Brazil, see ÁR Oquendo, *Latin American Law* (New York, Foundation Press, 2006) 710ff.

in private law the impact was confined to rather specific matters. One example is the introduction of the 'Torrens system' for the recording of land titles[66] in the Dominican Republic in 1920, as a result of the US military intervention of 1916–22.[67]

More generally, common law influences occurred in the field of commercial law, even if, at least in a formal sense, this area had been strongly shaped by the legislative model of France and its dichotomy of *Code civil* and *Code de commerce*. Thus, the nineteenth century saw the adoptions of numerous Latin American commercial codes,[68] a trend that was only reversed in the late twentieth century when, mostly under the influence of Italian law, several countries merged their civil and commercial codes into a 'Code unique'.[69] But as regards its substance, the French *Code de commerce* had been much less influential; instead, legal institutions of the English-speaking world seeped into the commercial law of Latin America.[70] We see, for example, that a number of Latin American states enacted legislation on trusts or trust-like devices.[71] Also the style of drafting commercial contracts in Latin American law firms seems to have been heavily influenced by Anglo-American legal culture. As regards its systematic and conceptual framework, however, Latin American private law firmly continued to follow the tradition of Continental Europe.[72]

iii. Eclecticism, but Also Originality

A third conclusion is that the approach of the Latin American legislatures was distinctly eclectic.[73] They were ready to take into account any foreign model that was available to them. An indispensable tool in this respect was the *Concordance entre les Codes civils étrangers et le Code Napoléon* by Antoine de Saint-Joseph, written in 1840,[74] which granted its users access to a great number of existing

[66] On which see, eg, BC Shick and IH Plotkin, *Torrens in the United States: A Legal and Economic History and Analysis of American Land-registration Systems* (Lexington, MA, Heath, 1978).

[67] See JA Bonilla Atiles, *Legislación de Tierras Dominicana: El Sistema Torrens*, 2nd edn (Santo Domingo, Libraría Dominicana, 1974) 51ff.

[68] See J Olavarría Avila, *Los Códigos de Comercio Latinoamericanos con una Introducción de Derecho Comparado Externo* (Santiago, Editora Jurídica de Chile, 1961).

[69] As was done in the Paraguayan Civil Code of 1985, the Brazilian Civil Code of 2002, and the Argentinean Civil and Commercial Code of 2014. See generally on the unification of civil law and commercial law, JP Schmidt 'Code Unique' in J Basedow, KJ Hopt and R Zimmermann (eds), *The Max Planck Encyclopedia of European Private Law*, vol I (Oxford, Oxford University Press, 2012) 210–14.

[70] See Eder (n 59) 59–60; David (n 5) 12; Kleinheisterkamp (n 2) 285–87.

[71] For references, see A Braun, 'The State of the Art of Comparative Research in the Area of Trusts' in M Graziadei and LD Smith (eds), *Research Handbook on Comparative Property Law* (Cheltenham, Edward Elgar, 2016) 121, 124, 130.

[72] López-Medina (n 7) 360 rightly criticises the widespread idea of the French nature of Latin American private law, but takes things too far with his claim that it does not even belong to the civil law family any longer (even if the usefulness of such abstract categorisations is admittedly quite limited).

[73] Kleinheisterkamp (n 2) 293–94.

[74] Also very influential was Saint-Joseph's parallel work for commercial law: *Concordance entre les Codes de commerce étrangers et le Code de Commerce Français* (Paris 1844). One of the first to emphasise

codifications (including, for example, those of different Swiss cantons).[75] It is hardly imaginable how, in a place so remote from Europe, the drafters would otherwise have gathered the necessary information.

As a result of this widespread eclecticism, the Latin American countries might be described as 'mixed legal systems', not so much because of the co-existence of civil law and common law, but because of the co-existence of, say, French, German, Spanish, Portuguese and Italian ideas within one legal order.[76] In a similar vein, Latin American private law has been described as a 'comparatist's dream',[77] and for a German scholar, for example, the study of a good Latin American treatise can be a very efficient way of familiarising herself with the law of France or Italy. Accordingly, Latin American scholars often have a much broader comparative knowledge than their European colleagues.[78]

Admittedly, the 'copy and paste' method was sometimes carried out rather haphazardly, which resulted in serious technical inconsistencies.[79] However, to regard the nineteenth-century Latin American civil codes as entirely unoriginal[80] would be to overlook an important point. As mentioned earlier, sophisticated codifiers such as Andrés Bello took over foreign rules because they aptly formulated the sought-after solution; in other words, the foreign rule was not so much copied in its substance, but rather in its form. In this way, European codes such as the *Code civil* served as a 'catalyst' for newly founded states, which had to build up a legal system in a very short time with very limited personal and material resources at their disposal.[81] Besides, in some instances the Latin American codifiers also decided to leave the well-trodden European paths, in order to take into account domestic idiosyncrasies.[82] A good example of this is provided by the law of succession. While, generally, many features of the Iberian tradition were continued in this area (eg, the strong limitation of freedom of testation by the institute of forced heirship),[83] in some matters a

the role of Saint Joseph's works for the development of Latin American private law seems to have been KH Nadelmann, 'Kritische Notiz zu den Quellen der Rechte Süd- und Mittelamerikas' (1955) 20 *Rabels Zeitschrift für ausländisches und internationales Privatrecht* 500–03.

[75] For an overview, see Parise (n 25) 825 n 5.

[76] No relevant part, in turn, has been played by the customary law of the indigenous people for the development of Latin American private law. Some recent Latin American Constitutions, however, grant indigenous tribes a certain legal autonomy, see S Lanni (ed), *I diritti dei popoli indigeni in America Latina* (Naples, Edizioni Scientifiche Italiane, 2011).

[77] KS Rosenn, 'Teaching Latin American Law' (1971) 19 *American Journal of Comparative Law* 692. In a similar vein David (n 5) 12–13.

[78] On this point, see also Section V. below.

[79] Eder (n 59) 53. For examples from the Peruvian Civil Code of 1984, see Kleinheisterkamp (n 2) 294; for an example from the Costa Rican Civil Code of 1886, see Scholl (n 14) 114–15.

[80] As was the predominant view for a long time, see David (n 5) 1.

[81] Kleinheisterkamp (n 2) 274.

[82] Momberg (n 27) 413. See also JC Rivera, 'En defensa de los códigos (el viejo y el nuevo)' (2015) 182 *La Ley* LXXIX, 28 September 2015, 1–2, who provides various examples of quite modern solutions in the Argentinean Code of 1869.

[83] See the detailed overview by A Guzmán Brito, 'La pervivencia de instituciones sucesorias castellano-indianas en las codificaciones hispanoamericanas del siglo XIX', in José de la Puente Brunke and

very modern attitude prevailed.[84] The Latin American regimes on intestate succession, for example, often granted the surviving spouse a position that was much more favourable than in many European legal orders at the time, which still reflected the concern that ancestral estates might end up in the hands of the other family. As many fortunes in the New World had been built up from scratch owing to the joint effort of both spouses, these considerations were considered irrelevant here.[85]

iv. *The Limited Influence of the* Code Civil

To conclude this item and return to its starting point, I shall briefly illustrate why someone who came to Latin America expecting to find all the characteristic features of French private law would quickly be disabused of this notion. Three examples should suffice.

(1) Except for the few early copies of the *Code civil*, no Latin American civil code has followed its structure. While the *Code civil* deals with the law of obligations and the law of succession (and even with matrimonial property law) in a single book with the somewhat artificial title 'Des différentes manières dont on acquiert la propriété', the Latin American codes, in an approach where the influence of Roman law is again evident, clearly separate the law of obligations from the law of succession.[86]

Jorge Amado Guevara Gil (eds), *Congreso del Instituto Internacional de Historia del Derecho Indiano: Derecho, instituciones y procesos históricos vol III* (Lima, Fondo Editorial de la Pontificia Universidad Católica del Perú, 2008) 31–88. Another example is the determination of the order of heirs in intestate succession according to the 'three-line system', see JP Schmidt, 'Intestate Succession in Latin America' in K Reid, MJ de Waal and R Zimmermann (eds), *Intestate Succession* (Oxford, Oxford University Press, 2015) 118, 122ff.

[84] For further discussion of the following topic, see Schmidt (n 83) 119–20, 141–42.

[85] A further issue where the existing tradition was broken with concerned the succession rights of collateral relatives. From early on, most Latin American codes followed a very restrictive approach in this regard, and today most countries draw the line after the fourth degree of kinship, or even before that (Germany, in turn, still admits unlimited family succession, while France for a long time allowed collaterals up to the 12th degree to inherit). This focus on the core family is at least partly motivated by a wish to redistribute wealth, as in the absence of close family members, the estate devolves upon state institutions. See Schmidt (n 83) 135–36. Besides, the aim was probably to limit the cases in which estates were inherited by relatives still living in Europe, see E Holthöfer, 'Fortschritte in der Erbrechtsgesetzgebung seit der französischen Revolution' in H Mohnhaupt (ed), *Zur Geschichte des Familien- und Erbrechts: Politische Implikationen und Perspektiven* (Frankfurt am Main, Klostermann, 1987) 121, 131.

[86] In Gaius' scheme of *personae, res, actiones*, which was later repeated in Justinian's *Institutiones*, the law of succession and the law of obligations form, next to property law in the strict sense, more or less independent subgroups within the wide category of *res*, see JF Stagl, 'Das didaktische System des Gaius' (2014) 131 *Zeitschrift der Savigny-Stiftung für Rechtsgeschichte (Romanistische Abteilung)* 313–48. For the genesis of the structure of the Chilean Civil Code, see A Guzmán Brito, 'La formación del sistema general del "Código Civil de Chile" y los sistemas de los códigos existentes hacia 1852' in D Martinic and M Tapia (eds), *Sesquicentenario del Código Civil de Andrés Bello. Pasado, presente y futuro de la codificación* (Santiago, Lexis Nexis, 2005) 123–69.

(2) Almost all Latin American legal orders have embraced the concept of the 'juridical act', a creation of German Pandectism,[87] which serves as the overarching category for all acts by which individuals self-determine their legal relationships in the exercise of their private autonomy.[88] The *Code civil*, by contrast, only deals with specific types of juridical act, especially contracts, and does not provide an overarching regime.[89]

(3) Under French property law, ownership of movables is transferred by pure consent, while the Latin American countries, again in the spirit of Roman law, require the delivery of the object, a *traditio*.[90]

Also, on a more general level, it is hard to agree with the opinion that the *Code civil* 'continues to serve [in Latin America] a taxonomic function as the intellectual superstructure upon which all legal thought is built',[91] or that the Latin American legal systems owe their place within the civil law tradition to it.[92] After all, we must not forget that the *Code civil* was of course not a *creatio ex nihilo*: in its form, it was a product of the idea of codification, which owed much to the systematisation efforts of natural law writers;[93] in its substance, the *Code* drew heavily on the *ius commune*. Therefore, its concepts and categories are much older than the *Code civil* itself (as we have seen, many can be traced back to Roman law), and they did not come to Latin America exclusively via France.

An even stronger exaggeration of the role of French law may be found in the assertion that if one day a 'droit latino-américain à proprement parler doit naître de la diversité des droits actuellement appliqués dans ces pays, ce ne pourra être qu'un système à base de droit français'.[94] In view of the great variety of influences on Latin American private law that we have seen, this assessment is clearly to be rejected.

[87] For its origin and functions, see JP Schmidt, 'Juridical Act' in J Basedow, KJ Hopt and R Zimmermann (eds), *The Max Planck Encyclopedia of European Private Law*, vol II (Oxford, Oxford University Press, 2012) 1016–20.

[88] While in Arts 1445ff CC Chile, the role of the *acto jurídico* is still very limited, the codes of Argentina (Arts 944 CC 1869 and Arts 257 CC 2014), Brazil (Arts 81ff CC 1916 and Arts 104ff CC 2002) and Peru (Book II CC 1984) contain a fully fledged doctrine of juridical acts.

[89] The concept of the 'acte juridique' was finally introduced into the *Code civil* in 2016, but this change has been rather cosmetic in nature, since there is still no independent regime for juridical acts. Instead, the rules on contracts apply 'en tant que de raison', see Arts 1100, 1100-1 *Code civil*, as amended by the *Ordonnance n° 2016-131 du 10 février 2016 portant réforme du droit des contrats, du régime général et de la preuve des obligations*. It should be pointed out that French legal scholarship, as a result of German influence, adopted the concept of the 'acte juridique' several decades ago, and that there had been several earlier attempts to include it in the *Code civil*. See JP Schmidt, 'Der "juridical act" im DCFR: Ein nützlicher Grundbegriff des europäischen Privatrechts?' [2010] *Zeitschrift für Europäisches Privatrecht* 304, 308.

[90] See, eg, Art 676 CC Chile. For a comprehensive comparative analysis of the transfer of movable property in the Iberian and the Latin American legal orders, see A Röthlisberger, *Traditionsprinzip und Konsensprinzip bei der Mobiliarübereignung: Eine vergleichende Untersuchung zu den iberischen und lateinamerikanischen Kodifikationen* (Zürich, Schulthess, 1982), who stresses, among other things, that the influence of the *Code civil* in Latin America is often overrated (III, 119).

[91] Mirow (n 7) 191.

[92] Garro (n 26) 605.

[93] See Schmidt (n 26).

[94] I Zajtay, 'Les destinées du Code civil' (1954) 6 *Revue Internationale de Droit Comparé* 792, 802.

IV. Idealism and Realism in Latin American Contract Law

As was outlined in the preceding sections, the Latin American codifiers (at least the more sophisticated ones) did not just blindly copy the European models, but also sought to take into account the social reality in their countries. Indeed, one might regard this as a fundamental and almost self-evident requirement for successful legislation. A particular rule that works well in Europe (or any other part of the world) might be entirely unsuitable in the Latin American context, where law generally has to operate under very different conditions. The Latin American societies are characterised not only by a particular cultural and ethnological mix between indigenous, European, and, especially in the case of Brazil, African elements, but also by huge social and economic asymmetries.[95] One might add that faith in, and respect for, the state, its institution and the rule of law are, arguably, markedly lower than in Europe,[96] and that as a result, formal legal regimes are often bypassed or substituted by informal social practices.[97]

However, again, we must be careful not to over-generalise. It is good to remember that Latin American societies are not only very different from European societies, but also from one another.[98] One might actually find several countries even within one and the same Latin American country, with huge differences especially between life in the big cities and life in the rural areas.[99] What is remarkable, in any event, is how little the Latin American reality(ies) were reflected, at least for a long time, in Latin American contract law.

As mentioned earlier, the elites of the newly independent Latin American states were strongly attached to the ideals of the European bourgeoisie. These ideals found their expression in a very formal and liberal private law, which basically rested on three pillars: formal equality of all citizens, ample freedom of ownership and ample freedom of contract.[100] Correspondingly, the Latin American legislatures were only fleetingly, if at all, concerned with issues such as contractual justice or protection of the weaker party. Brazil may seem to be an extreme example,

[95] See also A Ferrante, '¿Es correcta la elección del método de cálculo de la reducción del precio en los principios latinoamericanos de contratos?' (2014) 22 *Revista Chilena de Derecho Privado* 9, 13.

[96] See, eg, Samtleben (n 54) 332; Kleinheisterkamp (n 2) 265.

[97] For Brazil, see the classic study by KS Rosenn, 'The Jeito: Brazil's Institutional Bypass of the Formal Legal System' (1971) 19 *American Journal of Comparative Law* 514–49, and more recently PR Fortes, 'How Socio-Legal Norms Emerge within Complex Networks: Law and (In)Formality at Ipanema Beach and its Developmental Implications' (2014) 10 *FIU Law Review* 183–213.

[98] See also Eder (n 59) 39: 'While there are elements of unity and resemblance in the twenty republics to the South, the differences are more important'.

[99] For Brazil, these contrasts are sometimes expressed in the term 'Belindia': for a small part of the population, the living conditions resemble those of Belgium, while for a large part they resemble those of India.

[100] See Zweigert and Kötz (n 4) 86–87, 143–44.

yet it may still be regarded as representative of the general trend: the Civil Code of 1916[101] not only rejected the institute of usury, but also the *laesio enormis*, despite its long tradition in Portuguese law. The author of the corresponding draft of 1899, Clovis Bevilaqua, had argued that in the economic situation of the time, the determination of prices could calmly be left to the free play of market forces.[102] In a similar vein, the Code did not contain the principle of good faith, and exceptions from *pacta sunt servanda* were not even allowed in cases where both the Portuguese tradition and general considerations of fairness would have suggested they be allowed. Hence, a farm tenant, for example, who had seen his crop destroyed due to force majeure, still had to pay the full rent.[103]

It seems remarkable that in their liberal zeal, the Latin American codes went even further than some of their European counterparts. The German Civil Code (BGB), for example, had at least received the famous 'drops of socialist oil' and included specific rules for the protection of employees, lessees or debtors in general.[104] But in Latin America, the conditions for a very liberal private law were, of course, even less present than in Europe. Citizens were in fact tremendously unequal, and for the many who were without any significant possessions, freedom of ownership and freedom of contract were no more than pretty words written on a piece of paper. The situation was described aptly by René David, according to whom the Latin American codes of the nineteenth century

> reflétaient avant tout l'idéal de justice d'une classe dirigeante, europééne par son origine et sa culture. Ce droit tenait peu compte des conditions de vie, des sentiments ou des besoins des autres parties de la population, tenues dans un état de complet ou demi-esclavage.[105]

It has to be remembered in this context that Brazil had not abolished slavery until 1888, and that this formal act had not of course turned former slaves into educated and well-off opera-going citizens overnight, but rather had created a mass of new proletarians.

One reason for the rather liberal design of the Latin American contract law regimes was, of course, that the ruling classes were mainly concerned with their

[101] For a more detailed overview of the characteristics of the Brazilian Code of 1916, see Schmidt (n 44) 51–56.

[102] C Bevilaqua in *Projecto do Código Civil Brazileiro. Trabalhos da Commissão Especial da Câmara dos Deputados, vol VI* (Rio de Janeiro, Imprensa Nacional, 1902) 51–52. For further analysis, see Schmidt (n 44) 367–68. The 19th century saw the abolition of the *laesio enormis* also in a number of other Latin American States, see Caffera, Ch 5 in this book.

[103] Art 1214 CC Brazil 1916, which according to A dos Santos Justo, 'O Direito Luso-Brasileiro: codificação civil' (2004) 25 *Revista Brasileira de Direito Comparado* 167, 192, marked a departure from 'medieval solidarity'. An earlier draft had still provided that the tenant could request a reduction of the rent, but in the end, as in many other instances, the interests of the property-owning classes prevailed.

[104] R Zimmermann, *The New German Law of Obligations: Historical and Comparative Perspectives* (Oxford, Oxford University Press, 2005) 163–65, who also points out that important measures of protection for industrial workers were already contained in special legislation (168–69).

[105] David (n 8) 266–67. Similar Eder (n 59) 54: 'The codes were largely for the upper class only, especially the landed aristocracy'; O Gomes, *Raízes históricas e sociológicas do código civil brasileiro* (Rio de Janeiro, Forense, 2003) (first published in 1958) 34.

own interests, and with the economic development of the country in general.[106] During the legislative proceedings of the Brazilian Code of 1916, for example, various drafts to improve the protection of industrial workers had been tabled, but in the end were all rejected, one of the arguments being that the economy should not be burdened with additional costs.[107] At the same time, the Latin American codifiers hoped that by following the ideals of the European bourgeoisie, they would help their societies to develop not only economically, but also culturally, so that the gap between ideal and reality would eventually disappear, or at least narrow.[108] Finally, one probably also has to take into consideration that in their perception of law as an abstract, logical and largely self-referential system that did not necessarily need to be in tune with reality or social custom,[109] nineteenth-century Latin American codifiers were simply children of their time.

In any event, these hopes remained largely unfulfilled. Even in early 20th-century Latin America, the exceedingly liberal conception of contract law proved unable to deal satisfactorily with both the old and the new challenges (just as it failed to do in Europe). In Brazil, for example, tenants, loan debtors and purchasers of immovable property increasingly became confronted with business practices that were highly unethical, but completely legal under the laissez-faire approach engrained in the Code of 1916. The desire to combat these developments found expression in a number of specific statutes of protection that were adopted in the 1920s and 1930s,[110] and also Brazilian courts and legal scholarship sought to mitigate the strictness of the law, by referring to unwritten doctrines such as good faith or *clausula rebus sic stantibus*.[111] However, apart from the Mexican Civil Code of the Federal District of 1928, which had a distinctly socialist imprint,[112] it took several decades before the tendency towards a more social and less formal contract law began to be reflected in the Latin American codifications. In Argentina, for example, it was not until 1968 that provisions on *laesio enormis*, change of circumstances and abuse of rights were introduced into its *Código Civil*,[113] with Paraguay following suit in its second Civil Code of 1985.[114] The new Brazilian Code of 2002 contains rules on abuse of rights (Article 187), control of standard contract terms (Articles 423, 424) and change of circumstances (Article 478), as well as a general clause on good faith (Article 422), and thus shifted the paradigm of its

[106] The aim of the Argentinean Code of 1869 to facilitate the circulation of wealth and to 'colonise' the country is stressed by Rivera (n 82) 1–2.

[107] Gomes (n 105) 32ff.

[108] David (n 8) 267.

[109] Eder (n 59) 53–54, mentioning as examples the elaborate provisions on prenuptial contracts and the wife's dowry, legal institutions which were completely irrelevant in social practice.

[110] See Schmidt (n 44) 58–60.

[111] See, eg, A Silveira, *A bôa fé no direito civil* (São Paulo, Paulista, 1941); Schmidt (n 44) 426–27 with further references.

[112] See Eder (n 59) 56–57.

[113] Law 17.711. For further changes this reform encompassed, see Rivera (n 82) 2, who also states that it affected the very pillars of the Code from 1869, of which 'little or nothing remained'.

[114] Garro (n 26) 608.

predecessor of 1916.[115] The most modern Latin American contract law regime is undoubtedly found in the new Argentinean Civil and Commercial Code of 2014, which also deals with consumer contracts.[116] Other Latin American contract law regimes, in contrast, still have not seen any fundamental reforms since their enactment roughly 150 years ago. Chilean law, for example, to this day does not accept the termination or adaptation of contracts in the case of change of circumstances.[117]

What is perhaps even more important is that the Latin American legal orders have been more static than their European counterparts also in another regard, namely the contribution of the courts to the development of contract law. As is well known, the German experience in particular is very rich in this respect and offers many examples where courts, by invoking good morals or the principle of good faith, have sought to make contract law more flexible and socially oriented. Examples we can mention include the control of standard contract terms, also in business-to-business-contracts, the adaptation of contracts in case of change of circumstances, or the many scenarios discussed under the heading of 'abuse of a right'.[118] These doctrines went on to be 'exported' to many other European countries,[119] eg, to Spain[120] and Portugal.[121]

In Latin America, in turn, judges have, overall, been much more reluctant to interfere in contractual matters.[122] The principle of good faith, for example, was always applied in a rather restrictive manner (if it played any role at all). A more activist stance began to develop only towards the end of the twentieth century, also as a result of the 'constitutionalisation' of private law.[123] Since then, however,

[115] For further analysis, see Schmidt (n 44) 461ff.

[116] See Arts 1092ff. The decision to include a general framework for consumer contracts into the Code was inspired by German law, see p 116 of the explanatory notes: www.nuevocodigocivil.com/wp-content/uploads/2015/02/5-Fundamentos-del-Proyecto.pdf.

[117] Momberg (n 27) 427.

[118] See Zimmermann (n 104) 26–27, 173–75, 205ff; S Whittaker and R Zimmermann, 'Good Faith in European Contract Law: Surveying the Legal Landscape' in S Whittaker and R Zimmermann (eds), *Good Faith in European Contract Law* (Cambridge, Cambridge University Press, 2000) 18ff.

[119] For an overview, see F Ranieri, 'Good Faith' in J Basedow, KJ Hopt and R Zimmermann (eds), *The Max Planck Encyclopedia of European Private Law*, vol I (Oxford, Oxford University Press, 2012) 790–94; MW Hesselink, 'The Concept of Good Faith' in AS Hartkamp et al (eds), *Towards a European Civil Code*, 4th edn (Alphen aan den Rijn, Kluwer Law International, 2011) 619–49.

[120] See C Eckl, *Treu und Glauben im spanischen Vertragsrecht* (Tübingen, Mohr Siebeck, 2007) 70ff.

[121] See especially the monumental work by A Menezes Cordeiro, *Da Boa Fé no Direito Civil*, vols I and II (Coimbra, Alemdina, 1984).

[122] See Eder (n 59) 64 ('Equity is unknown in their judgements').

[123] Quite dramatic examples may be found in the jurisprudence of the Colombian Constitutional Court, such as the cases of credit debtors unable to fulfil their obligations vis-à-vis the bank because they were kidnapped or displaced by armed conflict (see *Corte Constitucional* T-520/03: www.corteconstitucional.gov.co/relatoria/2003/T-520-03.htm, and *Corte Constitucional* T-312/10: www.corteconstitucional.gov.co/RELATORIA/2010/T-312-10.htm). It should be pointed out that the prominent role of the Colombian Constitutional Court in private law relationships is also, or even primarily, explained by procedural factors: the *acción de tutela*, which is available against infringements of a fundamental right, is a much faster and more efficient way to obtain protection than a procedure before the ordinary courts, which usually lasts many years (I am very grateful to Catalina Salgado Ramírez for her valuable information on Colombian law).

in some countries, such as Brazil, the pendulum seems to have swung to the other extreme, with judges now taking ample liberties to intervene in contracts (though often on a formal legal basis).[124] Also the new Argentinean Code of 2014 leaves much room for judicial discretion, a fact that has not escaped criticism.[125] Overall, one can note a growing appetite in Latin America to use contract law, and private law in general, as an instrument for social change and redistribution of wealth. In view of the huge social and economic imbalances that characterise the Latin American societies, this vision is very understandable. To what extent private law can, and should, really fulfil that role is, of course, an entirely different matter.

To sum up: for a long time, the contract law of the Latin American legal orders did not show any particular cultural imprint, being even more formal and liberal than their European counterparts. A trend towards a 'more social' model of contract law, accompanied by an increase of judicial discretion, only emerged rather slowly, and the intensity of this movement varies greatly between different Latin American states. As a result, contemporary contract law in Latin America is marked by the competition between different paradigms and the tensions resulting therefrom (we witness a similar phenomenon in Europe, of course[126]). As will be discussed later, this posed a considerable challenge for the drafters of the PLACL.

V. 'Nationalist' vs 'Universal' Spirit: The Methodological Divide Between Europe and Latin America

It follows from the preceding sections that a blackletter rule comparison between Latin American and Continental European contract laws would uncover scarcely

[124] In Brazil, the decisive turn was brought about by the Consumer Code of 1990 (Law 8078/1990), which gives the judge ample freedoms to strike down contract clauses as 'abusive', even when they were negotiated individually (see Art 51), or to interpret contracts in favour of the consumer (Art 47). The role of the Consumer Code is increased by the fact that its concept of 'consumer' in Article 2 is wide enough to include certain commercial parties. For a detailed analysis, see Schmidt (n 44) 237ff.

In contrast, the importance of the much-debated Article 421 of the Brazilian Civil Code of 2002, which refers to the 'social function of the contract', must not be overstated. As far as can be ascertained, Brazilian legal scholarship has not managed to give clear contours to this concept, which as a result is invoked for pretty much any rule of contract law, even *pacta sunt servanda*. This comes as no surprise, as the term 'social function' is far too vague to be meaningful. Every legal rule or institution fulfils a 'social function', insofar as it attempts to regulate a certain matter of life in a society. The decisive question is therefore not whether a contract has a social function, but in what it actually consists. For further discussion, see Schmidt (n 44) 471ff.

[125] Rivera (n 82) 3, who furthermore remarks that the discretion which existed under the former Code had occasionally been 'abused' (n 30).

[126] For the tensions between the more liberal-oriented national contracts laws of the EU Member States and the mostly consumer-oriented contract law enacted by the EU, see H Eidenmüller, F Faust, HC Grigoleit, N Jansen, G Wagner and R Zimmermann, 'The Common Frame of Reference for European Private Law—Policy Choices and Codification Problems' (2008) 28 *Oxford Journal of Legal Studies* 659, 678ff.

any fundamental differences. Rather, the national solutions, if not actually identical, appear as minor variations on common and familiar themes. However, in another regard there is actually a huge gulf between the two geographic regions, or at least between some of their members, and it is a gulf that is rarely perceived, for it is hidden under the surface of the written law. It concerns the role of foreign sources[127] in legal scholarship and practice, and matters of legal methodology in general.

A. The Nationalisation of Legal Scholarship in France and Germany

Legal comparatists and legal historians have often lamented that the European codification movement of the eighteenth and nineteenth centuries broke up the intellectual unity that existed under the *ius commune* and led to a fragmentation not only of legislation, but also of legal scholarship.[128] Legal scholarship now became confined to national borders and was forced to lead an existence that Rudolph von Jhering famously described as 'humiliating and undignified'.[129] Prime examples of this process are French and German law. Even if the (in)famous dictum attributed to Bugnet—'Je ne connais pas le droit civil, je n'enseigne que le Code Napoléon'[130]—was hyperbolic probably even in the nineteenth century, its underlying rationale remains largely unchanged. For if we delve into a standard German or French textbook, there is a high probability that we will encounter no references whatsoever to foreign sources. Instead, a German writer will exclusively focus on German legal provisions, on German legal literature and German case law, while a French writer will do the same for her country.[131] In both jurisdictions, one has to turn to works of comparative law to find information on

[127] Here and in the following account, 'source' is used in the wide sense and thus includes both legislation and legal writing, cf S Vogenauer 'Sources of Law and Legal Method in Comparative Law' in M Reimann and R Zimmermann (eds), *The Oxford Handbook of Comparative Law* (Oxford, Oxford University Press, 2006) 869, 877–78.

[128] See, eg, Zimmermann (n 104) 5–6; Zweigert and Kötz (n 4) 15. In Germany at least, this development was greatly reinforced by reforms of legal education, see J Liebrecht, 'Formando juristas en Alemania: estructuras, método e ideales' (2015) 13 *Academia. Revista sobre Enseñanza del Derecho* (25) 37–74.

[129] In the original: 'Eine demüthigende, unwürdige Form für eine Wissenschaft!' R von Jhering, *Geist des römischen Rechts auf den verschiedenen Stufen seiner Entwicklung*, 7/8th edn (Leipzig, Breitkopf & Härtel, 1924) 15.

[130] Quoted after F Gény, *Méthode d'interprétation et sources en droit privé positif*, vol I, 2nd edn (1919, reprint Paris, Librairie générale de Droit et de Jurisprudence, 1954) 30.

[131] See, eg, Gordley (n 60) 491, according to whom French jurists 'take it for granted … that French law is to be found by consulting exclusively the French judges and French scholars who have interpreted the Code'. See also B Markesinis and J Fedtke, *Judicial Recourse to Foreign Law. A New Source of Inspiration?* (London, UCL Press, 2006) 66, who identify 'a lack of dedicated and focused study of foreign law by the present generation of French academics'. It seems doubtful, however, whether earlier generations worked differently.

other legal systems. Also, there is, at least traditionally, a very clear divide among scholars, between those who deal exclusively with domestic law (and these are the overwhelming majority), and the handful of miserable people who dedicate part of their time to comparative law. Finally, also the use of comparative law in court practice, advocated very prominently already a long time ago by Raymond Saleilles[132] and Konrad Zweigert,[133] never achieved a real breakthrough.[134] As a result, it is still very rare for French and German courts to refer to foreign sources in purely domestic cases.[135]

B. The Survival of the *Ius Commune* Spirit in Other Countries of the Civil Law Tradition

It is doubtful, however, to what extent the development of legal scholarship in France and Germany can be regarded as representative. Other European countries, such as the Netherlands,[136] Italy,[137] Spain or Portugal, have always remained much more open to foreign legal sources. This fact was keenly observed by John H Merryman and led him to the conclusion that these countries are actually more typical examples of the civil law tradition than are Germany and France.[138] As might be expected, his bold statement was sharply rejected by established comparatists from the respective countries, such as René David[139] and Hein Kötz.[140]

[132] R Saleilles, 'La Fonction juridique du Droit comparé' in Fritz Berolzheimer (ed), *Rechtswissenschaftliche Beiträge. Juristische Festgabe des Auslandes zu Josef Kohlers 60. Geburtstag. 9. März 1909* (Stuttgart, Enke, 1909), 164–75 (reprint Aalen, Scientia, 1981).

[133] K Zweigert, 'Rechtsvergleichung als universale Interpretationsmethode' (1949/50) 15 *Rabels Zeitschrift für ausländisches und internationales Privatrecht* 5–21.

[134] T Coendet, *Rechtsvergleichende Argumentation: Phänomenologie der Veranderung im rechtlichen Diskurs* (Tübingen, Mohr Siebeck, 2012) V.

[135] In 2000, Kötz counted little more than a dozen decisions in which the German Federal Supreme Court (*Bundesgerichtshof*) had referred to foreign law, and in most cases it was only done to give further support to a solution it had arrived at already on the basis of German law: H Kötz, 'Der Bundesgerichtshof und die Rechtsvergleichung' in H Kötz, *Undogmatisches: Rechtsvergleichende und rechtsökonomische Studien aus dreißig Jahren* (Tübingen, Mohr Siebeck, 2005) 120, 127–30 (first published in CW Canaris et al (eds), *50 Jahre Bundesgerichtshof, Festgabe aus der Wissenschaft*, vol II (Munich, Beck, 2000) 825–43). See also Markesinis and Fedtke (n 131) 72–82.

[136] For examples from Dutch court practice, see Kötz (n 135) 132.

[137] Markesinis and Fedtke (n 131) 64 find that 'the overall state of *academic* comparative studies [in Italy] is among the healthiest in Europe—if not the world' (emphasis in the original). The fact that the use of foreign law in Italian judgments is not openly declared is mainly explained by the statutory prohibition on judges citing doctrinal writers, see A Braun, 'Professors and Judges in Italy: It Takes Two to Tango' (2006) 26 *Oxford Journal of Legal Studies* 665, 670ff.

[138] Merryman (n 4) IX; see also JH Merrymann, DS Clark and JO Haley, *Comparative Law: Historical Development of the Civil Law Tradition in Europe, Latin America, and East Asia* (New Providence, LexisNexis, 2010) 629–30.

[139] See David's review of the first edition of Merryman's *Civil Law Tradition* (1969): (1970) 34 *Rabels Zeitschrift für ausländisches und internationales Privatrecht* 360, 361–62.

[140] See his review of one of Merryman's other works in (1980) 44 *Rabels Zeitschrift für ausländisches und internationales Privatrecht* 538, 539–40.

Yet Merryman makes an important point, which takes on additional importance in the Latin American context. Because here, the national isolation of legal scholarship definitely never happened; instead the 'universal' spirit of the *ius commune* survived the arrival of the codifications largely unscathed, as if Latin American scholars felt compelled to continue the openness that had characterised their legislatures in the nineteenth century.[141] As a result, the distinction between professors of domestic law and professors of comparative law does not make any sense to Latin American lawyers; they are comparative lawyers by nature.[142] For a Latin American textbook writer, it is the most common thing in the world to make abundant references to foreign sources, also because an exclusive focus on domestic law would be regarded as a lack of erudition (however, as we will see later, 'foreign' in this context basically means 'European').[143] It should be stressed that this approach is not limited to the doctrinal level, but also finds its way into case law. As a result, comparative law in Latin America is a 'highly practical discipline'.[144] A curious paradox can be seen in the fact that in the area of private international law, a much more restrictive spirit prevails as regards the willingness to apply foreign law, as a result especially of the 'territorialistic' approach adopted by Bello.[145] Hence, while Latin American scholars and courts are happy to imbue their domestic law with foreign legal ideas, the direct application of foreign law in cross-border situations is something they rather seek to avoid.

C. Downsides of the Latin American 'Spirit of Universality'

This Latin American openness to (certain) other legal systems must, on the one hand, be regarded as a virtue. It is an attitude that legal scholarship in Europe, particularly in France and Germany, is only slowly beginning to recover.[146] Besides, it has allowed the Latin American courts a considerable degree of flexibility, as well as the constant modernisation of private law without the need for legal reform.[147]

[141] Some comparative scholars have even regarded this 'universal spirit' of the Latin American legal orders as their defining characteristic, as opposed to the 'nationalist spirit', which supposedly 'enslaved the European legal systems', see Castan Tobeñas (n 19) 62; Schipani (n 12) 223–24 (stressing also that many Latin American civil codes permit reference to 'general principles of law' and hence do not claim a national legal monopoly); Catalano (n 12) 63.

[142] In a similar vein, López-Medina (n 7) 360–61.

[143] See Eder (n 59) 63–64.

[144] Kleinheisterkamp (n 2) 285.

[145] See J Samtleben, 'El principio de la territorialidad en América Latina' in J Samtleben, *Rechtspraxis und Rechtskultur in Brasilien und Lateinamerika* (Aachen, Shaker, 2010) 370ff, first published in *Primer Seminario Nacional de Derecho Internacional Privado* (México, DF, UNAM, 1979, 171ff).

[146] See R Zimmermann, 'Comparative Law and the Europeanization of Private Law' in M Reimann and R Zimmermann (eds), *The Oxford Handbook of Comparative Law* (Oxford, Oxford University Press, 2006) 539, 548ff.

[147] At the conference at which this contribution was first presented, this point was particularly stressed in the discussion by a Latin American participant.

On the other hand, however, the Latin American 'spirit of universality' appears to be problematic for a number of reasons, at least in the way it is often handled.

i. Problems of a Methodological Nature

a. The Absence of Clear Criteria for Comparison

A first concern is that the frequent recourse to foreign legal sources does not seem to follow any clear methodological criteria.[148] Even the choice of legal system to which a writer or a court refers often strikes us as rather arbitrary. A doctoral student might feel compelled to include German law in his analysis, for example, not because German law was influential or particularly noteworthy in the subject-matter in question, but simply because 'Germany is an important jurisdiction'. Apart from arbitrary, the references to foreign legal systems are frequently also excessive, as if the quality of a work depended on the number of jurisdictions mentioned.[149] The analysis of a particular foreign law itself is often limited to blackletter law and thus remains rather sketchy and superficial. Of course, these shortcomings are frequent also in comparative legal writing from other parts of the world. But when comparative references are well-nigh ubiquitous, as in Latin American legal writing, the problem becomes much more visible.

b. The Unclear Status of Legal Sources

A second concern is that the relationship between comparative arguments and domestic law does not seem to have been clearly sorted out.[150] If we wish to respect the binding nature of a code, it is not clear to what extent reference to foreign sources is actually permissible, even if they are only invoked as persuasive authority. For contemporary private law is of course fundamentally different from the period of the *ius commune*, at least in one regard: while there was a common base of legal sources back then, especially in the form of the *Corpus Iuris Civilis*, which permitted a legal discourse across borders, such a common point of reference ceased to exist with the advent of the national codifications.

Where a specific provision was directly taken over from French law, for example, it can of course make a lot of sense to look at how French courts and scholars interpret this norm, if one is looking for guidance and inspiration. But what happens if domestic law contains a gap? Can that gap be filled (or even detected) by

[148] See also, for the Brazilian context, the critique of OL Rodrigues Junior, 'Fonte estrangeira pode fundamentar decisão nacional?' *Consultor Jurídico* 12 December 2012, www.conjur.com.br/2012-dez-12/direito-comparado-recurso-estrangeiro-fundamentar-decisao-nacional.

[149] For an extreme example, see Kleinheisterkamp (n 2) 295.

[150] The question of when and how comparative law can be used in domestic cases is admittedly a very difficult one; in favour of an open approach, J Gordley, 'When Is the Use of Foreign Law Possible? A Hard Case: The Protection of Privacy in Europe and the United States' (2007) 67 *Louisiana Law Review* 1073–102. For an in-depth study of the philosophical dimension of comparative reasoning, see Coendet (n 134).

reference to foreign law, or would it have to be detected and filled from within, in order to respect the decisions of the domestic legislature and pay tribute to the requirement of systematic coherence? This is at least what most French and German lawyers would think;[151] recourse to a foreign solution would thus be an additional, but never a decisive argument.[152]

In Latin America, things sometimes go even further, namely when foreign authorities are cited not only to supplement, but even to oust domestic law. This is not to suggest that foreign sources are necessarily invoked *contra legem*, but that domestic law is simply disregarded. As a result, the difference between domestic law and foreign law, between the law as it is and the law as it should be, becomes blurred.

This attitude of 'taking domestic legislation less seriously' can actually be traced back to colonial times, when the lawyers of the Spanish empire often made little effort to apply the existing statute law, generally regarded as chaotic and defective, but turned directly to Roman law, which, although formally not even recognised as a subsidiary legal source,[153] was the law in which they had been trained and whose quality they regarded as far superior.[154] The situation in the law of Portugal (and thus also Brazil) was similar, although here Roman law was at least expressly named as a subsidiary legal source that could be supplemented with the writings of Accursius and Bartolus, provided they did not contradict the *communis opinio doctorum*. As a consequence, in legal practice the citation of real or imaginary authorities became more important than the discussion of the royal legislation.[155] When, in 1769, the *Lei da Boa Razão* (ie the 'Law of Good Reason') sought to strengthen domestic law and limit the influence of Roman law, recourse to non-domestic authorities only shifted, but did not diminish. Since subsidiary legal sources as of then had to pass the test of 'good reason', which was supposed to

[151] The dismissive remark of Zweigert and Kötz (n 4) 18 that '[t]he purely logical techniques at our disposal are insufficient, and it is unconvincing to play with analogy or the *argumentum e contrario*' is certainly not representative of the German legal community at large. The rigorous and sometimes overly formalistic methodological approach of German lawyers is a result of the highly technical training they receive at university, see Liebrecht (n 128) 46–50.

[152] See, eg, the interesting study by CW Canaris, one of the leading figures of German private law scholarship, on the question to what extent the 'Unidroit Principles of International Commercial Contracts' or the 'Principles of European Contract Law' can be used by courts in order to further develop German law: CW Canaris, 'Die Stellung der "UNIDROIT Principles" und der "Principles European Contract Law" im System der Rechtsquellen' in J Basedow (ed), *Europäische Vertragsrechtsvereinheitlichung* (Tübingen, Mohr Siebeck, 2000) 5, 6–7, 29–31. According to Vogenauer (n 127) 875–76, most lawyers (ie from any jurisdiction) 'would almost certainly be reluctant to accord to comparative law the status of a "source of law"'.

[153] J Barrientos Grandon, *La Cultura Jurídica en la Nueva España (Sobre la recepción de la tradición jurídica en el virreinato)* (México, UNAM, 1993) 113.

[154] See Kleinheisterkamp (n 2) 265–66, with further references. Apparently, in other parts of Europe the respect for statute legislation was greater, but also here ways were found to favour the application of Roman law, especially via the maxim *statuta sunt stricte interpretanda*. See N Jansen '*Ius Commune*' in J Basedow, KJ Hopt and R Zimmermann (eds), *The Max Planck Encyclopedia of European Private Law*, vol II (Oxford, Oxford University Press, 2012) 1006, 1008.

[155] FC Pontes de Miranda, *Fontes e Evolução do Direito Civil Brasileiro* (Rio de Janeiro, Pimento de Mello, 1928) 65–68; Braga da Cruz (n 46) 36.

be embodied, inter alia, 'in the modern laws of the civilised nations',[156] a massive and often arbitrary[157] importation of foreign legislation and foreign writings on the *usus modernus pandectarum* ensued.[158] This passion for citing foreign authorities, sometimes tagged as *bartolismo*,[159] survives in Brazil to this day,[160] and most Brazilian lawyers regard it as a tradition to be cherished. Critical voices, which point to its harmful consequences, still seem to be few.[161]

c. Taking Foreign Doctrines Out of Their Specific Normative Context

These methodological concerns are aggravated by another consideration: the European legal doctrines that are so frequently cited in Latin America were usually not at all developed in a 'spirit of universality'. Instead, their point of departure was the respective national law, and their conclusions are not intended to apply beyond national borders. Hence, it is problematic to extract these doctrines from their specific national context and transplant them to a different legal environment (not to mention even the risk of them being misunderstood[162]). For the sake

[156] As was specified shortly after the *Lei da Boa Razão*, in 1782, by the Statutes of the University of Coimbra, see L Cabral de Moncada, *Estudos de História do Direito*, vol I (Coimbra, Por Ordem da Universidade, 1948) 103.

[157] See the criticism by A Teixeira de Freitas, *Consolidação das Leis Civis*, 3rd edn (Rio de Janeiro, Garnier, 1876) XXXII: '[T]he famous statute from 1869, which under the heading of *good reason* gave arbitrariness free rein'.

[158] Kleinheisterkamp (n 2) 266.

[159] The term seems to have been coined by the eminent Brazilian comparatist C do Couto e Silva, *Principes fondamentaux de la responsabilité civile en droit brésilien et comparé* (course delivered at the Faculté de Droit et Sciences Politique de St Maur (Paris XII), 1988); see also J Martins-Costa and G Branco, *Diretrizes Teóricas do novo Código Civil brasileiro* (São Paulo, Saraiva, 2002) 193.

[160] C do Couto e Silva, 'O direito civil brasileiro em perspectiva histórica e visão de futuro' (1988) 97 *Revista da Informação legislativa* 163, 167, 171–72; id, 'Miguel Reale, Civilista' (1991) 72 *Revista dos Tribunais* 53, 54 (drawing a parallel with the *ius commune*). The Brazilian penchant for citing foreign sources has often been noted and pointed out by European observers, see, eg, T Ascarelli, 'Osservatione di diritto comparato privato italo-brasiliano' (1947) 70 *Il Foro Italiano* 98–99; ET Liebmann, 'Istituti del diritto comune nel processo civile brasileiro' in E Redenti (ed), *Studi in onore di Enrico Redenti*, vol I (Milan, Giuffrè, 1951) 581, 591; R David, 'Le droit brésilien jusqu'en 1950' (= *Cours de droit civil comparé*, Doctorat, 1949–1950, 210–394) in A Wald and C Jauffret-Spinosi (eds), *Le Droit Brésilien d'hier, d'aujord'hui et de demain* (Paris, Société de Législation Comparée, 2005) 25, 111, 137–39; David (n 8) 243.

[161] But see the convincing criticism of the 'doctrinal syncretism' in contemporary Brazilian legal scholarship by OL Rodrigues Junior, 'Dogmática e crítica da jurisprudência (ou da vocação da doutrina em nosso tempo)' (2010) 891 *Revista dos Tribunais* 65, 83–84; also F Medina [Book review], 'Anwendung und Auslegung von Recht in Portugal und Brasilien: Eine rechtsvergleichende Untersuchung aus genetischer, funktionaler und postmoderner Perspektive; zugleich ein Plädoyer für mehr Savigny und weniger Jhering, de Benjamin Herzog' (2016) 3 *Revista de Direito Civil Contemporâneo*, 393, 406–11.

[162] A phenomenon not rare at all, see López-Medina (n 7) 358 n 23, and also OL Rodrigues Junior, 'A influência do BGB e da doutrina alemã no Direito Civil brasileiro do século XX' (2013) 938 *Revista dos Tribunais* 79, 113–14, who also points out another danger, namely that a particular doctrine is imported which in its country of origin is already regarded as outdated or refuted, or which has meanwhile been abandoned by its own creator. The Spanish translation of Karl Larenz's treaty on the law of obligations of 1958, for example, continues to be widely used in Latin America, even though later editions of the book saw some important changes.

of illustration, we can cite various examples from Latin American court practice and legal writing.

A first example is the application of the German doctrine of *Vertrag mit Schutzwirkung zugunsten Dritter* (contract with protective effect vis-à-vis third parties) by the Colombian Supreme Court of Justice in 2009.[163] This doctrine was mainly developed to overcome specific limitations in the German law of delict,[164] which, however, are absent in Colombian law. Therefore, one may suspect that the Colombian Supreme Court imported an antidote for a disease from which the 'patient' did not actually suffer.[165]

Another similar example is the reception of certain categories from the Italian law of delict, such as the *danno esistenziale*, which were developed by Italian legal scholarship to overcome the rather restrictive regime on the compensation of non-economic loss in the *Codice civile* of 1942.[166] These categories were picked up quite uncritically by some Latin American scholars and courts and used to carry out questionable extensions of tort liability.[167]

As a further example, there is the question of whether, under Brazilian law, a contractual offer is binding on the offeror. Many Brazilian scholars seek to solve the matter by recourse to French legal writing, ignoring the fact that Brazil, unlike France, has an express rule on this matter that was actually inspired by German law.[168]

A final example, again taken from Brazilian law, is recourse to the 'duty to mitigate the loss', as developed under English law, in order to deal with the situation where a creditor has failed to take reasonable steps in order to reduce the damages arising out of non-performance. Not only is it doubtful whether Brazilian law actually contains a gap in this matter, but the received doctrine is frequently also understood in a way that hardly corresponds to the English 'original'.[169] From a general point of view, it is interesting that Brazilian scholars and judges for once do not seek inspiration in the countries of the European Continent, where in particular § 254 of the German BGB on contributory negligence would be an obvious point of reference, but instead turn to the common law. The reason for this

[163] *Corte Suprema de Justicia*, Casación Civil, 1 July 2009.

[164] See Zweigert and Kötz (n 4) 461.

[165] For a thorough and critical analysis, see JM Rodríguez Olmos, 'Deberes de protección, "aun frente a terceros", en la dogmática alemana' (2011) 20 *Revista de Derecho Privado* 301–46.

[166] See Braun (n 137) 675–76.

[167] For a sharp criticism of the Peruvian development in this regard, see LL León, 'Inflando los resarcimientos con automatismos. El daño al proyecto de vida y otros espejismos de la magistratura peruana' (2008) IV.8 *Foro Jurídico* 61–74, also available at: works.bepress.com/leysser_leon/7.

[168] See Art 427 CC Brazil and § 145 BGB. For further analysis, see JP Schmidt, 'La revocación de la oferta en el Derecho contractual de los países latinoamericanos y en el Derecho uniforme' (2010) 30 *Roma e America* 136–39.

[169] For a comprehensive analysis and sharp criticism of the numerous misconceptions of the 'duty to mitigate the loss' in Brazilian legal writing and court practice, see DP Novais Dias, 'O *duty to mitigate the loss* no direito civil brasileiro e o encargo de evitar o próprio dano' in *Revista dos Tribunais. 100 anos, Doutrinas essenciais: Obrigações e Contratos*, vol III (São Paulo, Revista dos Tribunais, 2011) 683ff (first published in (2011) *Revista de Direito Privado* 89ff).

preference seems to lie in the widespread misconception that the idea embodied in the 'duty to mitigate the loss' was first developed in English law, and from there taken over by the Continental legal orders.[170]

d. Undermining the Aims of Codifcation

Of course, the picture painted here is deliberately a bit one-sided. Not all scholars and courts proceed in this way, and numerous Latin American voices have criticised this dash after the 'latest legal fashion'.[171] Still, one is sometimes tempted to sum up the *mos latinoamericanus*[172] in the rule: foreign *legal writing* trumps domestic *legislation*.[173] The irony lies in the fact that the foreign doctrines that are so readily accepted were usually built on a particular normative base, which, at least indirectly, thereby ends up being taken more seriously than the domestic legislation.

The problem with this approach is not only that it undermines the normative force of domestic law, but that it also undermines the very idea of codification, namely to create a comprehensive and self-contained regime, which renders the law more accessible and understandable. Even if the original ambitions attached to codification by Bentham and others, namely that it would enable 'every man [to be] his own lawyer'[174] and make the professional advocate redundant, remained unfulfilled,[175] the reduction of the relevant sources still means a huge simplification for legal practice. If, in contrast, unfettered recourse to foreign sources is still permissible, the legal complexity that codification sought to abolish remains, and this state of affairs is problematic not only from a technical, but also from a social point of view. For if successful legal reasoning, whether in court or in scholarly writing, requires ample references to foreign law, it quickly turns into an elitist exercise, from which all those are excluded who are 'only' familiar with domestic law.[176]

[170] See Dias (n 169) 684, 691–92, who also points out that this view is already refuted by the fact that § 254 BGB clearly pre-dates the case of *British Westinghouse* of 1912, in which the mentioned doctrine was first laid down.

[171] See especially León (n 167).

[172] This expression has already been used, though in a different context, by A Guzmán Brito, '*Mos latinoamericanus iura legendi*' in DF Esborraz (ed), *Sistema Jurídico Latinoamericano y Unificación del Derecho* (México, Porrúa, 2006) 81.

[173] Similar Kleinheisterkamp (n 2) 295.

[174] '[A] lawyer, by whom he can neither be plundered or betrayed': J Bentham, 'Letters to the Citizens of the Several American United States' (1817) in P Schofield and J Harris (eds), *The Collected Works of Jeremy Bentham, Legislator of the World: Writings on Codification, Law, and Education* (Oxford, Oxford University Press, 1998) 113, 123, 137–38.

[175] See R Zimmermann, 'Codification: History and Present Significance of an Idea' (1995) 3 *European Review of Private Law* 95, 107–08.

[176] See also Kleinheisterkamp (n 2) 296–97, who furthermore points out that it was precisely for these reasons that Latin American legislatures sought to restrict, as much as possible, the scenarios in which their judges have to apply foreign law (see also text following n 145 above).

ii. Obstructing the Development of Domestic Law

As mentioned above, the constant legal modernisation for which the 'universal spirit' allows is often regarded as one of its advantages. Simultaneously, however, it has the drawback of stifling the potential of domestic law, which often seems to be underrated.[177] The French *Code civil* or the German BGB certainly do not offer greater possibilities for scholarly creativity than their Latin American counterparts. It is just that German and French scholars seem to make much more of an effort in this regard. To paraphrase Jhering: they do not bother to fetch a thing from afar when they have got one as good or better at home.[178] In view of all the scholarly (but also legislative) efforts that have gone into the fine-tuning and updating of the *Code civil* and the BGB since their enactment, it is also logical that today, no one in France or Germany would dare to suggest their wholesale substitution by a new national code (leaving aside the question of a European civil code). In contrast, the Latin American legal orders have always been much more ready to 'dump' their existing codes, which had been little cultivated anyway, and enact new ones instead (a notable exception is the Chilean Code of 1855, which continues in force).[179]

This lack of esteem for domestic law—in which one might also detect a lack of self-confidence—is also reflected in Latin American legal textbooks and treatises. Scholars from outside Latin America (but domestic practitioners as well) who turn to them in search of information on a particular legal problem are often disappointed, especially by the marginal attention or even lack of it that is paid to domestic court practice. Instead, many textbook writers prefer to show how well they are acquainted with 'classical' European legal scholarship.[180] It was again René David who keenly observed an interesting paradox: although Latin American jurists are rarely pure academics, but instead also spend a considerable amount of time on legal practice, their scholarly writings are often distinctly theoretical, as if they carefully sought to never mix their two professions.[181]

The Latin American approach is sometimes justified by pointing to the foreign origin of the respective codes, which supposedly made it natural, or even necessary, to follow the respective models also later on.[182] This argument is only partly convincing, however. It would mean, for example, that German and French lawyers would also have to continue to refer to Roman sources in the application of the BGB and the *Code civil*, since this is where most of the provisions have

[177] See also Kleinheisterkamp (n 2) 296; Rodrigues Junior (n 162) 114.

[178] Jhering (n 129) 8.

[179] For an overview, see Schmidt (n 44) 84–85.

[180] See also Garro (n 26) 611; Pizarro Wilson (n 23) 16. An extreme example from Brazil is FC Pontes de Miranda's monumental 60-volume *Tratado de Direito Privado* (Rio de Janeiro, Borsoi, 1954–69), in which the author draws so constantly and heavily on German legal scholarship that one is sometimes not sure which jurisdiction he is actually writing about. See also the criticism by Kleinheisterkamp (n 2) 296.

[181] David (n 5) 13–14.

[182] Eder (n 59) 63, and Hernández-Bretón (n 18) 41.

their roots. There is probably no rule in modern private law that can claim to be entirely original, but this does not of course mean that one is barred from interpreting it autonomously. Sooner or later, a legal order should learn to stand on its own feet, so that recourse to foreign sources is only necessary in exceptional cases.

A more understandable motive for resorting to foreign sources is another one, namely the lack of sufficient domestic materials (ie court decisions, scholarly articles, etc) to draw upon (although this is hardly a valid point for large jurisdictions such as Argentina or Brazil). In Europe, this explains why especially lawyers from smaller jurisdictions, such as Austria, Switzerland, Portugal or The Netherlands, are happy to seek inspiration elsewhere. Yet the argument is again ambiguous, as there is a risk of getting stuck in a vicious circle: the less one cares about cultivating the home-grown product, the more one will become dependent on foreign imports. Also, lawyers might lose sight of the concrete problem at hand, and instead be caught in fruitless controversies as to how the respective foreign doctrine is to be understood 'correctly'.

iii. Eurocentric, Rather than Universal

A final criticism of the methodological *mos latinomericanus* is that its geographical focus is actually not universal at all, but clearly eurocentric.[183] Only rarely will a Latin American scholar have an interest in and know much about the law of his *neighbouring countries.*[184] There has been surprisingly little exchange even among legal orders that basically share the same civil code, such as Chile and Columbia. By the same token, legislative reform in twentieth-century Latin America has very rarely been inspired by sources from within the continent, unlike in the nineteenth century.[185] The Brazilian Civil Code of 2002, for example, which was drafted in the early 1970s, shows clear influences from Italian, German and Portuguese law, but not from any Latin American jurisdiction.[186] Similarly, the new Argentinean Civil and Commercial Code of 2014 was influenced considerably, at least if one is to judge by the explanatory notes of its drafters, by non-Latin American sources.[187]

[183] As seen above, this interest is hardly reciprocated. The legal exchange between Europe and Latin American is therefore largely a one-way-street, albeit a very busy one.

[184] See also Garro (n 26) 610–11. Even Bevilaqua (n 13) felt a certain embarrassment when he had to describe the laws of the Latin American countries for his treatise on comparative law, and realised that he actually knew little about them: 'Though being our neighbours, the American States are much less known among us than the European ones, to which we continue looking'. Bevilaqua goes on to name the sources he relied on for information on Latin America, and they are mostly European (101 n 1).

[185] Momberg (n 27) 415–16; A Garro, 'Contract Law in Latin America: Building of a "Latin American" *Ius Commune* on Contract Law' in I Schwenzer (ed), *35 years CISG and Beyond* (The Hague, Eleven International Publishing, 2016) 253, 256.

[186] See Schmidt (n 44) 545–46.

[187] Besides Italian and German law, the law of Quebec is mentioned several times in the explanatory notes (n 116), eg, 10, 40, 49, 52, 54, 57, 58, 100, 116, 122, 138, 153, 172, 198, 221, 233, 238.

It seems doubtful, therefore, whether this code really has a particular 'Latin American cultural identity'[188] (although it did, of course, draw heavily on the practical experiences gained under the former code). At least, it is not easy to give any clear examples of substantial private law rules[189] from the new code that would be typically Latin American and at the same time *not typically European.*[190]

What are the reasons for the underdeveloped state of the intra-Latin American legal discourse? Why did the fruitful exchange of legal ideas between Latin American jurists in the nineteenth century wither in the twentieth century? Lack of information seems to be one factor. For a Brazilian scholar, for example, it will often be easier, and not necessarily more expensive, to buy legal literature from Italy or Germany than from Peru or Colombia. Another, probably even more important factor is what has been tagged the 'Cinderella complex';[191] most Latin American scholars will automatically assume that European legal scholarship is of a higher quality and therefore more authoritative.[192] To be sure, European legal literature is often produced under conditions that most Latin American academics can only dream of. A German professor, for example, is not only paid well enough so that he can focus exclusively on his academic life, he also has a team of research assistants at his disposal and enjoys access to well-equipped public libraries.

We see, therefore, that what René David described in 1953 as a phenomenon of the past actually still seems to be a fitting description of our times: 'Les droits de l'Amérique latine gravitaient dans l'orbite de la science juridique de l'Europe continentale. Les juristes de l'Amerique latine reconnaissient unanimement le suprématie, et l'éminente supériorité, des juristes du continent européen'. Or, as a North American author put it (albeit to make an even more radical point): 'Latin American societies are not European, only their jurists pretend to be'.[193] Therefore, if Europeans often gain the impression that Latin American private law is entirely free from originality (which is clearly not the case), they can hardly be blamed.

[188] For this claim, see p 4 of the explanatory notes (n 116), and also Parise, Ch 3 in this book. Admittedly, the explanatory notes contain frequent references to other Latin American legal orders, but it seems doubtful whether they outweigh the non-Latin American sources.

[189] The case of private international law, which is included in the Argentinean Code of 2014, is a different one, as here the numerous regional Conventions ratified by Argentina obviously needed to be taken into account. For a general overview, see DP Fernández Arroyo, 'Main Characteristics of the New Private International Law of the Argentinean Republic' (2016) 80 *Rabels Zeitschrift für ausländisches und internationales Privatrecht* 130.

[190] One might perhaps mention Art 965 in this context, according to which contractual rights are to be regarded as property rights. Most European observers would probably regard such as rule as self-evident and therefore superfluous, but one could also see it against the background of repeated state intervention in private contractual relationships in recent Argentinean history, especially the forced conversion of bank deposits from dollars to pesos that occurred in 2001–02 (known as the *pesificación*).

[191] López-Medina (n 7) 360. In Brazil, the inferiority complex which the nation is perceived to suffer from has been given the name of *complexo de vira-lata* (mongrel complex), and it is also detected in the behaviour of legal scholars, see OL Rodrigues Junior, 'Problemas na importação de conceitos jurídicos', *Consultor Jurídico* 8 August 2012 (www.conjur.com.br/2012-ago-08/direito-comparado-inadequada-importacao-institutos-juridicos-pais).

[192] López-Medina (n 7) 365.

[193] JL Esquirol, 'The Fictions of Latin American Law (Part I)' [1997] *Utah Law Review* 425, 470.

It must be noted, however, that even where European sources are concerned, there is usually no truly universal approach. Instead, most Latin American authors have their favourite countries, and their choice is usually not defined by objective criteria, such as the subject-matter in question, but by personal factors, such as language skills, access to literature, and academic ties to certain institutions or colleagues (again, this is of course a general phenomenon in comparative legal writing, but in Latin America it seems to be more manifest). As a result, one author will draw heavily on French law, another on Italian law, a third on German law, etc. The result can be a problematic 'intersection' of foreign influences in the respective country, eg, when a provision that derives from one legal order is later interpreted in the spirit of another legal order.[194] More generally, this approach can lead to the formation of different 'schools of thought' within one Latin American legal jurisdiction and the fragmentation of the internal discourse.

D. Conclusions

While in terms of blackletter rules and the general conceptual framework, European and Latin American private law are basically located on the same continent, in terms of legal methodology, and in particular the use of comparative law, they are separated by a deep and wide ocean (though, as we have seen, we must also distinguish between the different European legal orders). Lawyers from neither side of the Atlantic seem actually to be aware of these differences in their respective methodological approaches.[195] If it is true that 'comparative legal studies are most fruitful when they focus on styles and techniques rather than on substantive law',[196] the issue definitely deserves further investigation.

The critical remarks presented here should not, of course, be understood as a plea for Latin American lawyers completely to abandon the use of comparative law. But there seem to be strong arguments for a more reflective and critical handling of foreign sources, and for a greater effort to work out solutions on the basis of domestic law first.

VI. Possible Aims and Purposes of the PLACL

What conclusions can be drawn from the history and characteristics of private law, and especially contract law, in Latin America for the aims and purposes of the

[194] See the example of the effects of a contractual offer in Brazilian law (n 169 above).

[195] On the general difficulty in understanding a foreign system's methods, see Vogenauer (n 127) 885–86.

[196] This was one of the conclusions in D Harris and D Tallon (eds), *Contract Law Today: Anglo-French Studies* (Oxford, Clarendon Press, 1989) 394.

PLACL? We can distinguish between practical purposes and academic purposes. I argue that the latter are, at least at present, much more important than the former.

A. Practical Purposes of the PLACL

At first glance, one might regard the PLACL as a first step towards 'hard' legal unification in Latin America, something which academics in particular have often deemed not only desirable, but also entirely natural, in view of the similarity of the Latin American private laws and their common cultural, linguistic and historical heritage.[197] However, not only does experience clearly suggest a lack of political will to achieve unification of substantive private law in Latin America (of the numerous attempts made none was ever successful);[198] in view of the still rather low level of economic and political integration, it is also very doubtful whether, at present, there is any practical need for it. The two most important integration projects, namely the 'Andean Community of Nations' (CAN)[199] and the 'Common Market of the South' (Mercosur),[200] have, after a promising start, been stagnating for years now. If even in the European Union, with its considerably higher level of political integration and intra-regional trade, it is debated as to what extent the existing legal diversity actually creates additional transaction costs and therefore barriers to the internal market,[201] the argument for legal unification is even more difficult to make in the Latin American context, where it cannot even be justified by the need to overcome barriers of a linguistic nature.[202] For centuries now, the Latin American countries have been closer to Europe and the United States than to each other, both economically and culturally,[203] and intra-Latin American infrastructure continues to be clearly underdeveloped. It is almost as if Latin America continued to be haunted by the ghosts of its colonial past, when the Spanish

[197] See, eg, Rauchhaupt (n 59) 140–42; Esborraz (n 12) 236, with further references.

[198] For an overview with further references, Esborraz (n 12) 32–38; Ferrante (n 95) 14–20, who surprisingly affirms the existence of a 'clear political will' for the unification of substantive private law (15, 17). Attempts at the regional harmonisation of private international law were more successful, see the overview by DP Fernández Arroyo, *Derecho Internacional Privado: Evolución y Perspectivas* (México, Porrua, 2003) 33ff, or J Samtleben, 'Métodos de armonización del derecho internacional privado en América Latina' (2010) 30 *Roma e America, Diritto Romano Comune, Rivista di Diritto dell'Integrazione e Unificazione del Diritto in Europa e in America Latina* 193–208 (published also in *Derecho internacional privado—derecho de la libertad y respeto mutuo—, Ensayos a la memoria de Tatiana de Maekelt* (Asunción, CEDEP, 2010) 203–21).

[199] See RA Porrata-Doria Jr, 'Andean Community of Nations (CAN)' in R Wolfrum (ed), *The Max Planck Encyclopedia of Public International Law*, vol I (Oxford, Oxford University Press, 2012) 385–88.

[200] See JP Schmidt 'MERCOSUR' in R Wolfrum (ed), *The Max Planck Encyclopedia of Public International Law*, vol VII (Oxford, Oxford University Press, 2012) 110–17.

[201] See, eg, H Eidenmüller, N Jansen, FM Kieninger, G Wagner and R Zimmermann, 'Der Vorschlag für eine Verordnung über ein Gemeinsames Europäisches Kaufrecht' [2012] *Juristenzeitung* 269, 286

[202] Linguistic unity or proximity would of course *facilitate* legal unification in Latin America, but this does not constitute a substantial argument for why it should be done.

[203] See J Samtleben, *Internationales Privatrecht in Lateinamerika* (Mohr, Tübingen, 1979) 140–41.

Crown, in its extraordinary zeal for centralisation and control, expressly forbade trade or even communication between the American colonies.[204]

A second practical purpose of the PLACL that immediately comes to mind is that mentioned in their Article 1, namely to govern international contracts, or even purely domestic contracts, if there is a corresponding agreement between the parties. I argue that also in this respect, the role of the PLACL will only be marginal. This is at least the lesson we can draw from the practical experiences with the UNIDROIT Principles of International Commercial Contracts (PICC), which now extend over a period of more than 20 years. Despite their widely acknowledged substantive quality and the vast amount of literature that has already been written on them, the PICC are only very rarely chosen as the law applicable to a contract.[205] There are a number of reasons for this, but the main reason seems to be that the PICC simply cannot cater for the needs of commercial practice, in that they are unable to provide a comprehensive contract law regime.[206] While contracts in real life are always specific contracts, such as sales contracts, service contracts etc, the PICC contain only rules on general contract law and are therefore necessarily incomplete. Besides, they inevitably open themselves to mandatory state law (Article 1.4 PICC). As a result, it is hardly recommended for parties to subject their contract to the PICC, or at least, to do so exclusively, as this will leave too many issues without express regulation. One may presume that under the PLACL, the situation would not be very different, as they contain the same limitations as the PICC: they do not provide rules for specific contracts, and they cannot avoid the application of mandatory state law (Article 2 PLACL).

Possibly, the PLACL might serve as a kind of regional 'background law', as has been argued for the PICC on a global level.[207] This would mean that the PLACL could be used for the interpretation and supplementation of domestic or international uniform law (eg, the CISG), a purpose that is also mentioned in their Article 1(4). Besides, the PLACL might serve as a model for legislative reform.[208] A basic requirement for such a role as 'background law' would be that the PLACL either fulfil a 'restatement function' or a 'model function',[209] or a combination of both. Hence, the PLACL must either accurately depict the law as it currently exists in the

[204] See, eg, MC Mirow, *Latin American Law: A History of Private Law and Institutions in Spanish America* (Austin, TX, University of Texas Press, 2004) 19–20.

[205] R Michaels, 'The UNIDROIT Principles as Global Background Law' [2014] *Uniform Law Review* 643, 646–47; for an overview of the empirical data, see S Vogenauer, 'Introduction' in id (ed), *Commentary on the UNIDROIT Principles of International Commercial Contracts (PICC)*, 2nd edn (Oxford, Oxford University Press, 2015) 1 para 49.

[206] See Michaels (n 205) 663–64; id, 'Umdenken für die UNIDROIT-Prinzipien: Vom Rechtswahlstatut zum Allgemeinen Teil des transnationalen Vertragsrechts' (2009) 73 *Rabels Zeitschrift für ausländisches und internationales Privatrecht* 866, 872–74.

[207] See Michaels (n 205) 657ff.

[208] This last aim was regarded as the main one by the drafters of the PLACL, especially in light of the fact that Chile and Colombia have not carried out any substantial reforms in the law of contract since the 19th century, see Momberg (n 27) 424.

[209] See in the context of the PICC, Michaels (n 205) 664–65.

Latin American countries or, where they depart from the current state of the law, must derive their authority from the substantial quality of the proposed solutions. At this stage, it does not always seem clear to which category each of the PLACL provisions belongs. This is something that should be pointed out in the commentaries, which yet have to be written.

B. Academic Purposes of the PLACL

The PLACL could fulfil academic purposes in two respects: one concerns the strengthening of a 'Latin American legal identity', the other the intra-regional legal discourse.

i. The PLACL as an Expression of the 'Latin American Legal Identity'

a. Putting Latin America on the Map of Mainstream Comparative Law

In mainstream comparative law, the PLACL could help to increase the 'visibility' of Latin America and to give the continent its own voice. They could remind comparative scholars from other continents that private law in Latin America is not a simple offshoot of French law, or of European law in general, and provide them with a concrete text to look at and work with. Conversely, the PLACL could enhance the self-esteem and the self-awareness of jurists from Latin America and curb their urge to follow European trends.

b. The Difficult Emancipation from Europe

However, the assertion of such a 'regional legal identity'[210] would, of course, require Latin American contract law to be different in fact from its European counterpart, something which is not self-evident in view of the strong and continuous influences described earlier. While in areas such as family law and, especially, the law of succession, some characteristics can be readily identified which the Latin American countries have in common and by which at the same time they distinguish themselves from most European countries,[211] in contract law things are much less straightforward. Here, one might instead argue for the existence of different groups within Latin America, for example a Chilean group, which is closer to French law, and a Brazilian-Peruvian group, which shows more influence from German and Italian law.[212] Countries such as Chile, Argentina and Brazil

[210] cf Pizarro Wilson (n 23) 16; Momberg (n 27) 425.

[211] For examples from succession law, see text accompanying n 83 above. As an example from family law, one may mention the widespread recognition of cohabitation, or de facto marriages, which started several decades earlier than in Europe, see Schmidt (n 83) 151 with further references.

[212] For an earlier attempt at identifying different groups within Latin American, see Rauchhaupt (n 59) 128.

do, of course, share a kind of common core of contract law, with similar general principles and concepts,[213] but whether these similarities are really greater than those between, say, Chile, Spain and Germany, or Brazil, France and Italy, is not clear. One may therefore ask pointedly: what prevented the drafters of the PLACL from simply copying the Principles or European Contract Law (PECL) or the PICC? Exactly which provisions of these texts would be unsuitable for the Latin American context? Or, to turn the question round: what makes the PLACL 'Latin American', apart from the origin of their drafters?

No doubt, these questions pose a challenge to the PLACL, as their drafters did not fail to realise.[214] But at the same time, it is a challenge that offers a great opportunity for further emancipation from the European tradition. The PLACL could, and should, help us to understand to what extent contract law is, or should be, different in Latin America. For example: is there more or less need for formalism? Should Latin American contract law be more debtor friendly?[215] Has contract law in Latin America been shaped by certain scenarios or types of contract that have been litigated most frequently before the courts?[216] Preliminary contracts for the sale of land, for example, were once described as 'the most Brazilian of all contracts',[217] due to their frequency and relevance in everyday life.

Also, the personal scope of application of the PLACL is important. Did their drafters mainly have business-to-business, or also business-to-consumer and consumer-to-consumer contracts in mind?[218] Did they think of large businesses, or also of small and medium-sized enterprises? Any European who walks the streets of a large Latin American city immediately notices the host of ambulant vendors and realises that here, the concept of a 'small business' acquires a meaning that is quite different from that with which he is familiar.

In the search for a 'Latin American identity', one should of course not try to be original just for the sake of originality. As Ole Lando once remarked: 'Contract law is not folklore'.[219] It is driven to a large extent by economic needs and purposes, and these are basically the same everywhere in the world. If, furthermore, we take into account the close intellectual ties between Europe and Latin America, it would be surprising if the respective principles of contract law differed greatly from one another. Finally, Latin American particularities would probably show in

[213] Garro (n 26) 608.

[214] See Pizarro Wilson (n 23) 16; Momberg (n 27) 425.

[215] See Schipani (n 12) 227–32 on the principle of *favor debitoris* and the *beneficium competentiae*.

[216] In the context of Australian law, see MP Ellinghaus, 'An Australian Contract Law?' (1989) 1 *Journal of Contract Law* 13, 19–20, and in the context of English, French and German law, see Kötz, 'Rechtskreislehre' (n 16) 103.

[217] Osório de Azevedo Jr, 'Promessa de venda' in *Enciclopédia Saraiva do Direito*, vol 62 (São Paulo, Saraiva, 1981) 86.

[218] Art 1(1) PLACL does not make any distinction. On the other hand, the absence of any specific protective devices suggests that the PLACL were not designed for consumer contracts.

[219] See, eg, O Lando, 'The Principles of European Contract Law and the Lex Mercatoria' in J Basedow (ed), *Private Law in the International Arena: Liber Amicorum Kurt Siehr* (The Hague, Asser, 2000) 391, 394.

specific contract law, and not so much in general contract law, which inevitably is quite abstract from reality.[220]

c. In What Sense Are the PLACL 'Latin American'?

When I looked briefly at the PLACL, I only spotted two, rather formal, aspects that might be labelled as characteristic of Latin American law. One is that they are occasionally quite doctrinal in nature. By doctrinal I mean that the PLACL do not only seek to lay down rules and principles, but in a certain way also aim at fulfilling didactic purposes. Articles 8 and 9 are very illustrative in this sense, defining what a contract is and what its essential elements are. Provisions of this kind are very typical of the Chilean Code;[221] likewise, the Argentinean Code, both the old and the new, contains many textbook definitions, which in the eyes of many Europeans would be better left to legal writing to sort out. Of course, in a text such as the PLACL, which has to bring together lawyers from different legal orders, definitions can help to avoid misunderstandings. Still, as regards basic concepts such as 'contract', I have my doubts as to whether a definition is really needed, and whether it is actually possible to find a definition that is entirely satisfactory.

A second feature of the PLACL that one might regard as characteristic of Latin American contract law is their choice to list the 'causa' in Article 9 as an essential element of the contract. Although the concept is of French origin, of course, its dissemination in Latin America has been much wider than in Europe.[222] The PECL and the PICC, in any event, both consciously rejected it, and even in France the '*cause*' was finally suppressed with the 2016 reform of the *Code civil*.[223] It might therefore be regarded as surprising if this notion were able not only to maintain, but even to strengthen its existence in Latin America. But of course, the question again is: do the PLACL wish to be descriptive or prescriptive?

d. The PLACL Between Restatement and Model Law

It seems that there is much to say in favour of first restating the Latin American contract law regimes before trying to improve them (following herein also the

[220] In the discussions at the conference from which this contribution originates, repeated requests were made to name a rule from the PLACL that had a specific 'Latin American flavour' (an expression from Agustín Parise), but no clear example could be provided.

[221] The Chilean Code contains numerous provisions on matters of terminology at the beginning of each book and almost every sub-section, as if it were trying to combine a code with a textbook, see Nelle (n 35) 106–07.

[222] Yet it is absent from, among others, the Paraguayan Code of 1985 and the Brazilian Code, both that of 1916 and that of 2002 (for a complete overview, see Esborraz (n 12) 223–32). The drafter of the 1916 Code, C Bevilaqua, explained that the concept of the '*cause*' had 'apparently entered the French Civil Code due to a misapprehension'. *Código Civil dos Estados Unidos do Brasil*, vol I (edição histórica) (Rio de Janeiro, Rio, 1979) Art 90 (p 339) n 3.

[223] See, eg, M Séjean, 'The French Reform of Contracts: An Opportunity to Tie Together the Community of Civil Lawyers' (2016) 76 *Louisiana Law Review* 1151, 1157f.

approach of famous codifiers Bello and Teixeira de Freitas),[224] even were this to come at the price of a text that is less attractive, be it from the perspective of legal scholarship or of commercial practice (as explained above, this last concern should not be taken too seriously anyway). For if the PLACL jumped immediately to Latin American contract law as it should look in the future, we would lose an important opportunity to know what it looks like now, which in many respects is also the way it has looked for the last 150 years.

However, it should be stressed that the two approaches do not necessarily exclude each other. A good example may be found in Article 1(1) PLACL, according to which they apply to both 'civil' and 'commercial' contracts. This distinction was characteristic of Latin American contract law throughout the nineteenth and large parts of the twentieth centuries, and it was expressed not only in the dualism of civil code and commercial code, but also in the distinction between university chairs of civil law and university chairs of commercial law (less so in the existence of commercial courts). In one way, Article 1(1) PLACL can thus be regarded as descriptive. At the same time, however, the provision is also prescriptive, because it does not attach any normative significance to the distinction and thus overcomes it. This decision is certainly to be welcomed, as separate regimes for 'civil' and 'commercial' contracts are indeed hard to justify, both from a theoretical and a practical point of view,[225] as the Brazilian Teixeira de Freitas pointed out back in the nineteenth century.[226]

ii. The PLACL as Trigger and Reference Point for the Intra-regional Legal Discourse

Even if, after all, no true Latin American characteristics of contract law were to be found, the effort of drafting the PLACL will still have been worthwhile. This is because also in that case, they can fulfil what I regard as their most important purpose: to strengthen, or rather to spark, a truly intra-Latin American legal discourse. As explained earlier, Latin American scholars usually know very little about the law of their neighbouring countries, and regional conferences in which matters of substantial private law are discussed are still very rare.[227] The elaboration of the PLACL has not only forced their drafters to take their attention away

[224] Both proceeded in two steps: first consolidation, then codification. See A Guzmán Brito, 'Codificación y consolidación: una comparación entre el pensamiento de A. Bello y el pensamiento de A. Teixeira de Freitas' in S Schipani (ed), *Augusto Teixeira de Freitas e il diritto latinoamericano* (Padua, CEDAM, 1988) 255–67.

[225] See also Eder (n 59) 48: '[T]he needless distinction between "civil" and "commercial" law, with separate codes and embarrassing conflicts'. For a comparative discussion, see Schmidt (n 69).

[226] See Schmidt (n 44) 163ff.

[227] The picture is different in the areas of private international law or arbitration, for example, where Latin American conferences are organised on a regular basis, eg, by the Asociación Americana de Derecho Internacional Privado (ASADIP). López-Medina (n 7) 355, in contrast, claims the existence of an active dialogue also in the area of substantive private law.

from Europe, and to turn it to their own continent;[228] the PLACL will also serve as a common point of reference in the future intra-regional discourse (which can also be used for teaching purposes). The same goes for the collection of the country reports[229] that served as a preparatory step for the elaboration of the PLACL, which is easily the most comprehensive and up-to-date work of its kind in the area of contract law.[230] For once, the national reporters were barred from referring to the writings of the cherished European authorities and instead had to focus on national legislation, national legal writing and national case law.[231]

In their function as trigger and reference point for the intra-regional legal discourse, the PLACL could even be considered as 'the starting point for the development of a new a Latin American *ius commune*'.[232] To my mind, it is apt not to speak of a rediscovery here, but rather of something that still needs to be created.[233] It is true, of course, that there was far-reaching legal unity under the Spanish colonial rule, but it excluded Brazil, by far the biggest and most populated country in Latin America. Besides, it seems questionable whether the extremely complex and patchy colonial legal regime is really something one wants to tie in with. Instead, we should accept the fact that the Latin American legal orders have been developing largely independently from each other over roughly the last 150 years, and that beyond the general framework of the civil law tradition, the existence of a common core of Latin American contract law still needs to be proven. This is corroborated by the fact that the elaboration of the PLACL, contrary to what an uninformed observer might expect, has so far proved to be an extremely difficult task due to the many conflicting views within the drafting group, both on technical matters and on policy decisions.[234]

[228] See also Pizarro Wilson (n 23) 16, and Parise, Ch 3 in this book: 'Latin Americans need to know more about each other'. Similarly in the discussions at the conference at which this contribution was first presented, one member of the drafting group from Chile stated that for him, one of the most exciting aspects of elaborating the PLACL had been the opportunity to get to know the laws of other Latin American countries.

[229] Including the laws of Argentina, Brazil, Chile, Colombia, Paraguay, Uruguay and Venezuela, see C Pizarro Wilson (ed), *El derecho de los contratos en Latinoamérica (Bases para unos Principios de Derecho de los Contratos)* (Bogota, Universidad del Rosario and Universidad del Externado de Colombia, 2012).

[230] For a study that includes all Latin American countries, but focuses on the concept of contract, see Esborraz (n 12) 63ff. In matters of family law and the law of succession, the intra-regional discourse seems to be more advanced. See, eg, LB Pérez Gallardo (ed), *El derecho de sucesiones en Iberoamérica: tensiones y retos* (Bogotá, Temis, 2010) and Á Acedo Penco and LB Pérez Gallardo (eds), *El divorcio en el derecho iberoamericano* (Bogotá, Temis, 2009).

[231] In a similar vein, Momberg (n 27) 425.

[232] Momberg (n 27) 428.

[233] In this sense also ibid, and Garro (n 185) 265. Others, in turn, claim that a Latin American *ius commune* has never ceased to exist, see Esborraz (n 12) 32–33, with further references.

[234] At the conference from which this contribution originates, this was mentioned several times by members of the drafting group. On conflicting views on fundamental policy decisions, see also Momberg (n 27) 426–27.

VII. Conclusion

The PLACL offer a variety of opportunities for both law and lawyers in Latin America. They could spark a new interest by comparatists in the continent and help to overcome the prevailing eurocentric taxonomies. They could show us the status quo of contract law in Latin America, but also offer proposals for its modernisation. They could help Latin American lawyers to become more self-aware and more self-confident, and stimulate the discourse between them. They could make transparent what Latin American and European contract law have in common, and where they differ (and why). But the PLACL should also not let us forget that in matters of legal methodology, the differences between Europe and Latin America are much greater than any blackletter comparison will ever tell us.

All these opportunities are too good to be missed. However, the success of the PLACL is not guaranteed. Latin America has a long history of projects of legal harmonisation and integration that started very promisingly but ultimately failed to fulfil expectations. The wish to write a new chapter in this regard should be sufficient motivation for the members of the drafting group to bring their work to a successful finish. They should take their time and refrain from rash decisions, as the success of the PLACL will depend decisively on their substantial quality.

5

The Economic Conditions of Contract in South American Law: An Historical Approach

GERARDO CAFFERA*

I. Introduction

The economic conditions of a contract are the benefits to be received and the burdens to be assumed by each of the parties through the performance of the contract. A relevant question regarding those conditions is *who* should determine *how* they should be distributed.

There are three possible answers. First, *absolute freedom of contract*: only the parties to the contract determine appropriate distribution with no limitation or interference of any kind. Secondly, at the other extreme, *absolute regulation of economic conditions* (such as prices fixed by the government): this possibility has limited historical relevance but may be applied from time to time to certain goods or during critical periods (eg, in wartime). Thirdly, *limited freedom of contract (or freedom of contract with limitations)*: while the parties are in principle free to determine which distribution is appropriate, there are some limitations to that freedom. Thus, under certain circumstances, their agreement may be declared null or reformed on the basis of what the law considers to be an inappropriate distribution. Of course, in this third model, the nature, flexibility or scope of these limitations to freedom of contract may differ.

A draft of a set of *Principles of Latin American Contract Law* (PLACL) was recently issued by a group of academics under the sponsorship of the Fundación Fernando Fueyo Laneri.[1] The discussion of this draft at the Faculty of Law of the

* I am grateful for the useful comments and advice received from Stefan Vogenauer, Rodrigo Momberg, Arturo Ibañez and Alberto Pino from the University of Oxford and Sergio Cámara from the Universidad de la Rioja (Spain).

[1] See the Appendix to this volume for the bilingual version of the PLACL.

University of Oxford[2] motivated this historical survey. The main provisions of the PLACL regarding the economic conditions of the contract are Articles 5 and 37. The model adopted by those articles is that of freedom of contract with limitations. Article 5 PLACL provides that 'the parties are free to enter into contracts and to determine their content'. Therefore, as a matter of principle, the parties may freely choose the economic conditions of the contract. Article 37 PLACL, on the other hand, sets a limit. That provision deals with gross disparity (*excesiva desproproción*) in the distribution of economic burdens and advantages. Its first two paragraphs read as follows (emphases added):

> (1) A party may seek the adaptation of a contract or any of its clauses, or to annul the contract, if it or they give the other party an *excessive advantage in contravention of the requirements of good faith*.
>
> (2) *All circumstances must be taken into account* when considering the existence of gross disparity, in particular the dependence of the aggrieved party and its extraordinary economic distress, urgent needs, ignorance or lack of experience. Moreover, the relationship of trust existing between the parties as well as the nature and purpose of the contract must be taken into consideration.

Good faith in its objective version is usually conceived as a standard of honest, loyal and transparent behaviour. This characterisation of good faith supports an interpretation of Article 37 according to which, for the defect of gross disparity to arise, the disparity should be the consequence of behaviour against good faith. Thus, the mere existence of a relevant disproportion in the distribution of burdens and benefits is not sufficient to declare the contract null or subject to judicial modification. A subjective element (ie the advantage-taking party acting against good faith) should also be present.

I pose two questions regarding the gross disparity provision of the PLACL. First, does it represent a long-standing concept within Latin American contract law? Secondly, if the first answer is in the negative: does it represent the *standard* towards which the national law of Latin American jurisdictions is currently moving? If both answers are in the negative, the conclusion would be that Article 37 of the PLACL represents a normative claim. Other questions would then be pertinent, but they are not addressed in this chapter.

In order to answer the first two historical questions, I propose a historical analysis. First, a survey of the first hundred years of the formation of Latin American contract law, which took off after its emancipation from Spain and Portugal. The objective of this first step is to determine if the absence of gross disparity is a requirement that somehow belongs to the long-term identity of Latin American contract law. The second step consists of an inquiry into the changes in Latin American contract law in the last hundred years in order to determine if the PLACL are in line with that evolution. I argue that, historically speaking, the

[2] *The Future of Contract Law in Latin America*, Keble College, Oxford, 25 June 2015, organised by the Institute of European and Comparative Law of the University of Oxford.

absence of gross disparity in the contract was not an essential requirement within the long-term identity of Latin American contract law. In that respect, there was from the outset a marked difference from Spanish and French law. Some use or influence of Jeremy Bentham's ideas may have inspired a divergence with European Continental law.

On the other hand, the legislative changes that have occurred over the past hundred years were not uniform and, furthermore, the gross disparity provision in the PLACL does not match the direction of any of those changes, even if some of them, at first glance, may seem similar. The scope of those changes was in some cases narrower and in others wider than the PLACL proposal. Thus, my claim is that the PLACL proposal on gross disparity is not *descriptive* of Latin American law as it *has always been* or as it *already is* or as it is *tending to be*. The PLACL gross disparity provision is, therefore, a normative claim by the drafters of the PLACL as to how Latin American contract law *should be*. We do not know what their reasons for advocating this solution are and so cannot assess them. However, this descriptive inquiry may be helpful in order to extract the basic features of the historical evolution of freedom of contract in Latin American law. Among other things, this may be a relevant input for a future discussion of the normative claim made by the drafters of the PLACL.

Some methodological aspects should be clarified first. To begin with, the historical functional equivalents of the gross disparity provision in the civilian tradition were *laesio* (*lesión*) and usury laws. Roughly speaking, *laesio* limits the price of goods in sales and other contracts while usury law limits the price of money (interest) in loans and financial transactions.

Secondly, there were, and still are, two types of *laesio* and usury laws. *Laesio* may be objective or subjective. Objective *laesio* consists exclusively of a disparity between economic burdens (usually evidenced by a relevant deviation from market prices), is philosophically supported by the ideal of commutative justice and relies on the existence of a *iustum pretium*. Subjective *laesio* requires, in addition to the objective disparity of values, an abuse of the weaker position of the party taken advantage of, and therefore is more akin to protection of the autonomy of that party. *Laesio* leads to revision of the contract or its nullity. In terms of its scope, *laesio* may affect *all* types of contract or only *some* of them (eg, only land transactions). Limitation of interest rates by usury laws are also of two types: *rigid* usury, in which the limit is expressed as a concrete maximum percentage *per annum* (eg, 5 per cent or 12 per cent); or *flexible* usury, in which the limit is expressed as a certain margin above market rates (eg, 1.5 times the market rate).

Thirdly, *laesio* is also applicable in family and succession law or to some contractual sanctions. However, this chapter is only concerned with *contract law* and *adequate* performance of contract. This restriction sets aside two areas: *laesio* in sanctions for breach of contract and *laesio* in succession and family law. In South American law, provisions limiting the autonomy of the parties in those areas do exist. However, these are not limitations of the freedom of the parties to decide on the core economic equation of the contract (eg, the price that is paid). Therefore, those rules are not concerned with the crucial function of contract analysed here: the determination of the content of exchanges in a market.

Finally, this chapter refers only to seven *South* American jurisdictions: Argentina, Brazil, Colombia, Chile, Paraguay, Uruguay and Venezuela. Reports on the contract law of those countries were published by the promoters of the Principles under the title *El Derecho de los Contratos en Latinoamérica: Bases para unos Principios de Derecho de los Contratos* (The Law of Contract in Latin America: Basis for a Set of Principles of Contract Law).[3] As suggested by the title of that publication, the drafters of the PLACL based their work on the information contained therein. As these jurisdictions belong to South America, in this chapter I avoid further references to *Latin American* law and limit my assertions to *South American* law. Obviously, some important jurisdictions in South America (Peru, Ecuador and Bolivia) are still missing.

II. *Laesio* and Usury in Colonial South America

Laesio did not exist in classical Roman law. According to Zimmerman, the idea was built 'upon the frail foundations of two texts from Justinian's Code',[4] which allowed a certain Aurelianus Lupus to rescind a contract under which he had sold a tract of land for less than half its value. Thereafter, medieval jurisprudence expanded the underlying principle to all kinds of contract. Scholastic and natural lawyers came to consider equality of exchange (commutative justice) as a basic principle of contract law. The *iustum pretium* (deviation from which entailed *laesio*) was the price estimated in common, ie the market price. If the seller received less than half the value or the buyer paid more than one-and-a-half times that value, the contract might be rescinded. Some natural lawyers even asked for further expansion of *laesio* to *any* deviation from the *iustum pretium*, at least in the case of expensive goods. By the nineteenth century, however, *laesio* had been discredited. For instance, in accordance with a more liberalistic approach, the French Civil Code retained *laesio* as a remedy for the seller of land (Article 1674) when there was a deviation of at least seven-twelfths from the *iustum pretium*.

On the other hand, usury laws limited the price (*interest*) to be paid by the borrower in a loan agreement. The different historical approaches to interest may be synthesised in three basic models: (a) *total prohibition of interest* accompanied by civil and criminal consequences, such as total or partial nullity of the agreement or penalties; (b) *restriction of interest rates*, where interest is admitted but within

[3] C Pizarro Wilson (ed), *El Derecho de los Contratos en Latinoamérica: Bases para unos Principios de Derecho de los Contratos* (Bogotá, Fundación Fernando Fueyo Laneri, 2012).

[4] For this paragraph: R Zimmermann, *The Law of Obligations: Roman Foundations of the Civilian Tradition* (Oxford, Oxford University Press, 1996) 259.

a maximum set directly or indirectly by the law: directly through a concrete rate (rigid usury) expressed in the law or, indirectly, where the maximum is set at a certain margin above the usual interest charged in the market (flexible usury); and finally, (c) *freedom of interest*, where the parties are left to determine the interest rate freely and with no limitation. The laws establishing a total prohibition of interest or its restriction to a certain maximum are known as *usury laws*. Within the civilian tradition, usury laws restricting interest have been predominant.[5] Roman law intervened from early on, prohibiting usurious interest rates. The so-called *centesimae usurae*, ie the prohibition of interest rates exceeding 12 per cent per year, was maintained essentially unchanged throughout the Imperial period down to the sixth century. Justinian, influenced by Christian ideas, reduced the maximum interest rate to 6 per cent. During the Middle Ages, the development of usury laws was dominated by canon law, which totally prohibited the charging of interest. The total prohibition of interest in canon law came under attack in the wake of the Reformation, 'from Calvin in regard to its theological justification [and] from Carolus Molinaeus and Clausius Salmasius as far as its legal basis was concerned'.[6] From then on, the preferred model of usury law was one that allowed interest, but with restrictions. Grotius considered that charging interest was not repugnant to natural law in so far as the rate represented a just consideration.[7] This intermediate model of restriction rather than total prohibition was henceforth to dominate the legal landscape. At the level of positive law, in France, after a brief period of freedom of interest following the Revolution, a maximum rate was re-established by an Act of 3 September 1807. It remained in force until 1918 and, after a few years, limitation of interest was reintroduced in 1935.[8]

In Spanish South America, *laesio* and usury laws, as part of the Spanish legal system, were in force for centuries. Spanish law remained applicable in South America after independence until the new countries introduced their own legislation. In the matter of *laesio*, Spanish law originally endorsed a liberal approach: the *Liber Iudiciorum* (Fuero Juzgo) of the first half of the thirteenth century explicitly rejected *laesio* as a defect of contract. As this was a compilation of previous laws promulgated by the early Visigothic kings, it may have expressed a long tradition stretching back into time and identical to classical Roman law. However, during that same thirteenth century, Law 56 Title 5 *Partida* 5 (1256–1265) established that 'the sale that has been done for less than half of the price that [the thing] was worth by the time of the sale can be undone'.[9] The rule applied to movable

[5] The following paragraph draws on Zimmermann (n 4) 167–75.

[6] ibid, 174.

[7] H Grotius, *The Rights of War and Peace*, Book 2 (Indianapolis, IN, Liberty Fund, 2005) ch 12, para XXII.

[8] Institut für Finanzdienstleistungen (IFF) and Zentrum für Europäische Wirtschaftsforschung (ZEW), *Study on interest rate restrictions in the EU, Final Report for the EU Commission DG Internal Market and Services*, Project No. ETD/2009/IM/H3/87 (Brussels, 2010) 50.

[9] '[S]e puede desfacer la vendida que fuese fecha por menos de la meytad del derecho prescio que podier valer en la sazón que la ficieron' (The text is written in medieval Spanish).

and immovable assets. It was later expanded to all kinds of contract by the *Ordenamiento de Alcalá* (1348) and the *Novísima Recopilación de Castilla* (1805), which extended *laesio* to all types of contract such as rental agreements and barters, among others.[10] On the other hand, under the *Auto Acordado 16, Título 21 Libro 5* of the *Recopilación Castellana*[11] issued by King Phillip IV on 14 November 1652, interest rates under Spanish law were restricted to a maximum of 5 per cent in general private law transactions and 6 per cent in commercial ones.

As to Portuguese law, in force in Brazil before and after independence, similar limitations were in place. The Portuguese *Ordenações Filipinas* of 1603 have been described as a regulation that 'perspires from every pore the intervention of the state in the economy'.[12] *Livro IV, Título XIII* of the *Ordenações Filipinas* established that sales of movable or immovable assets affected by *laesio enormis* (difference of 50 per cent from the market price) were subject to rescission unless the difference from the *iustum pretium* was paid by the buyer or reimbursed by the seller.[13] On the other hand, the *Ordenações Filipinas* almost totally prohibited the charging of interest (Book IV Title LXVII), accepting it only for certain exempted transactions. However, an Act (*Alvará*) promulgated on 17 January 1757 admitted interest in loans and other transactions though restricting it to a maximum of 5 per cent per year.[14]

III. South American Contract Law in the Nineteenth Century

A. Progressive Liberalisation of Contract

South America emancipated from Spain and Portugal between 1810 and 1830. The laws of the home countries remained in force in the new nations for several decades and were only progressively replaced by national legislation. In the field of contract law, this replacement began in earnest during the second half of the nineteenth century (only Bolivia making a head start in the 1830s). From 1855 onwards, national civil codes were enacted and the laws of the home country

[10] O Rivera Farber, 'La lesión en los contratos civiles' (1993) 103 *Revista de Derecho Notarial Mexicano* 170–80.

[11] G Torres García, *Historia de la Moneda en Colombia* (Bogotá, Imprenta del Banco de la República, 1945) 135.

[12] A Rubens Didone, *A influencia das ordenacoes portuguesas e espanhola na formacao do direito brasileiro do primero império* (http://repositorio.uscs.edu.br/bitstream/123456789/292/2/tese%20doutorado%20Prof%20Didone.pdf) 26.

[13] C Mendes de Almeida (ed), *Ordenações Filipinas*, vol 4 (Rio de Janeiro, Instituto Philomathico, 1870) 793.

[14] ibid, 1044.

displaced. As pointed out earlier, the models of Spanish and Portuguese law were ones of limited freedom of contract: as regards loans, usury at a *fixed rate* was in force, and *laesio* applied to *all* contracts. These models were the most restrictive that South America will ever know. Beginning in the 1830s, there was a progressive move towards liberalisation. The French Civil Code was the most quoted source of inspiration but other influences were at work. The first step in this liberalisation process was that of usury laws being totally abolished or markedly softened. The ideas of the famous English philosopher and jurist Jeremy Bentham inspired reforms or were used as arguments at this first stage. The second phase was the abolition of *laesio* in five of the seven jurisdictions addressed in this chapter and a severe restriction of its scope in the other two. As a consequence, during the last decades of the nineteenth century and up to the 1920s or 1930s, South American contract law was much more liberal than its recurrent model: French law. The following sections explain this evolution.

B. The First Step: Abolition of Usury Laws

Beginning in the 1830s and ending in the 1870s, usury laws were totally abolished in five of the seven jurisdictions analysed in this chapter: Venezuela, Argentina, Uruguay, Paraguay and Brazil. In the other two jurisdictions (Chile and Colombia), after a period of total liberalisation of interest rates, usury laws were reintroduced, but in a flexible form. Broadly speaking, this situation did not change until the 1930s. Bentham's doctrine on interest rates inspired many of the reformers or was used by them as an argument. He proposed *complete* freedom of interest rates on three grounds: (a) analogy with the absence of restrictions on the price of other goods, (b) irrationality of the *moral* condemnation of usury, and (c) ineffectiveness of usury laws as protective instruments. The appropriateness of abolishing the usury laws was supported by Bentham on the basis of *analogical reasoning*. The price of money lent (interest) should be agreed freely, as was the price or rent of land *or any other goods*. He supported an *absolute* version of freedom of contract: '[W]hy a policy, which, as applied to exchanges in general, would be generally deemed absurd and mischievous, should be deemed necessary in the instance of this particular kind of exchange, mankind are as yet to learn'.[15]

Bentham's ideas about usury were known in South America through his books. In addition, there is evidence of Bentham directly advocating his policy to at least one South American leader. In a letter dated 13 August 1825, Bentham commended to Simón Bolívar his ideas about the abolition of usury laws. In it, he revealed that his ideas had been considered in the House of Commons.[16] Another actor related

[15] Jeremy Bentham, *Defence of Usury* (London, 1787) 13.

[16] L O'Sullivan and C Fuller (eds), *The Correspondence of Jeremy Bentham*, vol 12: July 1824 to June 1828 (Oxford, Clarendon Press, 2006) 148.

to Spanish America was José Joaquín de Mora, a liberal Spanish professor of law who spent time in London, Buenos Aires, Santiago de Chile, Peru and Bolivia during his exile from Spain. There are some notes in Bentham's Memorandum Book 'connecting Mora's name with Defence of Usury',[17] an indication he was probably working on a translation. Furthermore, Bentham's ideas were endorsed by his Spanish commentator, Ramón Salas,[18] and his Argentinean follower, Pedro Somellera. The latter was a professor in Buenos Aires and the author of a book on Principles of Civil Law published in 1824, which explicitly followed Benthamite doctrine. It was used as a textbook at the University of Buenos Aires. While considering loans (*mutuo*) and interest, Somellera wrote: 'The convention between the contracting parties is what the law sanctions'.[19] The general principle was provided earlier in the chapter: 'Complete freedom in contracts: here is the general rule … let the individual interest operate'.[20]

In 1832, the Chilean legislature discussed a Bill aiming to abolish usury laws. It has already been noted by a Chilean scholar that the Act may have been the result of Benthamite influence.[21] In addition, the records of parliamentary discussions contain evidence of that influence. The documents for the session of 25 June 1832 include a report, also published in the press, defending the abolition of usury, which in some cases is a mere paraphrase of *Defence of Usury*.[22] The Act was promulgated on 14 September 1832. Its second Article reads:

> It is legal … to stipulate through private agreements the interest that the parties want and these agreements shall be respected, it not being acceptable to argue against them the defence of usury.[23]

As a consequence, Spanish usury laws were tacitly abolished.[24] The author of the Bill was Manuel José Gandarillas, a lawyer and politician of liberal economic ideas who was active in the 1830s among a group of local jurists and politicians strongly influenced by Bentham.[25] However, the Act left open an indirect way of challenging the validity of the interest rate: *laesio*. It was a more flexible limit as it depended

[17] C Fuller (ed), *The Correspondence of Jeremy Bentham*, vol 11: January 1822 to June 1824 (Oxford, Oxford University Press, 2000) 266–67. The notes correspond to 23 April and 9 September 1823.

[18] Ramón Salas' comment in J Bentham, *Tratados de Legislación Civil y Penal*, vol 5 (Madrid, Ramón Salas tr, 1821) 155.

[19] P Somellera, *Principios de Derecho Civil dictados en la Universidad de Buenos Aires*, vol 1 (Buenos Aires, Imprenta de los Expósitos, 1824) 195–96.

[20] ibid, 189.

[21] A Guzmán Brito, *Andrés Bello Codificador*: vol I (Santiago de Chile, Ediciones de la Universidad de Chile, 1982) 102.

[22] (1832) 113–14 El Correo Mercantil Santiago de Chile, 27 June 1832. The author is not identified and there is no title for the article.

[23] Congreso de Chile, *Sesiones de los Cuerpos Legislativos de Chile*, Sesión 18 de julio de 1832, www.historiapolitica.bcn.cl.

[24] V Letelier, *Génesis del Derecho* (Santiago de Chile, Editorial Jurídica de Chile, 1967) 185.

[25] B Subercaseaux, *Historia de las Ideas y de la Cultura en Chile*, vol 1 (Santiago de Chile, Editorial Universitaria, 1997) 20.

on the market. Twenty-three years later, the Civil Code of Chile explicitly recognised this defence. Its Article 2206 established that:

> Conventional interest shall have no other limits than those indicated by special statutory laws, except if, not being limited by statutory law, it exceeds by half the interest that is proved to have been currently in use at the time when the agreement was made, in which case the judge shall reduce interest to such current interest.

In Brazil, complete freedom to determine interest rates was adopted by an Act of 24 October 1832. Its first and fourth Articles provided:

> Article 1. Interest or price of money, of whichever species, shall be that which the parties agree on. …
>
> Article 4. All statutes and provisions to the contrary are hereby repealed.

The enactment was attributed by a Brazilian scholar to the widespread influence of Bentham's book, *Defence of Usury*, among lawyers and at law schools in the 1830s.[26] This development was followed by the Commercial Code of 1850, which only forbade the capitalisation of interest (*anatocismo*).[27] The Brazilian Civil Code came relatively late compared to the rest of South America. Although the Constitution of the Brazilian Empire promised a civil code 'as soon as possible', the code was only enacted in 1916 when the empire had already become a republic.[28] With regard to interest rates, the Brazilian Civil Code of 1916 followed the 1832 Act. The code was enacted at a time described by Brazilian scholars as 'a time of exacerbated individualism'.[29] The civil code regime was one of 'wide' freedom.[30] Article 1262 of the Code reads as follows:

> It is permitted … to apply interest to the loan of money or other fungible assets. That interest can be fixed below or above the legal rate … with or without capitalisation.

Bentham's extreme doctrine of freedom of contract also left its mark on Venezuela. An Act of 10 April 1834 established absolute freedom of contract, including the complete liberation of interest rates. A book published in Venezuela in 1845 by Fermín Toro, a local lawyer, provides evidence of the Benthamite inspiration of the supporters of the liberal legislation.[31] The defenders of the Act were, according to him,

> the partisans of a speculative rigour that allows every damage, every extortion … if it is exercised in the name of the freedom of industry and with the object of increasing

[26] Mendes de Almeida (n 13) 871.

[27] A Ramos Rodrigues, 'Da evolução normativa da limitação de juros no Brasil e a necessidade constitucional de instaurar-se uma nova etapa' (2002) 11-III Ambito Juridico, http://www.ambitojuridico.com.br/site/index.php?n_link=revista_artigos_leitura&artigo_id=4961&revista_caderno=9.

[28] D Vieira Ferreira, *O Codigo Civil Annotado* (Rio de Janeiro, Leite Ribeiro, 1922) xx–xxxiii.

[29] Ramos Rodrigues (n 27) quotes S Rodrigues, *Direito Civil—Parte Geral das Obrigações*, vol II, 2nd edn (São Paulo, Saraiva, 1965) 338.

[30] C Sahb Batista Lopes and M Richter Ribeiro, 'A disciplina dos juros no direito brasileiro após o advento do Código Civil de 2002' (2014) 9 *Meritum—Belo Horizonte* 15, 23.

[31] F Toro, *Reflexiones sobre la Ley del 10 de abril de 1834* (Caracas, Imprenta de Valentin Espinal, 1845) 66.

> wealth ... Say and Bentham ... would tell us that all of this is natural and legitimate [and] that the nation as a whole benefits from this.[32]

The Venezuelan Civil Code of 1867 in its Article 1547 followed the 1834 Act in declaring that the parties were 'entirely free' to agree on the interest rate. The same approach was taken by the Civil Codes of 1873, 1880, 1896, 1904 and 1916 (Articles 1676, 1684, 1720, 1728 and 1820, respectively),[33] although these all left open the possibility of other special legislation fixing a maximum. This approach was more liberal than that adopted by the Chilean Code: there was no limit enshrined in the code.

Colombia abolished usury laws in the 1830s. An Act was passed on 26 May 1835, the first article of which repealed the Spanish rules.[34] The Colombian historian Torres García has no doubt that it 'was the natural outcome of the propaganda of Bentham's doctrine developed in New Granada (Colombia) by General Santander'.[35] In 1873, a federal code was enacted along the lines of the Chilean model[36] and the same limit on interest rates *was* included. In 1887, after Colombia became a unitary republic, the 1873 Civil Code for the federation was adopted with minor changes as the Civil Code for Colombia. The Colombian Civil Code established a limit of one-and-a-half times the market rate for interest.[37]

In Uruguay, a Bill was defended in the Senate in 1838 by Antonino Domingo Costa using the analogical argument,[38] albeit without explicit reference to Bentham:

> [T]he laws in force ... limit interest rates to five and six per cent and call usurious those that exceed such percentages, but they submit to the absolute freedom of the parties the determination of rents, as if the property of an immovable asset was something different from the property of money.[39]

The Bill was passed on 2 April 1838 and established absolute freedom: 'the legal interest of money shall be that agreed by the contracting parties'. In 1852, the future author of the Commercial Code expressed similar ideas in the journal *La Constitución*: 'money is a merchandise just like any other'.[40] When the Commercial Code of Uruguay was enacted in 1865, the provisions of the 1838 Act were incorporated into it. The commission that reviewed the draft of the code remarked that 'our country has the glory of ... breaking with all ... the absurd preoccupations with usury'.[41] When the Uruguayan Civil Code was enacted in 1868, its Article 2177

[32] ibid, 7.

[33] A Pietri, *El Código Civil de 1916 y sus diferencias con el de 1904 e indicación de los artículos correspondientes con éste y en el de 1896* (Caracas, Litografía del Comercio, 1916) 469.

[34] Torres García (n 11) 136.

[35] ibid, 140.

[36] A Uribe Misas, *Código Civil de Colombia* (Madrid, Instituto de Cultura Hispánica, 1963) 17–18.

[37] Pizarro Wilson (n 3) 245.

[38] E Acevedo, *Anales Históricos del Uruguay*, vol 1 (Montevideo, Casa A Barreiro y Ramos, 1933) 507.

[39] ibid.

[40] E Acevedo (hijo) (ed), *Eduardo Acevedo Años 1815–1863. Su obra como codificador, ministro, legislador y periodista* (Montevideo, Imp. 'El Siglo-ilustrado', de Mariño y Caballero, 1908) 157.

[41] M Herrera y Obes et al, 'Informe de la Comisión Correctora' in *Código de Comercio para el Estado Oriental del Uruguay* (Montevideo, Imprenta de la Tribuna, 1866) ii.

also provided for the complete freedom of interest rates. In the relevant notes, the codifier indicated that it was 'against the European Codes', thereby consciously departing from French or any other civil law influence.[42]

The Argentinean Civil Code was drafted by Dalmacio Vélez Sarsfield. The relevant provision concerning interest rates on loans reads: 'Interests may be attached to the obligation and the interest agreed between creditor and debtor is valid'.[43] In his note to this provision, Vélez Sarsfield commented that 'Regularly the European codes are against freedom of contract in the matter of interest on capital'.[44] He had been one of the professors of political economy at the Faculty of Law of the University of Buenos Aires in the 1820s.[45] It was said that when he 'went to Buenos Aires to teach in the first years of his public career he learned [from Political Economy] ... translated into that individualistic liberalism of *Bentham* and Adam Smith'.[46]

Finally, in 1876, Paraguay adopted the Argentinean Civil Code as its own and therefore freedom of interest rates was enacted to the same extent adopted previously by Argentina. Thus, by 1876, five of the jurisdictions addressed in this chapter had *totally* abolished usury laws and two (Chile and Colombia), after some decades of complete liberalisation, had readopted them. However, even in the latter two cases the usury laws were reintroduced in a more flexible (market-driven) format, different from the rigid version adopted by Spanish law.

C. The Second Step: Abolition of *Laesio*

As explained above, Spanish and Portuguese law were still in force in South America after its independence. *Laesio*, which was conceived as a 50 per cent deviation of the price from the market value, was a defect of contract. In the course of the nineteenth century, *laesio* was abolished or relaxed to such an extent that, in the end, South American law came to allow much more space for freedom of contract than the *Code Napoléon* did. By the beginning of the twentieth century, five of the seven legal systems considered in this chapter had totally abolished *laesio*. These were the same as those that had completely abolished usury. The other two systems had retained *laesio* but limited it to sales and barters of land. In other words, the same impulse that had led to the abolition of usury laws continued with the abolition of *laesio*. The radical liberal stand on usury may have been the driving force behind

[42] ibid, 298–99.

[43] Código Civil de la República Argentina, redactado por el Dr. Dalmacio Vélez Sarsfield y aprobado por el Honorable Congreso de la República el 29 de setiembre de 1869. Edición Oficial (New York, 1870) 157.

[44] ibid.

[45] A Chaneton, *Historia de Vélez Sarsfield*, vol 1 (Buenos Aires, Editorial Universitaria de Buenos Aires, 1937) 121–22.

[46] E Martínez Paz (ed), *Catálogo de la Biblioteca Dalmacio Vélez Sarsfield* (Córdoba, Imprenta de la Universidad Nacional, 1940) xix (emphasis added).

this second step. Bentham's main argument was based on the assumption that interference with the price agreed by the parties was such an unsound policy that no one would accept it. By analogy, he argued, the price of money (interest) should not be limited either. This was a sound argument within common law systems that did not allow the courts to evaluate the adequacy of price or consideration in contracts. It became problematic, however, when translated to South American law: *laesio* was in force there and therefore the basic assumption supporting Bentham's argument was not applicable. The contradiction disappeared in five of the seven jurisdictions addressed in this chapter when the reform was pushed further, and *laesio* was also totally abolished. These changes are described in the following paragraphs in chronological order.

The Chilean Civil Code of 1855 restricted *laesio* to sales and barters of land, following the example of the French Civil Code. However, a minor modification was introduced: whereas the French Civil Code only granted this remedy to the seller, the Chilean Code also made *laesio* available to the purchaser. Article 1889 of the Chilean Civil Code reads:

> The seller suffers *laesio enormis* when the price that he receives is less than half the fair price of the thing that he sells; and the buyer suffers *laesio enormis* when the fair price of the thing that he buys is less than half the price that he pays for it.

The rule of Article 1889 is restricted to the sale of immovable assets by Article 1891 and is applicable to barters of land in accordance with Article 1900 of the Civil Code. The reduction of *laesio* to sales and barters of land was achieved in several steps. In the first draft of the code, *laesio* was still referred to as a defect of any contract jointly with duress, *dolus* and mistake.[47] However, when the code was enacted, that provision was amended and *laesio* was excluded as a generally applicable institution. On the other hand, Bello may have suffered a defeat in this area. His first drafts of the Civil Code contained an additional *subjective* requirement for a *laesio* claim to proceed. According to those drafts, the party alleging *laesio* should prove that it was ignorant of the value of the thing at the time of the contract. Furthermore, if ignorance was proved but was the result of negligence, it was not to count as ignorance for legal purposes. However, the original drafts were amended and this extra requirement, which would have further restricted the field of *laesio*, was not enacted.[48]

The Venezuelan Civil Code of 1867 entirely expelled *laesio* from the field of contract law. Its Article 1072 stated:

> No obligation or agreement shall be rescinded on the ground of *laesio* even if it is *enormissima*[49] except in the cases of the following article.

[47] A Bello, *Código Civil de la República de Chile*, vol II (Caracas, Ministerio de Educación, 1955) 390.
[48] ibid, 678.
[49] *Laesio enormissima* in the civil tradition was that in which there was a difference of 100 per cent from the market price.

The 'following article' indicated that rescission of contracts was possible in all the cases 'specifically' determined by the law. A closer look through the code reveals that the only cases where *laesio* remained applicable involved succession and family law. This solution was maintained by the subsequent Code of 1873 and its successive reforms. It is widely acknowledged that the 1873 Code and the successive codes of Venezuela were based on the Italian Civil Code of 1865 and the previous Venezuelan Code of 1867.[50] The *laesio* rule was taken from the 1867 Code. Article 1247 of the 1873 Venezuelan Civil Code reads as follows:

> Rescission grounded on *laesio* cannot be claimed, not even in the case of minors, except in the cases and under the conditions specifically expressed by the law.

The Civil Codes of 1896, 1904 and 1916 had similar provisions in their Articles 1277, 1283 and 1376 respectively. As in the case of the 1867 Code, the cases where *laesio* was applicable belonged to succession and family law. This restrictive application of *laesio* remained a characteristic of Venezuelan contract law.[51]

The Uruguayan Civil Code of 1868 followed the same line on *laesio* as that Uruguayan law had already adopted for usury. *Laesio* was totally and explicitly abolished. Article 1238 of the Uruguayan Civil Code (still in force as Article 1277) provided that *laesio* was *not* a defect of contract. In his comments, the codifier noted that this solution was against Spanish law and the Justinian, French Austrian, Prussian, Louisiana and Sardinian Codes. Significantly, he supported his decision by reference to the remote example of the *Liber Iudicorum* (Fuero Juzgo) referred to above and to the laws of the Gothic kings of Spain (a book dating back to 1600, *Forus antiquus Gothorum regum Hispaniae*, was quoted in his comment).[52] The commission in charge of revising the Code recommended the abolition of *laesio* on three grounds. First, there was no other genuine price for an article than the price agreed between the parties to the contract. A total departure from the doctrines of *iustum pretium* was thus acknowledged. Secondly, the parties should act responsibly: 'people must enter into contracts prudently and if they do not and they sustain damage thereby, the law should not help them'.[53] Finally, *laesio* provided a platform for dishonest litigation which was not favourable to the development of commerce. The reform was a radical one in that it instituted complete freedom regarding the economic conditions of the contract. Usury and *laesio* were totally abolished. This went further than any of the civil law models at hand (notably French law).

[50] Pietri (n 33) v. A Urbaneja, *El Código Civil de 1873, el Código de Procedimiento Civil 1873, el Código de Comercio de 1873* (Caracas, 1973).

[51] J Otis Rodner, *El Contrato y la Inflación: el Uso de las Cláusula de Valor en Venezuela* (Caracas, Editorial Sucre, 1983) 53. Pizarro Wilson (n 3) 591–92.

[52] T Narvaja, *Fuentes, Notas y Concordancias del Código Civil de la República Oriental del Uruguay* (Montevideo, Tipografía y litografía oriental, 1910) 190.

[53] Report of the *Comisión Revisora* quoted by A Reta-Ofelia Grezzi, *Usura: la Ley 14887 y sus Antecedentes* (Montevideo, Fundación de Cultura Universitaria, 1979) 29.

In Argentina, Vélez Sarsfield, the drafter of the Civil Code of 1869, followed the same path he had adopted in the matter of usury and totally excluded *laesio* from the Argentinean Civil Code. He simply did not refer to *laesio* in the code. Vélez Sarsfield made explicit his rejection of *laesio* in his comments, arguing that, although 'almost all the codes' accepted *laesio* as a defect of contract, the discrepancies between these codes suggested that there was not 'a uniform principle to establish this theory'. Furthermore, he felt that people would not be responsible for their acts if the law allowed them to amend all their mistakes.[54] On these grounds, *laesio* was eradicated from Argentinean contract law, which adopted the principle of absolute freedom of contract with regard to its economic aspects. It was a solution as radical as that taken by Uruguayan law since it abolished *both* usury and *laesio*. Again, the widespread influence of Benthamite doctrine in Argentina, coupled with a critical assessment of the European codes, may explain this position, which was more extreme than that provided by the usual models.

The 1873 and 1887 Colombian Civil Codes followed the solutions of the Chilean Civil Code in respect of usury and *laesio*. Both codes restricted objective *laesio* to sales and barters of land. The only requirement was a deviation of 50 per cent from the market price (Articles 1947 of the Civil Code and 32 of Act 57/87).[55] As was the case in Chile, *laesio* was applicable to other areas outside contract law, such as the division of inheritances, or to sanctions such as penalty clauses, or to some guarantees as a reflection of the limitation of interest rates (mortgage and *anticresis*). As explained above, these are not considered as additional limitations of freedom of contract since they fall outside contract law or are trivial corollaries of the substantive rules already described.

Paraguay enacted its first civil code in 1876. By an Act of 19 August 1876, the 'liberal' Argentinean Civil Code was adopted in Paraguay[56] and remained in force until 1985. Accordingly, the comments made regarding Argentina are likewise applicable to Paraguay: absolute freedom of contract prevailed and *laesio* was fully abolished.

Finally, the Brazilian Civil Code of 1916 did not include *laesio* as a defect of contract. In accordance with its Article 147, contracts were voidable in case of mistake, *dolus*, coercion, simulation or fraud; no mention was made of *laesio*. Furthermore, *laesio* was not even applicable to sales of land (Articles 1122ff). In other words, the liberalistic approach was a full one, covering every contract. The position of the Brazilian legal system was identical to that of Uruguay, Argentina, Venezuela and Paraguay.

[54] Código Civil de la República Argentina (Buenos Aires, 1883) 254–55.

[55] Pizarro Wilson (n 3) 245.

[56] A Guzmán Brito, *La Codificación Civil en Iberoamérica: Siglos XIX y XX* (Santiago de Chile, Editorial Jurídica de Chile, 2000) 457.

D. South American Contract Law at the Beginning of the Twentieth Century

A picture of how the economic conditions of contract in South American law had been regulated by the end of the nineteenth century or the beginning of the twentieth century emerges from the analysis of seven jurisdictions. The principle of freedom of contract was widely accepted. The restrictions of Spanish and Portuguese law had been totally set aside or relaxed. In general terms, the reform went further than French law, a much-favoured source of inspiration during this period. This outcome may be partially credited to the influence of Bentham's early book, *Defence of Usury*, as indicated above. By the 1830s, Bentham's ideas began to be turned into positive law in South America: usury laws were abolished. This may have partially inspired subsequent developments with regard to *laesio*, which was *totally* abolished in a majority of the countries analysed (Argentina, Uruguay, Brazil, Paraguay, Venezuela) or restricted to sales and barters of land (Chile, Colombia). This liberal conception of contract went beyond the usual French model, which retained *laesio* for land sales. With regard to interest rates, France maintained the *fixed* limit of its 1807 Act for civil transactions, repealing it for commercial transactions in 1886[57] and for civil transactions only in 1918. On the other hand, by the end of the nineteenth century *no usury law at all* existed in five of the South American jurisdictions analysed above and a flexible model applied in the other two (Chile and Colombia).

In terms of the questions posed at the beginning of this chapter, all these aspects are evidence that a strong conception of freedom of contract was part of the features of this formative period of South American contract law. This conception was reflected in the first pieces of legislation enacted after independence (abolition of usury laws) and, later, in the civil codes (abolition or restriction of *laesio*). Equality in exchange or similar requirements were not a characteristic of South American law. Contrariwise, a strong version of freedom of contract, represented in its most extreme forms by complete abolition of *laesio* and usury law, was actually a regional feature. Therefore, gross disparity as described in the PLACL cannot easily be understood as a foundational or essential aspect of the identity of South American law when its two centuries' history is taken into account. Certainly, this liberal approach may not come as a surprise, given the historical context of these developments. However, my claim is that South American private law was *more* liberal than French law, a common source of inspiration during this period. Therefore, the idea of gross disparity as a defect of contract sits uncomfortably with the long-term history of South American law. Nevertheless, it

[57] Torres García (n 11) 126.

would be premature to end our historical inquiry here. The next section addresses changes in South American legislation in the last hundred years.

IV. South American Contract Law in the Last Hundred Years

A. Overview

As already indicated in the introduction, the next question we must answer is whether the gross disparity provision of the PLACL reflects a tendency underlying the *more recent* changes in South American contract law. While at first glance, it may seem that the answer should be in the affirmative, this is not in fact the case. Certainly, over the past four or five decades, a legislative shift to protect weaker parties (eg, in consumer law) and a renewed interest in equality in contract have been perceivable. Three of the seven jurisdictions addressed in this chapter have adopted subjective *laesio* in their civil codes. This species of *laesio* requires two elements: an objective disparity in the distribution of economic burdens *and* the need for such disparity to be the result of some weakness of the disadvantaged party. While this of course looks similar to the PLACL provision, the perceived changes did not go in the same direction as the PLACL. In the following paragraphs I will show, on the one hand, how several jurisdictions have remained attached to their nineteenth-century models and, on the other hand, that subjective *laesio* as adopted in three jurisdictions evidences considerable differences with the gross disparity described in the PLACL. Based on that analysis, I argue that the PLACL provision, for one reason or another, does not fit any of the models of *laesio* in force in the South American legal systems nor does it reflect the trend of the last decades.

B. Evolution of *Laesio*

In order to address *laesio* as it has been applied over the past 100 years, we must first make a distinction between consumer contracts and non-consumer contracts. The former are contracts in which a business entity (a professional supplier of services or goods) enters into a contract with a consumer (a person that intends to satisfy its own needs). The latter (non-consumer contracts) are those contracts usually referred to as private-to-private contracts. These include transactions between business entities but also transactions between two consumers, ie any transaction that is *not* a business to consumer one. The enactment of consumer protection legislation from the 1970s onwards introduced some new aspects into the field of *laesio*. I shall first address the situation with regard to private-to-private transactions, moving on to the situation in respect of consumer contracts in a second step.

i. Laesio *in Private-to-private Contracts*

As to private-to-private contracts, two trends can be identified among the seven jurisdictions addressed in this chapter. A first group of four jurisdictions is formed by the countries that have maintained the original approach of their nineteenth-century civil codes and, thus, totally exclude *laesio* or restrict it to sales and barters of land. Chile, Venezuela, Uruguay and Colombia belong to this group. In Chile, *laesio* remains restricted to sales and barters of land and the same applies to Colombia. In Uruguay, the Civil Code retains its original provision stating that *laesio* is not per se a defect of contract. Finally, the Venezuelan Civil Code of 1982, like its predecessors, does not include *laesio* as a defect of contract.[58] This group of jurisdictions represents a model based on freedom of contract with a narrow or zero scope for *laesio*. A second group is formed by three countries that have introduced a *new* version of *laesio* in their civil codes in the last five decades. This new version requires not only the existence of an economic disparity between the obligations of the parties, but also that this disparity be the result of a certain weakness of the disadvantaged party that has been exploited by the advantage-taking party. This group includes Argentina, Paraguay and Brazil. The legislative trend in those countries is more akin to the PLACL provision with, however, two crucial differences. These are explained below.

In Argentina, a reform of the Civil Code enacted in 1968 introduced a subjective version of *laesio*. According to the 1968 reform, Article 954 of the Argentinean Civil Code reads:

> Nullity or modification of an act may … be requested when one of the parties *exploiting the need, lack of reflection or lack of experience of the other* has obtained an unjustified and *obviously* disproportionate advantage.
>
> In the absence of evidence to the contrary, there is a presumption that such exploitation existed when there is a *notable* disproportion between the burdens.

This Argentinean version of *laesio* was different from the original Spanish one. Whereas the latter only referred to a disproportion in value, the concept of *laesio* enacted in 1968 required two components: economic disproportion (the objective factor) and the exploitation of a weaker party (subjective factor). This is what legal scholars usually describe as qualified or subjective *laesio*. Argentinean authors in the immediate aftermath of the introduction of *laesio* into Argentinean contract law indicated that this defect of contract should be more properly called *exploitation of the weakness or needs* of the other party. In their view, the economic disproportion was a mere consequence that was taken into account to grant a remedy, but was not of the essence of the defect. *Laesio* was seen, therefore, as connected

[58] Pizarro Wilson (n 3) 591.

exclusively with the process of formation of the consent of the parties.[59] The new Argentinean Civil and Commercial Code, which came into force in 2015, also includes *laesio* as a defect of contract in terms that are almost identical to those of the 1968 reform. The most relevant paragraphs of Article 332 of the 2015 Code read as follows:

> Nullity or modification of an act can be requested when one of the parties *exploiting the needs, psychical weakness or lack of experience of the other* has obtained an unjustified and *obviously* disproportionate economical advantage.
>
> In the absence of evidence to the contrary, there is a presumption that such exploitation existed when there is a *notable* disproportion between the burdens.

The only difference with the 1968 reform is the substitution of the expression *lack of reflection* (*ligereza*) by *psychical weakness*. However, given that Argentinean authors related the meaning of *ligereza* to the situation of alcoholics, drug addicts, mentally diminished persons and spendthrifts,[60] this syntactic difference does not actually imply a variation from the original text as interpreted within the Argentinean legal community. Furthermore, the substitution of the word *ligereza* for the expression 'psychical weakness' (*deficiencia psíquica*) was advocated by Argentinean scholars almost immediately after the 1968 reform was enacted.[61]

Three aspects of the Argentinean rules on *laesio* (the 1968 and 2015 versions) must be highlighted. First, there is no requirement that the disproportion be gross or that there be an excessive advantage. It is sufficient that the disparity be obvious, evident, ie easy to perceive. The only reference to an excessive advantage (*notable desproporción*) concerns the rebuttable presumption of exploitation it entails. Accordingly, as far as the objective element of *laesio* is concerned, any disadvantage is sufficient. Secondly, there is no arithmetical threshold for establishing which disproportion is relevant. If the disproportion is obvious, any disparity may be relevant provided that it is accompanied by the exploitation of one party by the other. This characteristic sets apart the Argentinean model from the old Spanish law and from the French Civil Code, with their requirements of 50 per cent or seven-twelfths' difference with respect to market price. Inspiration may have been drawn from the German or Swiss Civil Codes.[62] Finally, the subjective element (abuse, exploitation) can only exist if the disadvantaged party is one to which one of the limited number of situations mentioned in the rule applies: need, psychical weakness or lack of experience. As vague as these terms may be, they limit the scope of *laesio*. Not just any abuse (or, to use PLACL language, not just any act against good faith) is sufficient for *laesio* to come into play. Only cases of abuse affecting needy, inexperienced or mentally weak victims are relevant.

[59] P. Garrido and L Andorno, *Reformas al Código Civil Ley 17.711 Comentadas* (Buenos Aires, Zavalía Editor, 1971) 166, approvingly quoting López Olaciregui's comments.
[60] ibid, 163–64.
[61] ibid, 164.
[62] ibid, 165.

The Paraguayan Civil Code of 1986 includes a solution which is almost identical to that of Argentina. Its Article 671 states:

> If one of the parties to the contract, by exploiting the need, lack of reflection or inexperience of the other obtains a manifestly unjustified advantage which is disproportionate with what the other party receives, the latter may request the nullification or the equitable modification of the contract. In the absence of evidence to the contrary, there is a presumption that such exploitation existed when there is a *notable* disproportion between the burdens.

Finally, as already mentioned, the Brazilian Civil Code of 1916 did not include any references to *laesio*. This was recently changed by the new Civil Code of 2002. A general provision dealing with *laesio* was introduced which adopted a subjective model. Article 157 of the 2002 Brazilian Civil Code states:

> There is *laesio* when a person, under pressing need or due to lack of experience, assumes an obligation manifestly disproportionate with the value of the opposing obligation.

With regard to the objective element of *laesio*, the Brazilian Code (like its Argentinean and Paraguayan counterparts) does not require the disproportion to be excessive or gross, but only that it be evident (manifest, obvious). On the other hand, the subjective element is in some respects different from that required by Argentinean and Paraguayan law. First, there is no focus on the behaviour of the party that takes an advantage. Exploitation or awareness of the other party's weakness is not an element of *laesio*.[63] All that matters is the existence of certain kinds of weakness of the disadvantaged party. Secondly, psychical weakness (*ligereza*) does not form part of the list of relevant problems of the disadvantaged party that may give rise to a claim of *laesio*.

ii. Laesio *in Consumer Contracts*

In relation to consumer contracts, two trends coexist. First, a majority of the jurisdictions analysed in this chapter apply to consumer contracts the same rules that apply to any contract. Five of the jurisdictions belong to that group: Argentina, Chile, Uruguay, Paraguay and Colombia. The most recent example is the Argentinean Civil Code of 2015, which explicitly excludes the possibility of controverting price clauses in consumer contracts on the basis of the mere existence of a disproportion. Its Article 1121 states that the relation between the price and the good or service procured cannot be declared abusive. In Argentina, for a similar sort of claim to progress, the subjective requirements of *laesio* under the Civil Code rules should be met. This was already the situation in Argentinean law before the 2015 Code entered into force.[64] In Uruguay, Article 30 of the Consumer Protection Act (Ley 17.250) excludes *laesio* as a case of abuse but, differently from

[63] Pizarro Wilson (n 3) 157.

[64] RL Lorenzetti, *Consumidores* (Buenos Aires, Rubinzal-Culzoni Editores 2003) 258–59.

Argentina, no other chance of controverting the price in itself remains, as there is no rule on *laesio* in the Uruguayan Civil Code.

Second, a different trend is followed by Venezuela and Brazil. These countries have re-established objective *laesio* within the ambit of consumer contract law. The Venezuelan model retains freedom of contract for private-to-private transactions, but within the field of consumer protection, Article 6 of the Act for the Protection of Consumers of 2 September 1974[65] and the more recent 2010 *Ley para la Defensa de las Personas en el Acceso a Bienes y Servicios* introduced what (those Acts) refer to as *generic usury*. Under Article 144 of the 2010 Act, this is a criminal offence committed by anyone who 'procures for him or herself or for a third party, directly or indirectly, a benefit that implies a notoriously disproportionate advantage when compared with the benefit that he procures to the other party'. The sanction for this offence is a one- to three-year prison sentence. The rule applies also to parties that receive interest at a rate that exceeds the rates allowed by the Central Bank of Venezuela. This is the most radical move in South American law in respect of *laesio* and usury. First, the version of *laesio* adopted is a purely objective one and there is no requirement of exploitation or wrongdoing on the part of the advantage-taking party nor of any special weakness characterising the other party. Given that this Act applies to consumer transactions, the weakness may be said to be presupposed as a generic characteristic of any consumer. Secondly, under Venezuelan consumer protection law any disproportion is sufficient to claim that generic usury has been incurred. These differences set apart the Venezuelan Act of 2010 from the other legal systems in South America that accept objective *laesio* (ie Chile and Colombia) and, obviously, from those that only accept subjective *laesio*. A third difference is that the consequences are related not only to private law but also to criminal law.

In the case of Brazil, Article 6 of the Consumer Protection Code provides that consumers have the basic right to 'modify the contractual clauses that establish disproportionate burdens (*prestacões*)'[66] and Article 51 considers any clause that puts the consumer at an 'excessive disadvantage' to be abusive. These provisions have been interpreted as creating a specific type of objective consumerist *laesio*.[67] Lima Marques explains that Article 6 of the Brazilian Consumer Code allows the judge to 'modify the clause referring to the price … in charge of the consumer, if it is disproportionate' and characterises this situation as a case of *laesio*.[68] The existence of *laesio* under Brazilian consumer law 'does not depend on the good or bad faith of the supplier that imposes it on the consumer'.[69]

[65] Otis Rodner (n 51).

[66] Pizarro Wilson (n 3) 158.

[67] ibid.

[68] C Lima Marques, *Contratos no Código de Defesa do Consumidor: O Novo regime das relacoes contratuais*, 6th edn (São Paulo, Editora Revista dos Tribunais, 2011) 949.

[69] ibid, 940.

iii. Summary

To summarise: in the past decades, three main trends emerged regarding *laesio* in South America. First, in respect of private-to-private contracts, four jurisdictions retained their original approach to *laesio* (Chile, Colombia, Uruguay Venezuela). Secondly, in the same field, three other jurisdictions adopted *subjective laesio* applicable in the case of exploitation of inexperience, need or psychical weakness of one party (Argentina, Paraguay and Brazil). Finally, while the majority (five countries) kept a uniform system for consumer and non-consumer contracts, two jurisdictions (Brazil and Venezuela) adopted a separate regime for consumer contracts consisting of a model of objective *laesio*.

C. Evolution of Usury Law

By the beginning of the twentieth century, usury laws in South America had been reduced to their historical minimum. Of the seven jurisdictions considered in this chapter, only two retained limitations on interest rates under flexible (market-driven) versions with a limit set at 1.5 times the market rate. The other five held on to the model of absolute freedom for interest rates for a long time. This scenario changed between the 1920s and 1940s. The economic crisis of 1929, affecting exports, was one of the principal reasons for this change,[70] although in one case the upheavals caused by the First World War prompted an earlier reaction.[71] Another crucial change in the history of usury law in South America was the development, starting in the 1930s, of national central banks, which slowly began to assume competence in monetary matters.[72] That development determined a tendency directly or indirectly to entrust the regulation of interest rates to the monetary authorities. The powers granted to central banks ranged from fixing maximum rates to indicating, in an authoritative manner, which were the relevant current market rates to be taken into account in determining maximum rates. The repealed Uruguayan Decree/Law 14.887 of 1978 and the recent regulations issued by the Central Bank of Argentina relating to consumer credits[73] are examples of the former modality. Chilean Act 18.010 of 1981 (as amended by successive reforms) and the recent Act 18.212 (2007) of Uruguay are examples of the latter. As a result of these changes, it may be concluded that usury law was readopted, in one form or another, throughout South America in the course of almost a century. If we look at the history of independent South America comprehensively, usury may be seen to have gone through two remarkably contrasting phases. The first

[70] Sahb Batista Lopes and Richter Ribeiro (n 30) 24.

[71] For example: Uruguayan Act number 5.180 of 1914.

[72] C Marichal 'Historiografía de la banca latinoamericana: su despegue, 1970–1993' (1995) 2 *América Latina en la historia económica* 73–90.

[73] Banco Central de la República Argentina, *Comunicación A'5615*, in force since 1 July 2014.

(which lasted almost a century) was one in which absolute freedom of contract prevailed, accompanied, in a minority of countries, by a flexible (market-driven) version of usury. This was a phase that contrasted sharply with the original Spanish and Portuguese law and, in general, with the civil law tradition. A second phase (likewise, spanning almost a century) was one in which usury was reintroduced, either in a rigid or a flexible form.

A brief and, probably, incomplete list of examples of the legislation enacted in six of the relevant jurisdictions is given in the following paragraphs in order to support my overview of the evolution of usury law.[74]

(a) Chile. Except for a short period, Chile substantially retained the solution of its 1855 Civil Code (limitation of interest to 1.5 times the market rate). In 1929, Act 4.694 reiterated the same limit.[75] In 1953, Act 11.234 made two relevant changes: a stricter limit was set, at 1.2 times the market rate. Twenty years later, in 1974, Decree-Law 455 reintroduced the original maximum of 1.5 times the market rate. Act 18.010 of 1981, currently in force with some modifications, also establishes the limit for interest rates at 1.5 times the market rate. The *Superintendencia de Bancos e Instituciones Financieras* is in charge of informing the applicable market rate (*interés corriente*) based on its periodical surveys of the financial system.

(b) Brazil.[76] Brazil kept its liberal regime in respect of interest rates until 1933. In that year, Decree 22.262, also known as the Usury Act, was enacted. Article 1 of that Act fixed the maximum rate at 12 per cent per year. However, on 15 December 1977, the Brazilian Supreme Court endorsed an interpretation that made this Act inapplicable to banks and financial institutions. The latter's transactions were held to be regulated by Act 4595 of 1964, which attributed to the National Monetary Council (formed by the Central Bank of Brazil and government officials) the task of determining maximum interest rates for the financial system. Finally, Articles 406 and 591 of the Brazilian Civil Code of 2002 established that if the loan is destined for economic purposes, the application of interest is presumed, and this interest, *sub poena* of reduction, cannot exceed the rate applied by the tax authority as punitive interest for taxes. While some Brazilian scholars discuss how the coexistence of the Usury Act and the new Civil Code are to be understood, roughly speaking it is clear that Brazil has since the 1930s moved to a rigid model of maximum rates determined by either one or the other of the aforementioned Acts or by the administrative authorities.

(c) Venezuela. Freedom of interest rates persisted in Venezuela until the Venezuelan Civil Code of 1942 was enacted. Article 1746 of that Code

[74] It was not possible to add information from Paraguay.

[75] For this paragraph: R Abeliuk, *Las Obligaciones*, vol I, 4th edn (Santiago de Chile, Editorial Jurídica de Chile, 2003) 355–61.

[76] For this paragraph: Sahb Batista Lopes and Richter Ribeiro (n 30) 15–66.

established two different limits. In the case of loans secured with a mortgage, the maximum was fixed at 12 per cent per year, while for all other loans, the maximum was fixed at 1.5 times the market rate (the Chilean model). Four years later, Decree 247 of 1946 on the repression of usury was issued, imposing a rigid limit of 12 per cent per year for all transactions. Finally, under the successive consumer protection Acts, the maximum rates are to be determined by the administrative authorities or by the Central Bank of Venezuela (which was granted the power to fix maximum rates under an Act of 30 December 1974).[77]

(d) Colombia. The Colombian Civil Code of 1887 is still in force in respect of interest rates. As explained above, Article 2231 of that Code established a limit of one and a half times the market rate for interest. This is a solution similar to that in force in Chile.

(e) Uruguay. The system of absolute freedom of interest introduced by the 1838 Act ended in 1914. Act 5.180 of 1914 established a system of rigid usury with a maximum rate of 12 per cent or 14 per cent per year depending on the existence or otherwise of a mortgage securing the credit. In 1972, Act 14.095 granted the Central Bank of Uruguay the power to determine maximum interest rates, a power which was not exercised until 1998. In the meantime, Act 14.887 fixed a flexible *maximum* of 1.75 times the market rate, related to the criminal offence of usury.[78] Finally, Act 18.212 of 2007 (as subsequently amended) abrogated all preceding Acts and set up a system of flexible usury. Depending on the amount of the transaction, maximum rates are nowadays established at 1.55 and 1.90 times the market rate to be communicated periodically by the Central Bank of Uruguay. Significantly, according to its Article 2, business-to-business transactions exceeding a certain amount are excluded from the scope of the Act and, accordingly, in those cases freedom of interest applies.

(f) Argentina. The new Argentinean Civil and Commercial Code of 2015 in its Article 771 grants power to the courts to reduce the interest rate 'whenever the rate agreed … exceeds, without justification and disproportionally, the average cost of money for debtors in similar transactions in the locality where the obligation was assumed'. This rule is applicable to any kind of loan. In parallel, for consumer credit transactions, the Central Bank of Argentina recently issued regulations establishing maximum rates ranging from 1.25 and 2 times a reference rate related to the rate for internal bonds issued by that bank, to be published periodically.[79]

[77] L Borjas, 'Régimen Legal de los Intereses' (1981) 6 *Revista de Derecho Público* 6–33. Otis Rodner (n 51) 66–71.

[78] Reta-Ofelia Grezzi (n 53) 27–47.

[79] Banco Central de la República Argentina, Tasas de Interés en las Operaciones de Crédito: Última Comunicación Incorporada A-5684: Texto Ordenado al 18/12/2014. Artículo 6.4.

To summarise: the South American jurisdictions analysed in this chapter experienced considerable changes between the beginning and end of the twentieth century. While at the beginning of that century, freedom of interest rates prevailed, such was not the case from the 1930s onwards. Nowadays, rigid or flexible forms of limitation exist in all the countries addressed in this chapter, with a more marked preference for flexible mechanisms. On the other hand, this area was placed under the regulatory competence of the central banks. More importantly, the issue became an essential part of governmental monetary policy following the economic crisis in the first half of the twentieth century.

D. The PLACL and Recent Trends in South America

The PLACL provision on gross disparity does not match the more recent trends discernible in the South American legal systems. First, in the matter of *laesio*, it does not tally with the legal systems that have retained their traditional solutions. Chile, Colombia and Uruguay grant limited or zero space to *laesio* and Venezuela has also kept the no-*laesio* solution for private-to-private transactions. Even where some of these systems do admit *laesio* (in respect of contracts for the sale and barter of land), they remain attached to an *objective* model that includes a precise *standard* of deviation (50 per cent of the market price) rather than a vague reference to *excess* as in Article 37 of the PLACL. Roughly speaking, on the one hand, the PLACL adopt subjective *laesio* for *all* contracts, whereas the four systems mentioned adopt, as a matter of principle, freedom of contract (with the exception of land transactions in two cases).

Secondly, still on the subject of *laesio*, the PLACL make no distinction between consumer and non-consumer transactions. If the PLACL are intended to cover consumer contracts (which is not clear), this uniformity would be in line with the majority of jurisdictions analysed in this chapter. Five of the seven jurisdictions addressed do not distinguish between consumer and non-consumer contracts for purposes of regulating *laesio*. However, there is a crucial difference: the underlying civil code rule in those countries differs from that in the PLACL. For example, in Chile, Uruguay and Colombia, the *non*-applicability of *laesio* to consumer contracts (except those related to land) is the rule, whereas in the PLACL, subjective *laesio is* applicable. The contrast with Brazil and Venezuela goes in the opposite direction. These two countries have adopted objective *laesio* for consumer transactions, whereas the PLACL (always assuming they are intended also to cover consumer contracts) adopt subjective *laesio*. Therefore, in some cases, the PLACL go far beyond some legal systems (eg, in adopting subjective *laesio* for *every* contract) while in others, they lag far behind (eg, in *not* adopting objective *laesio* for consumer contracts, unlike Brazil and Venezuela).

The third mismatch in the civil codes and the PLACL provision in matters of *laesio* deserves more attention. At first glance, the rules of the Argentinean, Paraguayan and Brazilian Civil Codes seem substantially similar to the PLACL provision on gross disparity. All these systems adopt subjective *laesio* and, despite the fact that these are only three of the seven jurisdictions considered, they may be evidence of a more up-to-date trend, given that their civil codes are the most recent ones.

However, there are marked divergences with the PLACL. On the one hand, as explained above, according to Article 37 of the PLACL, if a party *acting contrary to good faith* gains an *excessive* advantage over the other party, the latter may request the nullity or modification of the contract. On the other hand, the Argentinean, Paraguayan and Brazilian codes contemplate the situation from a different perspective: that of a *weak party* that, due to its mental deficiencies, being in need or lacking experience, is *taken advantage of* (exploited) by the other party.

Two relevant differences arise from this comparison. First, the subjective element is differently focused. The codes apply only in cases where the disadvantaged party suffers from a weakness or deficiency. The protected party should be psychically weak or suffering from need or lacking experience. All these are factors affecting the freedom of *that* party, which is not in the best condition to adopt an autonomous decision. Then there is a second requirement in Argentina and Paraguay (but not in Brazil): that the advantage-taking party exploited or abused the other's weakness. Inversely, the PLACL focus *only* on the advantage-taking party, not on the victim. For the purposes of the PLACL, it does not matter if the other party is in a situation of weakness or not. It is sufficient that the advantage-taker acted contrary to good faith (dishonestly). Even if the other party is in perfect condition to act autonomously (ie to self-protect him- or herself), the contract would be null or modifiable. Of course, the PLACL, in the second paragraph of Article 37, refers to the weakness of that party, but only as something to be especially taken into account, not as an essential requirement for the defect of gross disparity to arise. Secondly, regarding the objective element (disparity), while the codes only require that the advantage be manifest, ie easy to perceive, the PLACL require that it be *excessive* (not just *any* disadvantage is enough). Therefore, the PLACL provision is both wider and narrower than those in the codes. It covers more situations: not only cases where the disadvantaged party suffers from certain weaknesses, but any case where there is a dishonest act by the advantage-taking party. On the other hand, it excludes cases where the advantage is not excessive.

These two differences are not only quantitative, they also reflect two distinct approaches. While the codes seem concerned with the conditions required for the *existence* of autonomy, the PLACL seem focused on how autonomy is *exercised.* The rules on subjective *laesio* of the codes take note of deficiencies that may impair the freedom of one of the parties when making a promise or assuming an obligation. The exploitation of such deficiencies is *manifested* through the advantage that the other party gains, but the essence of the provision is the protection of persons who are not able properly to exercise their freedom. The contract in such cases is subject to nullification or modification. If both parties enjoy proper conditions for taking an autonomous decision, the Argentinean, Paraguayan and Brazilian civil codes do not open the door to nullity or modification: the agreement prevails. While the approach of those three codes implies an expansion of the classic rules intended to guarantee that contracts are the outcome of autonomous decisions, it is still a reflection of classic principles. Certainly, a new set of protections is added to the classic rules on capacity, mistake,[80] coercion and fraud (*dolus*), but the purpose and philosophy are the same: the contract is still conceived as the product of freely exercised private autonomy. The PLACL provision implies a different conception. As explained earlier, a situation of gross disparity may arise under the PLACL even between equally autonomous parties not affected by the kinds of weakness or insufficiency described in the three aforementioned codes. Both parties may be perfectly able to exercise their autonomy but the contract may nevertheless be rendered null or modifiable if one of them acted contrary to good faith. The PLACL are interested not only in preserving the *conditions for* an autonomous decision but also in directing *how* that autonomy is *exercised*. If the autonomy of the parties is not affected by any deficiency, it cannot be argued that the PLACL protect autonomy. Therefore, the only explanation is that the PLACL intend to direct the way in which autonomy is exercised. Whether this is or is not a sound policy is another question. My claim refers to another aspect: when compared with South American law, the PLACL adopt a quite different approach. The difference in play here is the same that goes from *protecting autonomy* to *regulating its exercise*.

Finally, usury is not contemplated by the PLACL. Not addressing this aspect, tied as it has become to national monetary policies and central bank regulations, seems a sensible approach. The question that remains to be answered is whether the gross disparity provision is intended to operate simultaneously with usury regulations, or not. So far, nothing in the PLACL text would prevent the parallel and potentially contradictory application of national usury laws and the PLACL (if they were to become applicable). If the PLACL are intended to work in parallel with national usury laws, this may create the problematic situation where a loan is perfectly legal according to a national usury law but voidable under the PLACL. For example, if the interest rate is below national regulations, the contract would be valid under national law but if the rate were considered 'excessive' under the PLACL rule, the contract would be voidable. This is not the sort of situation that promotes certainty. Perhaps the PLACL should indicate that, where usury laws are in place, the gross disparity provision would not be applicable. The subsidiary rules of limitation of interest rates included in the Chilean and Colombian civil codes are an original South American solution, which may be taken into account to amend this aspect of the PLACL.

V. Conclusions

The PLACL provision on gross disparity sparked this inquiry into South American law on the economic conditions of contract. The conclusion drawn here is that

[80] A Alterini, *Contratos* (Buenos Aires, Abeledo Perrot, 1998) 380–84, for example, suggests a parallelism between *lack of experience* and *mistake*.

the PLACL provision does not fit the long-term history of that law nor match the trends of the current legal systems addressed in this chapter. However, the PLACL provide an interesting basis for a much-needed exchange between the legal communities of South America. Suggesting that there are differences between those Principles and past and current trends in South American contract law is not meant to be the end of the debate. Taking gross disparity as a normative claim, as I think it is, and showing which are, for me at least, the divergences with South American contract law as it stands, may clear the field for a discussion as to whether (and how) South American contract law should be changed.

Leaving aside the PLACL, the above inquiry also allows us to extrapolate some general conclusions regarding South American contract law. First, in its formative years, South American contract law showed a marked tendency towards liberalisation. The main feature of its development was radical support of private autonomy and freedom-of-contract doctrines. This feature seems more salient when South American contract law is compared with French law. While in South American contract law there was a strong tendency to eliminate *laesio* and usury, French law retained *laesio* for land transactions and rigid usury for loans. This contrast is relevant, given that French law is usually considered the main model for South American contract law. My claim is that this divergence with French law was influenced by the widespread use of the Benthamite ideas on usury during the 1830s. Other reasons remain to be explored.

Second, the recent tendency represented by Venezuela and Brazil to reintroduce objective *laesio* for consumer transactions has not generated consensus. This is evidenced by the Argentinean Code of 2015, which expressly rejects the idea.

Third, the reintroduction of subjective *laesio* from 1968 onwards in three jurisdictions (Argentina, Paraguay and Brazil) actually implies a reinforcement of autonomy as the regulatory ideal of contract law. As explained above, the modern rules on *laesio* differ from the old ones. They are concerned with the weakness that hinders the autonomy of one of the parties to the contract, but they do not seem interested per se in the economic equation at stake. While the old rules of *laesio* relied on the idea that there was a fair price for goods (*iustum pretium*), the new provisions take disproportion as a mere additional requirement. Objective disparity plays the role of a limiting device. Its function seems to be that of cooling down the temptations of litigants to abuse defences based on such malleable claims as those of 'being in need' or 'lacking experience', for example. The codes admit those defences, but the admission comes at a price: to render the contract null an economic disproportion must *also* exist. The subjective requirement fits the idea of freedom of contract. The requirement of objective disparity is not the key aspect of subjective *laesio* but a limit to potential abuses of the defence: a tribute to certainty.

6

The Principles of Latin American Contract Law and the CISG

PILAR PERALES VISCASILLAS*

I. Introduction

There can be no question that the debate on international commercial contract law and on contract law in general has been gathering pace since the adoption and subsequent success, first of the 1980 Vienna Convention on the International Sale of Goods (CISG),[1] which is now law in 83 states around the world,[2] and then of the UNIDROIT Principles of International Commercial Contracts (PICC). The (draft) Principles of Latin American Contract Law (*Principios Latinoamericanos de Derecho de los Contratos*, PLACL) are one of the latest efforts in drafting uniform substantive rules in the area of regional contracts, both civil and commercial, which seem to have a better chance of success compared to other initiatives in the region that have apparently failed for lack of perseverance on the part of their promoters.[3]

* This chapter was written as part of the Research Project of the Ministry of Science and Technology (Spain) (DER-2013-48401-P) and (DER2016-78572-P) headed by the present author.

[1] As rightly considered by A Veneziano, 'A Review of the Most Successful Instruments for the Worldwide Unification of Contract Law Cannot But Start With the CISG' (2013) 58 *Villanova Law Review* 522. This is somehow forgotten both by some regional instruments such as the CESL or by the case law, which at times prefer to look to regional instruments, even non-binding ones or still in draft form, rather than to the CISG, which is not only hard law but the internal law in the country: for a short critical review of this regional trend in the case law of Spain: P Perales Viscasillas, '¡Larga vida al Derecho Mercantil de Obligaciones y Contrato! (A propósito del Dictamen del Consejo de Estado al Anteproyecto de Ley de Código Mercantil en la parte de Teoría General de Obligaciones y Contratos)' (2015) 13 *Revista Mercantil La Ley* 4–10.

[2] The list of contracting states may be found at the UNCITRAL website: www.uncitral.org.

[3] R Momberg, 'Harmonization of Contract Law in Latin America: Past and Present Initiatives' [2014] *Uniform Law Review* 13–14 describes other academic initiatives in the region that seek to follow the European initiatives to some extent, such as the Group for the Harmonization of Latin American Private Law with the aim of creating a Code on the Law of Obligations, and the Latin American Code of Contract Law (*Bases para un Código Latinoamericano de contratos*) under the first Latin American Congress of Private Law.

Latin America is no stranger to the world of unification of private law, albeit in the area of private international law (PIL) or conflict-of-laws rules. Since the end of the nineteenth century, several initiatives have been taken in this area and 26 instruments have been drafted under the auspices of the Inter-American Specialized Conference on Private International Law (CIDIP).[4] Most of these were hard law instruments (Conventions), but a shift towards more flexible instruments, such as model laws, and more substantive instruments, such as those in the area of consumer protection, seems to be taking place.[5]

The PLACL are not a PIL instrument but a so-called uniform international (commercial?) contract law instrument (or, in Spanish, *derecho uniforme del (comercio?) internacional* (DUCI)). The instruments that fall into the category of uniform law are neutral and flexible as to their content and application and share the common goal of providing uniform rules to be applied globally around the world, particularly in the area of commercial contracts, although the PLACL go further as they cover private law contracts in general. The aim of uniform law is to provide legal certainty by diminishing the importance of the conflict-of-laws rules and replacing this insecure system with a set of universally applicable rules.

Within this uniform law, the most successful instrument is the CISG, not only because of its worldwide acceptance by a large number of countries that have ratified it, including 13[6] out of 19 Latin American countries,[7] but also because of the influence it has had in the creation and consolidation of a body of uniform and international commercial law and in the birth of regional private law instruments,[8] thereby creating a common understanding of contract law and building the modern theory of general contract law that we have today.

The merits of the CISG can be measured not only in terms of the large number and economic weight of the countries that have ratified the Convention, but also in terms of the quality, novelty and worldwide span of the solutions it offers, from a purely technical and legal perspective. However, the Convention, as an international treaty, does have some drawbacks. First, it might be quite cumbersome to amend or modify it;[9] secondly, despite its broad substantive coverage, the CISG leaves important areas of the sale of goods contract to domestic law; thirdly, the

[4] See Momberg (n 3) 8–10, explaining the evolution in Latin America.

[5] ibid, 10.

[6] Argentina, Brazil, Chile, Colombia, Cuba, Dominican Republic, Ecuador, El Salvador, Honduras, Mexico, Paraguay, Peru and Uruguay.

[7] The states that have not so far ratified the CISG are: Bolivia, Costa Rica, Guatemala, Nicaragua, Panama and Venezuela. At least Guatemala is on the way to a possible ratification. I have not included Belice, Haiti and the French possessions, but note that Guyana has ratified the CISG, as well as Saint Vincent and the Grenadines.

[8] See R Illescas Ortiz and P Perales Viscasillas, *Derecho Mercantil Internacional. El Derecho Uniforme* (Madrid, Centro de Estudios Ramón Areces, 2003) 18.

[9] Notwithstanding the above, there are some indirect tools to update an International Treaty. See: 2006—Recommendation regarding the interpretation of Arts II(2) and VII(1) of the Convention on the Recognition and Enforcement of Foreign Arbitral Awards (New York, 1958); or the 2005 United Nations Convention on the Use of Electronic Communications in International Contracts (Art 20).

CISG only covers contracts for the international sale of goods, so that some other important types of international commercial contract do not enjoy an international uniform law regime.

In the wake of the success of the CISG, several other instruments, mostly with a material or territorial scope different from that of the CISG, have sought to offer *soft law* solutions that can either be applied in conjunction with the CISG or as competing instruments by means of voluntary application to the contract. These contractual instruments are mostly based on, or inspired by, the CISG since, despite the fact that the latter is restricted to international sale of goods contracts, it regulates areas that belong to general contract law.

Eloquent proof of the impact of the CISG on other international or regional instruments is provided by what I call the first generation of soft law instruments, and in the area of international uniform commercial law the first such were the UNIDROIT PICC (1994, modified and enlarged in 2004 and 2010),[10] created under the leadership of Professor Michael Joachim Bonell under the institutional auspices of UNIDROIT, and the Principles of European Contract Law (PECL), which have a broader scope of application (both civil and commercial contracts) but are limited to regional EU contract law. The PECL were drafted by the Commission on European Contract Law, also known as the Lando Commission after its Chairman, Professor Ole Lando.[11] The PECL were intended as the first stone in the building of a future European civil code.[12] However, it is probably more realistic to expect some kind of unification to be achieved at the level of general principles and rules, although it is not clear what form these would ultimately take: whether they would be collected in a binding or a soft law instrument.

In any event, several initiatives have evolved in Europe since 1997. First, the Study Group on a European Civil Code, under the direction of Professor Christian von Bar, drafted the different chapters that would make up the 'future' civil code published in 2009 as the Draft Common Frame of Reference (DCFR), which I consider to be a second generation soft law instrument since it also covers consumer transactions and deals with a variety of private law contracts, mostly commercial, such as agency, franchise, distribution, lease, etc, and even regulates property and non-contractual matters. Secondly, although it has recently been withdrawn, there

[10] In fact, the 2004 and 2010 editions generally cover general contract law institutions that are not covered by the CISG: authority of agents, contracts for the benefit of third parties, set-off, limitation periods, assignment of rights and contracts, transfer of obligations, conditions, plurality of obligors and obligees, unwinding of contracts and illegality. UNIDROIT is working on a future revision of the Principles focusing on long-term contracts (to be published in 2017). In this regard, the PLACL might be extended, so as to provide specific rules for long-term contracts since they do not even include the classic rule in Art 5.1.8 PICC nor any rules for the implied determination of the contract; these are very important in long-term transactions.

[11] http://frontpage.cbs.dk/law/commission_on_european_contract_law/index.html.

[12] The PECL were published in three parts. The first two were published in 1999 (see O Lando and H Beale (eds), *Principles of European Contract Law, Parts I and II* (Alphen aan den Rijn, Kluwer Law International, 2000). Part III was published in 2003.

was the European Union Proposal for a Regulation on a Common European Sales Law (CESL) of 11 October 2011,[13] whose antecedents may be found in the DCFR and the PECL. The CESL was initially intended to be incorporated into the legislation of the EU Member States, although for the contractual parties, it would have been an opt-in instrument.[14] It was restricted to sale of goods contracts although apparently, within the EU, it was intended to be broader in scope, covering consumer transactions as well as B2B contracts. The second generation of instruments is thus considered in the institutional framework of the EU and covers a broad subjective scope of application since consumers are included.

Finally, I will refer to a third generation of soft law instruments that are regional in their scope of application,[15] unlike global instruments, and are not confined to commercial law so that they cover private law in general, but have no institutional support and thus are purely academic initiatives. This, in my view, is quite important, particularly since the drafters are very ambitious, thinking in terms of fully fledged or semi-legislative instruments.

Another important point is that regional and international instruments share the objective of 'de-nationalisation of rules and principles'[16] by 'spelling out a number of "fundamental", "general" or "underlying principles" of contract law',[17] but often arrive at different formulations stemming from the different territorial scope of application and subject-matter that sometimes leads to a different legal angle or perspective on certain legal institutions. Particularly the creation of the second- and third-generation instruments has sparked intense debate worldwide on general commercial contract law, more generally on private law, on regional versus universal harmonisation of the law, as well as the role of soft law instruments as opposed to hard law instruments. The role of the CISG, its limits and drawbacks

[13] www.ec.europa.eu/justice/contract/files/common_sales_law/regulation_sales_law_en.pdf.

[14] See, for a critical view: P Perales Viscasillas and R Illescas Ortiz, 'The Scope of the Common European Sales Law: B2B, Goods, Digital Content and Services' (2012) 11 *Journal of International Trade Law & Policy* 241–58; and I Schwenzer, 'The Proposed Common European Sales Law and the Convention on the International Sale of Goods' (2012) 44 *Uniform Commercial Code Law Journal* 457–81.

[15] There are also several other regional initiatives, eg, in the Caribbean the OHADAC Principles on International Commercial Contracts, 2015, OHADAC standing for 'Organization for the Harmonization of Business Law in the Caribbean'; in Africa the Uniform Act on General Commercial Law by OHADA, the Organization for the Harmonization of Business Law in Africa, which is working on a Preliminary Draft Uniform Act on Contract Law; and in Asia the Principles of Asian Contract Law, PACL. The latter two are still under development. For information on the current development of the Asian Principles: S Han, 'Principles of Asian Contract Law: An Endeavor of Regional Harmonization of Contract Law in East Asia' (2013) 58 *Villanova Law Review* 589–99, the PACL being very similar to the PLACL in nature, although English was the working language.

[16] See J Ramberg, 'The Creativity of Arbitrators in the Context of the UNIDROIT Principles of International Commercial Contracts' [1998] *Uniform Law Review* 655 in relation to the PICC and the PECL.

[17] S Vogenauer, '"General Principles" of Contract Law in Transnational Instruments' in L Gullifer and S Vogenauer (eds), *English and European Perspectives on Contract and Commercial Law: Essays in Honour of Hugh Beale* (Oxford, Hart Publishing, 2014) 292, who also states: 'The exact number and the precise content of these principles differ across the instruments. However, all of the texts deal, in one way or another, with at least some of the five principles that I will discuss in this contribution: freedom of contract; the binding effect of contracts; good faith and fair dealing; freedom from formalities; and the duty to co-operate'.

as an international commercial contract law instrument, forms the core of this discussion.[18]

It will come as no surprise that a proposal on possible future work by UNCITRAL in the area of international contract law was put forward by Switzerland on the occasion of the UNCITRAL Commission session in 2012.[19] In this regard, CISG Advisory Council (CISG-AC) Declaration No 1 (The CISG and Regional Harmonization)[20] supported the Swiss Proposal, considering some of the shortcomings of regional as opposed to global unification. One of the most obvious dangers of regional unification is that the solutions proposed will not be in line with the CISG. That is what happened with the CESL, which, although apparently mirroring the CISG, in fact adopted some solutions that departed from the basic foundations of the CISG, particularly as regards *pacta sunt servanda* and freedom of contract, thereby producing a text that was heavily consumer oriented due to the combination in a single text of B2B and B2C transactions. This goes a long way in explaining the failure of the CESL and the success of truly uniform and international texts such as the PICC.[21]

The PLACL bear a strong imprint of the CISG, hence the Convention is a mandatory point of reference for them, but their resemblance to the PECL[22] and the PICC is even more striking, both in the intended scope of application (Preamble) and in terms of the issues covered. The PLACL and the PICC might be considered, at least theoretically, as competing instruments as *opt-in* instruments for the parties. However, absent an express agreement of the parties on the express inclusion of the PLACL into the contract and considering the direct application of the CISG to international sale of goods contracts, they ought really to be considered more as complementary than as competing instruments.

[18] The idea of elaborating a 'Global Commercial Code' was put forward by G Hermann, 'Law, International Commerce and the Formulating Agencies—The Future of Harmonisation and Formulating Agencies: The Role of UNCITRAL', paper presented at the *Schmitthoff Symposium 2000. Law and Trade in the 21st Century.* Centre of Commercial Law Studies, London, 1–3 June 2000. After that, it was suggested that UNCITRAL should embark on an international Convention related to the general part of contract law: MJ Bonell, 'Towards a Legislative Codification of the UNIDROIT Principles?' in CB Andersen and UG Schroeter (eds), *Sharing International Commercial Law across National Boundaries: Festschrift for Albert H Kritzer on the Occasion of his Eightieth Birthday* (London, Wildy, 2008) 69; but, slightly differently: MJ Bonell, 'Do We Need A Global Commercial Code?' [2003] *Uniform Law Review* 472. See finally O Lando, 'Principles of European Contract Law and UNIDROIT Principles: Moving from Harmonisation to Unification?' [2003] *Uniform Law Review* 132, also in favour of an international Convention drafted by UNIDROIT.

[19] Forty-fifth session, New York, 25 June–6 July 2012. A/CN.9/758, available at http://daccess-dds-ny.un.org/doc/UNDOC/GEN/V12/534/54/PDF/V1253454.pdf?OpenElement. For an explanation of why a uniform instrument is needed, see I Schwenzer, 'Who Needs a Uniform Contract Law, and Why?' (2013) 58 *Villanova Law Review* 723–32.

[20] Available at www.cisg-ac.org.

[21] For the PICC as the basis of the future contract law instrument: HD Gabriel, 'UNIDROIT Principles as a Source for Global Sales Law' (2013) 58 *Villanova Law Review* 661–80. Most of the papers included in the cited *Villanova Law Review*, vol 58, consider the PICC as one of the basic pillars of a uniform contract law regime together with the CISG.

[22] Apparently this was the main source of inspiration: AM Morales Moreno, 'Los Principios Latinoamericanos de derecho de los contratos. Un debate abierto sobre las grandes cuestiones jurídicas de la contratación' (2014) 1 *Anuario de Derecho Civil* 230.

II. A General Comparison Between the PLACL and the CISG: Origin, Scope of Application and Issues Covered

In terms of the drafting process, the scope of application and the issues covered, there are several important differences between the PLACL and the CISG that are generally summarised in Table 6.1.

Table 6.1: Origin, Scope of Application and Issues Covered: PLACL v. CISG

	PLACL	CISG
Type of instrument	Academic initiative Soft law only?	International Convention Hard law. Law of 13 Latin American countries
Objectives or purposes	Preamble — to offer to the parties or the judge a choice of law to govern the contract — to build a *lex mercatoria* in Latin America or a Latin American *ius commune* — to interpret and supplement international uniform law instruments, domestic laws or contracts governed by international uniform law — to be a model for national or international legislators	To enhance legal security around the world by providing uniform international rules to be applied in international sale of goods contracts independent of the legal, political or economic system of the parties
Geographical scope of application	Dual scope: — regional: contracts related to countries located in South America, the Caribbean and jurisdictions of the Americas governed by civil law systems — domestic and international contracts	Universal scope: — international: all the countries in the world
Systems of law	Civil law systems	Civil and common law Generally all the legal systems in the world
Objective scope of application (type of contract)	Private law (civil) and commercial contracts	International sale of goods contracts. But: Art 3 and case law that expands CISG scope of application

(continued)

Table 6.1: ***(Continued)***

	PLACL	**CISG**
Subjective scope of application	B2B Consumer contracts?	B2B, exceptionally see Art 2(a) CISG
Issues covered by the instruments (chapters)	— Preamble and General Principles	— General provisions and scope of application
	— Formation of the contract	— Formation of the contract and *modification*
	— *Defects of the contract: mistake, fraud, threat and gross disparity*	— NO, Art 4(a) except in exceptional cases.
	— *Nullity of the contract*	— NO, Art 4(a)
	— *Simulation*	— NO, Art 4(a)
	— *Effects of a contract on third persons*	— NO, Art 4
	— Interpretation	— YES, Art 8
	— Performance of contractual obligations	— YES, similar principles apply
	— Non-performance of contractual obligations	— YES, similar principles — *Final (Treaty) Provisions*
Drafters/ drafting process	Private/academic initiative Original text in the Spanish language Questionnaire/drafting teams/general meeting	UNCITRAL, UN body Six official languages Through consensus

Some general comments with regard to the scope of application of both instruments as shown in Table 6.1 follow below.

A. Origin: Drafters and Methodology

First, as to the drafters of the two instruments, there is no need to go into any great detail on the origin and drafting process of the CISG. Suffice it to say that the CISG was drafted under the auspices of the United Nations Commission on International Trade Law (UNCITRAL)[23] and is thus the product of a true process

[23] UNCITRAL was established in 1966 by Resolution 2205 (XXI) of the UN General Assembly. On UNCITRAL, see *A Guide to UNCITRAL: Basic facts about the United Nations Commission on International Trade Law* (UNCITRAL, Vienna, 2013).

of *consensus* between states and private actors worldwide[24] with a direct interest in the process.[25]

The PLACL are the result of a private initiative among academics that began in 2010 with the support of the French *Fondation pour le droit continental* and the Chilean Fernando Fueyo Foundation, which is attached to the Diego Portales University in Chile.[26] The group is composed of academics from Argentina, Colombia and Chile, further extended to Brazil, Paraguay, Uruguay and Venezuela.[27] Scholars have noted the absence of other relevant countries as one of the drawbacks of these Principles, together with the lack of legitimacy and support as a private initiative.[28] In fact, it has been recognised that they are, 'at the most, South American',[29] but as a common factor, they are all parties to the CISG except for Venezuela, which has signed but not ratified the Convention.

Turning to the drafting methodology,[30] a questionnaire was first distributed to national reporters in key areas of contract law in order to identify the current status in the relevant domestic laws; these national reports were eventually collected in a book. In a second step, drafting teams were appointed to draft not only the rules, but also the comparative notes and comments that will, at a later stage, become part of the comments that will accompany the final text. Thirdly, the reports were evaluated in general meetings and organised by commissions that examined and approved the black letter rules. Although I have not been able to track down the relevant information, it seems that Spanish was the working language; however, there is now an English translation of the black letter rules which is appended to this book.

B. Type of Instrument and Scope of Application

With regard to the nature of the instrument, the PLACL, as mentioned above, can be classified as an academic instrument. Although theoretically they belong

[24] 'These instruments are negotiated through an international process involving a variety of participants, including member States of UNCITRAL, which represent different legal traditions and levels of economic development; non-member States; intergovernmental and non-governmental organisations. Thus, these texts are widely acceptable as offering solutions appropriate to different legal traditions and to countries at different stages of economic development. In the years since its establishment, UNCITRAL has been recognised as the core legal body of the United Nations system in the field of international trade law': see *The UNCITRAL Guide*, p. 1, available at www.uncitral.org/pdf/english/texts/general/06-50941_Ebook.pdf.

[25] 'The notion is generally understood to mean adoption of a decision without formal objection and vote': A/CN.9/653, no 11; y A/CN.9/638/Add.4, pfos. 6-21. The UNCITRAL Rules on Procedure and the different working methods may be found at www.uncitral.org/uncitral/en/about/methods_documents.html.

[26] For further details: Momberg (n 3) 14.

[27] ibid.

[28] ibid, 17

[29] ibid.

[30] The methodology is aptly described by Momberg (n 3) 15–16. The book referred to in the text is: C Pizarro Wilson (ed), *El derecho de los contratos en Latinoamérica: Bases para unos principios de derecho de los contratos* (Chile, Fundación Fernando Fueyo Laneri, 2012).

to the category of *soft law* instruments, ie, instruments that become applicable when the parties have chosen them as their 'law' governing their contract[31] so that their binding force only derives from the agreement of the parties (*opt-in* instrument), it is too early at this point to predict the future of this instrument as a *soft law instrument* and whether they will gain acceptance not only by practitioners including them in their contracts, but also as an instrument that might play a wider role.

Although the most obvious application of the PLACL is by way of agreement of the parties, the Preamble, which follows the Preamble of the PICC as well as that of the PECL, expands their natural scope of application by expressly describing their intended application in a variety of situations, such as when the parties have agreed that their contract be governed by general principles of law, the *lex mercatoria* or the like; that they may be applied when the parties have not chosen any law to govern their contract; to interpret and supplement international uniform law instruments, domestic law or contracts governed by international uniform law; and finally, as a model for national or international legislators.

Unlike the PICC Preamble, which states that they '*may* be applied' for the many intended roles, except for the agreement of the parties (*shall* be applied), the PLACL are even more ambitious and always use the wording 'shall be applied'. Therefore, rather than a recommendation to the courts or to national legislators about the applicability of the Principles when the contract is silent in their regard, we can infer that the purpose of the drafters was to recognise the automatic application of the Principles to the contract not only when it is derived from the will of the parties, but also in the variety of situations described in the Preamble.

I take the view that the drafters should consider softening the language in a similar fashion to the PICC. Coming from such a young, novel and academic initiative, a rule of prevalence of this nature[32] cannot count on any official support or legitimacy, and as such it seems to me that such imperative language may prove to be counter-productive for the purported application of the PLACL, ie, at the end of the day, it is intended to become a fully fledged or semi-legislative tool.

This pro-Principle approach taken by the PLACL would not collide with the so-called pro-Convention principle adopted in the CISG. The pro-Convention principle, on the one hand, dictates an interpretation in favour of the applicability of the CISG,[33] and as a consequence an international and uniform interpretation

[31] See PICC Preamble and Art 1:101(2) PECL.

[32] Although this is not expressly stated by the drafters, the intention is to displace the possible application of the PICC, as is evident where the Preamble (Art 1.2) considers that 'These Principles shall be applied preferentially over any other principles of contracts to contracts connected to countries located in South America, the Caribbean, and jurisdictions of the Americas governed by the civil law system'.

[33] See CISG-AC Opinion no 4, Contracts for the Sale of Goods to Be Manufactured or Produced and Mixed Contracts (Article 3 CISG), 24 October 2004. Rapporteur: Pilar Perales Viscasillas, Universidad Carlos III de Madrid, para. 4.4 (at www.cisg-ac.org). On the *favor conventionis* principle: Martínez Cañellas, *La interpretación y la integración de la Convención de Viena sobre compraventa internacional de mercaderías de 11 de abril de 1980* (Granada, Comares, 2004) 316.

(Article 7) would cut transaction costs, inhibit forum shopping and exclude conflict-of-laws rules.[34] On the other hand, this principle claims an extensive and broad interpretation of the gap-filling rule, attracting to the CISG several matters that might otherwise fall outside its scope. In this regard, a large portion of the CISG is to be considered as general contract law rules, and since there is no general contract law treaty this justifies a broader application of the Convention. Other general principles include the principle of *in dubio pro Conventione*,[35] which considers the preference in the applicability of the CISG before domestic law and over the purely domestic or national public order;[36] and the principle of equality between buyers and sellers that was, for example, considered decisive in the interpretation of Article 74, where it was concluded that attorneys' fees were not covered by that provision.[37] The principle of equilibrium between buyer and seller is therefore a general principle within the CISG, as shown also in the mirror structure of obligations and remedies under the CISG that might be used to equilibrate the interpretation of a contract and the strict application of any of its provisions. From this point of view, the central focus of the CISG is the international character of the transaction, the equality between the parties that implies not only a presumption of equal bargaining power, but also a principle that might favour contractual equilibrium where needed, and finally, the need to look for economic results that are reasonable in international trade. Therefore, the idea that the CISG focuses only on the economic dimension of the contract is unreal, untrue and unjust.

Another point that the drafters might consider is the lack of correspondence between the intended scope of the PLACL and the first portion of the Preamble. Article 1(1) PLACL states that 'These Principles set forth general rules applicable to domestic and international contracts, whether private or commercial in nature', but it does not limit this statement to Latin American contracts, as the title suggests.[38] Furthermore, the second paragraph of Article 1 also refers to the scope of application, using wording that is not very clear, stating: 'These Principles apply preferentially

[34] See F de Ly, 'Uniform Interpretation: What Is Being Done? Official Efforts' in F Ferrari (ed), *The 1980 Uniform Sales Law: Old Issues Revisited in the Light of Recent Experiences* (The Hague, Sellier European Law Publishers, 2003) 335, 341. Support for the idea of the CISG reducing transaction costs: K Lehn, 'The CISG: Perspectives from an Economist' in HM Flechtner, RA Brand and MS Walter (eds), *Drafting Contracts Under the CISG* (Oxford, Oxford University Press, 2007) 263–65.

[35] As considered by several authors: J Lookofsky, 'In Dubio Pro Conventione? Some Thoughts About Opt-outs, Computer Programs and Pre-emption under the 1980 Vienna Sales Convention (CISG)' (2003) 13 *Duke Journal of Comparative and International Law* 263, 263ff; Martínez Cañellas (n 33) 130–31. Also in CISG-AC Opinion No 16, Exclusion of the CISG under Article 6, Rapporteur: Lisa Spagnolo, Monash University, Australia. Adopted by the CISG Advisory Council following its 19th meeting, in Pretoria, South Africa on 30 May 2014, Opinion no 1, and comment 1.

[36] Martínez Cañellas (n 33) 131.

[37] CISG-AC Opinion no 6, Calculation of Damages under CISG Article 74. Rapporteur: John Y. Gotanda, Villanova University School of Law, Villanova, Pennsylvania, USA. Adopted by the CISG-AC at its Spring 2006 meeting in Stockholm, Sweden, para. 5.4 (at www.cisg-ac.org).

[38] More correct are the PACL: 'These Principles are intended to be applied as general rules of contract law in the Asian Countries'.

over any other principles of contracts to contracts connected to countries located in South America, the Caribbean and jurisdictions of the Americas governed by the civil law system'. It would seem to use a criterion based not only on geographical position but also on the legal system governing the countries concerned. It is not clear whether Latin America and 'jurisdictions of the Americas governed by civil law systems' refers to the same countries, the latter being apparently wider in scope and theoretically perhaps including Louisiana and Quebec. On the other hand, it is also doubtful whether the common law countries in the Caribbean are also included.

From my point of view, the most important role that the PLACL might develop in practice is not mentioned as such in the Preamble: the PLACL might serve as a tool for a comprehensive discussion of contract law in Latin America, educating students, lawyers and professors about the modern institutions, principles and theories that govern contemporary contract law, thanks, in particular, to the instruments developed under the auspices of UNCITRAL and UNIDROIT. They can be used as a point of reference for scholars and as materials to be included in academic curricula. A change in mentality from old institutions to new is sorely needed in this area. As a consequence, one of the roles foreseen by the drafters of the Principles, ie, as a model for national or international legislators, should be the ultimate goal of the drafters.[39]

Whether the Principles will succeed in the other roles established in the Preamble is very difficult to predict. Agreement of the parties as to the incorporation of the Principles into their contracts seems difficult to achieve: first, not many contracts are governed by soft law instruments as such, so lawyers tend to include a specific law, whether national or international, or the parties might not even have considered the inclusion of a choice-of-law clause;[40] secondly, the Principles are too new and thus offer no legal certainty as to their application and interpretation by the courts; furthermore they also lack legitimacy, and there is as yet no body of scholarly writings and case law, nor is there a system to help ensure uniformity of interpretation in this area. All these issues would form an obstacle to their incorporation into contracts; moreover, even if a soft law instrument were to be included, other instruments might better serve the parties, particularly in international contracts, ie, the UNIDROIT Principles for International Commercial Contracts. As pointed out by several scholars, the most difficult task is not to create a uniform text but to promote[41] and maintain uniformity.[42] To support and

[39] Momberg (n 3) 14 considers that 'the main purpose of the PLACL is to provide a source of inspiration for the reform and modernization of contract law in Latin America', particularly, as pointed out by the author, in the case of Chile and Colombia.

[40] One way to promote the use of the Principles might be to develop, as UNIDROIT did, some model clauses to guide their use. See: *Model Clauses for the Use of the Unidroit Principles of International Commercial Contracts* (Rome, UNIDROIT, 2013).

[41] R Sorieul, E Hatcher and C Emery, 'Possible Future Work by UNCITRAL in the Field of Contract Law: Preliminary Thoughts from the Secretariat' (2013) 58 *Villanova Law Review* 498–99.

[42] ibid, 499–507; and M Bridge, 'An Overview of the CISG and an Introduction to the Debate about the Future Convention' (2013) 58 *Villanova Law Review* 487.

preserve uniformity a powerful infrastructure is needed, and I doubt whether the promoters of the PLACL have the necessary tools and resources to achieve that goal.

After reviewing the PLACL, I cannot detect any particularly Latin American flavour ('Latin American juridical identity')[43] or particularities that justify the title of the Principles, still less a 'Latin American *Lex Mercatoria*' or 'Latin American *ius commune*' that the courts might use to interpret or supplement domestic and international uniform law.[44] On the contrary, I see a purely academic text that at first glance is in line with the principles and rules embodied in both the CISG and the PICC, however 'original' the drafters apparently wished to be for fear of being branded a sub-product or copy of the CISG, and in other instruments (PECL or DCFR).[45] In fact, the drafters of the Principles departed from the CISG by dealing with validity issues, which are matters excluded from the scope of the CISG except in certain cases such as mistake in the goods,[46] but not from the PICC, which do deal with those validity issues in a similar fashion. Besides, it seems difficult

[43] In the words of Momberg (n 3) 15.

[44] Too optimistic: ibid, 14, 18. Indifferent: Han (n 15) 558: 'So long as the PACL is a product of comparative law study and is built on the basis of the existing Asian laws, there is no need to worry that there is not any distinguishing Asian feature', but he did find at least one: the creditor's rights of subrogation and revocation, which are not found either in the PECL nor in the PICC. See also: P Perales Viscasillas, 'CISG Interpretation and the Principles of Latin American Contract Law' in *I Congreso Iberoamericano de Derecho Internacional de los Negocios: 360° de la Compraventa Internacional* (Colombia, Universidad del Externado, 2017) (forthcoming).

[45] Momberg (n 3) 15.

[46] But the matter of validity should be examined in the light of the Vienna Convention. In doing so, account should be taken of the fact that Art 4 CISG stipulates that the Convention governs only the formation of the contract of sale and the rights and obligations of the seller and the buyer arising from such a contract; the validity of the contract falls outside its scope. This article seems to be clear as to its meaning and sphere of application: on the one hand, any issue arising in an international contract of sales related to the validity of the contract is omitted from the Vienna text ('except as otherwise expressly provided in this Convention'), so it should be solved in accordance with the agreement of the parties or, subsidiarily, with the national law; on the other hand, the formation of the contract as well as the rights and obligations of the seller and the buyer are governed by the Convention. Notwithstanding this clear formulation, the application of Art 4 CISG is blocked by three factors: (1) the Vienna Convention does not give a definition of the term 'validity'; (2) the different national legal systems are not unanimous when it comes to classifying the issues connected with the validity of the contract, as we have already seen; (3) lastly, some situations connected with validity are regulated by both the Convention and the national law: the clearest example is Art 55 CISG, which is exclusively applied when the contract has been validly concluded.

For a detailed discussion of some validity issues under the CISG (remedies for tortious behaviour): UG Schroeter, 'Defining the Borders of Uniform International Contract Law: The CISG and Remedies for Innocent, Negligent, or Fraudulent Misrepresentation' (2013) 58 *Villanova Law Review* 553–87, stating that the list in Art 4 CISG 'is neither inclusive nor exclusive', and indeed that domestic dogmatic classification of an issue such as tort should not have any impact in terms of the interpretation of the CISG: ibid, 557–63. See also: CISG-AC Opinion No. 12, Liability of the Seller for Damages Arising Out of Personal Injuries and Property Damage Caused by Goods and Services under the CISG, Rapporteur: Hiroo Sono, School of Law, Hokkaido University, Sapporo, Japan. Adopted by the CISG Advisory Council following its 17th meeting in Villanova, Pennsylvania, USA, on 20 January 2013.

to pinpoint the particularities of Latin American legal systems when some solutions were reached by way of a compromise, thereby denoting a policy decision by the drafters, including some innovative solutions as compared with the Latin America idiosyncrasy,[47] and when there was a clear division between the so-called 'conservative jurisdictions' (Chile, Colombia, Venezuela and Uruguay) and the 'progressive jurisdictions' (Argentina, Brazil and Paraguay).[48]

A clear example is the strong presence of *causa* that is found in Article 9 PLACL as an essential element of the contract and of obligations (Article 39 PLACL).[49] Although at a first glance, the presence of *causa* among the Principles might be considered as a Latin American peculiarity omitted in the CISG and the PICC, this is not in fact the case, since it has also been omitted from the Brazilian and Paraguayan Civil Codes.[50] It is, however, doubtful whether the adoption of *causa* (*consideration* is the closest institution in common law systems) within the Principles is a good policy option, since both *causa* and consideration are irrelevant in international commercial contracts[51] where they have been substituted by mere consent.[52] Furthermore, in the section devoted to defects of the contract, no direct reference to *causa* is made, although this is an area in which, in some countries at least, there is a consolidated jurisprudence that annuls contracts due to essential mistake in the cause of the contract.[53]

Another example would be the strong presence of good faith in the Principles as compared with the single Article in the CISG, where good faith is only a principle of interpretation of the Convention (Article 7(1)). The question then arises whether this is a particularity of Latin American legal systems that might justify the text and its departure from the CISG. This is not the case, for two main reasons.

First, where we find issues expressly dealt with by both texts, good faith in the PLACL substitutes what are in the CISG the principle of reliance/*venire contra factum propium* (compare Article 18(2) PLACL with Article 16(2)(b) CISG) and the principle of reasonableness (compare Articles 19(4) and 23(1) PLACL with Article 18(2) CISG, and Article 102 PLACL with Article 77 CISG).

Secondly, although good faith under the PLACL is more clearly formulated as a principle or standard of behaviour of the parties (Article 7) during the negotiation

[47] Morales Moreno (n 22) 230, citing Carlos Pizarro.

[48] See Momberg (n 3) 16.

[49] Art 9 (Elements of a contract): consent, subject-matter and cause are the essential elements required to form a contract. Art 39 (Cause of the contract and obligation): (1) All obligations require a cause. A cause is presumed to exist as long as it is not proven otherwise, even if it is not expressed. (2) The cause of the contract must be lawful.

[50] Momberg (n 3) 17.

[51] See U Drobnig, 'Substantive Validity' (1992) 40 *American Journal of Comparative Law* 635 and B Nicholas, 'The Vienna Convention on International Sales Law' (1989) 105 *LQR* 214. See the Official Comments 1 and 2 to Art 3.1.2 PICC.

[52] A Garro, 'Reconciliation of Legal Traditions in the UN Convention on Contracts for the International Sale of Goods' (1989) 23 *The International Lawyer* 453–54.

[53] See, eg, in Spain with regard to B2B *Swap* contracts: STS 21 November 2012 (JUR 11052); STS 20 January 2014; STS 12 January 2015 (nº recurso 2290/2012), STSJM, 25 January 2015, STS 26 February 2015 (nº recurso 1548/2011), and STS 24 April 2015 (nº recurso 1509/2013).

of the contract (Articles 10 and 11) and as a principle of interpretation of the contract, under the CISG, good faith achieves those roles by means of the development of case law and scholarly writings. Specific manifestations of good faith are also found within the CISG, as it encourages parties to act in good faith, thus evidencing that good faith is also a substantive provision rather than a mere interpretative principle of the CISG. Manifestations of good faith as a standard of conduct are found in Articles 8, 16(2)(b), 29(2) and 80 CISG, which reflect the estoppel principle, also known as the *venire contra factum proprium*, which is also a general principle of the *lex mercatoria*. It is also found in Article 40 CISG and in the recognition of other general principles such as the duty to cooperate (Articles 32(3), 48(2) and 60 CISG), the loyalty principle[54] and the principle of mitigation of damages in Article 77 CISG. The case law has recognised that good faith not only plays a role within the Convention for purposes of interpretation, but also plays a seminal role throughout the Convention to modulate its content and provide a standard of conduct for the parties during the formation and performance of the contract. In this respect, a position closer to the civil law systems has been adopted, as opposed to the common law view in which there is no general recognition of the duties of good faith and fair dealing during the formation and negotiation of the contract.[55]

Notwithstanding the above, the PLACL reflect a stronger policy option in favour of contractual equilibrium between the parties, for example in the rules on the interpretation of the contract that are not expressly found either in the CISG or in the PICC (see Article 69 PLACL). At this point, it is not clear whether a concrete principle to protect the weaker party is derived from the good faith principle under the CISG. Although some scholars believe it is,[56] presumably considering the weaker party as consumers, in international trade the parties tend to be businessmen or professionals and thus equal or comparable bargaining power is presumed.[57] Consumer transactions fall outside the scope of CISG (Article 2 (a)).

Unlike the soft law instruments, the CISG is an international treaty (*hard law* instrument) that applies to international sale of goods contracts when states ratify, accept and approve the Convention and when certain conditions of applicability are met (Articles 1–6 CISG). Therefore, there is no need to mention the CISG as the applicable law when the conditions of application are met, but indeed a need

[54] *Appellate Tribunal of Helsinki* (Finland) 26 October 2000, CISG-Online 1078. The loyalty principle is expressly recognised in Art 5.1.3 PICC and Art 1:202 PECL.

[55] § 1-304 of the Uniform Commercial Code (UCC) (2001). The obligation of good faith states that: 'Every *contract* or duty within [the UCC] imposes an obligation of *good faith* in its performance and enforcement' (emphasis added).

[56] MJ Bonell, 'L'Interpretazione del Diritto Uniforme alla Luce dell'Art. 7 della Convenzione di Vienna Sulla Vendita Internazionale' [1986] *Rivista di diritto Civile* 223.

[57] In agreement with this conclusion: Martínez Cañellas (n 33) 145. Principle no I.9 of the Central list of principles of the *lex mercatoria*: 'no weaker party exists in international business transactions that needs to be protected as if it were a consumer' (Central at www.tldb.net).

to *opt out* from it expressly in order to exclude the Convention.[58] As an international treaty, the CISG is incorporated by states as national law, whereas the Principles are a set of rules without binding character either for individuals or for states. This could be deemed a disadvantage but is, on the contrary, a great advantage, since the Principles can easily be reviewed so as to adapt them to the demands of contract law practice. Indeed, the PLACL are not hard law, and they cannot be turned into hard law simply because their drafters express their intention to do so in the Preamble. As to the CISG, being an international treaty, the formal process of amending it can be quite arduous, but the way in which interpretation and gap-filling of the CISG has evolved over the past 35 years of application is eloquent proof of how the modernisation and adaptation of the Convention to the requirements of international trade has evolved over time.

C. Issues Covered

The PLACL are designed as a general code for private law contracts in Latin America. More than formulating principles, they draft specific and concrete rules of general contract law corresponding to the general theory of the law of contracts in civil law systems: formation of the contract through offer and acceptance, including rules on contract negotiation, defects of the contract (mistake, fraud, threat and gross disparity), and subject-matter, cause and formal requirements of the contract; nullity of the contract: absolute and relative nullity, its effects, simulation; effects of a contract on third persons (agency, contracts in favour of third parties, and promise that the third party will do something); interpretation; performance and non-performance of contractual obligations. The language of the text was adapted from the CISG, to more general terms such as 'the parties', or 'obligor'/'obligee'.[59]

The Principles cover the broad area of private law, meaning civil and commercial contracts, and thus, contrary to the PICC, do not limit their sphere of application to contracts which are considered to be commercial. This is problematic since, on the one hand, there are legal systems with a dual regulation depending on the nature of the contract (civil or commercial) and, on the other hand, some legal systems recognise only one regulation without prejudice to the existence of some special rules, usually intended to meet the specific needs of commercial

[58] Hence the exclusion of the CISG by opting into the PLACL is to be decided autonomously under the CISG. See CISG-AC Opinion No 16 (n 35), Opinion no 1; I Schwenzer, 'CESL and CISG' in EA Quintana Adriano (ed), *The Evolution of Global Trade Over the Last Thirty Years* (Mexico, Universidad Nacional Autónoma de México, 2014) 334, reflecting upon the CESL and the CISG.

[59] See Art 1(11) PICC for the definition of 'obligor' and 'obligee'. '"Obligor" refers to the party who is to perform an obligation and "obligee" refers to the party who is entitled to performance of that obligation'. The Official Comment points out that the terms 'obligor' and 'obligee' are used, irrespective of whether the obligation is non-monetary or monetary.

transactions, as happens in the Swiss or Italian legal systems. From my point of view, the solution adopted by the drafters of the PLACL is more in line with the European instruments (PECL and DCFR) and a sensible one, in that it will cover both civil and commercial contracts between two businessmen or between a businessman and a professional. Many legal systems do not recognise the latter as a businessman.[60]

Nevertheless, it is not entirely clear to me from the text of the Principles whether consumer transactions are excluded, as they usually are in international commercial instruments.[61] In principle, one might conclude that the lack of any express reference to them in the text and the fact that there are no specific provisions geared to protecting consumers are in line with the exclusion of B2C transactions from the scope of application of the Principles[62] and follow the classical trend in uniform commercial law of excluding from its sphere of influence transactions with consumers.[63] The main reason for excluding such transactions is the desire not to interfere with domestic mandatory rules designed to protect the so-called 'weaker party' in the contractual relationship; clearly, there is no weaker party in uniform international commercial law or, at least, the differences between the parties are not as pronounced as they frequently are in consumer transactions.

Even though at first glance the Vienna Convention restricts its sphere of application to sale of goods contracts, it has in fact been extended to other contracts, first by virtue of Article 3 CISG itself,[64] and secondly, by the development of scholarly writings and case law.[65] Furthermore, the CISG rules could be applied to every kind of international commercial contract (and even to national ones), since they regulate the obligations and rights of the parties in a manner typical of the general theory of contracts. The model role developed by the CISG and its impact on both domestic and international legislators with regard to the general theory of contract law, as shown, for example, in the introduction to this chapter, is not surprising. In terms of the issues covered by the CISG compared to the PLACL, the CISG does not cover all the aspects of validity such as defects, nullity and

[60] Art 66 PLACL might be seen as a provision which takes into account professional activities.

[61] See the Official Comment to the Preamble of the PICC; also Art 2(a) CISG.

[62] For example, silence or inaction as acceptance in Art 21 PLACL runs contrary to the well-established principle in consumer transactions where silence or inaction cannot be considered as acceptance, with no exceptions.

[63] This trend supposes, as an indirect effect, the implied conception of the business and professional character of the sphere of application of the Uniform Rules. See R Illescas Ortiz, 'El Derecho uniforme del comercio internacional: elementos de base' in *Estudios de Derecho Mercantil en Homenaje al profesor Manuel Broseta Pont*, vol II (Valencia, Tirant lo blanch, 1995) 1788.

[64] P Perales Viscasillas, 'Los contratos "mixtos" del artículo 3.1 de la Convención de Viena de 1980 sobre compraventa internacional de mercancías' in J Oviedo Albán (ed), *Contratos: Teoría General, principios y tendencias*, 2nd edn (Bogota, Ibáñez, 2012) 461–88; id, 'From and Before The CISG, To and Beyond the EU Directive 1999/44 on the Sale of Consumer Goods' (2001) 38 *Uniform Commercial Code Law Journal* 137–58; and CISG-AC, Opinion no 4 (n 33).

[65] P Perales Viscasillas, 'International Distribution Contracts and CISG' in I Schwenzer, YM Atamer and P Butler (eds), *Current Issues in the CISG and Arbitration* (The Hague, Eleven International Publishing, 2014) 43–58.

simulation of the contract, nor the effects of a contract on third persons, since those are issues excluded from the scope of the Convention (Article 4 CISG); and, indeed, the rules on the scope of application in both texts are radically different, as we have seen above.

III. The Principles of Latin American Contract Law and the CISG: A General Comparison of the Principles Embodied in Both Texts

Freedom of contract, binding force of contract and good faith are the only principles recognised outright by the drafters of the Latin American text. They are contained in section 2 (General Principles) of chapter 1 (Preamble) of the PLACL and others may be derived from the text and will be compared with those embodied within the CISG. The search for these other general principles is a tedious process of deduction or induction from the provisions of the PLACL,[66] but such a list of general principles has the important function of recognising a whole set of common provisions, widely acknowledged in other international and regional instruments of modern contract law,[67] that might guide judges, arbitrators and the contracting parties in developing domestic law and, of course, in the application and interpretation both of the Principles and the contract clauses themselves (Article 4 PLACL); furthermore, the Principles are a model to be considered by national[68] and international legislators as a framework around which to build specific rules.[69] The general principles function as a mechanism to protect against possible abuses and excesses by the parties. Accordingly, the Principles establish both intrinsic and extrinsic limits to the contract.

[66] To some extent, the same can be said when analysing the PICC or CISG. With regard to the PICC, Vogenauer (n 17) 300 has stated that: 'the PICC seem to envisage a complex structure of, first, top level principles ("fundamental", "basic" or "general" principles); secondly, intermediate or subordinate principles as "direct applications" of the former; and, finally, ordinary and specific black letter rules that are, at best, "indirect" applications of the first group'.

[67] See a recent comparison of the most important principles in the PICC, PECL, CISG, Acquis Principles, DCFR, and the CESL, and a hint of the reception of those principles into the draft codification in France: Vogenauer (n 17) 299ff, with special reference to the benefits of codifying general principles, albeit in a relatively small list and with a proposal of eight guidelines to codify them (ibid, 316–17).

[68] Inter alia, recently in Spain, Draft Commercial Code, Book IV (2014), taking from the PICC and the CISG the general principles of: freedom of contract, binding force of the contract, freedom of form, confidentiality, common intention of the parties in the interpretation of the contract, solidarity, cooperation, good faith and reasonableness.

[69] See for an approach to building general principles common to all contracts of the world as a first step in creating a global contract code, and indeed as a model or as gap-filler: O Lando, 'CISG and Its Followers: A Proposal to Adopt some International Principles of Contract Law' (2005) 53 *American Journal of Comparative Law* 401. For a historical reference to the codification of some principles, particularly in civil law countries with special reference to freedom of contract and good faith: Vogenauer (n 17) 293–99.

As has been rightly pointed out by Professor Vogenauer:[70]

> General principles of contract law at the outset of these texts help us better understand the general nature of the instruments. Their presence or absence, their exact formulation and their position within the overall context of a given instrument provide us with an idea as to how their black letter rules will attempt to strike the balance between freedom and social justice. Such guideposts are particularly useful in a transnational context where there is no shared background legal culture, as it exists in national jurisdictions. In the past, as this contribution has shown, general principles of contract law were not codified when they were either not yet fully established or so well-established that they were regarded as self-evident and their codification would have seemed superfluous, if not ridiculous. This is precisely not the case with the transnational instruments discussed in this contribution. They will be applied by lawyers with very different understandings of the role and function of contracts in law, society and the economy. In these circumstances, there are no self-evident or obvious solutions, and laying down a number of fundamental provisions will help them in gradually finding common ground.

As noted, although the PLACL have the word 'Principles' in their title, in fact only some of their provisions are principles in the traditional sense. Again in the words of Professor Vogenauer[71] in relation to the PECL and the PICC:

> This is intended to highlight their nonbinding or 'soft law' character. Only some of the provisions in these instruments are, however, 'principles' in the jurisprudential sense, ie, standards that guide, but do not necessarily determine the outcome of a given case and that can be outweighed by countervailing principles. From the perspective of legal theory, the majority of the articles of the PICC and the PECL are straightforward 'rules' that do not possess such a specific 'dimension of weight', but more or less dictate the outcome of a given case in an 'all-or-nothing' fashion.

No wonder, then, that he proposes to change the word 'principles' to 'fundamental provisions' in order to avoid 'the confusion that flows from the inconsistent use of the enigmatic term "principle" across different jurisdictions'.[72] However, it seems to us that common lawyers nowadays are more than used to the term 'principles', a notion already incorporated into their domestic legal systems by means of uniform law instruments, mainly the CISG, that have in common a provision dealing with interpretation and supplementation of the international instruments through the general principles on which they are based (cf Article 7 CISG).[73]

In conclusion, we shall extract some general principles from both the PLACL and the CISG, considering the word 'principles' in as flexible and broad a way as possible.[74] Some general legal principles are established, whether in the form of

[70] Vogenauer (n 17) 316.

[71] ibid, 310.

[72] ibid, 316–17.

[73] See P Perales Viscasillas, 'Article 7' in S Kröll, L Mistelis and P Perales Viscasillas (eds), *UN Convention for the International Sale of Goods (CISG)* (Munich, CH Beck, 2011) 40–141 (comparable rules).

[74] For the problems of terminology and classification with regard to languages and systems of 'Principles' under the different legal international and European instruments: Vogenauer (n 17) 310–12.

veritable principles (for example, freedom of form, Article 11 CISG), duties or rights (for example, a duty to cooperate is a clear principle of cooperation), or specific rules whence concrete principles are derived (for example, from Article 57(1)(a) CISG it is considered a principle that the place of payment of any monetary obligation under the CISG is determined by the creditor's place of business and as such fills an important gap for the interest rate within the CISG).

A. The Principle of Freedom of Contract (Article 5 PLACL)

The PLACL state the principle of freedom of contract in Article 5 (Freedom of contract): 'The parties are free to enter into contracts and to determine their content'. In this, they follow Article 1.1 PICC. This principle is also found in the CISG, where it is referred to as party autonomy under Article 6.[75] This Article requires little comment since it only stipulates a generally recognised principle in international and domestic private law. By virtue of the freedom of contract, the parties can conclude a contract as well as fix its content in the form they deem most convenient. This principle is mirrored in Article 4(1) PLACL (similar to Article 1.5 PICC), which permits the parties to exclude or modify the application of the Latin American Principles as well as modify or derogate from any of their provisions.

The freedom of contract principle in the PLACL, which is very broadly formulated, has some limits, inter alia:

(a) The freedom of the parties may not violate the law or public policy (Article 5).
(b) Public policy and mandatory rules, whether national, international or supranational, that are applicable in accordance with PIL rules (Article 2); this limitation also applies to the subject-matter of the contract (Article 38).
(c) The duty to act in good faith (Article 7); the principle of contract equilibrium is derived from this and is useful in assessing the content of the contract and thus the freedom of contract of the parties. Express recognition of this formula is recognised inter alia in the Principles, for example, in Article 37 (Gross disparity) and Article 69 (Ambiguous clauses), which also refers to criteria such as dependence of the aggrieved or affected party, its extraordinary economic distress, its (imperative) urgent needs, its ignorance, its lack of experience or its lack of bargaining skills.
(d) The limitation of usages and practices to the freedom of contract (Article 3(2)).
(e) Finally, there is the limitation adopted in chapter 2, section 2 of the PLACL. We are referring to Article 10, which, on the one hand, extends the freedom

[75] The principle of party autonomy is recognised by CISG-AC Opinion No 16 (n 35), Opinion no 1, and Comment 1.

of the parties to the pre-contractual stage, ie the stage preceding the offer, where it states that 'the parties are free to negotiate the contractual terms and to withdraw from the negotiations at any time', while on the other hand it curbs that freedom by penalising the party that acted in bad faith (Article 11(1) and (3)).

B. The Principle of *Pacta Sunt Servanda*

Article 6 (Binding force of the contract, similar to Article 1.3 PICC (Binding character of the contract)), indicates that: 'A contract validly entered into is binding upon the parties'. A contract that has been concluded in accordance with the rules on formation of the contract and has likewise been validly concluded, in compliance with the rules on validity or with the mandatory rules, is binding upon the parties. The contracting parties are thus obliged to comply with the terms of the contract.

The principle of *pacta sunt servanda* is solidly established and accepted in the various national legal systems, as well in the international arena, but is limited in its application by some rules in the Principles aimed at achieving a fair balance between the parties: Article 37 (Gross disparity), Article 69 (Ambiguous clauses), Article 70 (*Contra proferentem* rule), and Article 82 (Force majeure or acts of God).

As has been shown, freedom of contract and binding force of the contract are seminal principles in the Latin American instrument; however, both are subject to limitations. Too many restrictions would arguably lead to inconsistencies within the Principles[76] and dilute them beyond recognition, and so dissuade the parties from opting into the instrument due to lack of certainty as to the possible outcome of their agreement. This is what happened to the CESL, which was forced to introduce excessive limitations to party autonomy because it treated B2B relationships as consumer ones.

C. The Principle of Good Faith

The recognition of the principle of good faith (formulated in the PICC as 'good faith and fair dealing') as a mandatory standard of behaviour of the parties and not merely, as in Article 7(1) CISG, as a principle of interpretation of the Convention, was one of the greatest and best-founded innovations of the UNIDROIT Principles (Article 1.7 PICC). This provision has been the model for Article 7 PLACL.

Good faith under the PLACL has been deleted from the interpretative principles (as in Article 7(1) CISG) and relocated in an independent provision with a mandatory character ('Agreements limiting good faith shall have no effect whatsoever')

[76] As considered by Vogenauer (n 17) 314–15, in relation to the DCFR.

(Article 7(2)). At the same time, the PLACL give to good faith its natural content ('The parties must act in accordance with the requirements of good faith') (Article 7(1)).[77]

The principle of good faith takes a prominent place throughout the PLACL, in sharp contrast to the CISG, which only mentions it in Article 7(1). Accordingly, there is disagreement among scholars about the function that good faith might play under the CISG.[78] Under the PLACL, good faith is considered and applied throughout the life of the contract: during pre-negotiations (prior to the offer), during the formation strictly speaking, ie during the exchange of offer and acceptance that leads to the conclusion of the contract, and, lastly, during the performance of the contract.

The good faith principle is regarded as a *duty of the parties* in contract negotiation (Article 10 PLACL), including the duty to compensate for the loss caused by withdrawing from the negotiations in bad faith (Article 11(1) PLACL). It is also found in Article 18(2) PLACL (Irrevocable offer); Article 29(1)(b) PLACL (Grounds for mistake, as a duty on one of the parties); and Article 54(3) PLACL (Simulation and third parties).

Likewise, good faith is contemplated as a *general principle for the interpretation of the contract* (Article 71 PLACL), for example in fixing the time of acceptance and thus, expiry of the offer (Articles 19(4) and 23(1) PLACL), the time of performance (Article 74(1) PLACL), or in assessing gross disparity in order to adapt the contract (Article 37(1) PLACL) or the validity of limitation and exemption clauses (Article 111 PLACL), and as a *gap-filling tool* for the courts to adjust the contract (Article 37(3) PLACL).

However, its relocation should not be taken as an indication that good faith cannot be considered as a principle of interpretation of the PLACL, as it does in Article 7(1) CISG.

D. Other Principles

The Principles, as stated before, are important also in terms of filling the internal gaps of the text, as considered by Article 4(3) PLACL: 'Issues within the scope of these Principles but not expressly settled by them are as far as possible to be settled in accordance with their underlying general principles'. Since recourse to the general principles is an important tool for the interpretation both of the text of the Principles and the contract, and because some other principles—apart from

[77] The PECL also view the good faith and fair dealing principle in a manner very similar to that of the PICC. See A Hartkamp, 'The UNIDROIT Principles of International Commercial Contracts and the Principles of European Contract Law' (1994) 2 *European Review of Private Law* 343–44.

[78] Going too far: Schwenzer (n 58) 338, considering that a far-reaching principle of good faith under the CISG is hardly reconcilable with the need for certainty and predictability in commercial transactions and would not be recognised by common law lawyers.

those expressly mentioned in Articles 5–7 PLACL—may be found within the text, Table 6.2 offers a list of these principles (as well as some duties) and compares them with the general principles of the CISG.

Table 6.2: General Principles: PLACL v. CISG

	PLACL	CISG
Principle of the primacy of the instrument	YES (Art 1(2))	YES. The pro-Convention Principle
Freedom of contract/ negotiation and their limits	YES (Arts 5 and 9), and Art 6 (binding force of the contract, ie, *pacta sunt servanda*). Express limits considered, inter alia, public policy and mandatory rules (Art 2), and good faith (Arts 10 and 11)	YES. In more general terms (Art 6): party autonomy. No express limits except Arts 12 and 96
Principle of primacy of mandatory rules—public order	YES (Art 2)	NO. Matters dealt with by CISG are expressly regulated by it with exclusion of domestic law. But see the borderline with validity issues
Principle of good faith	YES. A strong presence. A *duty on the parties.* Imperative character (Art 7). A duty to follow in contract negotiations (Art 10) Good faith found in Arts 18(2), 29(1)(b) and 54. Also, good faith as a *general principle for the interpretation of the contract* (Art 71), as well as a *gap-filling tool* for the courts to adjust the contract (Art 37(3))	YES. A limited presence. As a principle of interpretation (Art 7(1)). Case law has considered good faith as a general principle in the formation and performance of the contract Other general principles derived from good faith are also found, such as estoppel or *venire contra factum proprium*
Primacy of usages and practices	YES (Art 3): source of the contract Also as a rule for interpretation, inter alia, Art 21 (silence), Art 65 (common intention of the parties), Art 74(1) (time of performance)	YES (Art 9): source of the contract. And also as an interpretative tool (Art 8(3))

(continued)

Table 6.2: *(Continued)*

	PLACL	CISG
Interpretation and supplementation of the instrument by the underlying general principles	YES. Seminal role (Art 4). Underlying general principles for the supplementation: yes. Self-sufficient system: no recourse to PIL (Art 4(3))	YES. Centrepiece of the Convention (Art 7) Underlying general principles for supplementation: yes Recourse to PIL (Art 7(2))
Principles of internationality and uniformity	YES. Art 4(2)	YES. Art 7(1)
Strong presence of *causa*: influence of civil law doctrine	YES. In Art 9 as an essential element of the contract, and of the obligations (Art 39)	NO. Irrelevance of *causa* and consideration in international contracts
Duty of confidentiality	YES (Art 12)	NO
Principle of 'reception' (reaching) for the effectiveness of declarations of intent	YES, inter alia, Arts 16, 17(2), 19(1), 22(1), 24, 91 (termination) Exceptions: acts of performance, contract is concluded when the act is performed (Art 22(3)); and acceptance by conduct, conclusion of the contract is when the offeror becomes aware of such conduct (Art 22(1))	YES, inter alia, Arts 15, 16, 23 Exceptions: acts of performance, contract is concluded when the act is performed (Art 18(3)); oral declarations: when the offeror becomes aware of it (Art 24)
Principle of contract formation through offer and acceptance	YES (chapter 2, section 3, Arts 13–24) Modification: no, but a reference in Art 8 Place of conclusion: yes (Art 40)	YES (Part II. Formation of the contract, Arts 14–24) Modification: yes, Art 29 No. Art 7(2)
Principle of reasonableness	YES. But less presence as compared with CISG: reasonable person (Art 28); (un)reasonable results (Art 3(2)); reasonable time (Art 85); reasonable measures (Art 102); reasonable terms (Art 103). In fact, substituted by the principle of good faith in order to determine certain aspects of the contracts (see above, good faith)	YES. (un)reasonable person, time, inconvenience, expenses, opportunity, excuse, length, delay, notice, measures, manner and substitute The term (un)reasonable is used in the CISG on 47 occasions*

(continued)

Table 6.2: *(Continued)*

	PLACL	CISG
Interpretation of the contract: (a) **Principle of primacy of the common intention of the parties**	YES. Art 64. Common intention prevails over the literal meaning of the words, plus Art 65 criteria for determining the common intention of the parties	YES. Impliedly in Arts 7(1) and 8(3), and developed by case law and scholars
(b) **Principle of systematic interpretation**	YES. Art 67	YES. Impliedly in Art 8 and developed by case law
(c) **Principle of preservation of the contract**	YES. Arts 68 and 69	YES. General principle within CISG (Arts 7, 8, 19(2) and 21(2))
(d) **Principle in favour of the contractual equilibrium**	YES. Arts 68 and 69	NO?
(e) ***Contra proferentem* rule**	YES. Art 70	Yes. It is derived from Art 8(2) and case law
(f) **Principle of good faith**	YES. Art 71	YES. Impliedly from Art 7(1) and developed by case law
Abandoning the principle of privity of contracts	YES. The principle of the relative effect of contracts has been overcome by the Principles, which also acknowledge rights and duties for third parties. See Arts 52, 54, 86(2)(a) and 93	NO. Art 4
Principle of termination (avoidance) and defective performance by notice	Termination. YES. Art 90 Effectiveness upon receipt Defective performance. YES. Art 85	Avoidance. YES. Art 26 Effectiveness following mail box rule (Art 27) Defective performance. YES. Art 39
The principle of separability after termination	YES. Art 91	YES. Art 81(1) CISG
The right to withhold performance	YES. Arts 92(1), 95 and 96	YES. Arts 58 and 71, 81(2), 85 and 86(1)

(continued)

Table 6.2: *(Continued)*

	PLACL	CISG
The synallagmatic principle	YES. Arts 92(1), 95 and 96 Concurrent performance principle	YES. Arts 58, 71, 81(2). Concurrent performance
Principle of full compensation and mitigation of damages	YES. Arts 100 and 102 Also the principle that interest is a separate remedy from damages	YES. Arts 74 and 77 Yes, the same in CISG: Art 78

Surprisingly, another well-known principle for both commercial contracts and private contracts in general,[79] the *Principle of freedom of form and proof*, is not recognised as such in the PLACL, probably because of the Article 96 reservation in the CISG made by Chile and Paraguay. Form and formal requirements are observed in accordance with the legal requirements that govern the contract or the law of the place where it is concluded (Article 40(1) PLACL).

Finally, contrary to the CISG, the PLACL do not mention subsidiary recourse to national law.[80] This exclusion is consistent with the creation of an autonomous, self-sufficient system.

IV. The Principles of Latin American Contract Law and the CISG: A Brief Comparison—Formation, Interpretation, Performance and Non-performance

Some general comments, comparing the general principles contained in the CISG and the PLACL and some of their specific provisions in regard to the matters covered by both instruments are set out below.

A. Formation of the Contract

The CISG rules on formation of the contract (Part II, Articles 14–24) provided the preferred model of two important instruments: the PICC and the PECL, followed by OHADA, DCFR and the failed CESL. Also important was the impact of the

[79] See Art 11 CISG and also Art 1.2 PICC (No form required) that states that: 'Nothing in these Principles requires a contract to be concluded in or evidenced by writing. It may be proved by any means, including witnesses'.

[80] The same approach is found in Art 3(2) UNCITRAL Model Law on Electronic Commerce (1996); Art 4(2) UNCITRAL Model Law on Electronic Signature (2001); Art 2(2) UNCITRAL Model Law on International Commercial Conciliation (2002); Art 2A UNCITRAL Model Law on International Commercial Arbitration (1985, as amended in 2006); and Art 4(2) UNIDROIT Model Law on Leasing (2008).

CISG on other international instruments such as The United Nations Convention on the Use of Electronic Communications in International Contracts (2005).

Although the civil and common law systems both analyse problems related to the formation of the contract by means of the traditional separation into two declarations of will (offer and acceptance),[81] there are also divergences between the two systems that, at first glance, appear insuperable. The CISG did attempt to solve them, but unfortunately some issues proved impossible to overcome. The PICC and the PECL for their part turned that lesson to account and managed to achieve a balanced set of rules between the different principles that inspire the two legal systems.

As far as the PLACL are concerned, the rules on contract formation are very similar, except that the CISG has no express rules on the definition and elements of the contract (Articles 8–9 PLACL) nor any rules on contract negotiations (Articles 10–12 PLACL). Section 3 (Formation of consent) covers the conclusion of the contract through offer and acceptance (Articles 13–24 PLACL) in a manner similar to the CISG as well as to other international or regional instruments (PICC, PECL, DCFR, CESL).

The main differences are as set out in the remainder of this section.

i. The Offer: Essential Elements

Under the CISG, for an offer to be considered sufficiently definite it must indicate the goods, their quantity and price (Article 14(1) CISG). Article 15 PLACL (Definition of offer) does not set any requirements for the definiteness of an offer as the CISG does, which makes sense if we consider the different scope of application of the two texts. The PLACL merely require that a proposal to conclude a contract must be sufficiently definite and indicate the intention of the offeror to be bound in case of its acceptance. The PECL and the PICC do not. The CISG follows the general civil law rule in this regard, which requires that the contracts—and hence, the offer—contain the so-called *essentialia negotii*, as opposed to the more flexible approach adopted by the PLACL as taken from common law systems in which the will of the parties (the agreement) and their intention to be bound by the agreement are the essential elements for the conclusion of the contract.

ii. 'Offers' to the Public

According to the Convention (Article 14(1) CISG), a proposal has to be addressed to one or more specific persons. If it is not, it would be considered an invitation to submit an offer, unless the contrary is clearly indicated by the person making the proposal (Article 14(2) CISG). As a consequence, the Convention requires that the offer be addressed to one or more specific persons; otherwise, that which is

[81] Also China's domestic law: see G Rougier-Brierre, 'Spécifités de la negociation et de la pratique contractuelle en Chine' [2007] *International Business Law Journal* 164.

addressed to the general public is considered an invitation to treat. That is to say, so-called public offers are not offers in the sense of the Vienna Convention unless the offeror clearly indicates otherwise, or rather, unless he expressly indicates that the declaration addressed to the general public is an offer. Notwithstanding the above, between those cases in which an offer is addressed to 'one or more specific persons' and those in which an invitation to make offers is addressed to the 'general public', there are certain intermediate situations whose legal classification is not clear (common cases of mailings of catalogues, prospectuses, pamphlets or similar tools to a certain number of people identified by name (the name of the company or personal details identifying the employer) and which contain all the other elements of Article 14 CISG). Such cases must be treated as though they were invitations to make offers[82] since, in international commercial trade, the use of such tools has a perfectly clear purpose: to convey information or to motivate the recipient to make an offer. This criterion has been followed by Article 11 of the United Nations Convention on the Use of Electronic Communications in International Contracts (2005).

The PLACL, following the PECL, take a slightly different approach, so that an offer may be made to one or more specific persons or to the public at large (Article 15(2) PLACL and Article 2:201(2) PECL). Such proposals would then generally be considered as offers, although they could also be considered as invitations to treat, depending on the circumstances (ie, an advertisement to sell a house) and the intention of the offeror. At the same time, a proposal to supply goods or services at stated prices made by a professional supplier in a public advertisement or a catalogue, or by a display of goods, is presumed to be an offer to sell or supply at the stated price while stocks last or the supplier's capacity to supply the service is exhausted. This approach is consistent with the fact that the offeree may be a consumer, but not with expectations in international commercial transactions; as a consequence, the preferred models should be the CISG and the 2005 UN Convention.

iii. The Offer: Withdrawal, Revocation and Expiration

The CISG distinguishes between withdrawal (Article 15) and revocation (Article 16) of the offer, as do the PLACL (Article 16).[83] Revocation of the offer is possible as long as the offer is not irrevocable and it reaches the offeree before he

[82] P Perales Viscasillas, *La formación del contrato de compraventa internacional de mercaderías* (Valencia, Tirant lo blanch, 1996) 287–300. See also Art 154(2) Civil Code of China: 'Exposing goods for sale with their selling price shall be deemed to be an offer. However, the sending of pricelists is not deemed to be an offer'.

[83] Also in the PICC (see Arts 2.1.3 and 2.1.4). But see Arts 2:202 and 2:203 PECL, which are devoted to the revocation and lapse of the offer. There is no rule like that contained in Art 15 CISG or Art 2.1.3 PICC in the chapter dedicated to the formation of the contract, the PICC relating to the withdrawal of an offer; and, in fact, there is no need for one, since the revocation rule in Art 2:202 PECL can also cover those situations in which the offeror changes his mind about sending an offer and takes back its

has sent his notice of acceptance (Article 16(1) CISG; similarly: Articles 2:202(1) PECL and 2.1.4(1) PICC). Both the PLACL and the PECL clarify that an offer may be revoked when its acceptance has been made by conduct before the contract is concluded, ie, when the offeror receives notice of such actions or performance begins (see Articles 17(2) PLACL and 2:205 PECL).

Aside from the possibility of revoking an offer, which is reserved to the offeror, the offeree may also terminate the offer by rejecting it (Article 17 CISG; similarly: Articles 19(1) PLACL, 2:203 PECL and 2.1.5 PICC). The rejection is effective when it reaches the offeror. The rejection of the offer prevents it from coming back to life—for example, if the offeree changes his mind about rejecting the offer and attempts to accept it again. The offer also expires when there is a counter-offer (see also Articles 19(1) CISG and 19(2) PLACL), or if the offer it is not accepted within the time fixed or, if no time is fixed, within a reasonable time (Article 18(2) CISG) or within a time that may be expected in good faith (Article 19(4) PLACL). The PLACL also explicitly cover the expiry of the offer when the offeror dies or is incapacitated prior to receiving the acceptance (Article 19(3) PLACL), contrary to what has been considered by scholars with regard to the CISG.[84]

iv. Irrevocability of the Offer

One of the most controversial rules in the CISG is the rule related to the irrevocability of an offer. Just as the Convention establishes the general rule in respect of the time when an offer can be revoked (until the dispatch of an acceptance or the conclusion of the contract), it also sets out when an offer can be considered irrevocable. An offer cannot be revoked (Article 16(2) CISG):

(a) if it indicates, whether by stating a fixed time for acceptance or otherwise, that it is irrevocable; or
(b) if it was reasonable for the offeree to rely on the offer as being irrevocable and the offeree has acted in reliance on the offer.

Under the Convention, it is not clear whether a fixed period of time for acceptance means that the offer is irrevocable, or that a time period exists for the offeree to accept the offer, past which time the offer expires. This ambiguity results from the very wording of Article 16(2)(a) CISG, which was written in the way it was because no agreement could be reached on the meaning of a fixed period of time for acceptance.

effectiveness by withdrawing his first declaration of intention that was sent. In any event, the withdrawal of a notice is a concept that extends to the offer and the acceptance and is regulated under chapter 1 in Art 1:303(5) PECL. It is a useful concept from a theoretical point of view. Also, in the US legal system, the word 'revocation' covers both cases: the withdrawal as well as the revocation of the offer. See P Winship, 'Formation of International Sales Contracts under the 1980 Vienna Convention' (1983) 23 *International Lawyer* 7. However, EA Farnsworth, *On Contracts*, 3rd edn (New York, Aspen Law and Business, 1999) no 3.17, n 1, follows the distinction, probably influenced by the CISG.

[84] See Perales Viscasillas (n 82) 215ff.

Although the PICC have not been able to solve the problem of interpretation under the CISG, the PECL, conscious of the divergent solutions under the Convention, solve the problem in their Article 2:202(3)(b), in accordance with which the revocation of an offer is ineffective if it states a fixed time for its acceptance. This seems to be consistent with the scope of application of the European Principles, which also cover consumer contracts. The PLACL follow the same approach as the PECL: Article 18(1) PLACL considers that an offer is irrevocable if the offeror has fixed a time for its acceptance and the offeror does not expressly reserve the power to revoke it.

Another way in which an offer may be considered irrevocable, even when the offeror has not indicated it, is when an offer creates the appearance to the offeree of being irrevocable to the extent that the latter relies on it as such and carries out some type of action related to it (*promissory estoppel*). This doctrine, which is derived from the common law,[85] is also recognised in civil law systems as the general principle of *venire contra factum proprium* as a specification of the good faith principle. In these situations, the offeror cannot revoke his offer (Article 18(2) PLACL, which expressly refers to reliance in good faith, Article 2:202(3)(c) PECL, Article 16(2)(b) CISG and Article 2.1.4(2)(b) PICC). Situations in which a period is set for acceptance could easily create the appearance to the offeree that the offer is irrevocable. Thus, if the offeree carries out some type of action related to the offer, such as investments in his company or the purchase of materials, hiring of experts, consultants, lawyers, etc., he can rely on the protection provided by the CISG.[86] In any of these situations in which the offeror has attempted to revoke an offer without being entitled to do so, the offeree may accept it.

v. Acceptance

An acceptance is the positive response to an offer. It must be made clearly and unconditionally by the acceptor. Acceptance can take place in three ways: by means of a declaration, an action or conduct, or even by means of silence or inaction (Articles 20(1) and 21 PLACL). The approach taken by the PLACL is the same as that in the CISG and indeed is also similar to that of the PICC and the PECL (see Article 18 CISG).[87] Express inclusion of the factors that allow silence to be considered as an acceptance is found in Article 21 PLACL (operation of law, the intention of the parties, customs and usages, or the prior conduct of the

[85] See section 90 Restatement (Second) of Contracts; Farnsworth (n 84) no 2.19 and no 3.25; JD Calamari and JM Perillo, *The Law of Contracts*, 3rd edn (St Paul, MN, West, 1987) nos 6-1 and 6-7.

[86] See section 87 Restatement (Second) of Contracts; Farnsworth (n 84) no 3.25ff.

[87] Perales Viscasillas (n 82) 534ff. See also Arts 1939 and 1940 Civil Code of Louisiana. The Principles, unlike the CISG, discuss acceptance by acts of performance but do not include a rule related to the time limit for acceptance when the offer is made orally. In the case of oral offers, the Convention requires that acceptance be immediate, unless circumstances indicate otherwise. In other words, the Convention establishes a more rigid period of time for acceptance when the offer is made orally than when it is made in writing (see Art 18(2) CISG).

parties); this is different from the CISG, but has no practical consequences since the case law and legal scholarship have already considered them.[88] Nevertheless, no value can be attached to a statement contained in an offer establishing that silence on the part of the offeree will be considered an acceptance since, in that case, the offeree would be bound from the very birth of the contract by a simple, unilateral declaration by the offeror.

vi. Counter-offer

Article 19 CISG overcomes the rigidity of applying the 'mirror image rule'[89] to contract formation, making a distinction between terms that materially alter the terms of the offer (counter-offer) and those that do not (acceptance). It might be that despite the immaterial terms added in the response to the offer, the offeror does not wish to be bound by them. Although, according to the Convention, the offeror is certainly not obliged to be bound, he must react to the response, otherwise his silence or inaction means acceptance of the immaterial terms (Article 19(2)).

A declaration of acceptance must coincide with each and every term of an offer in order to conclude a contract (Article 19(1) CISG and Article 2:208(1) PECL, Article 2.11(1) PICC). Such requirement is known as the 'mirror image rule', since the acceptance must be the exact reflection of the offer in a mirror. An exception is made for the possible introduction of new terms into the acceptance that do not substantially alter the offer. In that case, the acceptance will be valid, and the contract will consist both of the terms of the offer and those included in the acceptance that do not substantially alter the offer unless the offeror objects to the new terms without delay (Article 19(2) CISG, Article 2:208(3)(b) PECL, and section 2-207(2)(c) of the Uniform Commercial Code (UCC)); the offer does not expressly limit acceptance to the terms of the offer (Article 2:208(1) PECL, and section 2-207(2)(a) UCC); or the offeree does not make his acceptance conditional upon the offeror's assent to the additional or different terms and the assent reaches the offeree within a reasonable time (Article 14 CISG, Article 2:208(3)(c) PECL, Article 2.11(2) PICC and section 2-207(1) UCC).

On the other hand, if the element that is introduced in the acceptance adds new terms, modifies the terms of the offer or introduces any other type of limitation in the offer that substantially alters it, the contract will not be considered concluded,

[88] Perales Viscasillas (n 82) 512ff, and the scholars cited. They are: (a) legal provisions such as in Arts 19(2) and 21 CISG; (b) usages and practices established between the parties; and (c) the existence of a duty to respond. This is exactly how the courts in the United States understood it in one of the first cases to apply the Vienna Convention: *Filanto v Chilewich*, available at http://www.cisg.law.pace.edu/cases/920414u1.html.

[89] Art 1943 Civil Code of Louisiana: 'An acceptance not in accordance with the terms of the offer is deemed to be a counteroffer', and Art 160 Civil Code of China: 'An acceptance with amplifications, limitations or other alterations shall be deemed to be a refusal of the original offer and the making of a new offer'.

and the response to the offer will become a counter-offer (that is, if it meets all the requirements set by the Principles in order for it to be considered an offer in and of itself (see Article 2:208(1) PECL, Article 2.11(1) PICC, and Article 14 CISG and section 2-207 UCC).

The PLACL follow the same approach but include a case of rejection of the offer if the offer expressly demands full or partial acceptance of the proposed terms and the response alters any of the terms of the offer (Article 25(3)(a) PLACL).

Like the CISG, the PLACL contain no specific rule for the battle of the forms, contrary to Article 2.1.22 PICC or Article 2:209 PECL, which adopt the 'knock-out rule'.[90] There are no express provisions on non-negotiated terms, except for Article 70 (Clauses not negotiated bilaterally: these are to be interpreted against the party that proposed them). Unlike the CISG, the PLACL do have a rule on the place of conclusion of the contract (Article 40), while this issue is usually considered a matter that is outside the scope of the CISG and thus left to domestic law.[91]

Finally, it is worth mentioning that no rule similar to Article 29 CISG on modification of the contract is found in the PLACL, even though it has been adopted by other international instruments. The only reference to modification is found in Article 8 in connection with the definition of the contract.

B. Interpretation of the Contract

With the exception of Article 8, the CISG has no rules on the interpretation of the contract, and even this provision does not directly address the interpretation of the contract but rather, the interpretation of statements made by and conduct of a party. However, with respect to the interpretation of the contract, the general principles on which the CISG is based, particularly good faith and the international character of the Convention, may play an important role as well.[92] Furthermore, some principles of interpretation of the contract have been developed under the CISG.

The rules on the interpretation of the contract in the PLACL are more developed than those derived from the CISG. The PLACL follow the rules of the PICC, adopting the principle of primacy of the common intention of the parties (Article 64 PLACL and Article 4.1 PICC) and subsequently establishing the criteria for determining the common intention of the parties (Article 65 PLACL and Articles 4.1(2), 4.2 and 4.3 PICC). Although this principle is not

[90] CISG-AC Opinion No 13, Inclusion of Standard Terms under the CISG, Rapporteur: Sieg Eiselen. Adopted by the CISG Advisory Council following its 17th meeting in Villanova, Pennsylvania, USA, on 20 January 2013.

[91] See, P Perales Viscasillas, 'Articles 14 through 24. Chapter 12' in HM Flechtner, RA Brand and MS Walter (eds), *Drafting Contracts Under the CISG* (Oxford, Oxford University Press, 2007) 295–327.

[92] Cour de Cassation (France) 30 June 2004, CISG-Online 870. See also: A Zuppi, 'Article 8', in S Kröll, L Mistelis and P Perales Viscasillas (eds), *UN Convention for the International Sale of Goods (CISG)* (Munich, CH Beck, 2011) no 22.

expressly established in the Convention, it is derived from Article 7(2), which rejects the common law approach to interpretation based upon a strict and literal reading.[93] Moreover, it also derives from either Article 8 CISG in general, or from Article 8(3) CISG in particular, which also make it possible to look beyond the 'four corners of the contract';[94] in fact, the list of circumstances in that provision is in most cases replicated as the factors used to identify the common intention of the parties under the PLACL and the PICC.

The Principles also consider how to interpret words and terms of art (Article 66 PLACL and Article 4.3(e) PICC). Other principles of interpretation adopted by the PLACL derive from the PICC: the principle of systematic interpretation (Article 67 PLACL and Article 4.4 PICC), the principle of preservation of the contract (Article 68 PLACL and Article 4.5 PICC) as well as the principle of interpretation in favour of the contractual equilibrium in case of ambiguous clauses (Article 69 PLACL), the *contra proferentem* rule (Article 70 PLACL and Article 4.6 PICC), and finally, the principle of interpretation of the contract in accordance with good faith (Article 71 PLACL).

No specific rule for the supplementation of contracts, as in Article 4.8 PICC, has been adopted by the PLACL.

C. Performance of Contractual Obligations

Chapter 7 of the PLACL (Performance of contractual obligations) establishes principles similar to those derived from the CISG, such as the concept, place, time of performance, early performance or enforceability of an obligation. See, for example, for the concept of performance (Article 72 PLACL and Articles 30 and 53 CISG), and as gap-filler for the place of a monetary obligation, the place of the creditor (Article 73(3)(a) PLACL and 57(1)(a) CISG).[95]

However, in my view, the PLACL have an important lacuna since they do not take into account the fact that in regional and international contracts, the goods must be transported and thus a similar rule to Article 31(1)(a) CISG should have been considered in order to determine the place for the subject-matter of the

[93] See G Bell, 'How the Fact of Accepting Good Faith as a General Principle of the CISG Will Bring More Uniformity' (2005–2006) 16 *Review of the Convention on Contracts for the International Sale of Goods (CISG)* 5.

[94] Zuppi (n 92) no 26; P Huber and A Mullis, *The CISG: A New Textbook for Students and Practitioners* (The Hague, Sellier European Law Publishers, 2007) 12.

[95] Oberlandesgericht Düsseldorf (Germany) 2 July 1993, CISG-Online 74. The better rule derived from Arts 57(1) and 7 CISG is that such payment is to be made at the obligee's place of business. Therefore, one might go even further and infer that the place of payment of any monetary obligation under the CISG is determined by the creditor's place of business. However, there are opposing views, see UNCITRAL, *Digest of Case Law on the CISG*, Art 7 para 11, *inter alia*: Cour d'Appel de Paris (France) 14 January 1998, CISG-Online no 347, unable to derive a general principle, and thus the Court held that Art 57(1)(a) does not express a general principle on the place of payment, because in the cases it governs the seller and the creditor coincide.

obligation when the contract involves carriage of the goods. The rules to determine that place, in the case of specific goods, indicate the place where the goods were located when the obligation was concluded, and, for all other obligations, and as a residual general rule, the address of the obligor (Article 73(3)(b) and (c) PLACL, similar to Article 31(1)(b) and (c) CISG).

As to the time of performance (Article 74 PLACL), although the Principles purport to differentiate between cases where the performance can take place immediately or when a lapse of time is required, they do not in fact do so, since in both situations 'it shall be performed within the shortest time possible after the conclusion of the contract'. I do not see any difference between the two situations that seem to be intended to be different by the drafters.

D. Non-performance of Contractual Obligations

Chapter 8 of the PLACL (Non-performance of contractual obligations) (Articles 79–111) follow some of the principles enshrined in the CISG:

- The very same remedial system as in the CISG (compare Article 84 PLACL with Articles 45 and 61 CISG).
- The concept of fundamental breach (Article 80(d) PLACL) that is the basis for the termination of the contract (Article 89 PLACL and Articles 49(1)(a) and 64(1)(a) CISG). Fundamental breach is also rightly required for replacement (Article 87(2) PLACL and Article 46(2) CISG; different from the PECL), but the concept is formulated more broadly as compared with Article 25 CISG. In regard to terminology: 'termination' is chosen instead of 'avoidance', which is found in the CISG, so the PLACL follow the PICC and the terminology used in European legal texts.[96]
- The rule in Article 80 CISG is formulated in Article 81 PLACL.
- The concept of force majeure (Article 82 PLACL, which is an impediment under Article 79 CISG). As in the CISG, no specific hardship provision is found in the PLACL, so the PLACL may well develop an interpretation similar to that under the CISG.[97]
- The Principles also adopt the duty to communicate non-conforming performance within a reasonable time (Article 85(1) PLACL and Article 39(1) CISG).
- The principle of termination by notice (Article 90 PLACL and Article 26 CISG) and thus *ipso facto* rejecting avoidance of the contract. The Principles

[96] For a criticism of this point, arguing that it does not build up into a common and universal language: Schwenzer (n 58) 350–51.

[97] CISG-AC Opinion No 7, Exemption of Liability for Damages under Article 79 of the CISG, Rapporteur: Alejandro M Garro. Adopted by the CISG-AC at its 11th meeting in Wuhan, People's Republic of China, on 12 October 2007.

have, however, retained judicial termination, which is not excluded from the CISG if notice is made within the reasonable time stipulated in Article 26 CISG.[98]

— The Principles also follow the same (or very similar) legal scheme for the effects of termination (Article 91 PLACL and Article 81(1) CISG) and restitution (Article 92 PLACL and Article 81(2) CISG), price reduction (compare Article 88 PLACL with Article 50 CISG), suspension of performance (Article 96 PLACL and Article 71(1) CISG), damages (Articles 97 and 100 PLACL and Article 74 CISG) including substitute transactions (Article 103 PLACL and Articles 75–76 CISG). They also adopt the principle set out in Article 81(1) CISG whereby certain clauses survive despite termination of the contract (Article 91 PLACL), thereby recognising the separability principle in relation to dispute resolution clauses.

— The PLACL also consider the principle of concurrent performance (Article 95 PLACL and Article 58(1) CISG), the duty to pay interest plus damages (Articles 99, 78(2) PLACL and 78 CISG) and the duty to mitigate damages (Article 102 PLACL and Article 77 CISG).

As to the remedies as adopted in both texts, some differences may be observed:

— Specific performance under the PLACL (Article 86) does not have the same restrictions as provided in the CISG (Article 28) due to procedural constraints in domestic law, so that it is a primary remedy under the PLACL,[99] albeit subject to certain limitations in the case of non-monetary obligations: when performance is impossible, when it is extremely burdensome for the obligor or when it represents an injury to personal dignity.

— No *Nachfrist* remedy under the PLACL. Avoidance of the contract under the CISG goes hand in hand with the principle of *Nachfrist* (Articles 49 and 64 CISG). However, the PLACL do not include the *Nachfrist* remedy, which could be problematic in view of the essential role played by *Nachfrist* in the remedial system.

— The provisions on damages are very similar under both the CISG and the PLACL. However, the PLACL expressly consider non-monetary harm as a damage to recover (Article 98).

[98] See A Björklund, 'Article 26', in S Kröll, L Mistelis and P Perales Viscasillas (eds), *UN Convention for the International Sale of Goods (CISG)* (Munich, C.H. Beck, 2011) no 8.

[99] As considered by Morales Moreno (n 22) 236: 'La defensa de la supremacía de la pretensión de cumplimiento frente a la indemnizatoria, fue justificada en la propia esencia del contrato, el respeto a la palabra dada (pacta sunt servanda), principio básico en la tradición continental y francesa. Y en la prevalencia de la concepción ética del contrato, propia del derecho continental, frente a la puramente economicista, propia del derecho angloamericano'. But as Prof. Morales rightly states: 'deberíamos contar con un sistema procesal tan ágil, que permitiera satisfacer, de inmediato, el derecho del pasajero. Pero esto no es posible. Sin menospreciar el sustrato ético en el que se apoya el derecho de la contratación, hemos operar con cierto pragmatismo. Es muy deseable que todo deudor cumpla lo que prometió; pero de no ser así, lo importante es que el acreedor logre satisfacer su interés in natura a costa del deudor, por una vía alternativa'.

- The Principles also adopt a broader formulation of liability for harm, since in the event of fraud or gross negligence, the obligor is to be liable for all harm resulting from its non-performance (Article 100). The CISG contains no such wording and therefore leaves room for scholarly interpretation or judicial development in this area.
- Finally, contrary to the CISG, the Principles expressly provide for agreements relating to liability for non-performance (penalty clauses, earnest money (*arras*) and limitation and exemption clauses). An interesting point is that Article 99 PLACL is the only provision where interest is referred to, but the Principles fail to provide a solution for the interest rate, which is a highly debated issue under the CISG.[100]

[100] See CISG-AC Opinion No 14, Interest under Article 78 CISG, Rapporteur: Yeşim M Atamer, Adopted unanimously by the CISG Advisory Council following its 18th meeting in Beijing, China, on 21 and 22 October 2013, Black Letter Rule 9: 'In the absence of such agreement, the applicable rate of interest is the rate which the court at the creditor's place of business would grant in a similar contract of sale not governed by the CISG'. The same solution can probably be achieved by virtue of Arts 4(3) and 73(3)(a) PLACL.

Part II

The Principles of Latin American Contract Law: Comparative Analysis

7

The Notion of Contract and its Essential Elements in the Principles of Latin American Contract Law

IÑIGO DE LA MAZA GAZMURI

'Omnis definitio in iure civile periculosa est.'

Javoleno (D. 50. 17. 202)

This chapter is based on a presentation in which I was asked to explain the notion of contract and its essential elements in the Principles of Latin American Contract Law (PLACL). For the PLACL, contract *is* an agreement and its essential elements are consent, subject-matter and cause.

No matter how widespread the notion of contract as an agreement, it is nevertheless an intriguing idea and the PLACL are no exception to this. On the one hand, this is an agreement in which the parties, on the whole, do not deal on much of the content, so we might argue that much of the content of the contract is explained, at best, as a 'hypothetical agreement'. On the other hand, it is accepted that there is an agreement, even if the offer does not coincide entirely with the acceptance. Thirdly—and much more radically—it is accepted that there is an agreement even if one of the parties was unaware of some information which, had it been known to that party, would have led the latter to refuse to contract or to contract on terms very different from those in which it actually did.

This is probably the case for almost any European soft law text that aims to harmonise contract law and to define the contract as an agreement. However, the PLACL add a peculiarity which implies that the consent of the parties is not sufficient to form the contract. It requires two further elements: cause and subject-matter.

In the following pages I will take a closer look at these two issues. The first question is, what kind of agreement is the contract in the PLACL? And the second, why are cause and subject-matter required and what are the risks this represents?

I. The Contract As an Agreement

Article 8 of the PLACL defines the contract as follows:

> A contract is an agreement by means of which two or more parties create, transfer, modify, or extinguish a legal relationship of an economic nature.

This definition is similar to that provided by the Draft Common Frame of Reference (DCFR):

> II.—1:101: Meaning of 'contract' and 'juridical act'
>
> (1) A contract is an agreement which is intended to give rise to a binding legal relationship or to have some other legal effect. It is a bilateral or multilateral juridical act.

It also resembles the definition provided by Article 2(a) of the proposed Regulation to establish a Common European Sales Law (CESL):

> '[C]ontract' means an agreement intended to give rise to obligations or other legal effects.

It is, moreover, a definition which bears some resemblance to that of Article 1101 of the French Civil Code,[1] Article 1254 of the Spanish Civil Code[2] or Article 1438 of the Chilean Civil Code.[3]

In all these cases, the definition of contract links a constitutive act and a particular juridical relationship which is established through it. The structure of this definition probably finds its origin in the notion of legal business typical of the German Pandectist school, conceived as an act in which the author's will is directly geared towards the formation or dissolution of a juridical relationship.[4]

The idea of a contract as an agreement may already be discerned as such in the writings of Christian Wolff, who in turn took his cue from Molina, Grotius and Pufendorf.[5] This idea, according to Gordley, became popular among the Anglo-American, French and German jurists of the nineteenth century.[6]

Today, it appears to be in good health. For example, Treitel states: 'A contract is an agreement giving rise to obligations which are enforced or recognized by law'.[7] We find a similar definition in Bianca: 'The contract is an agreement between two

[1] 'Le contrat est un accord de volontés entre deux ou plusieurs personnes destiné à créer, modifier, transmettre ou éteindre des obligations'.

[2] 'El contrato existe desde que una o varias personas consientes en obligarse, respecto de otra u otras, a dar alguna cosa o prestar algún servicio'.

[3] 'Contrato o convención es un acto por el cual una parte se obliga para con otra a dar, hacer o no hacer alguna cosa. Cada parte puede ser una o muchas personas'.

[4] G Ferri, 'El negocio jurídico' (L. León, transl.), AA VV *Teoría general del negocio jurídico* (Lima, ARA Editores, 2001) 59–61.

[5] J Gordley, *The Philosophical Origins of Modern Contract Doctrine* (Oxford, Oxford University Press, 1991) 75.

[6] ibid, 163.

[7] G Treitel, *The Law of Contract*, 12th edn (London, Sweet & Maxwell, 2010) 1.

or more parties to establish, regulate or extinguish among themselves a patrimonial legal relationship'.[8] Meanwhile—though with much ado about the possibility of a general definition—Ghestin assumes the definition of Marty and Raynaud as a 'convention génératrice d'obligations'.[9]

The idea of agreement can also be found in Farnsworth, in the following terms:

> Books on the law of contracts usually begin by explaining what lawyers mean by the word *contract*. Sometimes lawyers use the word, as it is used in common speech, simply to refer to a writing containing terms on which the parties have agreed. But they often use the word in a more technical sense to mean a *promise*, or a set of promises, that the law will *enforce* or at least recognize in some way.[10]

Farnsworth's commentary warns of the possible difference between promise and agreement. A contract would actually be one or more promises to produce juridical effects. Furthermore, this is how it is defined by the *Restatement (Second) of Contracts*.[11]

Probably, however, the difference is not too relevant for the purpose of this chapter[12] because, as Smith notes, while the contract may be considered as an agreement or a promise, what is assumed is that it is a self-imposed obligation, an obligation arising from the will of the parties.[13]

It is noted that the idea of the contract as an agreement—or as a promise—would be something similar to the 'traditional version of the contract',[14] although, certainly, not the only one.[15] However, it would be particularly attractive, at least from a liberal perspective, for its relationship with values, such as private autonomy or freedom of the individual.[16]

This may be so, but what exactly does the statement that the parties agree mean in contract law? All concur that the term 'agreement' involves the will of the individual who decides autonomously and that this is precisely where its moral value resides. But what is the relationship between the will and the contract as an

[8] M Bianca, *El contrato* (F Hinestrosa and E Cortés transl.) 2nd edn (Bogotá, Universidad Externado de Colombia, 2007) 23.

[9] J Ghestin, *La formation du contrat*, 3rd edn (Paris, LDGJ, 1993) 5.

[10] EA Farnsworth, *Contracts*, 3rd edn (New York, Aspen Law & Business, 1999) 3.

[11] 'A contract is a promise or a set of promises for the breach of which the law gives a remedy, or the performance of which the law in some way recognizes as a duty'.

[12] However, the question about the difference between the contract as a promise and as an agreement has been discussed with some intensity. See, for example, R Barnett, 'Consent Theory of Contract' (1986) 86 *Columbia Law Review* 269 and J Penner, 'Promises, Agreements, and Contracts' in G Klass, G Letsas and P Saprai (eds), *Philosophical Foundations of Contract Law* (Oxford, Oxford University Press, 2014) 117–21. For a discussion of the role of promise in the contract from a historical and comparative perspective, see M Hogg, *Promises and Contract Law* (Cambridge, Cambridge University Press, 2011).

[13] S Smith, *Contract Theory* (Oxford, Oxford University Press, 2007) 57.

[14] ibid, 56.

[15] A good approximation to the theories of the contract is provided in P Benson (ed), *The Theory of Contract Law* (Cambridge, Cambridge University Press, 2007).

[16] See C Fried, *Contracts as a Promise* (Cambridge, MA, Harvard University Press, 1981). For an overview, see M Radin, *Boilerplate* (Princeton, NJ, Princeton University Press, 2013) 58–62.

agreement? Does the will explain the content of the agreement?[17] Does it justify its mandatory character?

These are, of course, formidable questions which I do not intend to address in this chapter. My purpose is much more modest. What interests me is to consider the use of the term 'agreement' by the PLACL, and I can suggest from the outset that it is a rather weak use, in at least three ways. The first concerns the content of the contract. It is perfectly possible to talk about contract even though the parties have not negotiated much of its content or even if they have not agreed on some part of the content. The second involves the treatment of what might be called 'defects' of the parties' will. There is agreement, even if some of the wills participating in it are extremely flawed. Finally, in the third sense, the use of the term 'agreement' is very weak because it is not possible to refer to a contract, even if the parties have agreed to contract, if two other essential elements of the contract, the cause and the subject-matter, are not present, in addition to that agreement.

In other words, what I will try to show is that the agreement of the parties—understood as a genuine meeting of their wills—does not necessarily—nor generally—explain the content of the contract, or require flawless wills, nor is it sufficient to constitute it. Within this scenario, my impression is that even when the PLACL are defined in the contract as an agreement, the importance attached to the will of the parties—and, therefore, their autonomy—is less than might appear because, once again, it is not the will of the parties that necessarily explains the content of the contract, nor is it its mandatory character, nor is it sufficient to constitute a contract.

II. Agreement and Content of the Contract

Without a doubt, two things would have to happen for the agreement of the parties to explain the content of the contract. The first is that the entire contents of the contract may have been negotiated. The second is that the parties agreed on

[17] It would appear to need to be very strong in the sense that it is the will or the agreement of the parties that would explain and justify the contract; as noted by H Dagan, 'Autonomy, Pluralism and Contract Law Theory' (2013) 76 *Law and Contemporary Problems* 19–38: 'The proposition that the commitment to individual autonomy is one of the most important foundations of contract is a truism, almost a cliché. Contract, in this common account, is the legal cousin of the social practice of promise and voluntary obligation, and the significance of that social practice to autonomy implies that contract law should be guided by the will of the parties or by their mutual consent. Accordingly, contract law, in this view, is both passive and structurally monist. It should be relatively passive due to the injunction to merely piggyback on people's expressions of their will, and it should be structurally monist—a unified body of doctrine guided by one regulative principle—because its normative underpinnings are the same irrespective of the type of contract at hand'.

the full content negotiated. This would be something like the traditional version of contract as far as its content is concerned.[18]

The first of those two things, however, never happens. With regard to the second, there may be disagreement on what the parties declared yet a perfectly valid contract may not be questioned. It is expedient to consider these issues separately.

A. The Necessary Incompleteness of Contracts

A perfect contract does not exist. That is, there is no contract in which the parties have agreed on all material aspects.[19] This idea seems to be widely accepted.[20]

A look at contract law, whatever the instrument used to regulate the subject-matter—codes, restatements, directives or soft law instruments—reveals the presence of a large group of rules aimed, so to speak, at filling the gaps left by the parties in terms of the content of the contract they plan to conclude. For example, in the case of a sale, it will not be uncommon for the declarations of will to confine themselves to the goods and the price, thereby leaving a huge number of issues open.

Partially at least, these issues are regulated by additional rules set in place for this very purpose, that of filling the gaps left by the parties.[21] The PLACL are no exception in this regard. The relevant rules are too numerous to detail them all, but by way of example, Article 73 indicates the place where the obligation should be fulfilled, Article 74 regulates the time for performance, Article 78 distributes the costs of implementation, and Article 84 establishes the remedies for breach of contract.

The peculiarity of these rules is twofold. On the one hand, they are understood to be incorporated into the contract without requiring the parties to indicate their

[18] In this sense, S Durany, 'Sobre la necesidad de que la aceptación coincida en todo con la oferta: el espejo roto' [1990] *Anuario de Derecho Civil* 43–44, 1011, 1113, states: 'Tradicionalmente los contratos se han considerado como el resultado de un proceso negociador individualizado en el que ambas partes contratantes conciertan personalmente los elementos del mismo. De esta manera, su acuerdo sobre los términos establecidos es completo, y el contrato se configura a su gusto. Así pues, dicho paradigma se caracteriza por: (1) un proceso de formación reciproco, donde ambas partes intervienen en la negociación; (2) un contenido del contrato establecido mediante negociaciones individuales. De esta manera, la legislación contractual contemporánea sienta sus bases sobre ambos postulados' (Traditionally, contracts have been considered as the result of a negotiation process where the parties personally agree its elements. Therefore, the agreement over the terms of the contract is complete, and the contract is modelled by their wishes. Thus, the paradigm is characterised by (1) a mutual formation process, where both parties intervene in the negotiation; (2) a contractual content established by individual negotiations. Therefore, contemporary contract law is based on both premises).

[19] O Ben Shahar, 'Agreeing to Disagree: Filling Gaps in Deliberately Incomplete Contracts' (2004) available at http://repository.law.umich.edu/cgi/viewcontent.cgi?article=1001&context=law_econ_archive, 5.

[20] As noted by R Barnett, 'The Sound of Silence: Default Rules and Contractual Consent' (1992) 78 *Virginia Law Review* 821, 821: '[B]y now everyone acknowledges the legal realist insight that all contracts are, by necessity, incomplete to some degree'.

[21] Using R Craswell's words, 'Contract Law, Default Rules, and the Philosophy of Promising' (1989) 88 *Michigan Law Review* 489, 504, it is possible to distinguish agreement rules and background rules in a contract.

willingness to do so. On the other hand, generally at least, these are rules that the parties may modify by agreement.

In what sense, then, can it be said that that part of the content of the contract on which the parties have not expressed agreement may be treated as the meeting of the wills of the parties? One possible answer is that given by Barnett[22] and Smith,[23] according to whom there would be something like indirect or tacit consent of the parties on these rules.

Yet, before we explore this idea further, it should be noted that such tacit or indirect consent of the parties does not function in the way demonstrations of unspoken will usually work, that is, to dispense with a number of acts that are undoubtedly taken for granted by the parties, but concerning which it is assumed either that the parties know and accept the rules, or that if they had not known of them, they would still have accepted them.

Of course, the presumption of knowledge is a factual issue that may perhaps be assumed in the case of sophisticated parties,[24] but is extremely questionable when inexperienced parties are involved. When ignorance of the rules is assumed, however, the presumption is much more ambitious since when all is said and done, the assumption is that had those parties negotiated them, they would have distributed the risks in precisely the way the legislator has done.

At all events, it is correct to say—regarding the issues not explicitly regulated by the parties—that there is an agreement which is, in a sense, quite weak: it is a hypothetical agreement and that kind of agreement, as Coleman has suggested, is more often associated with the idea of rational self-interest than with the notion of a genuine agreement.[25] To put it differently, if the justification for these rules is that they reproduce what rational parties would have negotiated, then the determining factor is the model of rationality which is used, leaving little, if any, room for explaining or justifying those rules in the light of the autonomy or will of the parties.

That being so, we must conclude that if the contract is an agreement, it is at best a hypothetical agreement, an agreement in which, hypothetically, the parties have agreed to adhere to additional rules on top of the will of the parties.[26]

B. Discrepancies Regarding the Content of the Contract

The problem addressed above is one of the incompleteness of the actual agreement between the parties regarding the content of their contract; but in addition, there is another issue where the question is not whether the actual agreement may miscarry on the content of the contract, but on something that, at least initially,

[22] Barnett (n 20).

[23] Smith (n 13) 67.

[24] See M Miller, 'Contract Law, Party Sophistication and the New Formalism' (2010) 75 *Missouri Law Review* 493.

[25] J Coleman, *Risk and Wrongs* (Oxford, Oxford University Press, 1992) 169.

[26] In this sense, even though a contract of adhesion is not involved, it would resemble it in that the act of will is limited to adherence to a predisposed set of rules. In the case of a contract of adhesion, they have been predisposed by the other party; in the case of other contracts, by the legislator.

sounds more challenging, ie, disagreement on something expressing the will of the parties. As we shall see, the PLACL address this issue in the context of the formation of consent.

Strict adherence to the notion of contract as an agreement seems to require that offer and acceptance be a complete match. This is what is generally known as the 'mirror image rule', which still seems to be largely accepted both in the *common law* and in the *civil law* traditions.[27]

Thus, for example, Frey has pointed out: '[A]t common law the acceptance must mirror the offer. Any deviation in the attempted acceptance would result in the attempted acceptance being a rejection of the offer and possibly a counter offer'.[28] Meanwhile, Ghestin notes that '[L]a formation du contrat exige une concordance exacte entre l'offre et son acceptation'.[29] That is, an acceptance which does not fully reflect the terms of the offer will be considered as a counteroffer. However, this is not the solution adopted by the PLACL. The wording of Article 25 ('Agreement with the terms of the offer') is significant in this respect.

> (1) A reply to an offer that contains additions, limitations, or modifications constitutes a counteroffer.
> (2) However, if the terms of the offer are not materially altered, the reply constitutes an acceptance, and the contract will be concluded with such additions, limitations or modifications.
> (3) Even when the limitations or modifications do not materially alter the terms of the offer, the reply will be understood as a rejection in the following cases:
>   (a) When the offer expressly demands full or partial acceptance of the proposed terms.
>   (b) When the offeror without delay informs the offeree of its objection to the changes.

Clearly, the PLACL provision does not, so to speak, require full concordance between the terms of the offer and those of acceptance. Discrepancies are perfectly admissible and, notwithstanding such discrepancies, the contract is still formed. In other words, the parties agree in their statements of will on part of the contents of the agreement, but the acceptance may contain additions, limitations or modifications regarding the offer and, to the extent that such additions, limitations or modifications do not materially alter the terms of the contract, they will be construed as part of it.

This rule, whose origins can apparently be traced to Swiss and US law[30] and whose closest precedent in the PLACL is Article 2.1.11 of the UNIDROIT Principles of International Commercial Contracts (PICC), is regulated in the context of

[27] A closer look in Durany (n 18).

[28] M Frey, *Essentials of Contract Law*, 2nd edn (Boston, MA, Delmar Cengage Learning, 2014) 38.

[29] Ghestin (n 9) 283.

[30] See R Anderson, 'Art 2.1.11' in S Vogenauer (ed), *Commentary on the UNIDROIT Principles of International Commercial Contracts (PICC)*, 2nd edn (Oxford, Oxford University Press, 2015) 317. It can also be found in identical or very similar terms in Art 19(2) United Nations Convention on Contracts for the International Sale of Goods (CISG), Art 2:208(2) Principles of European Contract Law (PECL) and Art II.-4:208(2) Draft Common Frame of Reference (DCFR).

the formation of consent; however, it determines the content of the contract, and establishes that those additions, limitations or modifications on which the parties did not reach an agreement are understood as part of the contract.

However, there is no need for exaggeration. Disagreement as to the content will occur only if, on the one hand, the additions, limitations or modifications contained in the amendment do not materially alter the terms of the offer. Furthermore, even if the acceptance does not materially alter the terms of the offer, the offer may not include any statement requiring total or partial acceptance and, even in the absence of such a statement, the offeree may express disagreement with the alteration provided he does so without delay.

We need not concern ourselves at this juncture with what constitutes a substantial alteration, nor need we examine the details of the statements of the offer or expressions of disagreement with the alteration.[31] The point is, rather, the change of emphasis that—for good reasons[32]—the PLACL place on the mirror image rule. In the traditional system, there is no contract if there is no perfect match between offer and acceptance. In the PLACL, discrepancy notwithstanding, the contract is formed unless the changes are significant or there is a statement in the offer or, finally, the offeree fails to express disagreement with the alteration without delay.

Disagreement as to the content of a contract that can arise in relation to the formation of consent is, as can be seen, slight because, on the one hand, it refers to non-essential aspects of the transaction and, secondly, it establishes protection mechanisms for the offeree. However, it also reveals an interesting effect: content that was not the product of the actual agreement of the parties is incorporated in the contract.

III. Agreements and Defective Will: The Case of Mistake

In an extremely influential piece on Spanish law, Díez-Picazo states the following:

> The traditional point of view considers the contract as an agreement, and therefore, as something that is a free and spontaneous creation of its authors. For the existence of a contract, serious, spontaneous and free consent is necessary. When some of these conditions of consent are not present, it is assumed that consent is vitiated, and the contract has an anomaly which implies or at least allows its invalidation.[33]

[31] On these topics, see ibid 316–20.

[32] Durany (n 18).

[33] L Díez Picazo, *Fundamentos de Derecho Civil Patrimonial* (Navarra, Thomson Reuters, 2007) 185: 'El punto de vista tradicional considera el contrato como un acuerdo de voluntades y, por consiguiente, como algo que es una obra libre y espontánea de sus autores. Para que exista contrato debe existir un consentimiento, que ha de ser serio, espontáneo y libre. Cuando alguna de estas cualidades o condiciones del consentimiento no se da, se dice que el consentimiento se encuentra viciado, de suerte que en el contrato existe una irregularidad que ha de determinar, o al menos permitir, su invalidación'. See also Ghestin (n 9) 447.

The PLACL show that, even if the contract is understood as an agreement, that assertion must be severely nuanced since it is perfectly possible that the will may turn out to be heavily flawed and yet the contract may be perfectly valid.

Here, we should take a moment to consider the regulation of 'flaw' that appears to illustrate this most eloquently: that of mistake.[34] Article 28 of the PLACL defines mistake as follows:

> Mistake means ignorance or an erroneous assumption relating to facts or to law when of such importance that a reasonable person in the same situation would not have concluded the contract or would have done so on materially different terms.

Meanwhile, Article 29 ('Grounds for mistake') provides the following:

> (1) Mistake vitiates a contract when:
> (a) It is caused by information supplied by the other party.
> (b) The other party knew or should have known of the mistake and did not disclose it against good faith.
> (c) Both parties made the same mistake.
>
> (2) In these cases, the contract is null if the mistake can be excused or the risk of its existence was not or ought not to have been assumed by the person who made it.

The concept of mistake is a broad one insofar as it includes (unlike, for example, the Chilean Civil Code) the so-called 'error de derecho'. The limitation of what can be regarded as a mistake is determined by the importance that a reasonable person would have attached to it. Thus defined, mistake is perfectly consistent with a proactive understanding of contract law. However, this is not the case with the grounds of mistake. For consent to be flawed, it is not enough that the mistake incurred by one party be extremely relevant. Something else is needed. Following the order of the article, mistake can be argued when it has been caused by the other party,[35] when the other party has breached a duty of information[36] or when it is a shared mistake.[37] But even in these three circumstances, the party that suffered the mistake should accept it if the mistake was inexcusable[38] or if it had assumed the risk of a mistake.[39]

[34] On the treatment of mistake in the PLACL, see I de la Maza, 'La excusabilidad del error' *inedit* (2015).

[35] On provoked mistake, see A Morales, *El error en los contratos* (Madrid, Editorial Montecorvo, 1982) 227.

[36] On pre-contractual information duties, see I de la Maza, *Los límites del deber precontractual de información* (Pamplona, Thomson Reuters, 2010).

[37] For an illustration of cases in which both parties suffer mistakes, but in respect of different issues, see Farnsworth (n 10) 623, n 1. For an example of shared mistake, the comments on the PECL (Lando/Beale (2000) 233) and those on the PICC (2010) 101 may be considered.

[38] On the question of excusability, see de la Maza (n 34).

[39] It deals with a well-developed idea in English law. There, however, the allocation of risk is a question preliminary to the discussion as to whether there was a mistake or not. In this sense, in *Associated Japanese Bank (International) Ltd v Credit du Nord S.A.* [1989] 1 WLR 255, 268, Steyn J handed down the following opinion: 'Logically, before one can turn to the rules as to mistake, whether at common law or in equity, one must first determine whether the contract itself, by express or implied condition precedent or otherwise, provides who bears the risk of the relevant mistake. It is at this hurdle that many pleas of mistake will either fail or prove to have been unnecessary. Only if the contract is silent on the point, is there scope for invoking mistake'.

The point here is not to explore the vicissitudes of such a complex notion as mistake, but to highlight a different matter since mistake only exceptionally vitiates the will. Therefore, in most cases it is perfectly possible to state that there is an agreement (or a perfectly valid contract) notwithstanding the fact that if a reasonable person had known there was mistake he would not have concluded the contract or would have done so on materially different terms.[40]

The way in which the PLACL regulate mistake reveals the rather exceptional character of this notion. That being so, it really does not seem relevant whether the parties reached an agreement—understood as a genuine meeting of minds—but rather, what matters is whether the *errans* deserve protection from the mistake. In general, they will not deserve protection if the declaration induced the other party to rely on a right to protection.[41] In that case, a contract would have all the appearances of an agreement.

If the contract is an agreement, then it is a curious agreement because, first, much of it is, at best, hypothetical; secondly, there may be no coincidence between what is offered and what is accepted and, more radically, it is perfectly possible that in fact there was no coincidence at all, except in apparent terms between the parties, since if one had not been wrong, it would not have contracted or would have done so on very different terms. But in the PLACL, that is not all. In the PLACL, not only is it an agreement in which the role of the will is inferior to that suggested by the use of the term 'agreement', but the agreement is not even sufficient to form a contract; subject-matter and cause are also required.

IV. Failure of the Agreement: Subject-matter and Cause as Essential Elements

It is time to turn to other soft law instruments. For example, Article 2:101 PECL ('Conditions for the Conclusion of a Contract') provides that:

(1) A contract is concluded if:
  (a) the parties intend to be legally bound, and
  (b) they reach a sufficient agreement without any further requirement.
(2) A contract need not be concluded or evidenced in writing nor is it subject to any other requirement as to form. The contract may be proved by any means, including witnesses.

[40] J Gordley, *The Jurists: A Critical History* (Oxford, Oxford University Press, 2013) 259 notes how strange this consequence is for the conception of contract as an agreement.

[41] This being so, at least when considering the situation of mistake and fraud, the PLACL do not seem to stray too far from the objective theory of assent that predominates in the common law. On the objective theory of assent, see Farnsworth (n 10) 116–32. Regarding the specific issue of mistake, see J Cartwright, *Misrepresentation, Mistake and Non-Disclosure* (London, Sweet and Maxwell, 1997) 404–07.

Similarly, Article 3.1.2 PICC states:

> A contract is concluded, modified or terminated by the mere agreement of the parties, without any further requirement.

These two provisions can be compared with Article 9 of the PLACL ('Elements of a contract'), which provides as follows:

> Consent, subject-matter, and cause are the essential elements required to form a contract.

If we take Huber's comment on Article 3.1.2 PICC, it is clear that it aims to exclude cause and consideration as a requirement of the contract.[42] However, if we shift the focus to Article 9 of the PLACL, the purpose is clearly seen to be exactly the opposite. Moreover, both the PECL and the PICC consider that the hypothesis of initial impossibility does not determine the invalidity of a contract. Thus, Article 4:102 PECL ('Initial Impossibility') provides:

> A contract is not invalid merely because at the time it was concluded performance of the obligation assumed was impossible, or because a party was not entitled to dispose of the assets to which the contract relates.

Article 3.1.3 PICC provides substantially the same. Moreover, the commentary on Article 4:103 PECL points out:

> In some legal systems a contract which, unknown to the parties, is impossible to perform, for example, because of the absence of an *object* or because the seller has no right to dispose of the goods it is purporting to sell, may be ineffective. Under the Principles this approach is not taken. Very often such cases will be ones of fundamental mistake under which either party affected may avoid the contract, but there may be cases when a party should be treated as taking the risk of impossibility and therefore should not be entitled to avoid the contract.[43]

Looking at Article 38(1) of the PLACL, we find the following statement:

> The subject-matter of a contract must be ascertained or ascertainable, possible, and lawful.

The subject-matter must be possible; if it does not exist—ie, in case of an original impossibility—there is a failure in one of the essential elements of the contract.

Moreover, comparing all these rules, the following emerges: both in the PECL and the PICC, the agreement (whatever it may mean) is sufficient to establish a contract. However, in the PLACL, the consent of the parties is not enough: subject-matter and cause are also required, elements which are considered 'essential' in the contract, ie, in the absence of these elements, the contract has no effect or, perhaps more exactly, it is null and void.[44]

[42] P Huber, 'Art 3.1.2' in S Vogenauer (ed), *Commentary on the UNIDROIT Principles of International Commercial Contracts (PICC)*, 2nd edn (Oxford, Oxford University Press, 2015) 467.

[43] Lando/Beale (n 37) 228. Italics in the original.

[44] There is ambiguity in the PLACL as to the consequences regarding the processing of nullity.

The requirement of a possible subject-matter and cause as essential elements of the contract, typical of the French Civil Code before its 2016 reform and generally reflected in Latin American civil codes, appears to be in retreat, a fact which does not make the lack of subject-matter and cause irrelevant. As to subject-matter, the problems raised by initial failure have moved from the area of validity of the contract to that of its non-compliance. As far as the cause is concerned, the functions that were once recognised (such as justifying the interdependence of obligations, safeguarding the legality of contracts, explaining the effects of simulation, protecting the commutativity of services or permitting a revision of the contract due to change of circumstances) seem to be redundant (thus, for example, in simulation)[45] or rather replaced by more fine-tuned instruments. To this—always referring to cause—we must add the extraordinary ambiguity of the expression ('cause'), which cannot fail to make its application difficult.[46]

V. Similarities and Usefulness

In a scenario such as this, we may wonder why the PLACL opted to keep both subject-matter and cause as essential elements of the contract. The answer seems to be twofold. In part, it is because the drafters of the PLACL wished to take account of the contract law rules applicable in the countries of the region and, on the other hand—but more specifically with respect to cause—because it was felt that they had performed some valuable functions.

As to similarities, it is important to note that, as a project, the PLACL pursue two objectives. The first—perhaps most obvious—of these is to systematise the similarities that exist at the level of the various national contract laws in Latin America: a kind of Latin American Restatement of Contracts. The second objective is to approximate the contract law applicable in the various Latin American countries to a paradigm such as that in the CISG, which was later translated into several civil codes, directives and soft law instruments.[47]

To some extent, the reasons for the presence of these two essential elements—subject-matter and cause—are coincidental. The different countries of the region consider them such. Where cause is concerned, this applies to the old Argentinean,[48]

[45] AM Morales 'Claves de la modernización del derecho de los contratos' in I de la Maza, AM Morales and A Vidal, *Estudios de derecho de los contratos* (Santiago, Thomson Reuters, 2014).

[46] A Morales, *Claves de la modernización del derecho de contratos* (Bogotá, Ibañez/CEDC, 2016) 62–70.

[47] In C Pizarro's words in 'Presentación' in C Pizarro and Fondation Pour le Droit Continental (eds), *El derecho de los contratos en Latinoamérica* (Universidad Diego Portales, Fundación Fernando Fueyo Laneri, 2012) 16, in the presentation of a book that originated in a questionnaire on contract law sent to academics in some of the countries in the region (Argentina, Brazil, Chile, Colombia, Paraguay, Uruguay and Venezuela), the PLACL aim to 'identify our national juridical identity' and 'to improve what has been done elsewhere'. With regard to the latter, this refers to the different soft law instruments that have sought to harmonise European contract law.

[48] Art 499.

Colombian,[49] Chilean,[50] Uruguayan[51] and Venezuelan Civil Codes,[52] but not to the Paraguayan[53] or Brazilian Civil Codes. As to subject-matter, this is considered in the old Argentinean,[54] Brazilian,[55] Colombian,[56] Paraguayan,[57] Uruguayan[58] and Venezuelan Civil Codes.[59] However, this is not all. Coincidence can be an argument, but it is not decisive. Were it so, there would be no way to explain why in areas such as remedies for breach of contract the PLACL at times move away—and, on occasion, considerably so—from the characteristic regulations of the Latin American countries and opt for a formula more closely modelled on the CISG. The second consideration is that both subject-matter and cause have proved serviceable in regulating contractual rights in Latin America.

For example, in the arduous discussions surrounding cause, it was noted that in Chile, 'cause' was used as a mechanism of commutative justice to shield the contractual balance from excessive penal clauses. It was also noted that in Colombia it was used, among other things, to explain group contracts and the effects of non-compliance of one with respect to the others. It was used for the same purpose in Argentina for both group contracts and chain contracts to explain the repercussions of what happens to one with respect to the others. In Argentina, it was also employed to resolve matters related to alterations arising from changed circumstances. Furthermore, in general, cause has been used to justify certain restitutions when a contract is terminated. As far as the cause of the contract is concerned, it has been used as a mechanism of moral control in contracts based on illicit motivations.

Cause, then, has played a useful role in what could be called Latin American contract law.

VI. The Dangers of Syncretism: Some Examples

If the aim was to identify and systematise the coincidences existing in the regulation of contract law in the countries of the region, there was justification for

[49] Art 1502.
[50] Art 1445.
[51] Arts 1261 nº 4 and 1287.
[52] Art 1142.
[53] In fact, in the Paraguayan Civil Code the removal of the cause is explained in the Preamble, as follows: 'In listing the essential requirements—or elements—of the contract, the draft omits the cause, closing the way to the many difficulties and controversies raised by the Napoleonic Code and its followers on the meaning and scope of this element. In fact, the same interests considered by jurisprudence under inaccuracy are protected by other standards; morality and good manners are not left without protection by the abolition of this element' (translation provided by the author).
[54] Arts 1169–75.
[55] Art 104.
[56] Art 1502.
[57] See, eg, Arts 299, 357, 396, 700 and 710.
[58] Arts 1261 nº 4 and 1287–89.
[59] Arts 1108, 1126–30.

introducing cause and subject-matter in the PLACL. The problem, however, is that this was not the sole objective. The intention was also—as eloquently evidenced by the treatment of notions such as mistake or of issues such as breach of contract and its remedies—to approximate the law of contracts to bring it more into line with European developments arising from the CISG.

This is a somewhat syncretic effort. That is, an effort that seeks to reconcile two different traditions, the codification of the nineteenth century and the CISG. It is also a risky endeavour. I will try to illustrate this with regard to the treatment of subject-matter and cause in the PLACL.

As we have already seen, subject-matter in the PLACL is an essential element of the contract. If it happens to be missing—a typical case of initial impossibility—we are apparently faced with a case of absolute nullity. This, of course, does not happen either in the PECL or in the PICC. In the former, the absence of subject-matter can be resolved under the rules on mistake or breach of contract.[60] In the PICC, however, recourse would have to be had to the rules of breach of contract.[61]

The point is that in the PLACL, both the notions of mistake and breach of contract follow the PECL and the PICC very closely. Perhaps we should recall the notion of mistake in the PLACL:

> Ignorance or an erroneous assumption relating to facts or to law when of such importance that a reasonable person in the same situation would not have concluded the contract or would have done so on materially different terms.

Everything indicates that it is a person's ignorance of something crucial to the extent that had he not been unaware, he would not have contracted. As a consequence, the definition of mistake covers the lack of subject-matter.

If we consider the notion of failure as laid down in Article 79 of the PLACL ('[N]on-performance is a failure to perform in the agreed manner'), it seems clear that if the thing that is owned does not exist, the debtor will fail to fulfil his obligation, therefore, the hypothesis of lack of subject-matter is also covered by the rules of breach of contract.

Things being as they are, it is not very clear whether there is any room left for subject-matter as an essential element of the contract. With respect to cause, it has been noted that one of its functions has been to help solve the problems raised by a supervening change of circumstances. However, this is explained by the absence of a rule that, in the respective civil codes, may resolve the problem in a more technically accurate manner.

At the time of writing this chapter, the PLACL do not have such a rule, but the idea is to incorporate it and so render cause superfluous, at least in this respect.

[60] See Art 4:119 PECL.

[61] See Art 3.2.4 PICC.

VII. Conclusion

The PLACL define the contract as an agreement and to that extent, there is nothing new under the sun. However, what is there beyond the intuitively obvious connection between the two expressions—contract and agreement? The answer, in my opinion, is that there is something less obvious. It may be noted that, within the set of factual circumstances required by the contract, one is the statement of two wills that, at least in appearance, match on some part of the content of the contract. Another is that the importance of this 'agreement' is less than is suggested by the definition of contract, since it is not sufficient to set the contract. Cause and subject-matter, two elements that seem to be in retreat in the harmonisation projects of European contract law, are also required. In the PLACL, this can be explained by their ambition to restate Latin American contract law, but it is a peculiar restatement in that it aims to approximate Latin American contract law to the paradigm of the contract law rooted in the CISG, and these two goals do not always produce consistent results.

VII. Conclusion

8

Formation of Contract under the Principles of Latin American Contract Law

RODRIGO MOMBERG

I. Introduction and Objective

This chapter is intended to provide an analysis, from a comparative perspective, of the rules on formation of contract contained in the Principles of Latin American Contract Law (PLACL). It takes as its point of reference the Latin American national systems represented in the Principles, but also includes transnational model rules, such as the United Nations Convention on Contracts for the International Sales of Goods (CISG), the UNIDROIT Principles of International Commercial Contracts (PICC), the Principles of European Contract Law (PECL) and the Draft Common Frame of Reference (DCFR), as well as the recently enacted reform of the French *Code civil*. The aim is to assess these provisions not only in the light of their regional background, but also from a transnational perspective, in order to determine whether they represent a restatement of Latin American law or a new approach to the subject, as well to make some suggestions on how to improve the regulation of this area of the law.

II. Definition and Elements of the Contract

In any juridical system, the concept and conditions for the existence or validity of a contract are of great relevance for the regulation of its formation. The rules on formation of contract are included in Chapter 2 of the Principles. The chapter is set out in five sections, covering the definition and elements of the contract (1), contract negotiation (2), formation of consent (3), defects of the contract (4) and subject-matter, cause and formal requirements (5).

This structure or systematisation reflects the choice of the PLACL to maintain the classic approach to the elements of the contract, found in most of the nineteenth-century codifications but retained also by modern Latin American codes. Article 9 (Elements of a contract) states that 'Consent, subject-matter, and cause are the essential elements required to form a contract'. This provision implicitly expresses the distinction between *essentialia* and *accidentalia negotii*, developed in the Middle Ages under the influence of Aristotelian logic,[1] a distinction that is still generally present in Latin American legal doctrine, where general treatises on private law refer to it in the chapters analysing the general category of juridical acts, and sometimes again in the chapters on obligations and contracts.[2] The Civil Codes of Chile (Article 1444) and Colombia (Article 1501) expressly recognise this distinction. The Civil Codes of Argentina, Uruguay and Venezuela implicitly refer to it in a number of provisions. Conversely, the Civil Codes of Brazil and Paraguay make no reference to it.

III. The Notion of Contract

In line with the civilian tradition, the Principles consider the contract as an agreement. The emphasis is on the agreement, on the existence of the consent of two or more wills. Article 8 emphasises that the agreement must be geared to the creation, transfer, modification or termination of a legal relationship of an economic nature.

The inclusion of a definition of contract is a traditional feature of Latin American codes. Only the Civil Codes of Brazil and Paraguay do not include such a definition. Neither the PECL nor the PICC define contract. The PICC also avoid any 'general provisions' and directly proceed to the regulation of offer and acceptance.

The concept of 'legal relationship' lies at the core of the definition of contract by the PLACL. The emphasis is on the agreement, but only if it is intended to produce legal effects.[3] In a corresponding provision of the DCFR, the concept of legal relationship is introduced but not further elucidated.[4] In this sense, the PLACL are more precise: the legal relationship is expressly characterised by its economic nature. This can be interpreted as aiming to exclude mere agreements in

[1] See R Zimmermann, *The Law of Obligations* (Oxford, Oxford University Press, 1996) 234.

[2] See F López de Zavalia, *Teoría de los contratos—Parte general* (Buenos Aires, Zavalia, 1971) § 4.I; R Abeliuk, *Las Obligaciones*, vol 1, 4th edn (Santiago, Editorial Juridica de Chile, 2003) para 43.

[3] In a similar way, also departing from the traditional definition contained in the repealed Article 1101 of the *Code civil*, the new provision defines contract as an agreement (*accord de volontés*) between two or more persons with the aim to create legal effects.

[4] N Jansen and R Zimmermann, 'Contract Formation and Mistake in European Contract Law: A Genetic Comparison of Transnational Model Rules' (2011) 31 *Oxford Journal of Legal Studies* 632.

the private sphere, which are not enforceable and give rise at best to moral duties or obligations; but also, more relevantly, as restricting the domain of contract to transactions with an economic content, something that has been highly disputed in legal doctrine and that seems closer to the common law tradition.[5]

In the Latin American legal tradition, a contract is part of a broader category, *convención* or bilateral juridical act, which requires two declarations of will or intent. The PLACL have abandoned that abstract terminology for the less technical, but more neutral and arguably more universal concept of agreement (*acuerdo*).[6] This is a departure from the position of Latin American civil codes, where contract is still defined as a *convención* or a juridical act.[7]

Therefore, the justification of the binding force of contracts is found in the will of the parties, rooted in the contract itself and with an effect similar to the law of the contracting parties.

A. The Retention of *la Causa*

However, consent is not sufficient to form a contract. Article 9 also requires subject-matter and cause (*objeto* and *causa*). This is the classic structure to be found in Latin American civil codes. The Civil Codes of Argentina (Article 281), Chile (Articles 1445, 1467 and 1468), Colombia (Article 1502), Uruguay (Articles 1261, 1287 to 1289) and Venezuela (Article 1141) still retain *causa* as an element of the contract. The new Argentinean Civil Code of 2015 includes *causa* (Article 281), even distinguishing between cause of the obligation (Article 726—source of the obligations) and cause of the contract (Articles 1012–1014). On the other hand, the Civil Codes of Brazil and Paraguay do not include *causa* as a requirement for the validity of a contract.

It is not the aim of this chapter to analyse these requirements. In this respect, the Principles depart from modern contract law. Neither the PICC, the PECL nor the DCFR include cause or other requirements for the conclusion of a valid contract. Article 3.1.2 of the PICC is especially illustrative: '(Validity of mere agreement) A contract is concluded, modified or terminated by the mere agreement of the parties, without any further requirement'. The Official Comments expressly state that the Article aims to make clear the rejection of consideration or cause as additional elements for the validity of a contract. Following this trend, the

[5] See L Díez-Picazo and A Gullón, *Sistema de Derecho Civil—El contrato en general. La relación obligatoria*, vol II, book 1, 10th edn (Madrid, Tecnos, 2012) 114.

[6] The notion of contract as a convention may be traced to Pothier, who defined contract as 'une espèce de convention': R Pothier, *Traité des obligations, T.1, Oeuvres de Pothier. Nouvelle édition* (Paris, Siffrein, 1821–24) 80.

[7] The Civil Codes of Chile (Art 1438), Colombia (Art 1495), Uruguay (Art 1247) and Venezuela (Art 1133) define contract as a *convención*; whereas the Argentinean Civil Code (Art 957) considers contract as part of the broader category of *acto jurídico*.

French reform of Book III of the *Code civil* has also abolished cause as an essential element for the formation of a contract, a decision that has sparked a major debate in French legal doctrine.[8]

The inclusion of subject-matter and cause in the chapter on formation is a consequence of these aspects being essential elements for the formation of a contract. Under the PLACL, a contract cannot be considered to exist if subject-matter or cause are absent. When cause and subject-matter are abolished as essential elements of the contract, as in the PICC or the PECL, the chapter of formation includes only the regulation of contract negotiation, offer and acceptance, and the authority of agents. The content of the contract is regulated in a separate chapter, and within it, some aspects that are remarkably absent in the PLACL: express and implied obligations, determination of the quality of performance, and price determination.

B. Formal and Real Contracts

Consensualism is not expressly recognised in the PLACL, even where the rules on formation of contract rely mostly on the existence of consent between the parties. Article 40 (Form and formal requirements) is particularly respectful of the formal requirements of domestic law. The principle of informality or freedom of form is not provided by the PLACL.[9]

Of course, the formalities required by national or international mandatory rules must be observed. The inclusion of Article 40 seems to be based on the fact that most Latin American countries retain the category of real contracts, rooted in the Roman contracts *re*, that is, contracts that require for their conclusion not only the agreement of the parties but also the delivery of the thing which is the subject-matter of the contract.[10] Accordingly, in the case of a real contract, even when the parties have reached agreement but no delivery has taken place, that agreement is unenforceable and may at the most be a ground of pre-contractual liability for the party reluctant to make the actual delivery. As with the requirements of cause or consideration, the category of real contracts is rejected by contemporary uniform contract law.[11]

[8] See generally C Grimaldi, 'Les maux de la cause ne sont pas qu'une affaire de mots' [2015] *Recueil Dalloz* 814–15.

[9] See notably Art 1.2 PICC. Also Arts 11 CISG, 2:101(2) PECL, II.-1:106(1) DCFR and 6 CESL. In all those instruments, the contract may be subject to formalities required by mandatory rules.

[10] See Civil Codes of Brazil (Arts 579 and 586), Chile (Art 1443), Colombia (Art 1500), Uruguay (Art 1252). The most common real contracts are *mutuum* (loan for consumption), *commodatum* (loan for use), deposit and pledge. The Civil Codes of Paraguay and Venezuela do not recognise real contracts. Notably, the new Argentinean Civil Code has suppressed the category of real contracts.

[11] See Official Comment to Art 3.1.2 PICC.

IV. The Consent of the Parties: Offer and Acceptance

Section 3 (Articles 13 to 26) of Chapter 2 of the PLACL is entitled 'Formation of consent' but, as stated above, the mere existence of an agreement is not sufficient to conclude a contract under the PLACL. However, the process of formation of consent receives more detailed and extensive regulation in the PLACL. Subject-matter, cause and formal requirements are addressed in Section 5, which devotes only one Article to each of those 'essential elements'.

Consent is not defined by the PLACL but clearly follows the well-known structure of offer and acceptance required for a contract to be considered as concluded. This is also the case for all the Latin American legal systems under scrutiny here, and is also a common feature of comparative contract law since, despite the evolution of means of communication and commercial practices, 'under all European and international legal regimes, the formation of contract is the manifestation of a consensus by means of offer and acceptance'.[12]

It is true that in some cases, the application of the model of offer and acceptance seems artificial (eg, multi-party contracts), while in others it is extremely difficult to ascertain what is an offer or an acceptance (eg, in complex and lengthy negotiations). However, the model has proved useful for the analysis of the process of formation *ex post* by the parties or the courts.[13] The model also gives certainty and predictability by providing a set of rules applicable to the process of formation of contract.[14]

A. Definition of Offer

The definition of offer is provided by Article 15(1) PLACL: 'A proposal for the conclusion of a contract constitutes an offer if it indicates the intention of the offeror to be bound in case of acceptance and if it is sufficiently definite'. The concept is similar to those included in other international instruments: Articles 14(1) CISG, 2.1.2 PICC, 2:201(1) PECL and II.- 4:201 DCFR. The new text of Article 1114 of the *Code civil* requires that the offer 'contains the essential elements of the intended contract', a definition that can be linked to the

[12] M Illmer, 'Contract (Formation)' in J Basedow, K Hopt and R Zimmermann (eds), *The Max Planck Encyclopedia of European Private Law* (Oxford, Oxford University Press, 2012) 378.

[13] P Perales, 'The Formation of Contracts & the Principles of European Contract Law' [2001] *Pace International Law Review* 376.

[14] J Cartwright, *Contract Law: An Introduction to the English Law of Contract for the Civil Lawyer*, 2nd edn (Oxford, Hart Publishing, 2013) 101–02.

aforementioned distinction between *essentialia* and *accidentalia negotii*.[15] Curiously, most of the Latin American codes do not provide a concept of offer.[16]

The definition expressed in Article 15(1) contains the two elements that have been routinely required by Latin American legal doctrine for the existence of an offer, that is, its seriousness (or intention to be bound) and its completeness. These requirements are examined in the following paragraphs.

B. Definiteness of the Offer

If we follow the classic Latin American doctrine, the definiteness or completeness of the offer means that the offer must include and specify all the (essential) elements of the contract, in the sense that its mere or bare acceptance will be sufficient to conclude it, without further elaboration or specification, at least with regard to those essential elements.[17]

However, in contemporary contract law, the requirement for the offer to be 'sufficiently definite' deserves more attention. Commenting on Article 2.1.2 PICC, it has been argued that definiteness is merely accessory to the parties' intention to be bound, especially when considering Article 2.1.14 PICC (contract with terms deliberately left open) and the provisions on open terms, implied terms, quality of performance and determination of the price.[18] In some jurisdictions, the sufficiency requirement is fulfilled 'even in the case of a reservation of future specification or in the case of the right of one party to subsequently determine specific contract terms unilaterally'.[19] The necessities of modern commercial practice and the existence of incomplete contracts have been cited as reasons for this broad understanding of sufficiency.

The assertion that the intention to be bound is the only 'real' requirement in international law instruments for the formation of a valid contract is confirmed by the Official Comments to Article 2.1.2 PICC, which state that indefiniteness is not an insurmountable problem for a proposal to constitute an offer, stressing that even essential terms of the contract may be left undetermined if the parties intend to be bound by the agreement and the indefiniteness may be overcome by other means such as the rules on interpretation or implied terms, the usages or practices between the parties, or any other applicable provision.[20]

[15] Art 1114: 'L'offre, faite à personne déterminée ou indéterminée, comprend les éléments essentiels du contrat envisagé et exprime la volonté de son auteur d'être lié en cas d'acceptation. A défaut, il y a seulement invitation à entrer en négociation'.

[16] Notably, the new Argentinean Civil Code defines offer in Article 972.

[17] Default legal rules may supplement the agreement of the parties, but those rules are mainly concerned with secondary obligations and not with the core of the agreement.

[18] L Mottago, 'Article 2.1.2' in S Vogenauer (ed), *Commentary on the UNIDROIT Principles of International Commercial Contracts (PICC)*, 2nd edn (Oxford, Oxford University Press, 2015) para 2. Art 2.1.14 PICC provides that 'If the parties intend to conclude a contract, the fact that they intentionally leave a term to be agreed upon in further negotiations or to be determined by a third person does not prevent a contract from coming into existence'.

[19] Illmer (n 12) 379.

[20] Official Comment to Art 2.1.2 PICC.

Accordingly, the Official Comments to Article II.-4:103 DCFR state that the parameter is not whether the object or the price of the contract is determined or determinable, 'but a broader one of whether the agreement reached is sufficient, or can be fleshed out sufficiently, for the contract to be given effect'.[21]

The difficulty of ascertaining with precision whether the offer or the agreement is sufficiently determined is demonstrated by the rules provided by the aforementioned Article II.-4:103(1) DCFR. The provision is rather obscure and even useless. It is self-evident that it will be a *sufficient* agreement if the terms of the contract have been *sufficiently* defined by the parties or can be otherwise *sufficiently* determined. In a deficient drafting technique, the key term, the adjective 'sufficient', is defined by its own adverb ('sufficiently').

Article 14(1) CISG contains the more precise rule with regard to the definiteness of the offer (but limited to the contract of sale): a proposal is sufficiently definite if it indicates the goods and expressly or implicitly fixes or makes provision for determining the quantity and the price. However, concerning the price, this rule has to be complemented with the rather contradictory Article 55.[22] The term 'implicitly' has been interpreted as referring to circumstances, either internal or external, by which the content of the contract may be determined.[23]

The case law related to Article 14 CISG has provided some examples of how to determine the sufficient definitiveness of an offer. For instance, it has been held that the terms as to quantity, quality and price may be implicitly fixed by the past practices established between the parties. Thus, proposals to purchase 'three truckloads of eggs',[24] 'a larger amount of chinchilla pelts of medium or superior quality'[25] and 'twenty truckloads of tomato concentrate'[26] were considered sufficiently definite. Likewise, the conclusion of a contract was not held to be prevented by the fact that the parties agreed on an approximate quantity of gas to be delivered where that statement reflected a common usage in the natural gas trade. Similarly, on the basis of industry customs, an agreement on the delivery of 'commercial quantities' of clathrate was considered to be sufficiently definite,[27] as was a framework agreement which provided that the buyer would purchase 'up to 250,000 pounds' per year.[28]

[21] Official Comment to Art II.- 4:103 DCFR.

[22] Art 55 CISG provides: 'Where a contract has been validly concluded but does not expressly or implicitly fix or make provision for determining the price, the parties are considered, in the absence of any indication to the contrary, to have impliedly made reference to the price generally charged at the time of the conclusion of the contract for such goods sold under comparable circumstances in the trade concerned'.

[23] U Schroeter, 'Article 14' in I Schwenzer (ed), *Schlechtriem & Schwenzer Commentary on the UN Convention on the International Sale of Goods (CISG)*, 3rd edn (Oxford, Oxford University Press, 2010) para 8.

[24] Landgericht Oldenburg (Germany) 28 February 1996, CISG-Online no 189.

[25] Oberster Gerichtshof (Austria) 10 November 1994, CISG-Online no 117.

[26] Oberlandesgericht Hamburg (Germany) 4 July 1997, CISG-Online no 1299.

[27] *Geneva Pharmaceuticals Technology Corp v Barr Laboratories Inc*, US Dist CT (SD NY), F Supp 201, 236, 282, 10 May 2002, CISG-online no 653.

[28] *Solae LLC v Hershey Canada Inc*, US Dist Ct (D Del), F Supp 2d 452, 456, 9 May 2008, CISG-online no 1769.

It is doubtful whether such a broad understanding of the definiteness of the offer is in accordance with Latin American contract law. Usually, Latin American case law and legal doctrine require that the offer must be complete, that is, include all the essential elements of the contract so that the mere acceptance of its terms by the offeree will form the contract.[29] The lack of rules on the content of the contract in the Principles is an additional difficulty. A rule such as Article 2.1.14 PICC does not sit easily with Latin American private law.

It is true that Article 38 PLACL provides that the subject-matter of the contract must be 'ascertained or *ascertainable*', but it is doubtful if that provision is broad enough for a contract to be considered valid in cases similar to those related to Article 14 CISG. In this sense, the traditional interpretation of similar provisions by Latin American doctrine has been restrictive.[30] If the PLACL purport to be suitable for commercial transactions, the option for the 'sufficient definitiveness' of the offer should be construed extensively, providing flexibility for the parties and the courts in addressing the problem of determining the existence of a contract and furthermore, its content.

The above-mentioned French reform, consolidating the case law of the Cour de Cassation, also allows a certain degree of indeterminacy in framework contracts and service contracts.[31]

C. Seriousness and Intention to Be Bound

To constitute an offer, the proposal must indicate the intention of the offeror to be bound in case of acceptance (Article 15(1) PLACL). This requisite is not further developed by the PLACL. Certainly, the offeror may express his intention explicitly, for instance by stating that the proposal is a 'binding offer', but in practice this is not the general rule. On the contrary, the most common situation will be that the proposal is formulated 'without obligation', 'subject to agreement', 'subject to confirmation' or with other terms that express the intention of the proponent not to be bound but merely to be ready to start the negotiations, implying that the proposal is only an invitation to make an offer (*invitatio ad offerendum*).

In most cases, the proposal will be silent in this respect and give no such indication. In order to determine if the proponent intended to be bound by his declaration, the proposal should in those cases be examined objectively, considering how it would be understood by a reasonable person in the position of the recipient.[32]

[29] See A Alessandri, M Somarriva and A Vodavonic, *Tratado de Derecho Civil. Partes preliminar y general* (Santiago, Editorial Juridica de Chile, 2011) para 1262: 'Las ofertas incompletas, o sea, las que no determinan todas las condiciones del contrato propuesto, no son propiamente ofertas'.

[30] See Arts 1003 Civil Code (CC) Argentina, 104(2) CC Brazil, 1461 CC Chile, 1518 CC Colombia, 1555 CC Venezuela, 1261 no 3 and 1283 CC Uruguay.

[31] Ass plén, 1 December 1995, Bull Ass plén no 9.

[32] H Kötz, *European Contract Law. Vol. 1: Formation, Validity, and Content of Contracts; Contract and Third Parties* (Oxford, Clarendon Press, 1998) 19.

Thus, in principle, a detailed proposal is likely to be construed as an offer.[33] Previous dealings between the parties and usages and practices are also relevant. If the proposal is made in the context of a commercial transaction, the proponent's intention to be bound is subject to a rebuttable presumption in some jurisdictions.[34] Since no presumption is established by the PLACL, in case of conflict as to the existence of a contract, the burden of proof is on the party alleging that the contract was concluded.

D. Offers to the Public

Article 15(2) PLACL recognises that an offer may be made to the public in general. In theory, it seems logical to consider that a proposal made to an indeterminate number of persons is not an offer, since otherwise any addressee would be entitled to accept it and therefore a large number of contracts would be concluded, generating an unreasonable burden for the proponent.[35] Also, in a commercial context, a supplier may wish to check some relevant characteristics of its customers, such as their creditworthiness, before a contract is concluded.[36] The same applies when the identity of the other party is relevant for the proponent, as in the case of *intuito personae* contracts.[37]

This recognition by the PLACL of the *possibility* that an offer may be made to the public can be explained by the fact that the *effectiveness* of offers to the public is disputed in comparative law. The intention of the PLACL seems to be to clarify that in certain circumstances a proposal to the public may be considered as an offer. In Latin American law, such offers are generally not binding (Argentina, Article 973; Chilean Commercial Code, Article 105; Paraguay, Article 685(2); Uruguay, Article 1262—requirement that the offer must be directed to a specific person; but see Brazil, Article 429, and Colombia, Article 848 Commercial Code). In France, offers to the public are considered valid, but in German and English law proposals to the public do not generally indicate an intention to be bound but only invitations to treat.[38]

However, legal systems that do not accept proposals to the public as offers nevertheless recognise major exceptions to that rule. Evidently, it is always possible for the proponent expressly to state that the proposal to the public is intended to

[33] R Schlesinger (ed), *Formation of Contracts: A Study of the Common Core of Legal Systems* (Dobbs Ferry, NY, Oceana Publications, 1968) 78.

[34] See Nottage (n 18) para 15, stating that it is 'arguably found in Anglo-Australian or French law'.

[35] See for an English case, *Grainger & Son v Gough* [1896] AC 325, HL. See also *Partridge v Crittenden* [1968] 1 WLR 1204, QBD.

[36] Nottage (n 18) para 8.

[37] H Beale, B Fauvarque-Cosson, J Rutgers, D Tallon and S Vogenauer, *Cases, Materials and Text on Contract Law: Ius Commune Casebooks for the Common Law of Europe*, 2nd edn (Oxford, Hart Publishing, 2010) 254.

[38] ibid, 254–57. But see *Carlill v Carbolic Smoke Ball Co* [1893] 1 QB 256, CA.

be an offer. Likewise, the circumstances under which the proposal is made may indicate that it constitutes an offer. Such will be the case if the proposal has sufficient content and clarity, and indicates, eg, the number of goods in stock or a time-limit for its acceptance, or contains expressions such as 'as long as stock lasts' or 'first-come-first-served'.[39]

To be considered as an offer, a proposal to the public must comply with the requirements established in Article 15(1) PLACL, that is, the intention of the offeror to be bound and sufficiency. Again, the intention to be bound must be ascertained objectively in order to differentiate this situation from an *invitatio ad offerendum*.

The PECL (Article 2:201(3)) and the DCFR (Article II.-4:201(3)) provide a presumption of offer in the case of public advertisements, catalogues or display of goods. These particular situations are not expressly addressed by the PLACL, but should be covered by the general rule of Article 15(2) PLACL. Thus, if the conditions required for a proposal to constitute an offer are fulfilled, it will be possible to consider such situations as an offer. This may make sense for consumer transactions, since it prevents the supplier from deceiving consumers by quoting false prices or from refusing to sell products or provide services without valid reason.[40] For consumer contracts, most Latin American jurisdictions follow the general rule in considering that proposals made to the public (consumers) are valid as offers, and therefore, that the consumer is entitled to enforce their terms.[41]

However, in a commercial context, for the reasons stated, the matter is more problematic. The PICC are silent in this respect and it has been argued that 'in case of doubt, proposals to the public constitute mere invitations to make offers'.[42] Article 14(2) CISG took the opposite approach of the PECL and the DCFR, providing that 'A proposal other than one addressed to one or more specific persons is to be considered merely as an invitation to make offers, unless the contrary is clearly indicated by the person making the proposal'. The CESL follows the same solution in its Article 31(3): 'A proposal made to the public is not an offer, unless the circumstances indicate otherwise'.[43]

Interestingly, Article 685 of the Paraguayan Civil Code seems to address the problem, providing a different treatment for the distribution of tariff or price

[39] E Terryn, 'Article 31' in R Schulze (ed), *Common European Sales Law (CESL): Commentary* (Baden-Baden, Nomos, 2012) para 7. The American case *Lefkowitz v Great Minneapolis Surplus Store*, 86 NW 2d 689 (1957) provides a good example, where the advertisement 'Saturday 9 AM Sharp 3 Brand New Fur Coats Worth to $100.00 First Come First Served $1 Each' was found to be to be an offer and not an invitation to treat.

[40] For instance, on discriminatory grounds.

[41] See Art 12 ley 17.250 *Defensa del Consumidor*, Uruguay; Arts 12 and 13 ley 19.496 *sobre Protección de los derechos de los consumidores*, Chile; and Art 7 ley 24.240 de *Protección y defensa de los consumidores*, Argentina

[42] J Kleinheisterkamp, 'Article 2.1.2' in S Vogenauer and J Kleinheisterkamp (eds), *Commentary on the UNIDROIT Principles of International Commercial Contracts (PICC)* (Oxford, Oxford University Press, 2009) para 18.

[43] For criticism of the solution, in particular from the perspective of consumer transactions, see Terryn (n 39) paras 9–10.

lists, presumably frequent in commercial relations, which do not constitute offers, and the public display of goods with an indication of price, where consumers will generally be involved, which is considered as an offer.

E. Effect, Withdrawal, Revocation and Expiration of Offer

i. Effect and Withdrawal of the Offer

Article 16(1) PLACL provides that the offer becomes effective when it reaches the offeree. If the offer is oral or made by an instantaneous means of communication, such as a telephone or video conference, the offer reaches the offeree immediately (Articles 675 CC Paraguay, 974 CC Argentina, 428(I) CC Brazil). If the offer is made by other means, it reaches the offeree when it enters the latter's area of control and he can inform himself of it.[44]

The PLACL distinguish between withdrawal and revocation of the offer. If the offer is retracted before it has become effective, the offer is *withdrawn*.[45] If the retraction takes place after the offer has become effective, the offer has been *revoked*.

As a logical consequence, Article 16(2) PLACL provides that an offer may be withdrawn before it reaches the offeree. This is something that is widely accepted, adding that a withdrawal is effective also if it reaches the offeree at the same time as the offer.[46] The rule is consistent with the freedom of the parties to enter into contracts (Article 5 PLACL), since it allows the offeror to change his mind and prevent the conclusion of a contract into which he no longer wishes to enter. Equally, the offeree for his part is also protected since he is unaware of the original offer and so cannot act on it.[47]

The ascertainment of the period during which the offeror may validly withdraw the offer is relevant in contracts *inter absentes*. Even considering that the offer becomes effective when it enters the area of control of the offeree and he can make himself acquainted with it, actual knowledge of the offer is not required. For instance, it is sufficient that the letter has been delivered to the house or place of business of the offeree; whether he has read it or not is irrelevant.[48]

ii. Revocation of the Offer

Determining whether an offer has become effective is more important if the offer cannot, as a default rule, be revoked. Comparative law mainly distinguishes three

[44] Kötz (n 32) 20.

[45] The withdrawal of the offer must not be confused with the *right of withdrawal*, which is granted to a party (generally, a consumer), under certain circumstances, to withdraw from a concluded *contract*.

[46] See for instance, Article 975 CC Argentina, Article 428(IV) CC Brazil, Article 15(2) CISG.

[47] L Nottage, 'Article 2.1.3' in S Vogenauer (ed), *Commentary on the UNIDROIT Principles of International Commercial Contracts (PICC)*, 2nd edn (Oxford, Oxford University Press, 2015) para 6.

[48] Beale et al (n 37) 266.

options with regard to the revocation of an offer. First, an offer may be revoked at any time until it has been accepted, which means that the offer is not binding at all. This is the position of English law. Secondly, under French law, the general rule is also the revocability of the offer until its acceptance, but the offeror can be liable in damages if revocation is abusive, that is, if he revokes the offer before the expiry of a given period he has fixed for acceptance, or before the expiry of a *délai raisonnable*.[49] Finally, in German law, the revocation of an offer has no effect until the expiry of the period fixed in the offer or, by default, a reasonable period. However, this binding effect can be excluded by stating that the offer is not binding (*freibleibend*).[50]

The PLACL take an intermediate approach in Articles 17 and 18 that is closer to the position adopted by the CISG (Article 16), the PECL (Article 2:202), the PICC (Article 2.1.4) and the DCFR (Article II.-4:202). The general rule is that the offer may be revoked before the offeree has dispatched its acceptance (Article 17(1) PLACL). However, this general rule is subject to important qualifications: the offer is irrevocable if the offeror has indicated that it is irrevocable or has fixed a time for its acceptance and the offeror does not expressly reserve the power to revoke it (Article 18(1) PLACL), and if the offeree has been able to rely, in good faith, on the offer being irrevocable (Article 18(2) PLACL). The cause of the offeree's reliance may be, eg, the conduct of the offeror, previous transactions between the parties or the nature of the offer.

This rule, which implies that, in general, the offer is not binding on the offeror, again reflects the principle of freedom of contract, but is also consistent with the freedom of the parties to negotiate and to withdraw from the negotiations at any time (Article 10(2) PLACL), which in the case of revocation of the offer is the time before the offeree has dispatched his acceptance. This rule reflects a good balance between the interests of the offeror and the protection of the offeree.

The consequence of irrevocability is not expressly stated in the PLACL. In theory, there are two alternatives: the offeror is liable to pay damages to the offeree for abusive revocation, but no contract is formed even though the offeree has accepted the offer; or the revocation has no effect and therefore the contract is concluded by the offeree's acceptance.

It can be argued that for the cases contemplated by Article 18(1) PLACL, where the intention of the offeror seems clear in order to indicate the irrevocability of the offer, a subsequent revocation should not prevent the conclusion of the contract if the offeree decides to accept the offer. Therefore, if the offeror refuses to perform, the offeree will be able to rely on the remedies for breach of contract provided by Section 2 of Chapter 8. However, in the case of Article 18(2) PLACL, the same conclusion should be qualified. The situation addressed by Article 18(2) is exceptional

[49] The reform of the French *Code civil* has confirmed the case law on this subject, expressly limiting damages to the negative interest. See Art 1116.

[50] For details, see Kötz (n 32) 22–23.

in relation to that of Article 18(1), and its aim is to protect the legitimate reliance of the offeree and therefore to compensate him for harm caused by that reliance. This interpretation is in line with the rules on contract negotiation provided by Section 2 of Chapter 2. Accordingly, the aggrieved offeree need not necessarily be considered as an obligee entitled to the full range of remedies provided for breach of contract. As in the case of contract negotiations, the general rule should be the award of reliance damages. Only in qualified circumstances should expectation damages or specific performance be available to the aggrieved offeree.[51]

F. Acceptance

i. Definition of Acceptance

Generally, Latin American codes do not provide a definition of acceptance. Article 20 PLACL defines acceptance as 'Any statement made by or other conduct of the offeree indicating assent to an offer'. This rule is similar to Articles 18(1) CISG, 2.1.6(1) PICC, 2:204 PECL, II.-4:204 DCFR and 34 CESL. At the core of the definition lies the necessity of an indication of assent by the offeree to the terms of the offer formulated by the offeror. Therefore, the acceptance must be unqualified, that is, it must correspond to the terms of offer, without introducing any alteration, modification or additions to those terms. This principle is reflected in Article 20(2) PLACL, and is generally accepted in uniform and domestic law.[52] However, the rule is not absolute and deserves some further clarification.[53]

ii. Form and Effects of Acceptance

Article 20(1) PLACL expressly provides that acceptance may be effected by any statement (or declaration) made by the offeree or by his conduct. Additionally, the offer may state a particular form for the acceptance to be effective. The provision coincides with those in Latin American codes, which usually provide that the acceptance may be effected in explicit or implicit (tacit) terms.[54] Exceptionally,

[51] In the same sense, J Kleinheisterkamp, 'Article 2.1.4' in S Vogenauer and J Kleinheisterkamp (eds), *Commentary on the UNIDROIT Principles of International Commercial Contracts (PICC)* (Oxford, Oxford University Press, 2009) paras 19–26, providing as an example the case of a general contractor, who can reasonably expect the offer (bid) of a subcontractor to be irrevocable until the main contract has been awarded, when that offer has been used for the calculation of the main bid, with the knowledge of the subcontractor.

[52] See Arts 19(1) CISG, 2:208(1) PECL, 2.1.11(1) PICC, II.-4:208 DCFR and 38 CESL. In Latin America, Civil Codes of Argentina (Art 978), Brazil (Art 431), Paraguay (Art 681), Uruguay (Art 1267) and Venezuela (Art 1137); and Commercial Codes of Chile (Art 103) and Colombia (Art 855).

[53] See below, at F.iii.

[54] See Civil Codes of Argentina (Art 979), Brazil (Art 432) and Paraguay (Art 674); and Commercial Codes of Chile (Art 103) and Colombia (Art 854).

silence may be considered as acceptance (Article 21 PLACL), a rule that again is generally accepted in uniform and domestic law.[55]

With regard to the effects of acceptance, Article 22 PLACL follows the trend of uniform law instruments, stating that a contract is concluded at the time the acceptance reaches the offeror.[56] The rule is mostly relevant for contracts *inter absentes*, since if the offer is oral, it must be accepted immediately, unless the circumstances indicate otherwise (Article 23(2) PLACL). It is true that, with the prevalence of immediate or instantaneous means of communication, the issue of the exact moment when an acceptance becomes effective has lost much practical importance.[57] As in the case of the offer, it is considered that the acceptance reaches the offeror when it enters the area of control of the offeror and he can acquaint himself with it, but actual knowledge of the acceptance is not required. Interestingly, the Official Comment to Article 1.10 PICC states that an electronic communication reaches the addressee when it has entered the addressee's server or when it has been delivered to his electronic mailing address.[58]

It is important to recognise the interplay between the revocability of the offer and the effectiveness of the acceptance. The PLACL provide a solution that acknowledges the interests of both parties: although the acceptance does not become effective before it reaches the offeror, a revocation of the offer must reach the offeree before he has dispatched his acceptance. This solution gives the offeree the opportunity to withdraw his acceptance if the withdrawal reaches the offeror before or at the same time as the acceptance (Article 26 PLACL). On the other hand, if the acceptance never reaches the offeror, no contract will be concluded.

On this subject, Latin American codes distinguish mainly between verbal (or *inter praesentes*) and *inter absentes* offers. In the former case, the offer must be accepted immediately.[59] In the other cases, the solution is not uniform: Articles 971 CC Argentina, 864 CCom Colombia and 1265 CC Uruguay provide that the contract is concluded with the reception of the acceptance or, in other words, when the acceptance reaches the offeror. Similarly, the Venezuelan Civil Code (Article 1137) provides that the contract is perfect from the moment the offeror has knowledge of the acceptance. The Brazilian (Article 434) and Paraguayan (Article 688) Civil Codes state that the contract is concluded when acceptance is dispatched; and the Chilean Commercial Code provides that the contract is concluded at the time of acceptance.

[55] See A León, *La voluntad y la capacidad en los actos jurídicos*, 4th edn (Santiago, Editorial Jurídica de Chile, 1991) 33–38.

[56] See Arts 18(2) CISG, 2.1.6(2) PICC, 2:205(1) PECL, II.-4:205 DCFR and 35(1) CESL. The rule is also followed in English law, with the relevant exception of the 'postal rule': if acceptance is communicated by mail, it becomes effective with the dispatch of the letter.

[57] Kötz (n 32) 25.

[58] Official Comment to Art 1.10 PICC.

[59] Civil Codes of Argentina (Art 980), Brazil (Art 428(1)), Paraguay (Art 675), Uruguay (Art 1263); Commercial Codes of Chile (Art 97) and Colombia (Art 850).

iii. Modified Acceptance

As stated above, acceptance must be unqualified, that is, it must reflect exactly the terms of the offer in order to form an agreement and therefore a contract. This is the so-called 'mirror-image rule'. Therefore, a simple 'yes' to the offer should be sufficient to conclude the contract. This rule is generally accepted in domestic and uniform law, and therefore, an acceptance that modifies the offer is regarded as a rejection of that offer and will be considered as a new proposal. Article 20(2) PLACL clearly establishes this rule: 'Modifications to an offer by the offeree constitute the proposal of a new contract'. Latin American codes and doctrine unanimously agree with this solution.[60]

However, some cases can be doubtful: if 50 things are offered for sale to a person who replies that he will buy 80, it is a matter of construction whether he is accepting the offer of 50 and asking for a further 30, or whether he is rejecting the offer and intends to buy either 80 or none.[61]

Contemporary uniform contract law instruments do not consider the mirror-image rule as absolute. If the acceptance differs from the offer in minor aspects, which do not alter or modify the substantive terms of the offer, those alterations become part of the contract, which is therefore concluded. The main rationale for this solution is that if the acceptance differs from the offer only in minor or accessory aspects, the offeror might remain inactive and only dispute the existence of an offer, alleging that on contract has ever been concluded if the contract turns out to have been a bad bargain.[62] This rule has been widely adopted in uniform law: Articles 19(2) CISG, 2.1.11 PICC, 2:208 PECL, II.-4:208 DCFR and 38 CESL.[63]

On the other hand, there is no such rule in the Latin American legal systems; on the contrary, the provisions in the various codes seem to be very strict in the sense that a modified acceptance always implies a new proposal. Nevertheless, in an innovative provision for Latin American contract law, Article 25 PLACL (Agreement with the terms of the offer) follows the trend of uniform law. Its first paragraph confirms the general rule (already stated in Article 20 PLACL) that '[a] reply to an offer that contains additions, limitations, or modifications constitutes a counteroffer', but its second paragraph provides that 'if the terms of the offer are not materially altered, the reply constitutes an acceptance, and the contract will be concluded with such additions, limitations, or modifications'.[64] To avoid

[60] See Civil Codes of Argentina (Art 978), Brazil (Art 431), Paraguay (Art 681), Uruguay (Art 1267) and Venezuela (Art 1137); Commercial Codes of Chile (Art 102) and Colombia (Art 855). The same can be said of the French reform, see Art 1118(3) of the revised *Code civil*.

[61] Example provided by Kötz (n 32) 31.

[62] ibid.

[63] The source seems to be the Swedish Contract Law Act 1915 and § 2-207(2) UCC (USA). For sources and criticism of the UCC rule, see R Anderson, 'Article 2.1.11' in S Vogenauer (ed), *Commentary on the UNIDROIT Principles of International Commercial Contracts (PICC)*, 2nd edn (Oxford, Oxford University Press, 2015) paras 5–6.

[64] The exception is confirmed (or pre-confirmed) in Art 19(2).

misinterpretations, the repetition of the general rule in Articles 20(2) and 25(1) PLACL should be corrected. In addition, the terminology of the two provisions does not coincide: in Article 20(2), the modified acceptance constitutes 'the proposal of a new contract', whereas in Article 25(1), it is a 'counteroffer'.

However, the offeror still has the option of avoiding the conclusion of the contract in case of modified acceptance if he states expressly that the offer requires full or partial acceptance of the proposed terms (Article 25(3)(a) PLACL), or if he informs the offeree, without delay, of his objections to the changes (Article 25(3)(b) PLACL).

The main difficulty with these rules is to determine when the terms of an offer are *materially* altered. The Official Comment to Article 2.1.11 PICC states that this is an issue that cannot be determined in the abstract but will depend on the circumstances of each case. The Official Comment to Article 2:208 PECL asserts that a term is material if the offeree knows or should have known that 'the offeror would be influenced in its decision as to whether to contract or as to the terms on which to contract'.[65] Article 19(3) CISG expressly provides a presumptive and non-exhaustive list of terms that are considered materially to alter the terms of the offer. Therefore, in principle, a modification of those terms, even a minor one, materially alters the terms of the offer and prevents the conclusion of the contract. However, this rule can be challenged. For instance, there is no reason to consider a slight or minor discrepancy in the price in a high-value transaction as material.

The case law related to Article 19(3) CISG shows that a case-by-case analysis is unavoidable.[66] Some criteria that have been proposed to assess the materiality of the terms include the reasonable expectations of the offeror, the nature of the terms altered (essential or accidental terms) or introduced (for instance, terms that in any case would have been implied in the agreement), and usages and prior practices between the parties.[67] In the same sense, it has been stated that '[t]he question is whether what has been introduced would have been regarded by a reasonable offeror as introducing a new term into the bargain rather than acceptance of the offer'.[68] In any case, the exceptions to the general rule should be strictly construed.

[65] Official Comment C to Art 2:208 PECL.

[66] See P Huber and A Mullis, *The CISG: A New Textbook for Students and Practitioners* (Munich, Sellier, 2007) 89–91, citing a French decision in which it was held that a term stating that the price would be modified by increases as well as decreases in the market price was not material. Art 38(2) CESL also provides a presumptive and non-exhaustive list of terms whose modification is considered materially to alter the terms of the offer. See also Anderson (n 63) paras 7–13.

[67] ibid, para 10.

[68] G Treitel, *The Law of Contract*, 13th edn by E Peel (London, Sweet and Maxwell, 2011) para 2-019, with references to English case law.

V. Missing Issues

Some important issues in respect of formation have been omitted from the PLACL. While it may be true that most of these are not usually contemplated in Latin American civil codes, the fact remains that, if the Principles purport to offer an alternative to commercial parties or to act as a guide to national courts and arbitrators, it would seem that the following issues should be addressed.

A. Letters of Confirmation

This issue is related to written confirmation (eg, 'confirmation of order' forms) sent after the conclusion of the contract, whether it was concluded orally or by informal communication. Here, one party intends to 'confirm' the contract by sending out a document containing the terms supposedly agreed. This document may include the standard terms of the party or even terms he believes were implied in the agreement. A problem may arise because in most cases, some of these terms will be new (they were never discussed by the parties) or they modify (generally secondary or accessory) terms already agreed.

Unlike modified acceptance, a letter of confirmation may be sent when the contract has been already concluded. However, the effect is similar: the additional or different terms contained in the letter of confirmation become part of the contract, unless they materially alter the contract or the recipient, without undue delay, objects to the discrepancy (Articles 2.1.12 PICC, 2:210 PECL and II.-4:210 DCFR).[69] There is no uniform approach in comparative contract law to this subject, but its omission could be criticised since it constitutes a useful tool to promote legal certainty, avoiding situations in which one party might try to back out of an agreement because of discrepancies in secondary or ancillary terms.[70]

B. Merger Clauses

It is common practice in international trade for the parties to insert a 'merger clause', intended to ensure that the writing embodies all the terms of the contract. The aim of such clauses is to protect the integrity of the writing, with the effect of

[69] The issue is not expressly included in the CISG, but 'the drafters decided that silence in response to such a letter cannot create a binding contract under the Convention's rules': U Schroeter, 'Introduction to Articles 14–24' in I Schwenzer (ed), *Schlechtriem & Schwenzer Commentary on the UN Convention on the International Sale of Goods (CISG)*, 3rd edn (Oxford, Oxford University Press, 2010) para 30.

[70] For criticism because of the lack of a similar provision in the CESL, see E Terryn, 'Article 38' in R Schulze (ed), *Common European Sales Law (CESL): Commentary* (Baden-Baden, Nomos, 2012) paras 12–13.

restricting the availability of evidence of prior statements or agreements, which is inadmissible if it is alleged to contradict or supplement the written contract. Since the PLACL do not reject or limit the admission of extrinsic evidence, and recourse to pre-contractual negotiations is expressly allowed by the rules of interpretation, the inclusion of a provision dealing with the validity of merger clauses would bring certainty to cases where the parties have agreed such a clause. The validity of merger clauses has been recognised, to different degrees, in all uniform international law instruments with the exception of the CISG.[71]

C. Standard Terms

The use of standard terms[72] is a common feature not only in business-to-consumer but also in business-to-business contracts. The standardisation of commercial contracts is widely recognised in legal literature, basically as an inevitable consequence of the modern mass-production economy.[73]

It is true that, traditionally, the regulation of standard terms has been absent from civil and commercial codes, and they were for a long time confined to consumer law instruments, mostly through the control of unfair terms. However, the trend nowadays is to incorporate the regulation of standard terms (including but not limited to unfair terms) into the general part of contract law. The German BGB, the Dutch BW and the DCFR are paradigmatic examples. In Latin America, the Civil Codes of Argentina (Articles 984 to 989), Brazil (Articles 423 and 424) and Paraguay (Article 691) include provisions which regulate the incorporation of standard terms into a contract, albeit to different degrees.

The trend is the same in uniform contract law, where the incorporation of matters related to standard terms has steadily increased. Thus, even though the CISG is silent in this matter, the PICC address it in Articles 2.1.19 (Contracting under standard terms), 2.1.20 (Surprising terms), 2.1.21 (Conflict between standard terms and non-standard terms) and 2.1.22 (Battle of forms). However, the PICC do not contain provisions dealing with the substantive control of unfair or abusive standard terms.[74] The PECL include provisions on terms not individually

[71] See Arts 2.1.17 PICC, 2:105 PECL, II.-4:104 DCFR and 72 CESL. In the case of the CISG, even though the CISG does not deal with merger clauses, it has been stated that in contracts governed by the CISG the effect of such a clause 'may be to prevent a party from relying on evidence of statements or agreements not contained in the writing. Moreover, if the parties so intend, a Merger Clause may bar evidence of trade usages'. See CISG-AC Opinion No 3, Parol Evidence Rule, Plain Meaning Rule, Contractual Merger Clause and the CISG, 23 October 2004, para 4.

[72] The PICC defines standard terms in Art 2.1.19(2) as those 'provisions which are prepared in advance for general and repeated use by one party and which are actually used without negotiation with the other party'.

[73] There is a vast corpus of literature on the subject. See generally, H Collins, *Regulating Contracts* (Oxford, Oxford University Press, 1999).

[74] Some provisions, applicable to any kind of contractual terms (negotiated and standard), may be used for the control of the substantive content of contract clauses: Arts 3.27 (Gross disparity), 7.1.6 (Exemption clauses), and the *contra proferentem* rule of interpretation of Art 4.6.

negotiated (Article 2:104), conflicting general conditions (Article 2:209) and, notably, unfair terms which have not been individually negotiated (Article 4:110). Since they are intended to apply also to consumer contracts, the regulation of standard terms is broader in the DCFR and the CESL, particularly with regard to unfair terms.[75]

The matter is not dealt with in the PLACL. Only a few provisions, which apply to terms of whatever kind, could be suitable for cases related to standard terms.[76] This is regrettable, and the fact that the PLACL are not intended to regulate consumer contracts is not a valid justification. The widespread use of standard terms in commercial contracts is sufficient reason to incorporate a minimum set of rules on the matter, in particular those dealing with the formal requirements for their inclusion in the agreement, the validity of surprising terms, their interpretation and the battle of forms. On the other hand, the control of the substantive fairness of standard terms is still a highly controversial matter, and the question of whether or not it should be included requires further debate and consensus in Latin American (and international) contract law.[77]

VI. Conclusions

This chapter set out to give an overview of the regulation of the formation of contracts in the PLACL. Even when the regulation of contract formation based on the model of offer and acceptance may vary between national legal systems, it seems that a uniform model has emerged in comparative legal discourse over the past 50 years.[78] As a consequence, the rules of the CISG, the PICC, the PECL, the DCFR and the CESL to a great extent coincide, and the same may be said with regard to the PLACL. In this sense, any deficiencies of the PLACL concern not so much the rules they include, but rather the issues they do not regulate.

The regulation of the definiteness of the offer and therefore, of the agreement, could be improved and should be addressed with the inclusion of provisions on open terms, implied terms and on the determination of the price. Since subject-matter and cause are regarded as essential elements of the contract, the natural place for such provisions would be the section on subject-matter.

Even though the PLACL are not intended to cover consumer contracts, the regulation of standard terms is another aspect that would deserve further attention.

[75] See DCFR, Book II, Chapter 9, Section 4 (Arts II.-9:401–II.-9:410), and CESL, Chapter 8 (Arts 79–86).

[76] Particularly, Art 37 (Gross disparity) and Art 70 (Clauses not negotiated bilaterally).

[77] In the same sense, see S Vogenauer, 'Introduction' in S Vogenauer (ed), *Commentary on the UNIDROIT Principles of International Commercial Contracts (PICC)*, 2nd edn (Oxford, Oxford University Press, 2015) para 53.

[78] Jansen and Zimmermann (n 4) 636–37.

Standard-form contracts are also common nowadays in commercial contracting and they should not therefore be disregarded in any body of rules dealing with contract law. As stated above, it would be appropriate for the PLACL to include rules dealing with the formal requirements for the inclusion of standard terms in the agreement, the validity of surprising terms, their interpretation and the battle of forms. It is a common feature of uniform contract law instruments that they regulate at least some core aspects of contracting under standard terms, and the PLACL should not be the exception.

9

Defects of the Contract under Articles 27 to 37 of the Principles of Latin American Contract Law

JOHN CARTWRIGHT

I. Introduction: Different Models of 'Defects' in the Formation of a Contract

Systems of contract law generally recognise that contracts are not validly formed where, at the moment when the apparent contract was entered into, one or both parties acted under a mistake, or one party was subjected to fraud, pressure or certain other forms of misconduct. There is certainly a common core of contract law in this area, although there are differences in the detail—sometimes very significant differences not only in the structure of the model adopted by different systems, but even in the result which legal systems will give in implementing their model.[1]

Some general points of comparison between the approaches of different legal systems in this area can be given at the outset, to form the basis for the following

[1] For comparative discussions, see H Kötz, *European Contract Law*, vol 1, trans T Weir (Oxford, Oxford University Press, 1997) chs 10 ('Mistake'), 11 ('Deceit and Duress'); K Zweigert and H Kötz, *An Introduction to Comparative Law*, 3rd edn, trans T Weir (Oxford, Oxford University Press, 1998) ch 31 ('Mistake, Deceit and Duress'); J Cartwright, 'Defects of Consent in Contract Law' in A Hartkamp and others (eds), *Towards a European Civil Code*, 4th edn (Alphen aan den Rijn, Kluwer Law International, 2011) ch 23 (and see chapters in earlier editions of this work by M van Rossum, 1st edn (Dordrecht, Martinus Nijhoff, 1994) ch 9; M Fabre-Magnan, 2nd edn (The Hague, Kluwer Law International, 1998) ch 14; M Fabre-Magnan and R Sefton-Green, 3rd edn (New York, Kluwer Law International, 2004) ch 22); R Sefton-Green (ed), *Mistake, Fraud and Duties to Inform in European Contract Law* (Cambridge, Cambridge University Press, 2005); J Cartwright, 'Defects of Consent and Security of Contract: French and English Law Compared' in P Birks and A Pretto (eds), *Themes in Comparative Law in Honour of Bernard Rudden* (Oxford, Oxford University Press, 2002) 153; J Cartwright and M Schmidt-Kessel, 'Defects in Consent: Mistake, Fraud, Threats, Unfair Exploitation' in G Dannemann and S Vogenauer (eds), *The Common European Sales Law in Context: Interactions with English and German Law* (Oxford, Oxford University Press, 2013) 373.

discussion of the approach taken by the Principles of Latin American Contract Law (PLACL).

A. What is Defective?

It is common for comparative lawyers in discussing this area to refer to the defects in *consent*, but sometimes we might speak of the defects of the *contract*. This is not just a matter of interchangeable terminology, however, since the choice of language will naturally relate to the basis of formation of the contract itself. Where the theory of contract formation is based on the parties' consent, it is natural to refer to that consent being invalid in order to explain why the contract is itself defective in consequence. But where the legal system uses different explanations for the creation of the contractual obligation, the language for the 'defects' in the formation of the contract may similarly differ.

B. What are the Grounds of Invalidity?

Legal systems commonly order this area under headings which can be translated into English as 'mistake', 'fraud' and 'duress', although even this apparent similarity can be misleading. Categories which appear to be the same in two systems might in fact have some significantly different rules, or be interpreted to cover different situations, at least at the margins. There are also, in some systems, other grounds of the consent (or the contract) being defective which are not universally acknowledged—in particular, some forms of exploitation of one party's weakness by the other party which fall outside the narrower category of duress.

C. What is the Remedy?

The natural and most common remedy in the case of defects in the formation of the contract is the invalidity of the contract. However, this common understanding masks a range of variations. Do the contractual obligations come into existence, subject to their being (retroactively) annulled, or are there circumstances in which the interference in the creation of the contract is so serious as to prevent the contract even coming into existence at all? If the obligations are annulled, what is the mechanism for the annulment: is a court order required, or is the party who seeks the remedy able to obtain it without the intervention of the court (for example, by giving notice to the other party)? What limits are there on the availability of the remedy, such as time limits for claims to be brought, and the impossibility of the parties' making restitution following the annulment of the contract? In addition to the generally recognised remedy of invalidity, there are other remedies under the law of some systems: damages may be available (either in addition to, or in place of, the invalidity of the contract); and the court might be given wider powers in some circumstances to intervene in the terms of the contract, for instance to adapt its terms.

D. What is the Theory Behind the Vitiating Factors?

The starting point for the vitiating factors discussed here is that they involve an interference with the party's decision to enter into the contract. Systems may differ, however, as to how significantly the party's consent must be affected; and even whether the interference with consent is in itself a sufficient reason for invalidity of the contract or whether it should require in addition that the other party was responsible for creating the situation by which the claimant's decision was interfered with, or acted wrongly in taking advantage of that situation. In some vitiating factors we can also see a focus on the inherent weakness of one of the parties vis-à-vis the other, or on the substantive unfairness of the terms of the contract, particularly in determining whether the 'weaker' party has been exploited. It is certainly too simple to describe this area as based on a defect in consent: even legal systems which base their theory of contract formation on the parties' consent have to provide a more finely nuanced account of the circumstances in which defects in consent will suffice to invalidate the contract, in order to avoid undermining the security of contracts. Legal systems take into account in different ways a range of issues in defining their vitiating factors and the scope of their operation: the degree of interference with the decision-making process of the party who seeks to avoid the contract (often put in terms of the causal link between the vitiating factor and the contract); the relationship of the parties (including their relative strengths, not only physical and economic but also in more practical terms, such as having, or having access to, information); the substantive fairness of the terms of the contract; and the behaviour of the party against whom the contract is sought to be avoided.

In order to evaluate the scheme of vitiating factors presented by the PLACL, it is useful to focus by way of comparison on some particular national legal systems and soft law principles. Many could be chosen, but here we shall include in the discussion certain contrasting systems and principles. Closely related to the Latin American jurisdictions are France and Spain; and the French system of contract law is particularly interesting to compare given that the provisions of the original Civil Code of 1804 have recently been subject to much critical review and have now been reformed.[2] Contrasting systems of contract law can be found in Germany and in England, which give respectively a different civil law and common law

[2] The new provisions of the Civil Code were created by Ordonnance no 2016-131 of 10 February 2016, and came into force on 1 October 2016. There is an authorised translation of the new provisions by J Cartwright, B Fauvarque-Cosson and S Whittaker at www.textes.justice.gouv.fr/art_pix/THE-LAW-OF-CONTRACT-2-5-16.pdf.

response to the questions we are considering here. In addition, these European jurisdictions have all been subject to review by the authors of recent sets of principles and rules of contract law which have no legal force, and may eventually be of only academic value,[3] but provide a critical assessment of contract law which is naturally of interest to the Latin American lawyer examining the proposed PLACL: the Principles of European Contract Law (PECL)[4] and other documents into which the PECL have been further developed: the Draft Common Frame of Reference (DCFR)[5] and the proposal for a Regulation on a 'Common European Sales Law' (CESL).[6]

In the remaining sections of this chapter I consider in detail the scheme of vitiating factors adopted by the PLACL, under the broad headings already set out above, but also drawing some comparisons with the national legal systems and soft law principles just mentioned.

II. The Scheme Adopted by the Principles of Latin American Contract Law

A. What is Defective?

Within Chapter 3 ('Formation of the contract') of the PLACL, Section 4 is headed 'Defects of the contract' (*De los vicios del contrato*); and this—rather than defects in *consent*—appears similarly in Article 27. This is an interesting formulation, since the Principles adopt the theory that a contract is based on consent. Although a contract is defined as an agreement (*un acuerdo*: Article 8), one of the three essential elements required to form a contract is consent (*el consentimiento*: Article 9). There is no reference, however, to 'consent' in Section 4—unlike European systems such as France[7]

[3] There was a proposal from the European Commission in 2011 (below, n 6) to create a Common European Sales Law, which would constitute an 'optional instrument': a self-standing set of contract law rules, common to all Member States and constituting a second regime of domestic contract law in each Member State, and which could be chosen by parties in cross-border transactions for the sale of goods, for the supply of digital content, and for related services. However, this was subject to criticism and was withdrawn at the end of 2014, and later replaced by a proposal for a Directive on contracts for the supply of digital content: COM(2015) 634 final (9.12.2015). No general harmonisation of the rules and principles of contract law in Europe is now in prospect.

[4] O Lando and H Beale, *Principles of European Contract Law Parts I & II* (The Hague, Kluwer Law International, 2000).

[5] C von Bar and E Clive (eds), *Principles, Definitions and Model Rules of European Private Law: Draft Common Frame of Reference (DCFR)* (Munich, Sellier, 2009).

[6] COM(2011) 635 final (11.10.2011).

[7] The new provisions of the *Code civil* ('C civ') (n 2) create a new sub-heading, under the heading of 'Consent' (itself a sub-heading of 'Validity of the Contract'), of 'Defects in consent' (*Les vices du consentement*). The consent of the parties is necessary for the validity of a contract: Art 1128; mistake, fraud and duress vitiate *consent*: Art 1130; and defects in consent are a ground of relative nullity of the *contract*: Art 1131. This continues the consensualist model which was already clear in the original

and Spain,[8] which follow the consensual model of contract formation and then generally group mistake, fraud, pressure, and so forth, under the general heading of defects in consent. German law, too, unifies the defects by reference to their underlying common rationale: the contract is based not on the parties' consent, but on their *declarations of intent*; and mistake, deceit and duress allow the party in question to avoid that declaration of intent.[9] The overarching category of defect in consent is even used by the DCFR and the CESL, although their rules for the formation of a contract are based not on consent but on agreement (objectively determined from the parties' words and conduct).[10] By contrast, the PECL, whilst drawing these defects together under the general heading of 'Validity', do not refer to 'consent' but only to the contract.[11] English law is different again, and does not even see a formal unity in defects such as mistake and pressure—the focus is on the validity of the contract itself rather than on the 'consent' of one or both parties, so the English lawyer does not naturally use any such phrase as 'defects in consent', and has developed separate grounds of avoidance of the contract for mistake, misrepresentation, duress, undue influence and under a doctrine of 'unconscionable bargains'.[12]

B. The Grounds of Invalidity

The defects of contracts recognised by the PLACL are listed in Article 27: mistake (*error*), fraud (*dolo*), threat (*intimidación*) and gross disparity (*excesiva desproporción*); and the following Articles define the elements of each of these defects. We shall discuss them in order, comparing each with the equivalent ground of invalidity recognised by the national jurisdictions and soft law systems covered by this chapter. Some significant elements of comparison will rest on how the text of the Principles might be interpreted, just as the laws of different national systems depend on the interpretation of their national texts. The comparison of the

C civ of 1804: see old Arts 1108 ('consent' as one of the requirements for the validity of a contract), 1109 (no valid *consent* in case of mistake, threats or fraud), 1110, 1113, 1116 (in consequence, the *contract* is null).

[8] Código civil ('Cc') Art 1265 (consent given by mistake, duress, intimidation or fraud is null), and 'consent' is one of the requirements for the validity of a contract: Art 1261; but then mistake invalidates the *consent* (Art 1266); duress or intimidation annul the *obligation* (Art 1268).

[9] BGB §§ 119 (mistake), 123 (deceit and duress).

[10] DCFR: Book II, Chapter 7: Section 2 is headed 'Vitiated consent or intention', but in the text it is the contract that is avoided, because the *contract* has been induced by mistake (II.-7:201), fraud (II.-7:205), coercion or threats (II.-7:206), or unfair exploitation (II.-7:207); and the contract is formed not by 'consent' but by agreement with intention to be bound, tested objectively (II.-4:101, 102). CESL: Chapter 5 is headed 'Defects in consent', but in the text it is the contract that is avoided, because the *contract* has been induced by mistake (Art 48), fraud (Art 49), threats (Art 50), or unfair exploitation (Art 51); and the contract is formed not by 'consent' but by a sufficiently certain agreement with intention to have legal effect, tested objectively (Art 30).

[11] PECL Chapter 4.

[12] J Cartwright, *Contract Law: An Introduction to the English Law of Contract for the Civil Lawyer*, 3rd edn (Oxford, Hart Publishing, 2016) 158.

grounds of invalidity is, however, incomplete without also considering their remedial consequences. Although the Articles which define the defects in contracts give some definition of the consequences (at least nullity of the contract), further detail is found not in Chapter 2 (Formation of the contract) but in Chapter 3 (Nullity of contract), which will also be mentioned here.

*i. Mistake (*el error*: Articles 28–31)*

The mistake may be of fact or of law (Article 28), and includes a mistake in expressing and transmitting intention (Article 31). In many legal systems, mistakes of law used not to be accepted as legally relevant, although in the modern law the extension has generally been made to include mistakes of law and it is natural to include them in a new text.[13]

The extension to cover mistakes in *expression or transmission of intention* has something of a Germanic flavour, with a focus on the (objective) outward expression of the (subjective) intention. The German approach goes further, and starts from a mistake in content of the declaration of intent, to which it then assimilates mistakes about essential characteristics of the thing or the person,[14] an approach which reflects the German emphasis on the declaration of intent rather than the intent itself. The PLACL, however, following their subjective approach to the formation of contracts,[15] naturally place first the mistake of fact or law, and then extend this to cover the expression of the intention—an approach also taken in the soft law systems.[16] English law, taking a strong objective approach to the formation of contract, and in particular to written communications and to contracts concluded in writing, limits operative mistakes generally and in particular in the case of written contracts, although it does provide remedies for mistake in limited circumstances.[17]

[13] Mistakes of law were included by interpretation of the original provisions of the French Civil Code: B Nicholas, *The French Law of Contract*, 2nd edn (Oxford, Clarendon Press, 1992) 89; F Terré, Ph Simler and Y Lequette, *Droit Civil. Les Obligation*, 11th edn (Paris, Dalloz, 2013) no 224, and the new provisions of the C civ (n 2) expressly include mistakes of law: Art 1132. Mistakes of law are also included by interpretation of the Spanish Civil Code: C Lasarte, *Principios de Derecho Civil*, vol 3, *Contratos*, 16th edn (Madrid, Marcel Pons, 2014) 23–24. English law generally excluded mistakes of law until the decision of the House of Lords in *Kleinwort Benson Ltd v Lincoln City Council* [1999] 2 AC 349. The German Civil Code (BGB) did not include mistakes of law, but in certain contexts they are included: BS Markesinis, H Unberath and A Johnston, *The German Law of Contract*, 2nd edn (Oxford, Hart Publishing 2006) 295–96. The soft law systems expressly include mistakes of law: PECL Art 4:103; DCFR II.-7:201(1); CESL Art 48(1).

[14] BGB § 119(1), (2). It then adds incorrect transmission: § 120. There is no equivalent provision in the C civ or the Cc.

[15] PLACL Art 9; above.

[16] PECL Arts 4:103, 104; DCFR II.-7:201(2), 202; CESL Art 48(1), (3), each of which refer to the expression or transmission not of the *intention*, but of a *statement* (perhaps also thereby reflecting a further distancing from the subjective notion of the agreement: n 10).

[17] For the effect of mistake in general within English contract law, see Cartwright (n 12) 163–76; J Beatson, A Burrows and J Cartwright, *Anson's Law of Contract*, 30th edn (Oxford, Oxford University Press, 2016) ch 8. For written contracts, see Cartwright (n 12) 67–68, 207–10 (objective interpretation); 165–67 (mistake in relation to written contracts).

'Mistake' is defined in Article 28, a text which is rather different from the approach taken by other systems. First, it is not usual in codes to have a definition of 'mistake' at all. To use the common meaning of the word, we might say that a mistake is a subjective state of misunderstanding of reality,[18] and one might even distinguish between 'mistake' and 'ignorance', the former requiring a positive state of mind.[19] The PLACL, however, give a definition of mistake, and one which departs from the common meaning of the word: it includes both ignorance and an erroneous assumption; and uses a test which is not subjective but objective, including a threshold of (objective) seriousness 'of such importance that a reasonable person in the same situation would not have concluded the contract or would have done so on significantly different terms'.

This form of drafting is rather curious, but its effect is in many respects similar to that of many other systems, which do not begin by giving a special, restrictive definition of 'mistake' but assume the (non-legal) definition of mistake as a subjective misunderstanding, and then add further rules to limit the range of actionable mistakes. Some such limitation on the scope of actionable mistake is inevitable: no legal system can sensibly provide for every mistake to nullify the contract, which would undermine contractual security: there must therefore be a sub-category of *actionable* mistakes—*legally relevant* mistakes—or some other technique to draw a line around those mistakes which may nullify the contract, and those which cannot.[20] French law, for example, uses the general (subjective) concept of mistake (*erreur*), but limits the scope of mistakes which nullify the contract: this was originally said in the Civil Code of 1804 to be mistakes as to the 'very substance' of the subject-matter of the contract, or as to the person of the other contracting party but only where the personality is the 'principal cause' of the contract.[21] This was widened by interpretation to include the 'substantial *qualities*' of the subject-matter or the person, although also narrowed to require the mistake to be 'decisive' (*déterminante*) and not inexcusable, and to exclude mistakes as to mere motive or value.[22] This developed definition of the scope of actionable mistake is now formally reflected in the revised text of the French Civil Code.[23] The approach taken by the PLACL, however, in limiting the definition

[18] See, eg, *Oxford English Dictionary Online* (Oxford University Press), December 2016, '*mistake*, n.: a. A misconception about the meaning of something; a thing incorrectly done or thought; an error of judgement. … c. In generalized use: misapprehension, misunderstanding; error, misjudgement'; *Le Petit Robert de la Langue Française*, 2017 edition (Paris, Le Robert, 2016), '*erreur*: fait de se tromper. Acte de l'esprit qui tient pour vrai ce qui est faux et inversement'; *Diccionario de la lengua española*, 23rd edn (Madrid, Real Academia Española, 2014) 'error. 1. Concepto equivocado o juicio falso'.

[19] J Cartwright, *Misrepresentation, Mistake and Non-Disclosure*, 4th edn (London, Sweet & Maxwell, 2016) para 12-03.

[20] German law is the least limited by its definition of mistake (*Irrtum*), placing instead a practical constraint on the party's raising mistake as a ground of avoidance of the contract by requiring him to compensate the other party: BGB § 122; below n 44.

[21] C civ (old) Art 1110.

[22] See, eg, Nicholas (n 13) 83–98; Terré, Simler and Lequette (n 13) nos 214–17, 220. In Spain, see similarly Cc Art 1266; Lasarte (n 13) 22–24.

[23] C civ (new) (n 2) Arts 1132–36.

of mistake to what a reasonable person would have done, is more emphatically objective than other systems which have a starting point of subjective mistake and have both subjective and objective elements in determining whether the mistake is actionable. The question elsewhere is therefore not generally whether a reasonable person would have acted on the mistake in entering into the contract, but on whether the mistaken party would have done so.[24] An assessment of whether the mistaken party would have been influenced by the mistake may well depend as a matter of evidence on how a reasonable person in that party's position would have acted,[25] but it is a significant formal shift to use the reasonable person not as evidence but as the substantive test.

Having defined the mistake in objective terms, the PLACL then place further limitations on which mistakes are *actionable*: the 'grounds for mistake' which vitiate the contract (*causales de error*: Article 29), within which the other party—the one who stands to lose the contract if the mistaken party is allowed to nullify it on the basis of his own mistake—must be involved in the mistake or its effects, and so have some form of responsibility for it. For the mistake to be legally relevant (a) it must be caused by information the other party supplied—although this may be innocent, and does not require him to know of the error;[26] or (b) he must have failed, contrary to good faith, to correct it when he knew or ought to have known the mistake; or (c) he must have shared the mistake.[27]

This formulation owes much to the PECL[28] and such a formulation is significantly different from the French and Spanish models since it excludes a purely unilateral mistake.[29] In this, it is closer to the English approach, where a unilateral mistake of fact or law is in principle insufficient:[30] either the mistake must be induced by the other party's misrepresentation,[31] or it must have been a shared ('common') mistake.[32] Grounds (a) and (c) in Article 29(1) of the PLACL relate to the English approach: induced mistake (misrepresentation), and common mistake, respectively. There are still significant differences, however: English law gives a much easier claim to the mistaken party who can plead his case as misrepresentation, with lower thresholds for liability: there is no requirement that the mistake caused by the misrepresentation be particularly serious, or that the misrepresentation be a determining cause of the contract—it need only be *a* cause (and the fact that it is objectively material is sufficient to entitle the court to infer that it was

[24] eg, C civ (new) (n 2) Art 1130; PECL Art 4:103(1)(b); DCFR II.-7:201(1)(a); CESL Art 48(1)(a).

[25] eg, in English law: *Redgrave v Hurd* (1881) 20 ChD 1, 21; *Mathias Yetts* (1882) 46 LT 497, 502 (Jessel MR: (objective) materiality of statement raises inference of reliance on it).

[26] Knowing supply of false information is also covered by fraud (*el dolo*): Art 32; see below.

[27] PLACL Art 29(1).

[28] PECL Art 4:103(1)(a); see also developments of this in the DCFR II.-7:201; CESL Art 48(1)(b).

[29] cf Lando and Beale (n 4) 237–38.

[30] *Smith v Hughes* (1871) LR 6 QB 597, 603, 606–07; *Statoil ASA v Louis Dreyfus Energy Services LP (The Harriette N)* [2008] EWHC 2257 (Comm), [2008] 2 Lloyd's Rep 685, [88].

[31] *Redgrave v Hurd* (n 25).

[32] *Bell v Lever Bros Ltd* [1932] AC 161 (HL) 218; see generally Cartwright (n 12) ch 7; Cartwright (n 19) ch 12.

a cause).[33] Common mistake, however, is very narrow: the courts see mistake as undermining security of contracts, and although a common mistake of fact or law may render the contract void, it does so only where the mistake is so serious as to make the performance of the contract physically or commercially impossible.[34]

Provision (b) in Article 29(1) goes much further, however, than English law, by extending nullity on the ground of mistake to a case of non-disclosure: where the other party knows or ought to know of the mistake and does not disclose it, contrary to good faith. Even in the strongest case—where the other party actually knows of the mistake, and realises that the mistaken party would not enter into the contract if he knew the truth—there is no duty in the English common law to disclose it, so there is no question of whether it was contrary to 'good faith' to remain silent: 'whatever may be the case in a court of morals, there is no legal obligation on the vendor to inform the purchaser that he is under a mistake, not induced by the act of the vendor'.[35] The civil law systems are much more open to imposing duties of disclosure,[36] and so it is not surprising that the PLACL should follow the lead of the PECL in bringing within the scope of the doctrine of mistake the failure to disclose a mistake which the other party knows or ought to know is being made, and also to define such a duty of disclosure by reference to the general principle of good faith.[37]

The grounds of mistake set out in Article 29(1) of the PLACL are then further limited by two rules set out in Article 29(2): they are operative only if the mistake is excusable, and if the risk of the mistake was not (and ought not to have been) assumed by the party making it. The 'excusability' principle allows a court to decide that, although the mistake is sufficiently serious to satisfy the normal test, the mistaken party is ultimately at fault in having made the mistake. Such a rule is used in, for example, French law[38] and Spanish law[39] and in some of the soft law systems.[40] It is also known as a (further) limitation on the already narrow doctrine

[33] *Attwood v Small* (1838) 6 Cl & Fin 232, 502; see also above n 25.

[34] *Bell v Lever Bros Ltd* (n 32); *The Great Peace* [2002] EWCA Civ 1407, [2003] QB 679 at [76].

[35] *Smith v Hughes* (n 30) 606–07 (Blackburn J). There are certain duties of disclosure, notably duties on traders to inform consumers about the goods they supply. But such duties are specific exceptions to the general rule against duties of disclosure and are generally made by statute to cover particular types of contract or particular types of party: Cartwright (n 12) 186–89; in more detail in Cartwright (n 19) Part 3.

[36] See, eg, J Ghestin and B Nicholas, 'The Pre-contractual Obligation to Disclose Information' in D Harris and D Tallon (eds), *Contract Law Today* (Oxford, Clarendon Press, 1989) 151, comparing French law and English law.

[37] PLACL Art 7; the general duty of good faith is not accepted in English law but is known and commonly applied in civil law systems: R Zimmermann and S Whittaker, *Good Faith in European Contract Law* (Cambridge, Cambridge University Press, 2000) ch 1. See also PECL, Art 1:201.

[38] C civ (new) (n 2) Art 1132. This was achieved for the original provisions of the Code by interpretation: Nicholas (n 13) 94–95.

[39] By interpretation: Lasarte (n 13) 23.

[40] Put, however, in the double negative: no avoidance if the mistake was inexcusable. This appears to place the burden of proof on the party seeking to resist avoidance: PECL Art 4:103(2); DCFR II.-7:201(2).

of common mistake in English law,[41] although the courts are reluctant to hold that a party was at fault in relying on a misrepresentation.[42] Similarly, in any legal system, the assumption of the risk of the mistake by a party ought in principle to exclude his having a remedy if the mistake occurs,[43] and such a provision in the PLACL is uncontroversial.

The approach to limiting actionable mistakes to take into account the other party's responsibility is different in German law: the party who makes a mistake is entitled to avoid his declaration of intent (and therefore the contract), an apparently broader general approach to avoidance for mistake. However, the price to pay is that he must compensate the other party's reliance loss flowing from reliance on the validity of the declaration of intent which is thereby avoided, although no such compensation is payable to a party who knows (or ought to know) of the mistake.[44]

The principal remedy for mistake in all legal systems is the avoidance of the contract, following from the fact that the mistake has vitiated the contract at the moment of its formation. The PLACL provide for nullity as the remedy,[45] although this is excluded in a case where the counterparty offers to perform it in the manner and with the content which accords with the mistaken party's intentions—that is, if the non-mistaken party can cure the mistake, the mistaken party cannot use the mistake to avoid the contract.[46] This follows the approach of the PECL,[47] which classify it as an 'adaptation' of the contract. It will be possible only in cases where the contract can be performed as if there were no mistake, which will cover cases such as mistakes in transmission, and in the content of the obligations, more easily than mistakes of fact or law, given that the parties cannot change the facts or the law into what they were erroneously believed to be.

Since the purpose of nullity is to protect the mistaken party, under the PLACL the nullity is not absolute but relative (Article 41), and can therefore be invoked only by the mistaken party, who may cure the defect by confirming the contract (Articles 46, 48). Nullity requires a court order, unless it is raised as a defence to an action before the court (Article 42); and once it has been ordered the contract is extinguished, each party being required to make reciprocal restitution in kind if possible, and otherwise by value of the benefits received (Article 50). Other systems follow a similar general line to the PLACL, but with some variations.

[41] *Associated Japanese Bank (International) Ltd v Crédit du Nord SA* [1989] 1 WLR 255, 268; *The Great Peace* (n 34) [76]–[80], [90]–[91].

[42] *Redgrave v Hurd* (n 25) 13–14 (Jessel MR: 'Nothing can be plainer … on the authorities in equity than that the effect of false representation is not got rid of on the ground that the person to whom it was made has been guilty of negligence').

[43] In France, it now appears in the reformed Civil Code (n 2) Art 1133; see also PECL Art 4:103(2); DCFR II.-7:201(2); CESL Art 48(2). In England, see *The Great Peace* (n 34) [84].

[44] BGB § 122; Cartwright and Schmidt-Kessel (n 1) 388–89.

[45] PLACL Art 29(2).

[46] PLACL Art 30.

[47] PECL Art 4:105; see also DCFR II.-7:203.

French law[48] and Spanish law[49] provide for relative nullity, which requires a court order, and which allows restitution in kind or by value, although there is no provision for the other party to deprive the mistaken party of restitution by offering to perform as if there were no mistake. German law allows the mistaken party to avoid the contract by simple declaration, without a court order; but requires him to pay the reliance losses of the other party (as long as the latter is innocent of the mistake).[50] In English law a common mistake—in those rather rare cases in which the test for a legally relevant mistake is satisfied[51]—renders the contract void, rather than voidable, and therefore no court order is required;[52] but misrepresentation, which is much wider and therefore more commonly relied on by claimants whose mistake was induced by the other party's words or conduct, renders the contract voidable and liable to be set aside by simple notice by the mistaken party, without requiring a court order.[53] The width of the ground of avoidance for misrepresentation (induced mistake) of fact or law is, however, counterbalanced by restrictions on its availability: not only must it be claimed within a reasonable time, but the court has a statutory discretion to refuse it in cases of non-fraudulent misrepresentation in non-consumer cases; and it will be denied if avoidance would prejudice an innocent third party, or if restitution in kind is not possible.[54] English law has not developed a general principle of restitution by value where the contract is avoided for misrepresentation.

The soft law principles also provide for avoidance of the contract for mistake, effected by notice (without a court order) and with restitution in kind or by value. However, they also add a remedy in damages where the non-mistaken party knew or ought to have known of the mistake.[55] This goes further than the approach generally adopted in the national systems within their doctrine of mistake, although they may bring such cases within 'fault' for the purposes of a claim under the general law of tort. In effect, the soft law principles categorise taking advantage of the other party's mistake (either knowingly or negligently) as a wrong giving rise to the duty to pay compensation.[56] The PLACL, although they follow the approach of the PECL in many respects in their rules of mistake, have not adopted this (and, it is submitted, it is not surprising that they have not done so).

[48] C civ (new) (n 2) Arts 1131, 1178, 1181, 1352 to 1352–9. For the (similar) law before the reform of the Civil Code, see Nicholas (n 13) 77–80; Terré, Simler and Lequette (n 13) nos 393, 418, 423–24.

[49] Cc Arts 1303, 1307.

[50] BGB § 122; n 44.

[51] See n 34.

[52] *The Great Peace* (n 34).

[53] *TSB Bank plc v Camfield* [1995] 1 WLR 430 (CA) 438.

[54] *Anson's Law of Contract* (n 17) 336–42.

[55] PECL Art 4:117; DCFR II.-7:214; CESL Art 55. Under the PECL and the DCFR there is also a right to damages for reasonable reliance on incorrect information, even if the mistake thereby caused does not give rise to the right to avoid the contract: PECL Art 4:106; DCFR II.-7:204. The PLACL give damages only for fraud: Art 33; below.

[56] The closest that national systems get to this as a general rule within their doctrine of mistake is German law, which does not require the non-mistaken party to pay damages, but he does forfeit the right to compensation for his reliance losses in such cases: n 50.

*ii. Fraud (*el dolo*: Articles 32–33)*

In common with most systems in the civil law tradition, the PLACL treat fraud as an independent vitiating factor, alongside mistake.[57] The distinction between mistake and fraud is sometimes explained as the distinction between a mistake that one makes oneself, and a mistake that is induced by the other party's deceitful words or conduct;[58] or the distinction between 'deceiving oneself' and 'being deceived'.[59] We have already seen that English law draws this distinction not in relation to fraud, but in relation to misrepresentation more generally, adopting a narrower doctrine of mistake than the civil law systems but a much broader doctrine of misrepresentation which encompasses innocent, as well as fraudulent, misrepresentation. Even in English law, however, the fact that the misrepresentation which induced the contract was fraudulent will also in some respects enhance the claims open to the party subjected to the fraud.[60] Indeed, the PLACL also identify induced mistake as one of the grounds of actionable mistake, without taking into account whether the inducement was fraudulent or innocent.[61] However, if the inducement is by deceit, the defect can be characterised as fraud, and in all systems which draw the line between mistake and fraud, more significant consequences attach to the party's claim based on fraud. As always, however, although different systems single out fraud for separate treatment, the systems do not treat it identically. As we shall see below, differences include whether fraud has to be active, or can also be committed by omission; whether it has to be committed by the other party to the contract, or can be by a third party; and whether the test of causation (and other restrictions which are placed on a claim for nullity of a contract based on mistake) are relaxed where fraud is proved.

The PLACL allow a contract to be vitiated by fraud committed by omission as well as by a positive act, and by a third party as well as by the other contracting party.[62] The extension to omissions is not surprising: most legal systems, even if they did not start by encompassing omissions within their definition of fraud, have recognised that there are circumstances in which a contract can be induced by deceitful silence which should be equated to deceitful words or conduct.[63]

[57] See, eg, French law C civ (new) (n 2) Arts 1130, 1132, 1137 (replacing the original Arts 1109, 1110, 1116); Spanish law Cc Arts 1265, 1266, 1269; German law BGB §§ 119, 123. The soft law systems take a similar approach: PECL Arts 4:103, 107; DCFR II.-7:201, 205; CESL Arts 48, 49.

[58] The new provisions of the French Civil Code (n 2) make this explicit in Art 1139 ('A mistake induced by fraud is always excusable').

[59] J Carbonnier, *Droit civil, vol 4, Les Obligations*, 22nd edn (Paris, Presses Universitaires de France, 2000) para 42 (one who commits a mistake 's'est trompé spontanément'; the victim of fraud 'a été trompée, ce qui suppose un trompeur').

[60] Cartwright (n 19) paras 4-50, 4-55, 4-63 (rescission); 5-01 (damages in the tort of deceit).

[61] PLACL Art 29(1)(a); n 27; see also n 55.

[62] PLACL Art 32(1).

[63] eg, in French law, the original C civ Art 1116 required fraudulent *manoeuvres*, but this was developed by the courts to include fraudulent silence (*réticence dolosive*): Ghestin and Nicholas (n 36). The new provisions of the French Civil Code (n 2) explicitly include intentional concealment: Art 1137. Similarly the interpretation of Cc Art 1269 in Spain: Lasarte (n 13) 28; and the courts in Germany have interpreted BGB § 123 to extend to fraudulent omission or silence, at least in cases where there is a duty of disclosure: Markesinis, Unberath and Johnston (n 13) 305.

However, this step has generally been taken cautiously, and often limited to circumstances in which the 'fraudulent' party has a duty to disclose the information which it (fraudulently) failed to do; and often also thereby linked to the general duty to act in good faith.[64] The soft law principles follow this by extending fraud beyond active misrepresentation only where the non-disclosure is contrary to the duty of good faith and fair dealing, or to a pre-contractual information duty.[65] The striking thing in the text of Article 32 of the PLACL is that it does not give any limit to the kinds of 'omission' which will constitute fraud.

It is striking also that under the PLACL, fraudulent acts or omissions of third parties count as much as those of the other party. The instinctive starting point is to limit fraud to that committed by the other party—it is the wrongfulness of the party's conduct that justifies his being deprived of the contract[66]—and so fraud by a third party may give rise to the vitiation of the contract by the *mistake* which is produced by the fraud, but not by *fraud* except where it is actually committed by the other party.[67] However, it is not a large step to say that, at least in the case where a contracting party knows of the third party's fraud, and perhaps also where he ought to know of it, but still takes advantage of the contract (and of the counterparty's consent induced by the fraud), he ought to be in no better position than if he had committed the fraud himself. This is the position which modern systems have generally adopted.[68] The PLACL, however, go much further in placing no restriction on the circumstances where a third party's fraud vitiates the contract. In this, they appear to base the vitiation of the contract purely on the interference with the deceived party's consent, rather than on a combination of the wrongfulness of the *other party's* conduct (active or passive) and the impact on the consent.

All legal systems naturally require a causal link between the fraud and the contract. This is generally put in terms of whether the party subjected to the fraud would not otherwise have contracted,[69] although rather curiously the PLACL ask whether *the parties* would not have contracted.[70] Where fraud is established, one might expect the law to intervene more readily than in the case of mistake—or, at least, not to have a higher test of causation than in the case of mistake. Most systems

[64] eg, in Germany: Markesinis, Unberath and Johnston (n 13) 305. It should not be surprising that English law, not recognising a general duty of good faith, has not taken this approach, and does not admit a wider ground of rescission for fraudulent non-disclosure: above text to n 35.

[65] PECL Art 4:107; DCFR II.-7:205; CESL Art 49.

[66] cf the Roman origins: *dolus* as a wrong giving rise to a defence, rather than as a vitiating factor in the contract itself: B Nicholas, *An Introduction to Roman Law* (Oxford, Clarendon Press, 1962) 164.

[67] Eg, France: C civ (old) Art 1116; Spain: Cc Art 1269.

[68] Germany: BGB § 123 (know or ought to know); England: *Royal Bank of Scotland plc v Etridge (No 2)* [2001] UKHL 44, [2002] 2 AC 773, [40] (knowledge); PECL Art 4:111 (know or ought to know, or not yet acted in reliance on the contract); DCFR II.-7:208 (know or ought to know, or not yet acted in reliance on the contract). CESL Art 49, however, is limited to fraud of the other party, and the French reform (n 2) has moved in this direction only to cover the situation where the third party is 'in collusion' (*de connivence*): C civ (new) Art 1138.

[69] eg, France: C civ (new) (n 2) Art 1130 (would not have contracted or would have contracted on substantially different terms, a test common to mistake, fraud and duress); Spain: Cc Art 1269.

[70] PLACL Art 32(1). The sections dealing with the other vitiating factors, however, refer to *the party* who is induced to enter into the contract: Arts 28, 34.

appear to use the same test of causation for mistake and for fraud. However, the PLACL are stricter for fraud, requiring clear proof that the parties would not have contracted without the fraud. Mistake covers the case where a (reasonable) party would not have contracted *or would have done so on significantly different terms*.[71] As in the case of other systems, however, proof of fraud and the required causation of the contract is sufficient; there is no place for a rule requiring the claimant's reliance on the fraud to be 'excusable', as in the case of mistake. As the revised French Civil Code says explicitly: 'A mistake induced by fraud is always excusable'.[72] But under the PLACL, following the same approach as the Spanish Civil Code, fraud by one party is only sufficient to vitiate the contract if there was no fraud also by the other party.[73]

Two remedies are generally available in all legal systems for fraud which induced the contract: nullity of the contract; and damages for losses caused. The regime of nullity for fraud generally follows the same pattern as for other defects in consent: and so under the PLACL it is relative nullity (Article 41), and can therefore be invoked only by the mistaken party, who may cure the defect by confirming the contract (Articles 46, 48). Nullity requires a court order, unless it is raised as a defence to an action before the court (Article 42); and once it has been ordered the contract is extinguished, each party being required to make reciprocal restitution in kind if possible, and otherwise by value of the benefits received (Article 50). Although the fraud induces a mistake, we have seen that the various legal systems provide some special rules within their remedial regime for mistake,[74] which are not applicable in cases of fraud: the PLACL, for instance, allow the non-mistaken party to prevent the nullity by offering to perform in accordance with the mistaken party's understanding;[75] and German law requires the party who wishes to avoid the contract for his own mistake to compensate the other party's reliance losses.[76] Such limitations on the availability of remedies for mistake have no place where the other party has induced the contract by fraud.

The fraud will give rise to damages—either in place of nullity if the contract is confirmed, or in addition to nullity if the party has suffered loss beyond that which is redressed by the restitution which follows the nullity. Most national systems treat the damages claim within the general law of tort (extra-contractual liability), but whether the system has a general principle of tort law,[77] or a more compartmentalised scheme of liabilities,[78] the intentional, dishonest infliction of loss will normally be covered. The soft law principles bring the damages claim

[71] PLACL Art 28; cf Art 32(2).
[72] C civ (new) (n 2) Art 1139; cf n 38.
[73] PLACL Art 32(2); cf Cc Art 1270.
[74] For the approaches of other legal systems in cases of mistake, see above text to fnn 50–54.
[75] PLACL Art 30; n 46.
[76] BGB § 122; n 44.
[77] eg, France: C civ (new) (n 2) Art 1240 (formerly Art 1382); Spain: Cc Art 1902.
[78] eg, Germany: BGB § 823; England: *Derry v Peek* (1889) 14 App Cas 337 (HL) (tort of deceit).

into their provisions dealing with fraud as a vitiating factor in contracts,[79] and the PLACL do likewise,[80] in each case covering not only the fraud committed by the contracting party himself, but also the fraud of third parties of which the contracting party knew or ought to have known. We have seen that the PLACL go beyond other systems in allowing nullity for third-party fraud even if the contracting party is not aware of it; but the damages claim is limited in that respect.[81] The text of the PLACL is, however, rather brief in saying simply that 'The defrauding party is liable for damages'.[82] The European soft law systems go further and make clear that the claim for damages is limited to the reliance interest—perhaps naturally, since they cannot appeal to the general law of tort as the basis of the claim. The PLACL are similarly limited to the contractual sphere, so it is perhaps surprising that there is no further definition of the basis of the damages.

*iii. Threat (*intimidación*: Articles 34–36)*

In the case of threats which induce a contract there is again a core consensus among legal systems but we also see differences, some of them very significant. The simplest case of—in the words of Article 34 of the PLACL—an 'unlawful threat of an imminent and serious harm' would be recognised by lawyers in most legal systems as a core case of duress, although some systems would expect to see more definition of what constitutes 'harm': whether it extends beyond physical harm to the person and property to cover harm to economic and other interests;[83] others, however, may be content with a simpler statement, similar to the PLACL, focusing on the 'unlawfulness' of the threat.[84] There is, however, disagreement among systems as to whether it is sufficient for the duress to emanate from a third party, or whether it must be from the other party to the contract, or at least from a third party of which the other party is aware or ought to be aware. This difference of approach marks out different underlying rationales for duress: whether it is simply the interference with the threatened party's consent that justifies the nullity of the contract, or whether the threat must be in some sense the responsibility of the other party (that is, the other party's fault is part of the equation). The PLACL allow a simple threat by a third party to vitiate the contract,[85] following a

[79] PECL Art 4:117; DCFR II.-7:214; CESL Art 55.

[80] PLACL Art 33.

[81] PLACL Art 33(2).

[82] PLACL Art 33(1).

[83] The scope is made clear in French law: C civ (new) (n 2) Art 1140 (following in this respect the old Art 1112) (person or wealth); and Spanish law: Cc Art 1267 (*intimidación*: person or property). English law extended *duress* to cover economic interests in the 1970s; and has used *undue influence* to cover less direct threats and influences: Cartwright (n 12) 191–93.

[84] eg, German law: BGB § 123. See also the soft law principles: PECL Art 4:108; DCFR II.-7:206; CESL Art 50.

[85] PLACL Art 34.

similar model to that of the French and Spanish Civil Codes,[86] and also following the original provisions of the French Code and the current Spanish Code in taking into account circumstances such as the age and personal condition of the party threatened,[87] and in excluding 'reverential fear'—action taken only out of a fear of displeasing a parent or other senior family member to whom respect is owed.[88]

The generally accepted remedy for threats is nullity, following the same model as for fraud: under the PLACL it is therefore relative nullity (Article 41) which can be invoked only by the threatened party, who may cure the defect by confirming the contract (Articles 46, 48). Nullity requires a court order, unless it is raised as a defence to an action before the court (Article 42); and once it has been ordered the contract is extinguished, each party being required to make reciprocal restitution in kind if possible, and otherwise by value of the benefits received (Article 50). Differences already noted for other systems' regimes of nullity also apply here.[89]

Unlike in the case of fraud, the PLACL do not make reference to any claim for damages in the case of loss caused by entering into a contract by reason of threats. The European soft law principles do so,[90] and it is surprising that this is not followed by the PLACL, given that they do not have general principles of tort law on which to rely for damages claims.[91]

*iv. Gross Disparity (*excesiva desproporción*: Article 37)*

Provisions on mistake, fraud and threats are known in all legal systems, even if the details may differ (and sometimes differ significantly, as we have seen above). More fundamental differences, however, are found among the systems in their approach to what the PLACL refer to as 'gross disparity'. Indeed, even among those systems which accept some form of defect in the contract on such a basis, the names given to the defect vary, sometimes emphasising the substantive unfairness in the terms of the contract,[92] sometimes emphasising the procedural unfairness by

[86] C civ (new) (n 2) Art 1142 (following in this respect the old Art 1111); Cc Art 1268. Similarly, BGB § 123. Other systems limit duress to threats by the other party (CESL Art 50), or where the other party knows of it (English law: *Royal Bank of Scotland plc v Etridge (No 2)* [2001] UKHL 44, [2002] 2 AC 773, [40]) or ought to know of it (PECL Art 4:111; DCFR II.-7:208).

[87] PLACL Art 35; C civ (old) (n 2) Art 1112 (this is not covered by the reformed provisions of the French Civil Code); Cc Art 1267. Rather curiously, perhaps, the PLACL follow the old French C civ (not included in the reformed French provisions) in including 'gender' explicitly as a relevant characteristic. Gender was included in the original text of the Spanish Cc, but was removed by Law 11/1990 on the ground that it was discriminatory.

[88] PLACL Art 36; C civ (old) (n 2) Art 1114 (this is not covered by the reformed provisions of the French Civil Code); Cc Art 1267.

[89] For the approaches of other legal systems, see above, text to nn 74–76.

[90] PECL Art 4:117; DCFR II.-7:214; CESL Art 55.

[91] The national systems do not include provisions for damages under their headings of threats/duress, but any claim for damages will be based on the general principles of tort law: above text to nn 77–78.

[92] 'Gross disparity': PLACL Art 37; 'excessive benefit or unfair advantage': PECL Art 4:109; 'unconscionable bargain': English law.

which one party has obtained the contract,[93] and sometimes emphasising the inherent weakness of the party who is given relief.[94] In fact, all doctrines which can be compared under this heading require some combination of procedural and substantive unfairness and one party taking advantage of a position of strength vis-à-vis the other.

The elements required by the PLACL for this defect in the contract are (i) an excessive advantage for one party, (ii) contrary to the requirements of good faith; (iii) taking into account (not as an independent requirement, but—rather unusually—in assessing the 'advantage') the aggrieved party's dependence, extraordinary distress, urgent needs, ignorance or lack of experience, as well as the relationship of trust between the parties, and the nature and purpose of the contract.[95] By its language this appears to be a narrow provision which will apply only in limited and rather extreme circumstances: the advantage must be excessive—and a mere excess of advantage is not sufficient unless it is also contrary to good faith; and there must be something by way of a particular personal weakness of the aggrieved party, or in the relationship between the two parties (dependence or trust), that justifies intervention by the court in the contract. In English law, some such cases might be covered by the doctrine of undue influence, which includes the use of a position of influence to obtain a contract, although there is no requirement of substantive unfairness in the terms of the contract except as evidence of the procedural unfairness of the stronger party.[96] However, English law also has a doctrine of 'unconscionable bargains', which requires the personal weakness of one party (based on such things as his poverty, ignorance or lack of advice), actively exploited by the other party in a morally culpable manner; and a resulting contract which is not merely harsh but oppressive in its terms.[97] This is a narrow doctrine, rarely invoked.[98] Other national systems which are considered here do not have an independent, directly comparable doctrine, although the new provisions of the French Civil Code, following earlier developments,[99] extend the doctrine of threats (*violence*) to cover it;[100] and in German law, some cases will be covered as a

[93] 'Unfair exploitation': DCFR II.-7:207; CESL Art 51; 'undue influence': English law. The revised French law includes within threats (*violence*) the case where a party '*exploits* the other's state of dependence': C civ (new) (n 2) Art 1143.

[94] In England, Lord Denning tried (unsuccessfully) to develop duress, undue influence, unconscionable bargains and related areas under a broad general heading of 'inequality of bargaining power', a title which emphasised the inequality of the parties, but in fact contained elements of substantive and procedural unfairness: *Lloyds Bank Ltd v Bundy* [1975] QB 326 (CA) 339; see *Anson's Law of Contract* (n 17) 404–07.

[95] PLACL Art 37(1) and (2).

[96] *CIBC Mortgages plc v Pitt* [1994] AC 200 (HL) 209; *Royal Bank of Scotland plc v Etridge (No 2)* [2001] UKHL 44, [2002] AC 773.

[97] *Fry v Lane* (1888) 40 Ch D 312; *Alec Lobb (Garages) Ltd v Total Oil (Great Britain) Ltd* [1983] 1 WLR 87, 94–95.

[98] *Anson's Law of Contract* (n 17) 400–03. It has been developed and applied more significantly in other common law jurisdictions, such as Australia, Canada and the United States.

[99] Nicholas (n 13) 108–10; Terré, Simler and Lequette (n 13) nos 247–48.

[100] C civ (new) (n 2) Art 1143.

particular application of the general provision on public policy.[101] The European soft law principles, however, include such a provision, although their formulation is more specific in requiring that the party who obtains the advantage knew (or ought to have known) of the weakness of the other party.[102] This will presumably be covered in the PLACL under the broader test that the advantage be contrary to the requirements of good faith.

The remedy varies again among those systems that accept such a principle. French law, in using the doctrine of threats (*violence*) to cover this case, will apply the general remedy of nullity which we have already seen; and English law also provides avoidance of the contract (at the weaker party's option) as the remedy for undue influence or unconscionable bargains. German law, however, in so far as it would bring a case within the doctrine of public policy, would render the contract not merely a (relative) nullity but void.[103] The PLACL, however, provide the aggrieved party with the remedy not only of relative nullity on the same model as for fraud and threats, but also adaptation of the contract by the court in order to make it consistent with the agreement that would have been reached by the parties in accordance with good faith (adaptation is available not only at the option of the aggrieved party, but also at the option of the other party in response to the aggrieved party's claim for nullity).[104] This follows the approach of the PECL and the DCFR,[105] although there (and in the CESL) damages are also available as a further remedy.[106]

C. What is the Underlying Theory of Intervention on the Basis of the Vitiating Factors?

It was noted in the Introduction that legal systems can differ in various ways in their general theory of the vitiating factors discussed in this chapter, and that one significant difference is in the balance between 'claimant-sided' and 'defendant-sided' grounds of relief:[107] that is, whether the reason for intervention in the contract is that the *claimant's consent* was defective, or that the *defendant's conduct* merits his being deprived of the right to enforce the contract. In all legal systems, there is some element of the 'claimant-sided' grounds of intervention within the vitiating factors, given that the core rationale for intervention is that the party seeking to be relieved of the apparent contract gave consent which was not perfect

[101] BGB § 138(1); Markesinis, Unberath and Johnston (n 13) 254–60; Cartwright and Schmidt-Kessel (n 1) 406.

[102] PECL Art 4:109(1); DCFR II.7-207; CESL Art 51.

[103] n 101.

[104] PLACL Art 37(1), (3), (4).

[105] PECL Art 4:109(2); DCFR II.-7:207(2).

[106] PECL Art 4:117; DCFR II.-7:214; CESL Art 55.

[107] cf P Birks and NY Chin, 'On the Nature of Undue Influence' in J Beatson and D Friedmann (eds), *Good Faith and Fault in Contract Law* (Oxford, Clarendon Press, 1995) 57, 58–59.

or was not given freely. Whether we describe the contract, or the consent, as being defective,[108] the interference with the claimant's consent is at the root of the problem. The defendant's conduct also plays a part, however, either in the core definitional elements of vitiating factors, or in the way in which the rules of the vitiating factors are in practice developed and applied. Here we consider how the PLACL strike this balance between claimant-sided and defendant-sided elements within the various defects of the contract.

The vitiating factor which in most legal systems presents a clearly claimant-sided rationale is *mistake*, given that the normal meaning of mistake has a subjective core and therefore remedies follow from the claimant's (subjective) defective consent. As we have seen,[109] this is also the starting point of the PLACL, which begin in Article 28 by defining mistake as 'ignorance or an erroneous assumption relating to facts or to law'. However, this is only the starting point, and within the PLACL there are limitations on the availability of remedies for mistake which point more towards the defendant-sided analysis. The rather curious definition of mistake,[110] which considers whether a reasonable person would also have been influenced by it in entering into the contract, adds an objective element to the very concept of 'mistake' but does not in itself affect the claimant/defendant balance. The 'grounds for mistake' set out in Article 29, however, do. Unilateral mistake of the claimant is not in itself a ground of vitiation of the contract: in addition, (a) there must also be information supplied by the other party, or (b) the other party must have known (or should have known) of the mistake and did not disclose it contrary to good faith, or (c) the other party must have made the same mistake.[111] These do not necessarily require 'wrongful' conduct on the part of the defendant, but do at least require some participation, or responsibility. Ground (b) is clearly based on the culpability of the defendant, since it requires a breach of the duty of good faith in failing to disclose a known mistake. Ground (a), however, can be satisfied by innocent, as well as culpable, misrepresentation; and ground (c), while also necessarily involving the defendant's innocent (subjective) mistake, at least limits the claimant's right to a remedy to the case where the defendant has participated by making the same mistake (regardless of how the mistake arose), and thereby has less reason to object to the claim that the contract is a nullity.

Fraud and *threat* are clearly claimant sided: it is the fact that the claimant was induced to conclude the contract by a deceitful act or omission[112] or an unlawful threat of an imminent and serious harm[113] that entitles him to annulment of the contract, rather than that the defendant (the other contracting party) was the source of the deceit or the threat. Article 32 is explicit on this point in relation to

[108] Above, sections I.A.1, II.A.
[109] Above, Section II.B.i.
[110] PLACL Art 28; above text to nn 20–25.
[111] PLACL Art 29(1); above, text to nn 26–36.
[112] PLACL Art 32; above, Section II.B.ii.
[113] PLACL Art 34; above, Section II.B.iii.

fraud, allowing the deceit of a third party as well as the other contracting party; Article 34 simply assumes it.[114]

Gross disparity, however, appears to be much more defendant sided. Although the circumstances to be taken into account include subjective elements such as the distress, needs, ignorance and lack of experience of the claimant, the core of this vitiating factor is the 'excessive advantage' which the contract gives to the defendant coupled with the requirement that this be 'in contravention of the requirements of good faith'.[115] The defendant's culpability in obtaining the excessive advantage is clearly in issue here.

Within the various grounds of defects of the contract, the PLACL therefore strike a balance: in some cases favouring the claimant's case because of the claimant's subjective defect in consent; in some cases requiring in addition the defendant's involvement or culpability in causing the claimant's situation or in taking advantage of it. In itself, this is not surprising. In the earlier sections of this chapter we have seen that national legal systems and soft law systems all strike some form of balance on this issue, and this is natural since the very nature of a contract, formed by the agreement between the two parties, requires us to consider both parties' positions where there is a challenge by one of them to the validity of the contract. The claim 'I should be free from the contract because my consent to it was not full or free' is met by the defendant's answer 'That is not my problem: why should I lose the benefit of the contract?' and all systems have to settle on their own view of the appropriate balance between the parties in such a debate. Perhaps the most striking difference on this point between the approach taken by the PLACL and the approach taken in other systems is that the PLACL *fraud* is claimant sided: the fact that there was fraud is enough even if the fraud was by a third party.[116] We may have concerns about undermining security of contract by reason of the claimant's subjective, unilateral mistake—concerns which respond to the defendant's argument 'why should I lose the benefit of the contract?'—and the PLACL appear to reflect this policy very clearly in the limitations they set on nullity for mistake by the addition of its grounds for mistake.[117] But once the mistake is induced by fraud, the claimant's right to nullity under the PLACL is enhanced, even if the defendant bears no responsibility for the fraud which is committed by a third party. It is difficult to see why the balance between claimant and defendant should be struck so differently there.

III. Concluding Remarks

As mentioned in the previous section, there are various balances to be struck in devising a set of rules governing defects in a contract on the basis of defects in the

[114] See further above text to nn 85–86.
[115] PLACL Art 37; above, Section II.B.iv.
[116] See above text to nn 66–68.
[117] PLACL Art 29(1).

consent of one or both parties; and we have seen that in their underlying rationale the PLACL strike a balance in relation to the claimant- or defendant-sided grounds for relief which is in some ways similar to other systems, but in some ways different.[118] We can also say that, more broadly, the PLACL present something of a compromise in their rules by comparison with the rules contained in the different national traditions and soft law systems found in Europe. In the course of the discussion throughout this chapter, we have seen how particular rules contained in the PLACL align with one or more of these other approaches. This is not the place to repeat the examples which have already been given, but we have seen some strong resemblances between the texts of the PLACL dealing with defects of the contract and the equivalent texts found in the PECL; and, among the national systems, stronger resemblances with the modern French and Spanish Codes than with the German Code or the English common law. This is not surprising: the Latin American contract law has strong historical links with the French tradition and, to that extent, is part of the French (or 'Romanistic') legal 'family'.[119] And the drafters of the PLACL have been able to use the fruits of the European lawyers' reassessment of their own national laws through projects such as the PECL and the DCFR. It is interesting, however, to note instances where the drafters of the PLACL have struck out on their own and have not fully accepted either a national or another soft law solution in their drafting of a particular rule. But it is also notable that the PECL themselves contain not only very strong continental European civil law influences, but also some significant input and influence from the European common law systems (and in particular, of course, English law). In the context of the defects in consent, this is seen, for example, in the rules of the PECL for mistake, which present a much broader general doctrine of mistake than is recognised in English law, but are functionally closer to English law when the English approach to induced mistake ('misrepresentation') is taken into account.[120] Although under the PECL actionable mistakes are in some significant respects wider than in English law, in particular in including cases of non-disclosure,[121] they do not allow for a unilateral mistake by the claimant as broadly as would the continental systems such as France, Spain and Germany; and by taking the approach of the PECL as the model for the grounds of actionable mistake in Article 28 of the PLACL,[122] the drafters have indirectly allowed some English law influences into their own approach.

[118] Above, Section II.C.
[119] Zweigert and Kötz (n 1) 113–14.
[120] Lando and Beale (n 4) 235–36; see also text to n 31.
[121] Above, text to nn 35–37.
[122] Above, text to nn 28–34.

10

Performance and Non-performance under the Principles of Latin American Contract Law

JEAN-SÉBASTIEN BORGHETTI

Honesty dictates that the author of this chapter should make it clear from the outset that it is doubtful whether the right person was chosen to address the issue of performance and non-performance under the Principles of Latin American Contract Law (PLACL).

A scholar purporting to analyse this remarkable piece of Latin American scholarship might be expected to master the language in which it was drafted, ie Spanish. Unfortunately, the author of this chapter, though he reads Cervantes' idiom, is not very familiar with it, and is thus not capable of catching certain linguistic nuances that might exist in the Principles. He wondered, for example, if any particular significance should be attached to the choice of the Principles' drafters to refer to *cumplimiento* and *incumplimiento* of the contract, rather than to *ejecución* and *inejecución*, which seem to be more readily used by at least some Latin American civil codes.[1] The two terms admittedly have very similar meanings, but it might be recalled that in Germany, when the *Bürgerliches Gesetzbuch* (BGB) was reformed, there was a debate among scholars as to whether the code should refer to *Pflichtverletzung* (violation of a duty) rather than to *Nichterfüllung* (non-performance), which also are quite closely related concepts, but nevertheless have slightly different meanings.[2] After discussing the matter with a Colombian lawyer, this author's feeling is that the use of the term *cumplimiento* was not intended to suggest a departure from the traditional solutions that may have been based on the concept of (*in*)*ejecución*,[3] but rather that it was a way of aligning the text with the legal terminology common to other international instruments such as the Vienna Convention on the International Sale of Goods, the Principles of European

[1] See, eg, Art 1603 *Código civil de Colombia*. Some codes speak both of *inejecución* and *incumplimiento*: see, eg, Arts 1314ff and 1426ff *Código civil del Perú*.

[2] See, eg, on the issue C Witz, 'La nouvelle jeunesse du BGB insufflée par la réforme du droit des obligations' [2002] *Recueil Dalloz* 3156.

[3] All the more so as the concept of *ejecución* is used to define *cumplimiento* in Art 79 PLACL.

Contract Law (PECL) or the stillborn Common European Sales Law (CESL).[4] This might be a misinterpretation, however.

This poor knowledge of the Spanish language is coupled with a limited acquaintance with Latin American legal systems. The author is, of course, aware of the strong European influences on these systems, especially from France, but also from Spain, Italy, Germany and Portugal, as well as of the more recent common law influences.[5] However, he has no in-depth knowledge of contract law in the various Latin American countries, or even in just some of them. This makes it difficult, at times even impossible, for him to grasp exactly where the PLACL stand vis-à-vis existing national laws.

The author's view of the Principles is therefore to a large extent uninformed. This ignorance might, of course, also have its positive side. Some things are better seen from the outside, as those on the inside are so used to them that they do no longer even take notice of them. The problem is that, of all non-Latin American lawyers, a French lawyer is probably the least apt to take a truly external view of the PLACL. There is no doubt that the French influence on these Principles remains strong, perhaps stronger than on many Latin American legal systems taken individually. This is manifest in the drafting style of the PLACL provisions, which tend to be quite general, even lofty, like those of the French *Code civil*—both in its original and its recently reformed version[6]—and depart quite strikingly from the legislative style of other legal traditions, such as that of England or Germany, or of other international harmonisation projects, which usually offer much more detailed provisions. The close proximity to the French legal tradition is also clear in the concepts used. An analysis of the provisions on performance and non-performance will provide several examples of this, but it may be said at this point that the Principles remain true to the concepts of *objet* (*objeto del contrato*; Article 38) and *cause* (*causa del contrato*; Article 39). These are typical of the Napoleonic codification[7] and yet have not found their way into the recent reform of French contract law:[8] it is as though,

[4] See J Basedow, 'Gemeinsames Europäisches Kaufrecht—Das Ende eines Kommissionsvorschlags' (2015) 23 *Zeitschrift für europäisches Privatrecht* 432.

[5] See, eg, H Valladão, *Le Droit latino-américain* (Paris, Sirey, 1954); A Wald, 'Le droit civil brésilien' [2010] *Recueil Dalloz* 1192; S Soleil, 'France—Amérique latine: les fondements d'un "cousinage" juridique' [2010] *Revue des contrats* 1036.

[6] The *Code civil* recently underwent a major reform. A regulation entered into force on 1 October 2016 (ordonnance n° 2016-131 du 10 février 2016 portant réforme du droit des contrats, du régime général et de la preuve des obligations) and recast the parts of the Code devoted to the general law of contract (ie, rules applicable to contracts in general, as opposed to rules applicable to specific contracts), to the general law of obligations (ie, rules applicable to all obligations, regardless of their source) and to the proof of obligations. The purpose of this reform was first of all to confirm existing law and to integrate solutions developed by case law into the Code, in order to make the French law of obligations more clear and accessible, but some substantive changes were also made.

[7] Very little is said about these two concepts, however, and it is doubtful what impact they would have if the Principles were to be implemented.

[8] The reformed *Code civil* has replaced the concepts of *objet* and *cause* with that of *contenu du contrat* (content of the contract; see Art 1128). Various provisions of the reformed *Code civil*, however, have explicitly confirmed the solutions which had formerly been achieved using these two concepts.

at least on certain points, the PLACL were more French than the new French law of contract![9]

The relationship between the PLACL and French law, whether old or new, is obviously not the subject of this chapter, but it is worth mentioning here that, while the proximity between these Principles and the French legal tradition rather puts the author of this chapter at his ease with the former, it also carries the risk that he will fail to realise how original and interesting some of their aspects may be as compared to other legal traditions, especially to the common law tradition.

So it is, however, and the author is very happy to have been given this opportunity to discover and study the PLACL, a fine and very interesting piece of legal scholarship. Besides, when it comes to international harmonisation projects in the field of contract law, the importance of national legal traditions is clearly on the wane. They have not disappeared, of course, and they certainly still exert an influence, but the fact remains that the various existing harmonisation projects have much in common. Whatever differences there may be among them stand out against the background of what might be called a stout 'common core'. This situation raises at least two questions. The first is, of course: what is specific in the PLACL, and how does it differ from, say, the PECL? The second question, which is nearly as obvious, is: what do the specific features of the PLACL have to do with the distinct cultural and legal identity of Latin America?

For the reasons mentioned above, the author of this chapter is not in a position to answer this second question. As to the first question, it would, of course, be too daunting a task to try and identify all common points as well as all differences between the PLACL and other harmonisation projects such as the PECL. Making a list of similarities and discrepancies is of limited interest in itself, and the size of this chapter would not allow it, anyway. What is more interesting is the issue of how these elements, taken together, sketch a distinct and coherent approach to contract.

In that respect, provisions on performance and non-performance, and especially the latter, are crucial, since it is well known that the distinctive conception of contract in a given legal system is often best reflected in the 'remedies' it offers in case of non-performance. Yet, it is not at all self-evident that international harmonisation projects should offer a fully coherent approach to contract (or to any other subject, for that matter). Given the way in which these projects are drafted, using various national and international materials, and relying on the expertise of lawyers with possibly very different backgrounds and conceptions, there is a definite risk of their turning into some kind of legal melting-pot, lacking any clear coherence or guidelines.

It is suggested that the PLACL offer a rather robust conception of contract. Nevertheless, such a piece of scholarship is necessarily a work of compromise: compromise

[9] It is quite obvious that the drafters of the Principles had a good knowledge of the French reform projects (a French law professor, Thomas Génicon, actually attended several meetings of the group which drafted the PLACL), and chose to follow them on certain points, but declined to do so on others.

between the various national legal traditions, between the preferences of the drafters, but also between continuity and innovation. While reflecting on these Principles, the author had the impression that the latter issue, ie the tension between continuity and innovation, must have been particularly strong when drafting the PLACL, and especially the provisions on performance and non-performance. One reason for this may be that this aspect of contract is one on which the old French *Code civil* and thus, presumably, at least some Latin American civil codes, were and are not wholly convincing. It is therefore a subject regarding which the desire to depart from the existing national provisions, if not from existing national laws,[10] may be quite strong. Besides, the various international instruments offer interesting counter-models in this respect.

The various influences and ambitions, however, as well as the tension between them, can come into play at at least two levels. The first level is that of concepts, the second that of rules and solutions. There is obviously some interdependence between the two, but they are nonetheless distinct, and it is therefore worth considering performance and non-performance in the PLACL, first of all from a conceptual perspective (I), and then from the perspective of the rules that have been adopted (II).

I. Concepts

It is probably at the conceptual level that the tension between tradition and innovation can be most strongly felt in the PLACL. The drafters clearly chose to modernise the approach to performance and non-performance, as compared to the Napoleonic tradition embedded in many Latin American civil codes.[11] Yet they also kept some of the features that are characteristic of this tradition. The Principles thus offer an interesting mix between tradition (A) and innovation (B).

A. Tradition

The Napoleonic *Code civil*, and some of the codes that have been significantly influenced by it, are rather short on the issue of the content of the contract. There are many provisions dealing with the different kinds of obligation that may be part of the contract,[12] but hardly any on how the content of the contract is to be ascertained. In the *Code civil*, which may be used as an example, the only explicit

[10] Which may have departed from the black-letter rules of the codes.

[11] The *Código civil de Chile* and the *Código civil de Colombia*, which were originally similar, were drafted by the great Latin American lawyer Andrés Bello in 1855. They are especially close to the French *Code civil*.

[12] See, eg, Arts 1168–1233 original *Code civil* and Arts 1304–1320 reformed *Code civil*.

provision on this issue is Article 1194 (ex-Article 1135), which provides: 'Contracts bind not only as to what is therein expressed, but also as to all the consequences that equity, usage, or law impose upon the obligation according to its nature'.[13] Part of the explanation for this (near) silence is probably that the issue of the content of the contract was already addressed, in the original *Code civil*, by the requirement that the contract must have a definite object (*objet défini*) and a licit cause (*cause licite*) in order to be valid (Article 1108), and is now addressed, in the reformed *Code civil*, by the requirement that the contract must have a content that is certain and licit (*contenu licite et certain*, Article 1128). The problem, however, is that the old provisions on object (Articles 1126–1130) and cause (Articles 1131–1133), as well as the new ones on content (Articles 1162–1171), apart from not being always very precise, only set limits on the freedom of the parties in setting the contractual content; but they give no indications as to how this content is to be ascertained. This, obviously, has an impact on the question of performance or non-performance, since the adequateness of performance must be assessed in connection with the content of the contract (as Article 72 PLACL makes clear).[14]

The PLACL, as has already been said, have retained the requirement that a contract should have an object (and a cause) in order to be valid. In line with this traditional 'French approach', but in stark contrast to other harmonisation instruments like the CESL, they do not deal explicitly with the issue of the content of the contract. This is all the more surprising, as the Principles do not have an equivalent for Article 1194 (ex-Article 1135) of the French *Code civil* either. In France, this provision has been used as the basis for the admission of implied contractual terms, which are otherwise not addressed by the Code. Under the PLACL, however, and absent any adequate provision on this issue, it is not clear how implied terms could be accepted. Of course, there is always the resource of contractual interpretation,[15] but this may not be sufficient in all cases, especially when the parties have made their intentions very explicit as to the content of the contract.

Another token of tradition in the PLACL, which also has to do with the content of contract, is their reliance on the concept of obligation. The original *Code civil*, and other codes after it,[16] refer less to the contract than they do to obligations.[17] Performance and non-performance, in particular, are addressed from the perspective of individual obligations, rather than from the perspective of the contract as a

[13] 'Les conventions obligent non seulement à ce qui y est exprimé, mais encore à toutes les suites que l'équité, l'usage ou la loi donnent à l'obligation d'après sa nature'. All citations of the *Code civil* in English are taken from the English translation accessible on the French law official website Legifrance (www.legifrance.gouv.fr) and written by David W Grunning.

[14] Also, object and cause are seen as necessary elements for the contract to be validly concluded; they are therefore considered from the perspective of the contract's conclusion, and not from the perspective of the contract's performance.

[15] See especially Arts 64, 65 and 70 PLACL. The latter article provides that 'Contracts shall always be interpreted in accordance with good faith'.

[16] See, eg, the *Código civil de Colombia* and the *Código civil de Chile*, as well as the *Código civil de Argentina* of 1871. The *Código civil del Perú* of 1984 also relies heavily on the concept of obligation, but the influence here seems to be predominantly German.

[17] The reformed *Code civil*, on the other hand, rather shifts the focus to contracts.

whole. In practice, this probably makes no great difference as the courts, disregarding the black letter of the code, tend to look at the contract from a broader perspective. Yet, from a theoretical point of view, focusing on the obligations rather than on the contract is not unproblematic. It is, indeed, doubtful if the whole content of the contract should boil down to obligations[18] and, by considering only the latter, there is a risk that part of the contract will remain out of sight. In the case of the PLACL, however, this risk is very small, due to other innovative aspects.

B. Innovation

When confronted with the traditional conceptual framework of the Napoleonic codes, the PLACL appear quite innovative on several counts. The mere fact that they use performance and non-performance as fundamental concepts is actually rather novel. Napoleonic codes typically regulate the 'effects' (*effets*) of obligations, but they offer no synthetic approach to performance and non-performance.[19] Typically, in the French *Code civil*, performance is dealt with under the concept of payment (*paiement*),[20] which is actually the same thing as performance; but non-performance, or rather the remedies for non-performance, did not use to be the subject of a systematic approach.[21] The PLACL offer a welcome modernisation in that respect.

Chapter 7 of the PLACL deals with the performance of contractual obligations. This is actually another example of the traditional obligation-based, rather than contract-based, approach. The rules contained in this chapter are for the most part a restatement of the traditional 'continental' rules on the payment of obligations. The first provision of the chapter, however, Article 72, offers a general definition of performance, which could apply to the contract taken as a whole as it does to individual obligations.[22] It also distinguishes implicitly between obligation and *prestación*.[23] This word is hard to translate into English,[24] but in substance designates what is to be provided under the obligation (or the contract). The *prestación* is thus the object of the obligation (or the contract), and it is that which the debtor/obligor must provide to the creditor/obligee in order to fulfil the

[18] On this issue, in the context of French law, see the seminal article by P Ancel, 'Force obligatoire et contenu obligationnel du contrat' [1999] *Revue trimestrielle de droit civil* 771.

[19] See, eg, the *Code civil*, the *Código civil de Chile* and the *Código civil de Colombia*.

[20] Arts 1235ff original *Code civil* and Arts 1342ff reformed *Code civil*; see also Arts 1568ff *Código civil de Chile* and Arts 1626ff *Código civil de Colombia*.

[21] This has fortunately been changed in the reformed *Code civil*; see n 37 below.

[22] Art 72 PLACL: 'Performance is the fulfilment of an obligation according to its terms'.

[23] This distinction, however, does not appear in the English translation of Art 72.

[24] The current English version of the PLACL usually translates *prestación* as 'performance', which seems adequate, but the two words are not exact equivalents, and it is sometimes necessary to use another English word to carry the meaning of *prestación* in a given context, such as 'obligation' (see Arts 72 and 79).

obligation (or the contract). This distinction was not clearly made in the original *Code civil*, but a rather similar one can be found in the BGB, which distinguishes between the *Schuldverhältnis* and the *Leistung*,[25] and it has just been introduced by the recent French law reform.[26] On the issue of performance, the PLACL thus adopt a conceptualisation that is more modern than that of many South American civil codes, even though the switch has not been complete, and some overlapping concepts, such as object and *prestación*, coexist.

It is on the subject of non-performance, however, that the PLACL take the most unmistakably modernising approach. True, the title of chapter 8 indicates that the Principles consider the non-performance of obligations, and not that of the contract as a whole; but the content of this chapter is otherwise rather innovative—as compared, once again, to the traditional Napoleonic approach. The chapter, first of all, is divided into two sections: 'non-performance in general' and 'means of relief for the obligee'. The first provision (Article 79) of the first section gives a definition of non-performance, which mirrors the definition of performance given earlier.[27] The second paragraph of this article offers an interesting precision: 'Defective performance includes all forms of non-conformity between that which was agreed and that which was performed by the obligor'. This might seem obvious, but, in the original *Code civil*, only radical non-performance and delayed performance were given any attention,[28] and defective non-performance was, so to speak, overlooked.[29] This more comprehensive conception of non-performance is, of course, most welcome.

The next article (Article 80) gives a definition of 'fundamental non-performance'. This notion is important, as some means of relief are only available to the obligee when non-performance can be regarded as fundamental.[30] It also indicates that the approach to (non-)performance is not as obligation-centred as the titles of the chapters suggest. As a matter of fact, fundamental non-performance, as defined in this article, will often be assessed at the level of the contract.

[25] See, eg, § 241 BGB.

[26] See especially Arts 1111-1, 1112-1, 1132, 1133, 1135, 1136, 1139, 1163, 1168, 1171, 1178, 1205, 1206, 1229 and *passim*.

[27] Art 79(1) PLACL: 'Non-performance is a failure to perform in the agreed manner'.

[28] Art 1147 *Code civil*: 'Le débiteur est condamné, s'il y a lieu, au paiement de dommages et intérêts soit à raison de l'inexécution de l'obligation, soit à raison du retard dans l'exécution, toutes les fois qu'il ne justifie pas que l'inexécution provient d'une cause étrangère qui ne peut lui être imputée, encore qu'il n'y ait aucune mauvaise foi de sa part'. ('A debtor shall be ordered to pay damages, in the proper circumstance, either on account of the non-performance of the obligation, or on account of the delay in performing, whenever he cannot establish that the non-performance was due to an external cause that cannot be imputed to him provided, moreover, there is no bad faith on his part'). This provision has passed practically unchanged in the reformed *Code civil*, but has now become Art 1231-5.

[29] This is still the case in the provisions of the reformed *Code civil*, even though case law and *doctrine* are more aware than they used to be of the specificity of defective performance, as opposed to radical non-performance.

[30] See below on termination.

Articles 81 and 82, which deal with force majeure and impossibility of performance, also constitute a conceptual clarification.[31] The original *Code civil* referred to force majeure, but did not clearly explain how the latter affects the contract.[32] It only provided that, in case of non-performance, the obligor must pay damages to the obligee, unless non-performance was the result of force majeure.[33] The underlying mechanism, which was not further clarified, was that force majeure creates a legitimate impossibility for the obligor to perform his obligation, which discharges the latter.[34] The PLACL adopt this system, but they clearly distinguish the 'cause'—force majeure—and its effect—impossibility of performance. They make clear that force majeure leads to the obligation (or the contract) being extinguished, or else suspended, if it renders performance impossible. Conversely, impossibility of performance releases the obligor only if it is due to force majeure.[35]

The second section of chapter 8 is probably the most innovative part of the PLACL, as compared to traditional Napoleonic civil codes. Following the standard set by some international instruments[36] and national reform projects,[37] it starts by listing the means of relief available to the obligee in case of non-performance, and then deals with them one by one. Without going into the details of these provisions at this point, it should be noted that the PLACL do not say a word about two well-known distinctions among obligations, which French law, and many Latin American legal systems after it, have adopted or established, and which as a rule have an impact on the assessment of non-performance and on its consequences: the distinction between obligations to do, not to do and to give (ie to transfer property),[38] and the distinction between *obligations de moyens* and *obligations de résultat*.[39] As these distinctions lead to more confusion than clarification, in the author's opinion, it is a very good thing that they should have not been retained.[40]

[31] Art 81 PLACL states that the obligee may not invoke non-performance due to its own acts or omission. This is the restatement of a traditional rule, which is not, however, formally expressed in many Napoleonic civil codes.

[32] On the other hand, the BGB does recognise the concept of impossibility (*Unmöglichkeit*), but does not really need the concept of force majeure.

[33] See Art 1147 (note 28) and Art 1148 original *Code civil*, which provided: 'Il n'y a lieu à aucuns dommages et intérêts lorsque, par suite d'une force majeure ou d'un cas fortuit, le débiteur a été empêché de donner ou de faire ce à quoi il était obligé, ou a fait ce qui lui était interdit'. ('Damages are not due when, because of a force majeure or a fortuitous event, the obligor-debtor either was prevented from giving or doing what he was obligated to give or did what he was forbidden to do').

[34] See, however, in the particular case of an obligation to deliver a thing, Art 1302 *Code civil.*

[35] This is also made explicit in the reformed *Code civil*: see Arts 1218 and 1351.

[36] See, eg, Arts 107ff CESL.

[37] This was also the approach of the French reform project of the law of obligations and has materialised in Arts 1217ff reformed *Code civil.*

[38] See, eg, Arts 1101 and 1126 original *Code civil.* This distinction is derived from Roman law; see R Zimmermann, *The Law of Obligations: Roman Foundations of the Civilian Tradition* (Oxford, Clarendon, 1996) 6; P Pichonnaz, *Les Fondements romains du droit privé* (Geneva, Schulthess, 2008) 1333.

[39] This distinction was first suggested by the French professor René Demogue, as a way to reconcile Arts 1137 and 1147 *Code civil*, which were regarded by some as contradictory; see R Demogue, *Traité des obligations en général*, vol 5 (Paris, Rousseau, 1922) no 1237.

[40] These distinctions are also absent from the reformed *Code civil.*

Instead, the Principles establish only one distinction, which is fully justified, and whose importance has become increasingly clear since the time when the Napoleonic civil codes were first drafted: that between monetary obligations and non-monetary obligations.[41]

From a conceptual point of view, then, the PLACL are something of a mix. They seek to retain part of the Napoleonic heritage, but integrate it into a more modern approach to the 'effects' of the obligations, centred on the distinction between performance and non-performance.

II. Rules

It is not possible in the context of this chapter to discuss all the rules and solutions contained in the two chapters of the PLACL dealing with performance and non-performance. Since the provisions on performance are mostly a restatement of traditional rules on the payment of obligations,[42] it seems more interesting to focus on the rules on non-performance (A). Something must also be said on the silence of the Principles on a certain number of issues, related especially to the extinction of the contract (B).

A. Non-performance

On the subject of non-performance, the PLACL remain true to a fundamental solution, which was adopted by the *Code civil* in 1804 (although it was later marred by the adoption of the distinction between *obligations de moyens* and *obligations de résultat*): the obligor must answer for any non-performance, regardless of his fault, and regardless of whether non-performance is attributable to himself personally or to someone he employed to perform the contract (Articles 79 and 82). It is only if non-performance was caused by force majeure, and is thus not imputable to the obligor, that the latter will escape any responsibility for it.[43] This being said, the means of relief offered to the obligee in case of non-performance, as well as the way in which they are regulated, mark a clear evolution as compared to the solutions of the Napoleonic *Code civil* and its followers. They reflect to a large extent the solutions that have been suggested in other harmonisation projects, and which can now be found in the new French law of contract,[44] testifying to the modernising intent of the drafters of these Principles.

[41] See especially Art 86(1) PLACL, dealing with specific performance. This distinction is also advanced in Arts 1343ff reformed *Code civil*.

[42] Compare Arts 72ff PLACL and the references cited at note 20.

[43] But, of course, the obligor may not avoid termination of the contract by the other party if he fails to perform, whatever the reason; see Art 83(1) PLACL.

[44] See Arts 1217ff reformed *Code civil*.

Interestingly, the PLACL address the issue of the correction of defective performance, a major practical issue, but which is nearly totally ignored by the *Code civil*[45] and its followers. The PLACL remain rather cautious on this matter, however. They require the obligee to give notice of defective performance to the obligor within a reasonable time after he should have become aware of it (Article 85(1)), and they expressly regard cure and replacement as particular types of specific performance, which are thus subjected to the latter's regime (Article 87).[46] They do not explicitly grant any 'right to cure' to the obligor, however, which means that, once the obligee has given notice of the defective performance, he may be free to choose any means of relief among those which are made available to him by the Principles, even if the obligor has offered to cure the defective performance. This is not very surprising, given the background of the Principles, but the solution clearly marks a limit to the concern for economic efficiency that is made manifest in other rules.

The PLACL recognise five means of relief for the obligee in case of non-performance: specific performance, price reduction, termination of contract, *excepción de contrato no cumplido*, and damages. Four of these are well known and are most probably already recognised in all Latin American legal orders. Price reduction, on the other hand, would be new to at least some of them.

Unsurprisingly, the PLACL deal first of all with specific performance. As is well known, unlike common law systems, civil law systems, including Latin American ones, attach great importance to specific performance, since they regard contract not just as a binding economic relationship, but also as a promise that must be kept. This conception can lead to some rather extreme results in some jurisdictions, for example in French law until recently, where a court can order specific performance even if its cost is totally unreasonable for the obligor.[47] The PLACL, while recognising specific performance as a usual remedy, and even possibly the normal one in case of non-performance, set important limits to it, at least for non-monetary obligations.[48]

First of all, specific performance cannot be demanded when it is impossible (Article 86(2)(a)). It is also ruled out when, even though it would be practically possible, it represents an injury to personal dignity (Article 86(2)(c)), or 'is extremely burdensome for the obligor, taking into consideration that the obligee may satisfy its interest by choosing another means of relief' (Article 86(2)(b)). While the second exception (injury to dignity) has long been acknowledged by

[45] Also in its reformed version.

[46] There is one exception, however, since replacement is only available in case of fundamental non-performance: Art 87(2) PLACL.

[47] See, eg, Cour de cassation, 11 May 2005, no 03-21.136, *Bulletin civil* III, no 103.

[48] Art 86 makes a distinction between monetary and non-monetary obligations. While specific performance can always be demanded for the former, it is subject to some restrictions as far as the latter are concerned.

authors and by case law,[49] the third is not at all self-evident in systems influenced by French law. This exception has actually also been adopted in the new French Civil Code,[50] but it is a subject of some debate, as several authors consider that abiding by one's word should be uppermost, and that economic considerations should not 'water down' the strength of the contract.[51] Undoubtedly, by accepting that specific performance cannot be demanded when it is extremely burdensome to the obligor, the Principles testify to the explicit penetration of economic considerations into continental 'Romanistic' legal systems, which used not to take them into account so clearly. Given the general trend observed in international harmonisation instruments and national reform projects, this is not really surprising.

The second means of relief is price reduction. In the original French *Code civil*, price reduction was not recognised as a general remedy, and, where it existed, for specific contracts, had as a rule to be authorised by the courts.[52] The PLACL take a much more modern approach and provide that 'in the event of defective performance, the obligee may accept this and reduce the price in proportion with the difference between the value of the performance at the time it was carried out and the value it would have had at that same time if the performance had occurred' (Article 88). The obligee can thus decide price reduction unilaterally, without his having to turn to the courts. That this solution should be found in the PLACL is rather natural. It has been adopted in other international instruments[53] as well as in the new French Civil Code.[54] Besides, since the Principles accept unilateral termination at the obligee's initiative, it is quite logical that they should also accept price reduction, which amounts to a partial termination of the contract: he who can do more (complete termination) should also be able to do less (partial termination in the form of price reduction).

The third means of relief mentioned by the Principles is *resolución*, ie termination. In the traditional French system, adopted in several Latin American Codes, *resolución* used to be a judicial sanction.[55] It was thus not possible for the obligee simply to give notice of termination to the obligor; in case of non-performance he had to go to court to ask the judge to grant termination, with the latter enjoying a fair amount of discretion in deciding if non-performance was serious enough to

[49] This is the case in France at least. The express reference to dignity may have been borrowed from the *projet Catala* (Art 1154).

[50] Art 1221 reformed *Code civil*, which excludes specific performance in case of gross disproportion between its cost for the obligor and its benefits for the obligee ('s'il existe une disproportion manifeste entre son coût pour le débiteur et son intérêt pour le créancier').

[51] See, eg S Picasso, 'L'exécution forcée des obligations contractuelles—Brève étude comparative des droits français et argentin' [2015] *Revue des contrats* 700.

[52] See, eg, Art 1644 *Code civil* for sales contracts.

[53] See, eg, Art 9:401 PECL.

[54] Art 1223 reformed *Code civil*.

[55] See, eg, Art 1489 *Código civil de Chile*, as interpreted by the courts, on which B Caprile Biermann, 'L'introduction de la résolution unilatérale pour inexécution—Rapport chilien' [2010] *Revue des contrats* 1067.

justify this means of relief. In some countries, including France, this rather burdensome system has been altered by the legislator,[56] or by the courts themselves, which have accepted termination by notice in certain circumstances.[57] The Principles adopt this possibility without relinquishing the traditional judicial termination. A contract may therefore be terminated either by decision of the court or by notice (Article 89(3)). In both cases, however, there must have been fundamental non-performance of the contract (Article 89). A third mode of *resolución* is through the application of a termination clause (Article 94). Such clauses have long been accepted in legal systems influenced by French law, and were traditionally a way to avoid the burdensome conditions of judicial termination. Even with the acceptance of termination by notice, they are still an interesting mechanism, in particular since they can provide that termination will be incurred even in case of non-essential non-performance.[58]

The fourth means of relief is *excepción de contrato no cumplido* (Article 95), here again a traditional mechanism,[59] whose principle is easily understood: unless performance by one of the parties must take place prior to performance by the other party, each party may refuse to perform if the other does not perform its own part of the contract. A more innovative aspect is the acceptance of what could be termed 'anticipated' *excepción de contrato no cumplido*, which allows a party to refuse to perform its own part of the contract when, prior to the date due for the other party's performance, the latter suffers a significant impairment to his ability to perform or to its solvency (Article 96).[60] It should be noted, however, that the Principles do not accept anticipated *termination* by one party in cases where it is clear that the other party will not wish or be able to perform its part of the contract.[61]

The fifth and last means of relief is, of course, damages. Provisions on damages in the PLACL are rather unsurprising.[62] They expressly state that non-monetary harm can be compensated (Article 98), a solution that has never really been

[56] See, eg, Art 1204 *Código civil de Argentina*; Art 1372 *Código civil del Perú*.

[57] In France, see the leading case Cour de cassation, 13 October 1998, no 96-21485, *Bulletin civil* III, no 300. In Belgium, see Cour de cassation, 2 May 2002, no C.01.0185.N [2003] *Revue générale de droit civil belge* 337.

[58] The rules of the PLACL on termination are once again very close to those of the reformed *Code civil* (Arts 1224–30).

[59] It is of course derived from the *exceptio non adimpleti contractus* of Roman law. Surprisingly, though, the French *Code civil* does not mention the mechanism, which the courts had to reintroduce into French law in the course of the nineteenth century. The Latin American civil codes usually explicitly mention the mechanism; see, eg, Art 1609 *Código civil de Colombia*; Art 1426 *Código civil del Perú*.

[60] The same solution is to be found in Art 1220 reformed *Code civil*.

[61] The same is true of the reformed *Code civil*.

[62] It should be mentioned that, in French law, the provisions of the original *Code civil* on contractual damages (Arts 1146ff) have been carried over into the reformed *Code civil* (Arts 1231ff), with only minor formal amendments. The reason for this is not that they were regarded as not being in need of reform, but that the government intends to reform the whole area of civil liability, including contractual liability, at a later stage. A reform project on civil liability was made public in March 2017, but it is still unclear if and when a final project will be discussed in Parliament.

debated in France, but was long refused by some Latin American legal orders—and maybe still is.[63] The Principles provide that, as a rule, a 'non-performing party shall be liable for harm it could have foreseen at the time of the conclusion of the contract and that results from its non-performance', but that 'in the event of fraud or gross negligence, the obligor shall be liable for all harm that results from its non-performance' (Article 100)—here again, a classical solution. It must be noted, however, that the Principles make no distinction between negative interest and positive interest, which has long been adopted in several legal orders but is still quite alien to the French legal tradition.[64] They also implicitly refuse the possibility to award punitive damages, thereby reflecting the solution that exists in an overwhelming majority of civil law systems.[65]

The PLACL also accept penalty clauses, as is traditional in civil law countries (Article 104), but within limits, which are likewise traditional: a court may, upon request by a party or on its own initiative, modify the amount of the penalty when it is manifestly excessive or derisory (Article 107). This acceptance of penalty clauses is, of course, in line with the priority given to specific performance, since such clauses can create a strong incentive for the obligor to deliver what he has promised.

The introduction into the PLACL of a duty to mitigate is more unexpected. Under Article 102(1): 'Compensation is subject to reduction when the obligee has failed to take reasonable measures to mitigate loss in good faith. Reduction shall correspond to the amount by which the loss could have been mitigated'. Such a duty to mitigate is alien to the French legal tradition and is still refused in France[66] and in many Latin American countries,[67] even though it has found its way into most international harmonisation instruments.[68] Its adoption by the PLACL is another token of the drafters' concern for economic efficiency, which was already apparent in the limit set on the obligee's right to demand specific performance.

One may actually wonder to what extent the duty to mitigate is compatible with the right to specific performance, however. In fact, in many cases of non-performance it is much more efficient, from an economic point of view, to terminate the contract and enter into another contract with someone else, than to

[63] For an explicit acceptance of compensation for non-pecuniary damage, see eg, Art 1322 *Código civil del Perú*.

[64] Even if it is attracting increasing attention; see, eg, in France, YM Laithier, *Étude comparative des sanctions de l'inexécution du contrat* (Paris, LGDJ, 2004) nos 108ff.

[65] On the debate which is taking place in some Latin American countries on the issue of punitive damages, however, see S Picasso, 'L'introduction des dommages-intérêts punitifs en droit des contrats—Rapport argentin' [2010] *Revue des contrats* 1107.

[66] Its adoption is, however, recommended in Art 1263 of the French reform project on civil liability (n 62).

[67] See J López Santa-María, 'Sobre la obligación de minimizar los daños en el derecho chileno y comparado' in F Mantilia Espinosa and F Ternera Barrios (eds), *Los Contratos en el derecho privado* (Bogotá, Legis, 2007) 325; C Pizarro Wilson, 'L'Introduction de l'obligation de modérer son dommage en matière contractuelle' [2010] *Revue des contrats* 1129.

[68] See, eg, Art 9:505 PECL.

demand specific performance from the original obligee.[69] The duty to mitigate, if strictly understood, could thus set a limit on the freedom of the obligee to choose his means of relief in case of non-performance and in some circumstances turn the right to terminate into an obligation. Admittedly, the PLACL have adopted a restricted version of the duty to mitigate, since it should only apply in cases where the obligee asks for damages, and not when other means of relief are relied upon. There may be a lack of consistency in recognising this duty only in certain cases, however, and, once the duty to mitigate is accepted, it may have a tendency to 'spill over', thus affecting the obligee's freedom to choose the remedy that suits him best.

One may wonder, therefore, if the PLACL are not taking the middle road as far as remedies for non-performance are concerned. The Principles still apparently regard specific performance as the first means of relief in case of non-performance, which is in line with the French and Latin American tradition, but they also give greater weight to considerations of economic efficiency; and it remains to be seen up to what point the priority given to specific performance and the concern for economic efficiency can be reconciled.

B. Lacunae

Surprisingly, the PLACL do not address certain traditional issues in the law of contract. As it is unlikely that the drafters simply forgot about them, one may wonder if they found them of little importance, or if they deliberately chose to remain silent on questions that are not of the utmost importance and on which they had difficulties reaching an agreement. Whatever their reasons, it may be worth mentioning these issues, which have to do with performance and non-performance.

First of all, the PLACL, although they contain a chapter on the effects of contracts on third parties (chapter 5), do not expressly formulate the privity-of-contract rule, in contrast to the French Civil Code.[70] This is rather surprising, even though it could be argued that this rule is implicit in any legal system, since it is hard to conceive how contract law could function without it.[71] Besides, the provisions on contracts in favour of third parties, which are the subject of the second section of chapter 5, only make sense if seen against the background of a privity-of-contract rule, which can thus be regarded as an implicit element of the PLACL.

More disturbing is the absence in the Principles of any provisions on the extinction of the contract, when this extinction is not a remedy for non-performance.

[69] See on this issue O Deshayes, 'L'Introduction de l'obligation de modérer son dommage en matière contractuelle—Rapport français' [2010] *Revue des contrats* 1139, no 17.

[70] See Art 1165 original *Code civil* and Art 1199 reformed *Code civil*.

[71] cf S Vogenauer, 'The Effects of Contracts on Third Parties: The *Avant-projet de réforme* in a Comparative Perspective' in J Cartwright, S Vogenauer and S Whittaker (eds), *Reforming the French Law of Obligations, Comparative Reflections on the Avant-projet de réforme du droit des obligations et de la prescription ('the Avant-projet Catala')* (Oxford, Hart Publishing, 2009) 235, 236–39.

Of course, a contract normally comes to an end through its being performed, but there are other hypotheses where the parties can put an end to a contract in the absence of non-performance and without performance having 'emptied' the object of the contract. This is the case, for example, when the parties have entered a long-term contract, with no fixed duration. It is generally accepted, at least in French law and in legal systems influenced by it, that, absent any specific term of the contract on this issue, any of the parties can terminate the contract at any time, simply by giving notice. Surprisingly, the PLACL do not expressly adopt or restate this rule, although it is highly unlikely that its drafters intended to reject it.

Equally surprising is the absence of any provision in the Principles concerning the fate of the contract in the case of a change of circumstances. This is a classical question, and most harmonisation projects accept that, if performance becomes excessively onerous for a party because of an exceptional change of circumstances, the contract may be terminated, or even sometimes modified by the courts.[72] Of course, such solutions directly run counter to the binding effect of contracts, and it is mainly for this reason that they are still rejected by some legal systems, but they have been accepted by other legal systems, including some Latin American ones,[73] and, very recently, the French one.[74] The PLACL actually do have a provision on gross disparity (Article 37), but the latter is considered only in so far as it exists at the time of the conclusion of the contract. It constitutes a ground for annulment or judicial modification of the contract, but cannot be used to address cases in which gross disparity is the result of a radical change of circumstances *post conclusionem*. This silence of the PLACL on change of circumstances may be interpreted as a sign that the drafters were unable to find an agreement on this delicate issue. The result, however, is that the contract will remain binding on the parties, whatever the change in circumstances.

[72] See, eg, Art 6:111 PECL.

[73] See, eg, Art 1198 *Código civil de Argentina*; Arts 478–80 *Código civil brasilero*; Art 868 *Código de comercio de Colombia*; Arts 1440–46 *Código civil del Perú*.

[74] See Art 1195 reformed *Code civil*.

11

The Provisions on Non-performance in the Principles of Latin American Contract Law

SABRINA LANNI*

I. Non-performance and the Battle for the Harmonisation of Contract Law in Latin America: The PLACL and Other Experiences

Latin American legal scholarship has been studying the harmonisation of private law, constantly questioning itself both on the features of the civil codes recently adopted in this area and on the ability of these codes to promote the harmonisation of private law in Latin America.

Special attention has been given to the issue of the harmonisation of contract law. The reasons for this are manifold; to mention but a few, they include the common characteristics of the Latin American civil codes, their shared derivation from Roman law, the existence of model codes that promote a cross-border Latin American civil law, and, last but not least, the ambition to implement supranational rules, in order to respond to the needs of an increasingly globalised society.

Whatever the reasons, this focus on the harmonisation of contract law has one specific goal in mind: to provide a common frame of reference in the matter of contracts for the Latin American countries. The example of the European Union and the various draft projects, like the Principles of European Contract Law (PECL) and the Principles of European Tort Law (PETL) dealing with private law in a region characterised by different systems, different languages and different models of civil code, is a particularly inspiring one for the Latin American legal system.

* This is a revised and updated version of a paper published in 'Osservatorio del diritto civile e commerciale' 2016 (1) *Il Mulino* 339–72. The author would like to thank Dr Federica Boldrini for her careful review of the English translation; it goes without saying that its final content remains the sole responsibility of the author.

Finally, the recommendations of the Latin American Parliament[1] for the creation of a model law aimed at the harmonisation of law in Latin America have breathed new life into the initiatives already taken in this respect and stimulated Latin American jurists to compare national and supranational legal systems.[2]

In recent years, some academic initiatives have got underway with a view to developing the Latin American juridical model. Two of these initiatives are still ongoing. The first, in order of time, was launched by the University of Rome 'Tor Vergata'.[3] The study group began its work in 1997, when a team of researchers came to Rome and spent two years studying the fundamentals of Latin American contract law, sponsored by UE-ALFA (SUMMA 1997/1999, TANTA 1998/2000, OMNEM 2004/2006). As a first step, the tasks of each component of the project were organised and weighed up first by Edgar Cortés Moncayo (Externado University of Bogotá), then by Angela Cristina Vierio (Rio Grande do Sul University).

The results of the ALFA projects and those of the study group set up in this context are still in draft form and have not yet been published. The draft as such may prove useful in itself, as source material for the future principles and their transposition, and for the purposes of interpretation of Latin American contract law.

The work is proceeding slowly because it contemplates not only contracts, but more generally also obligations.[4] The study group is proceeding on the basis of the essential idea that all Latin American systems conceive various types of juridical acts other than contracts—such as guarantees, offers, unilateral promises, torts and so on—even if not all of them use this term and not all have generalised rules.

The second academic initiative is that of the Principles of Latin American Contract Law (PLACL) proposed by the Chilean *Fundación Fernando Fueyo*, which is

[1] The Latin American Parliament (*Parlatino*) was created in 1964. It is a permanent regional organisation seated in Panama city (Panama) and composed of the countries of Latin America and of the Caribbean. It is an advisory assembly similar to the early European Parliament. Lately, *Parlatino* has prepared, mainly through its Commissions and with the valuable support of various international agencies with which it has inter-institutional cooperation agreements, many proposals of model laws in different fields (consumer law, generic drugs, nursing mother protection etc.).

[2] In Latin America, the realisation of *leyes-tipo, códigos-modelo* or *códigos-marco* (to harmonise single legal institutions or, more generally, certain areas of the law) has been strongly advocated by the *Parlatino* (see for the text 'Lineamientos metodológicos para la realización de estudios de armonización legislativa' [2006] *Roma e America. Rivista di diritto dell'integrazione e unificazione del diritto in Europa e in America Latina* 331). This requirement reflects a long-standing process in those countries; on the detail, see S Schipani, *La codificazione del diritto romano comune* (Turin, Giappichelli, 1999) 64–69; S Schipani and R Vaccarella (eds), *Un 'codice tipo' di procedura civile per l'America Latina* (Padua, Cedam, 1990); S Schipani and M Massa (eds), *Un 'codice tipo' di procedura penale per l'America Latina* (Padua, Cedam, 1994); A Gidi and E Ferrer MacGregor (eds), *La tutela de los derechos difusos, colectivos e individuales homogéneos* (Mexico, Porrúa, 2003). That process is currently in full development; for a discussion see R Correa Freitas, 'Un Modelo de Constitución para América Latina' [2012] *Revista Jurídicas UCES* 45–52; AAVV, *Modelo de Código Tributario para América Latina. Tendencias actuales de tributación* (Bogotá, ICDT, 2010).

[3] This was an initiative taken by Professor Sandro Schipani.

[4] The need for a general part on the law of obligations is in line with the idea of improving the movement of goods and services in an increasingly globalised society, and tallies with the need to encourage scholarly thinking on the unity and continuity of principles and values in the different Latin American legal systems; see E Cortés Moncayo, 'Oportunidad de una parte general de las obligaciones en un Código de contratos para Amèrica Latina' [2010] *Roma e America. Diritto romano comune* 92.

affiliated to the Diego Portales University, with the support of the French *Fondation pour le Droit Continental*.[5] This project is still under development and review, but has the great merit of promoting dialogue on the principles of Latin American contract law not only within Latin America, but in Europe as well: the attention given to the PLACL project by the Oxford Institute of European and Comparative Law will have a wide-ranging impact on the English-speaking countries and their jurists. Neither of these initiatives is intended to have binding normative force: they produce soft law rules, comparable to those contained in the PECL and in the Draft Common Frame of Reference (DCFR). This kind of soft law enactment can exercise great influence on the intense codification activity in the area of civil law in Latin America.

The topic of this chapter concerns a subject extensively covered in the PLACL: 'non-performance of contractual obligations' is, in fact, discussed in a specific chapter of the Principles (chapter 8), which defines non-performance, describes its features and peculiarities, and examines the consequences in terms of responsibility and the life of the contract.[6]

The norms contained in this chapter define some fundamental facets of non-performance. A general definition of the subject is supplied by the first paragraph of Article 79 ('Non-performance defined'), which states that 'non-performance is a failure to perform in the agreed manner'. Other rules are scattered around the text: among these, the second paragraph of the same Article 79 is particularly significant, in that it offers some clarification of the article, expanding the scope of its application by affirming that 'defective performance includes all forms of non-conformity between that which was agreed and that which was performed by the obligor'. The definition of further rules is evidently entrusted to the hermeneutic activity of legal practitioners, which are called upon to define the scope of application of this article.

In the light of these norms, the expression 'non-performance' identifies not only the non-realisation of the obligation that is due, but also its incomplete or defective execution: the concept of 'non-performance' is generic and includes non-compliance with any obligation relating to the contract. This means that the concept covers both the objective breach of the obligation and the non-execution of the principal or the secondary performance, pertaining to the fulfilment of the contract in the 'agreed manner'.[7]

[5] I omit references to this experience, which is the subject of the book of which this essay will form part; a reference point may be found on http://fundacionfueyo.udp.cl/proyecto-sobre-principios-latinoamericanos-de-derecho-de-los-contratos/.

[6] The chapter is divided into three sections: Non-performance in general (section 1: Arts 79–83); Means of relief for the obligee (section 2: Arts 84–102); Agreements regarding liability for non-performance (section 3: Arts 104–11).

[7] The concept of non-performance accepted in the PLACL seems to have its origins in the conceptual background provided by the Civil Code of Chile, which was, of course, well known to the Chilean co-authors of the Principles. Indeed, Art 1556 of that Code establishes that compensation for harm suffered includes the damage and the loss of profit, whether arising from the non-fulfilment of the obligation or from its defective or late performance.

The broad concept of non-performance which emerges from an analysis of the PLACL seems to be in line with the definition supplied by other traditions of legal scholarship. An interesting comparison can be made with § 280 of the reformed German Civil Code (BGB): legal doctrine holds that, in referring to the non-performance of a 'duty' and not of the non-performance of an 'obligation', this norm makes reference to all kinds of duty, even secondary and instrumental ones.[8] The text of the PLACL also evokes the way in which the subject is dealt with in the European legal harmonisation and unification projects and, in particular, the specific conceptualisation of the term 'non-performance' in Article 1:301(4) PECL.[9] It is, however, appropriate to point out that, even if referring to an objective notion of non-performance, the legal practitioner cannot but consider the reasons that determined the non-fulfilment of the contract.

The notion of non-performance does not appear to imply any illegality of the relevant conduct;[10] nonetheless, the civil lawyer is used to distinguish between attributable and non-attributable non-performance, as only the former gives rise to contractual liability even if, in both cases, the debtor may be required to fulfil the obligations deriving from the contract.

[8] See A Di Majo, 'Adempimento e risarcimento nella prospettiva dei rimedi' [2006] *Rivista di diritto civile* 68.

[9] The PECL and PETL are interesting points of reference for the subject of this chapter, since they use 'non-performance' as a general category, inherent in all forms of missing or incorrect performance. This approach clearly emerges in the definitional context of the PECL, especially from Art 1:301(4), which states that 'non-performance denotes any failure to perform an obligation under the contract, whether or not excused, and includes delayed performance, defective performance and failure to co-operate in order to give full effect to the contract'. This approach is confirmed by the interpretation of Art 1:301(4) in connection with Art 8:101 (on the remedies available) and Art 8:103 (on fundamental non-performance), showing a broad concept of 'non-performance' to include the 'accessory obligations' (cooperation, diligence, accuracy, punctuality, etc) that may appear as 'functional obligations' in the context of 'social contract', determining the duty of each party to cooperate in order to give full effect to the contract. Scientific support for this approach is offered by C Castronovo, 'La relazione come categoria essenziale dell'obbligazione e della responsabilità extracontrattuale' [2011] *Europa e diritto privato* 55–77, especially 67ff; the author considers 'relatedness' as a constant feature of the subjects that interact juridically, and suggests a rethink of these obligations as determining a 'relationship' rather than a 'duty'. This 'objective' and 'circumstantial' view of non-performance is taken not only in the PLACL, but also in some Latin American civil codes (ie the concept of *incumplimiento* in Art 512 of the old Argentinean Civil Code; see S Lanni, *L'inadempimento dell'obbligazione. La colpa: la prospettiva del codice civile argentino nel sistema giuridico latinoamericano* (Naples, ESI, 2012). Similar observations can be made with reference to the UNIDROIT Principles, where the concept of non-performance and its precise content does not give rise to an elaborate dogmatic reconstruction, as an effect of the different implications deriving from excusable and non-excusable non-performance (see, eg, Arts 7.1.2, 7.1.3, 7.1.4 PICC).

[10] The PLACL omit the reference to the word *culpa* in the regulation of non-performance. The evaluation of non-performance appears to be purely objective and detached from the rules regulating this subject in the Latin American civil codes. The word *culpa* and its reflections seem, however, to be assumed. I believe this assumption clearly emerges from the text of the PLACL in three different passages. First, *culpa* is invoked implicitly as a hypothesis (of *imputabilidad*) to determine when the non-performance is imputable to the obligor (Art 79(4)). Secondly, the obligor is considered liable for all the damages resulting from his non-performance in the event of 'fraud' or 'gross negligence' (Art 100(2)). Thirdly, the parties' freedom of contract is excluded as far as the effects of non-performance due to 'fraud' or 'gross negligence' are concerned (Art 111(a)).

The definition of a broad concept of non-performance fosters further reflection, in order to assess the impact of the principle of good faith in the PLACL, even beyond the legal provisions explicitly provided, as will be shown in the next part of this chapter. However, what I wish to emphasise here is that, considering the numerous cases of non-performance defined by the PLACL, the court is called upon to establish whether the contract should be terminated or should still be considered to exist. This power is anyhow largely restricted, since in the PLACL, the claim for performance of the contract is preferred to the possible compensation of its non-performance.[11]

The priority given to observance of the agreement is founded on the common principle *pacta sunt servanda* and on the prevalence of an ethical view of the contract over a purely economic one. The PLACL consider the termination of the contract, but have no rule comparable to § 281 BGB, which limits the right of the debtor to execution of the performance and allows the obligee to demand compensation in place of performance of the contract.[12]

The claim for compensation does not exclude the claim for performance, since it is not substitutive of the fulfilment of the contract, as is the case, instead, in the reformed German *Schuldrecht*, which refers to 'compensation' that 'takes the place' of unfulfilled performance ('statt der Leistung' § 281 BGB), even if the German legal doctrine also considers the possibility of 'compensation' as a 'consequence' which may coexist with incorrect or late performance ('neben der Leistung'), just as in the case of delayed performance.[13]

The interest in the fulfilment of contracts in the PLACL emerges in various different forms: as interest in the performance of duties arising from the contract; interest in the preservation of the contents of the executive agreement; interest in the protection of personal or material goods in the development of the contract; interest in obtaining even an imperfect performance; interest in limiting harm to other people.[14]

Several of these interests are supported in the PLACL by a framework of shared principles, whose identification would be reductive if limited to what is established in the *sedes materiae* of the legal text, specifically dedicated to the 'general principles' (section 2 of chapter 2). The norms contained in this context seem to define a general framework of contract law, which the drafters of the PLACL probably took as a point of reference. Their intention seems rather to have been to offer a modern and efficient contract law system, based on the combination of three fundamental principles which affect the whole legal text, namely freedom of contract (Article 5), binding force of contract (Article 6) and good faith (Article 7).

[11] See Arts 83(2), 84, 87, 88, 108.

[12] See AM Morales Moreno, 'Los principios latinoamericanos de derecho de los contratos. Un debate abierto sobre las grandes cuestiones jurídicas de la contratación' [2014] *Anuario de derecho civil* 240.

[13] On the issue of reform of the German *Schuldrecht*, see A di Majo, *Le tutele contrattuali* (Turin, Giappichelli, 2012) 101.

[14] The emergence in the PLACL of a specific interest in the performance is underlined by Morales Moreno (n 12) 240.

In this chapter, I therefore intend to investigate the measure on non-performance in the PLACL, in the light not only of the principles indicated in section 2 of chapter 2, but also of the principles that arise from an hermeneutic approach, based on the understanding of the whole legal text and of the legal system from which these principles have been deduced.

II. The Guiding Principle of the PLACL: Good Faith

Over the past several decades, there has been an extension of the good faith principle in Latin America, and it now constitutes a general principle of private law. As far as the law of obligations and contract law are concerned, this extension occurred in both areas in which the good faith principle is usually applied within the civil law system, that is, the subjective (concerning rectitude, honesty, fairness in determining the will of the parties) and the objective (concerning accuracy in the main performance and in the accessory duties, in order to guarantee the exact fulfilment of the obligation).[15]

Research into the causes of this reappraisal and a redefinition of the good faith principle have already been carried out within the Latin American specialist doctrine, which links the rethinking of this principle to the general transformation that has affected Latin American private law. Latin American private law appears to be in a state of constant construction, building on a new perception of civil code in which general principles are used as instruments to enable communication not only between different parts of the code itself, but also between different sources of law and different legal formants.

For this reason, the new Latin American civil codes intentionally couch their general clauses in 'open' and 'general' legal language. Over the past two decades, the explicit goal of Latin American legislators has been to leave to legal practitioners the task of integrating and developing legal rules, in consideration of the changing needs of contemporary society.[16] In this operation, special attention has to be paid

[15] On this, see J López Santa María, *Los contratos. Parte general* II (Santiago de Chile, Editorial Juridica de Chile, 1988) 391ff.; see also G Benacchio, 'Il ruolo della buona fede nel diritto comunitario' in *Convegno internazionale di studi in onore di Alberto Burdese* (Padua, Cedam, 2003) and FD Busnelli, 'Note in tema di buona fede ed equità', in L Garofalo (ed), *Il ruolo della buona fede oggettiva nell'esperienza giuridica storica e contemporanea. Atti del Convegno internazionale in studi in onore di Alberto Burdese* (Padua, Cedam, 2003) 189–201 and 225–57.

[16] With reference to good faith as an element of elasticity of the system, see J Martins-Costa, 'O direito privado como um "sistema em constituição": as cláusolas gerais no projeto do código civil brasileiro' [1998] *Revista dos Tribunais* 26. With reference to good faith as an instrument to achieve equitable solutions, see JM Iturraspe, *Justicia contractual* (Buenos Aires, Ediar, 1978) 138; F Amaral, 'A equidade no código civil brasileiro' [2003] *Revista de direito do Tribunal de Justiça do Estado do Rio de Janeiro* 71. Concerning the harmonisation of contract law in Latin America, it has already been observed that the growing application of good faith in different spheres of regulation has suggested to Latin American legislators the need for a wide-ranging definition of the principle itself: see S Schipani, 'Armonizzazione e unificazione del diritto: diritto romano comune in materia di obbligazioni e contratti in America Latina' [2004] *Roma e America. Diritto romano comune* 50.

to constitutional law, whose precepts are increasingly influential on private law issues.[17] Legal scholarship has indeed demonstrated that in several Latin American contexts, the law of obligations is strongly oriented towards a specific, so-called *principiológico* perception of good faith, which is offered as a guiding principle for a new generation of rules. Thus, good faith represents a fundamental principle of Latin American contract law: many Latin American national legal systems attribute central importance to the principle, even if some of these systems give the same recognition to particular rules with similar functions, in order to prevent parties from acting contrary to good faith. This happens in the older civil codes, belonging to the first codification movement, which are to some extent reluctant to make open references to good faith.

The situation changed with the recent Brazilian and Argentinean Codes. Even before the enactment of these Codes, the normative value of good faith had shifted from sectoral to general legislation, with the expansion of some contractual phases (eg, pre-contractual information) and the growing incidence of some sectors of regulation, such as liability for damages in respect of the consumer.[18]

The Brazilian experience provides a significant example of dogmatic development of the good faith principle as a general principle of law, aimed at achieving a degree of balance in every legal relationship. As stated by a copious jurisprudence, which has paid much attention to the use of general principles of law, with special reference to the application of good faith in the regulation of legal relationships, the Brazilian Consumer Law of 1990 made the application of good faith mandatory in legal relationships involving consumers. The same law positivised a series of 'derivative principles' already considered by legal practice as characteristic of the realisation of good faith, as a source of secondary duties, as a rebalancing element of the contract and as a limit to the proper exercise of rights. In this way, good faith was reappraised, shifting from being an uncodified general principle of law to its recognition as a fundamental principle of consumer law, and ultimately as a general principle codified in the new Civil Code.[19]

[17] In Latin America, constitutional law has penetrated into private law and its principles have been extended to various areas of the legal system, from consumer protection to privacy law, from environmental law to the discipline of indigenous property, etc. This phenomenon has been called the 'constitutionalisation' of private law (see G Badeni, *Tratado de derecho constitucional* (Buenos Aires, La Ley, 2006) 633) and implies a symmetrical 'civilisation' of constitutional law (see HC Talciani, 'Constitucionalización del derecho civil. Reflexiones desde el sistema jurídico chileno' in CV Armerngol, LB Pérez Gallardo and GM Carrillo (eds), *Derecho civil constitucional* (Mariel, Puebla, 2014) 14).

[18] In the Latin American national experience, consumer law has contributed to the shift of the good faith principle from sectional legislation (ie consumer law) to general legislation (ie civil codes), raising it from the guiding principle of consumer relations to the recognised guiding principle of obligations and contract law and, finally, to a general principle of private law.

[19] The new Brazilian Civil Code of 2002 indeed includes the good faith rule in the provisions on the interpretation of the legal transaction (Art 113), in the definition of abuse of rights (Art 187), as well as in the identification of the duties of the parties in connection with the conclusion and the performance of the contract (Art 422). Before its explicit acceptance in the new Civil Code, good faith represented an eminent principle of Brazilian civil law, which spontaneously regulated legal relations between the parties, even in a legislative framework such as the Beviláqua Code (of 1916), which did not expressly regulate this matter. Further information on the topic can be found in S Lanni, *America Latina e tutela del consumatore. Le prospettive del Mercosur tra problemi e tecniche di unificazione del diritto* (Milan, Giuffrè, 2005) 258ff.

Another important example of this trend can be found in the Argentinean legal experience, in which good faith is now recognised as a general principle of the new Civil Code of 2015. This recognition is the conclusion of a lengthy evolution concerning the systematic position of the principle itself, an evolution that started with the reform of the old Civil Code of 1869—that is to say, law 17.711, which properly codified the principle with reference to the effects of the contract (Article 1198)—and was completed with the promulgation of the current Code, in which good faith is placed between the key principles applicable to the exercise of rights (Article 9), and is the source of parallel rules applicable to specific contractual disciplines.

The reference to the new civil codes of Latin America takes on specific significance if we analyse the PLACL in connection with the search for a balance between tradition and innovation: the PLACL are based, in fact, on premises drawn from the new Latin American civil codes and from the infra-constitutional legislation of consumer law.

The PLACL rely heavily on good faith. First of all, they invoke it as a general principle, which ought to inspire both the conduct required of the contracting parties (Article 7) and the interpretation of the contract (Article 71). Secondly, they identify the operational incidence of the principle in relation to the various specific issues taken into consideration. The numerous references to good faith could be divided into two categories, the first associated with the different phases of the contract, the other connected to its different pathologies.[20]

With reference to the first issue, particular emphasis is placed on the duty to inform on aspects that could cause mistake in contract negotiation (Article 29), on the power of 'freedom of and withdrawal from' negotiation (Article 10), and in connection with the expectations raised by an offer that is considered irrevocable by the recipient (Article 18(2)), with the identification of the appropriate terms of the performance (Article 74(1)), and with the situation in which contractual terms, even if not made explicit by the parties, cause the offer to lapse (Article 23(1)).

On the other hand, as far as contract pathology is concerned, the good faith principle is applied by providing compensation for loss caused by withdrawal contrary to good faith (Article 11(1)), by imposing the adaptation of the contract or of some of its clauses in case of excessive advantage in contradiction with the requirements of good faith (Article 37(1)), by introducing the power of the courts to adapt the contract in accordance with the good faith of the parties (Article 37(3)), or to save a partially null contract (Article 47(2)).

In other words, the task of identifying the impact of good faith on the various steps of the contract, as well as its pathology, is left by the PLACL to the

[20] This implies a conception of the contract as a 'dynamic legal relationship', whose stages (from pre- to post-contractual) should all be subject to the principle of good faith: this concept is variously confirmed in Latin American doctrine; see C Lima Marques, *Contratos no código de defesa do consumidor* (São Paulo, Revista dos Tribunais, 2014); A Junqueira de Almeida Villaça Azevedo, 'Buena fe objetiva y los deberes de ella derivados' in M Cordoba (ed), *Tratado de la buena fe en el derecho II* (Buenos Aires, La Ley, 2004) 140.

hermeneutic activity of lawyers. In my opinion, this activity should be based on a dual perspective.

On the one hand, taking a scientific and systematic approach, I looked for elements of continuity between the PLACL and the Roman legal tradition, which not only influences the mindset of the jurists who have to apply those principles, but also represents the foundation of Latin American civil law as a whole. In this regard, it is worth remembering that good faith had a threefold function in the Roman contractual system: first, it determined the way of performing the contract, in order to preserve the synallagmatic character of the contract;[21] secondly, it aided in rebuilding the real intention of the parties through interpretation;[22] and thirdly, it integrated the contractual settlement of the parties themselves.[23]

That search proved positive: it is possible to identify these functions in the PLACL,[24] also considering that their importance was already highlighted by the comparative historical analysis carried out in the context of the harmonisation of European contract law,[25] with which the PLACL promote a dialogue in the framework of the Roman law tradition.

On the other hand, the second perspective that should guide the hermeneutic activity of Latin American lawyers interested in the PLACL seems to be connected with the definition of the extent and content of the broad rule established in Article 7: 'the parties must act in accordance with the requirements of good faith'. The principle of good faith proposed in the PLACL indeed looks like a meta-principle, according to which the legal practitioner is required to measure the non-performance of contractual obligations. This principle includes all the particular duties that the civil law doctrine derives from good faith, among which fairness, diligence, confidentiality, reasonableness, etc.

The PLACL do not make a formal distinction between the so-called primary and secondary duties deriving from good faith, nor do they consider the latter in a specific normative context. The legislative text does not include any reference to the practical applications of the good faith principle, that is to say, to the secondary duties of conduct which give the same principle its operational significance in the different contractual phases. This solution corresponds to that advanced during the preliminary work of the researchers who drafted the *Código tipo de obligaciones para América Latina*.[26]

[21] See D. 19,1,51 (Javolenus, Epistles, Book XI); Gai 4,61–63 and D. 16,3,31 (Tryphoninus, Disputations, Book IX).

[22] See D. 19,1,11,1 (Ulpianus, On the Edict, Book XXXII).

[23] See Gai 3,137.

[24] See Arts 3(1), 10(1), 13, 37(1), 64, 65, 69(2) PLACL.

[25] See G Luchetti and A Petrucci (eds), *Fondamenti romanistici del diritto europeo. Le obbligazioni e i contratti dalle radici romane al Draft Common Frame of Reference* (Bologna, Pátron Editore, 2010) 29ff.

[26] On the specific reasons for this choice, see LC San Martín Neira, 'Una noción de incumplimiento en la perspectiva de la armonización del derecho' in RM Hervias and GF Priori Posada (eds), *De las obligaciones en general* (Lima, Fondo Editorial, 2012) 335, where the author affirms that a broad concept of non-performance may include the breach of the contractual duties of good faith, since they form part of the contractual rule that the judge has to reconstruct case by case.

The secondary duties pertaining to good faith are not absent from the PLACL, but they are scattered throughout the normative text. This is the case of the duty of fairness, which emerges in different contexts in connection with the standards of conduct determining that '... indicating assent to an offer constitutes acceptance' (Article 20), or that '... differing from a declaration of acceptance ...' (Article 17) a party can revoke its offer, or even refuse to perform, if '... the conduct of the non-performing party gives the obligee reason to believe that it cannot rely on the party's future performance' (Article 80(c)). This is the case of the duty of diligence, which appears in connection with the means of relief available to the obligee (chapter 8, section 2), with reference to the case in which restitution is not possible, if the parties that terminated the contract could prove '... that the loss of the performance took place in spite of having acted with proper diligence ...' (Article 93).

A similar example is that of the duty of confidentiality derived from Article 37, containing an explicit reference to the 'relationship of trust existing between the parties', as well as from Article 12, included in a section on contractual negotiations, with an explicit mention of that duty ('... remedy for breach of this duty ...') as an expression of the broader duty to inform, which receives no specific normative acknowledgement in the Principles.

From a comparative point of view, the solution chosen by the PLACL to describe secondary duties of conduct pertaining to good faith differs from that adopted in other private law harmonisation and unification projects. In the latter, various distinctions have been proposed in relation to the centrality of good faith.[27] The DCFR, for example, draws a distinction between good faith, fair dealing, co-operation, reasonableness and confidentiality;[28] furthermore, the UNIDROIT Principles of International Commercial Contracts specify *venire contra factum proprium*, confidentiality, reasonableness and co-operation between the parties relating to the broader principle of good faith;[29] the Project for a European Contract Code[30] derives from good faith the duties to inform and to act with fairness, confidentiality and protection.[31]

[27] The central role of good faith in the various harmonisation and unification projects in the field of contract law is emphasised in F Ranieri, 'Il principio generale di buona fede' in C Castronovo and S Mazzamuto (eds), *Manuale di diritto privato europeo II* (Milan, Cedam, 2007) 495; S Grundman and D Mazeaud (eds), *General Clauses and Standards in European Contract Law* (The Hague, Kluwer Law International, 2007) XI; C Castronovo, 'Un contratto per l'Europa' in C Castronovo (ed), *Principi di diritto europeo dei contratti* (Milan, Giuffrè, 2001) XIIIff, especially XXIff and XXXff; R Zimmermann and S Whittaker (eds), *Good Faith in European Contract Law* (Cambridge, Cambridge University Press, 2008) 8ff. The prominence given to good faith in the drafts of a European code of contracts persuaded one Italian jurist to denounce what he calls the 'obsessive redundancy' of the principle itself (see M Barcellona, 'La buona fede e il controllo giudiziale del contratto' in S Mazzamuto (ed), *Il contratto e le tutela* (Turin, Giappichelli, 2002) 308), considering the frequency with which the terms good faith, fairness and reasonableness appear in the PECL (17 times).

[28] See Arts I.-1:103, III.-1:103, III.-1:104, I.-1:104, II.-3:302.

[29] See respectively Arts 1.8, 2.1.16, 5.1.2, 5.1.3 and Art 1.7 (2010 version).

[30] That is, the so-called 'Gandolfi project'.

[31] See Arts 6, 7, 8, 32, 44 and 99.

A comparison between these various harmonisation projects and the PLACL highlights the evolution of a different connection between the 'contractual' and the 'obligatory' relationship. It is well known that there is no coincidence in civil law systems between the two types of relationship: the 'contractual relationship' is inclusive of the different 'obligatory relationships' stemming from the contract itself.

That is not to say that the two relationships coincide in the PLACL, nor does it suggest an identification between the two; nevertheless, according to legal doctrine, the Principles do not seem to provide an adequate explanation of how the content of the contract integrates with a variety of duties deriving from good faith, which contribute to the determination of the exact content of the performance covered by the legal obligation.

Moreover, assessing the effects of the aforementioned relationship can contribute to a broader and more complete protection of the legal spheres of the parties from any detrimental act. Such an assessment is useful not only in relation to the general theory of contract, but also in order to identify the duties of good faith deriving from different types of contract. Indeed, the discipline of the various established forms of contract that come within the ambit of the PLACL themselves reveals a common core of duties relating to the main performance, as well as a number of accessory duties pertaining both to the debtor and to the creditor of the contractual obligation.

The PLACL underline the duty of the practitioner to assess the contract according to good faith in relation to a variety of functions, namely: the identification of the operative field of Article 7, the determination of terms and content of the contract in accordance with the limiting or integrative function of good faith, and the identification of the secondary duties of conduct deriving from the specific nature of the contract.[32] An analysis of the PLACL highlights the broad application of the good faith principle; this application is not limited to what emerges from the systematic collocation of the principle itself or from the accessory duties of conduct arising therefrom.

The references to good faith are so wide-ranging that some of the drafters of the PLACL are evaluating the risk of the creation of a judge-made law:[33] in the name of good faith, a judicial correction of the contractual settlement could be imposed, attributing arbitrary powers to the courts over the will of the parties, which would therefore be deprived of its force of law.[34]

[32] Consider the guarantee against eviction, which is not a mandatory rule in most specific contractual disciplines, unlike consumer law; for this reason, renouncing it may under no circumstances affect the obligation of the seller to refund the price determined in the contract, since this would alter the balance of the contract and its nature, which must respond to the imperative force of good faith. This theme has an interesting historical-comparative development, see MJ Schermaier, 'Bona fides in Roman Contract Law' in R Zimmermann and S Whittaker (eds), *Good Faith in European Contract Law* (Cambridge, Cambridge University Press, 2008) 86.

[33] See Morales Moreno (n 12).

[34] It is important to underline that this is not an isolated concern. In Latin America, the doctrine emphasises that, while it is true that the role of the judge is bound by the ethical and social guidelines of the legal system, the reference to supreme, axiological, historical values, or more generally to the

However, that risk appears to me to be limited, provided the lawyers attribute to the good faith principle its proper aim and use it as a 'bridge rule towards the principles' expressing the fundamental values of the Latin American legal system, with special reference to constitutional principles.[35]

III. Diligence of the Obligor and Its Effects on the Foreseeability of Harm

The principle of good faith dominates the legal content of the PLACL. The multiple functions of this principle, as referred to in the general rule established in Article 7, support the proper exercise of contractual rights, hence the application of good faith imposes the duty to establish and engage in contract negotiations in a framework inspired by diligence.

Diligence emerges as one of the parameters denoting the proper performance of the obligation as well as, at an earlier stage, of the secondary duties of behaviour, related to the exercise of good faith. The PLACL do not pay specific attention to diligence. The term in fact appears only twice, in relation to the impossibility of restitution either in spite of the 'diligence' exercised by the obligor (Article 93(1)) or in spite of the 'proper diligence' of the party that terminated the contract (Article 93(2)).

This concept is pre-assumed. It is part of the legal system of reference and its lack of conceptualisation does not interfere with the idea that conditions the use of this term in the law of obligations and contracts. *Diligencia, diligênza, diligenza, diligence, diligenţă*: all these refer to the concept underlined in the numerous civil codes promulgated in the Romance languages to indicate the standard of conduct expected from the parties in the various stages of the contractual relationship.[36]

structural values of the legal system, nevertheless confers on the judges themselves an unusual power, which tends to overlap with that of legal doctrine and is therefore used in a misleading fashion; see J Martins-Costa, *A boa-fé no direito privado* (São Paulo, Revista dos Tribunais, 2000) 246, 354, who emphasises the presence in Brazil of a 'modelagem brasileira' of good faith, with a strongly jurisprudential impact: ibid, 72 and there, n 5; see also E Mackay, 'Good Faith in Civil Law System. A Legal Economic Analysis' [2012] *Revista chilena de derecho privado* 149, 160. In Europe, the legal writing on the role and scope of application of the good faith principle in the DCFR underlines the ambiguity of this expression, stressing the need to curb the idea that the good faith principle can be used as a general instrument to adopt judicial interventions limiting the autonomy of the negotiating parties, also in consideration of the need to mediate between the civil law and the common law culture, since the latter is used to thinking more in terms of procedural remedies than personal rights; see G Vettori, 'L'interpretazione di buona fede nel codice civile e nel Common Frame of Reference (DCFR)' [2008] *Rivista di diritto privato* 336.

[35] On this point, I agree with the comment of Busnelli (n 15) 250, who refers to good faith as a 'norma-ponte'.

[36] To be more exact: not only a standard for the conduct of the parties but also an effort to fulfil the obligation in the best way. This is the rule concerning the *diligentiam praestare*, which belongs to man distinctly circumspect, prudent and shrewd ('… quae diligens pater familias in suis rebus praestare

Good faith and diligence appear as two integrated principles in the civil law codes. These two principles determine the lawfulness or unlawfulness of the action taken by the debtor; they are homogeneous criteria, or rather, flexible rules for the assessment of conduct that is delimited by the circumstances related to its performance.[37] These homogeneous criteria are not intended as synonyms; with regard to good faith, diligence presumes an effort to be made in fulfilling an obligation. Diligence is considered as the opposite of fault. It appears as one of the criteria suitable for the evaluation of non-performance under the PLACL and thus for the delimitation of the scope of Article 79(1), as well as one of the indicators used to determine when the non-performance is attributable to the obligor (Article 79(4)). How can diligence be evaluated? The answer is related to the hermeneutic activity of the legal practitioner.

From a comparative and historical point of view, the legal model of the first Argentinean Civil Code, only recently abolished, stands out among the codes of the Latin American legal system.[38] The analysis of the criteria used in the evaluation of the debtor's negligent conduct, as well as in charging the non-performance of the obligation to that debtor, disclose an interesting connection between the old (1869) and new (2015) Argentinean Civil Codes.

The concept of fault and the parameters for assessing diligence are linked to Articles 1724 and 1725 of the new Civil Code.[39] Article 1724 establishes that the 'fault lies in the omission of due diligence according to the nature of the obligation and to the circumstances of people, time and place' and, after specifying that it 'involves recklessness, negligence and unskillfulness in the skill or profession', Article 1725 goes on to state that

> for the evaluation of diligence [it] is essentially possible to enforce three main rules: (a) the greater duty to act with prudence and full knowledge of things evokes the greater diligence by the agent and greater capacity to foresee the harm; (b) when there is a

solet'), whose main source is located in D. 13,7,14, although different referrals to it may be found in the Digest, as is clear from CA Cannata, *Sul problema della responsabilità nel diritto privato romano* (Catania, Libreria editrice Torre, 1996) 45. The aforementioned effort inspires the research of E Cortés Moncayo, *La culpa contractual en el sistema jurídico latinoamericano* (Universidad Externado, Bogotá, 2009) 84ff, which pays specific attention to current trends expressed by reference to diligence in relation to the needs and limitations of the autonomy of contractual parties in the Latin American experience.

[37] See Cortés Moncayo (n 36) 63ff and 84ff, referring to fault and diligence as two sides of the same coin.

[38] See S Schipani, 'Codici civili nel sistema latinoamericano', in *Digesto delle discipline privatistiche*, Civil Law section (Turin, Utet, 2010) 298ff: contemplating the rule of the person, the supremacy of the protection of the person, not only as an individual but also as an expression of collective interests, the recognition of civil rights regardless of the quality of citizen. A synthetic framework of the topic may be found in the English literature in G Medina, 'Argentina on the Eve of a New Civil and Commercial code' in JC Rivera (ed), *The Scope and Structures of the Civil Codes* (Dordrecht, Springer, 2014) 58.

[39] With a view to emphasising the identity of the Argentinean model code, in terms of an historical comparative approach, it is interesting to note that the new *Código civil y comercial de la Nación* transposes the line of thinking proposed by the author of the old Civil Code, in respect of the valuation of the debtor's fault. Indeed, the combined provisions of Arts 512, 902 and 909 of the old Argentinean Civil Code are upheld and replicated in the new text of Arts 1724 and 1725.

> situation of special trust, it takes into account the nature of the legal act and the particular conditions of the parties; (c) to assess the behaviour, the particular condition or intellectual ability of a specific person are not taken into account unless the contracts required a special trust between the parties; the extent of liability is estimated in these cases by the special agent status (author's translation).

The rules derived from the new Argentinean Civil Code are assumed in the PLACL but not spelled out since they are part of the shared civil law system. Legal practitioners who take account of the harmonisation of civil law in Latin America, and specifically of the PLACL, are called upon to deal with these rules. They offer to the civil lawyer a reference parameter currently in vogue in Latin American jurisprudence, and provide the common lawyer with fundamental legal instruments for the solution of concrete cases.

It emerges clearly and in a timely fashion from the new Argentinean Civil Code that, in contracts involving a specific trust, the party who has caused damage to the legal sphere of others is responsible not only for displaying non-diligent behaviour, but also for having omitted the level of care linked to its professionalism or, more generally, to its capacity. This is a significant omission from the legal point of view, a very severe form of fault, which is opposed to the idea of honesty, fairness, loyalty or, in short, to what the good faith principle stands for. In summary, as expressed in the new Argentinean Civil Code, negligence represents a debtor's behaviour that does not correspond to the content of his circumstantial position.

An analysis of the legal text of the PLACL shows that neither the *bonus pater familias* parameter for the evaluation of diligence nor the theory of the differentiation of fault (*culpa lata—culpa levis—culpa levissima*) to establish the kind of contractual liability are accepted. These are common solutions in other Latin American legal systems; they are a matter of reference for Latin American civil law.[40] The legal text proposed by the new Argentinean Civil Code requires the legal practitioner to assess good faith and due diligence at all times.

The new Argentinean Civil Code measures good faith and due diligence in the debtor's conduct in accordance with distinctive attributes. The first connects it with a rule of fairness, which goes beyond the content of its performance and thus of the scope of the contract and which can be specified, either by legislation or by judicial review, as a reminder of good faith. The second is the antonym of fault, and exhorts the debtor to make the effort required for proper fulfilment of the obligation.[41]

[40] If we look at the choices made by the PLACL in the context of the new Latin American codifications a common perspective emerges. The new civil codes promulgated in recent decades in Bolivia, Guatemala, Cuba, Peru, Paraguay, Brazil and now in Argentina—with the exception of the Brazilian and Cuban Civil Codes (but also parts of the Peruvian Code)—underscore a shared perspective, namely adherence to a model code that expressly upholds a general legal provision such as that contemplated, well ahead of his time, by Vélez Sársfield in Art 512 of the Code, a model now being revived with renewed vigour in Art 1716 of the new Civil Code of Argentina.

[41] *Culpa* and *diligencia*: the legal framework of the binomial is outlined in Arts 9, 10, 159, 292, 315, 337, 340, 347, 361, 729, 774, 1079, 1317, 1340, 1358, 1483, 1536, 1710, 1724, 1735, 1743, 2026.

A distinction emerges between the first and second attributes, strengthened by the concept of good faith as a threshold for diligent conduct or, as Argentinean lawyers see it, as a powerful spotlight illuminating Argentinean private law in its entirety.[42] Compared with the new Civil Code of Argentina, this feature is implicit not only in the text of the PLACL as a whole, but also with reference to individual provisions, such as the rules on contributory negligence and comparative fault, or the provision dealing with the expansion of recovery in case of fraud or gross negligence.[43]

Another interesting question is the identification of the yardstick for diligence in cases of non-performance. In the new Argentinean Civil Code, as in the old one, the reference to the diligence of the *bonus pater familias* is no longer accepted as a criterion for assessing the debtor's fault; instead, the parameter of diligence linked to the nature of the obligation, as well as all the circumstances relating to the parties to the specific obligation and to the time and place thereof, were introduced.

This choice is not unfamiliar to the Latin American legal systems with which the PLACL are called upon to dialogue. The reference to the diligence of the *bonus pater familias* was not incorporated into the other new Latin America civil codes either. In general, this criterion may be said 'formally' to have failed in the new Latin American civil codes. Indeed, with the exception of the Code of Bolivia,[44] the criterion does not appear in the codes of Guatemala, Paraguay, Cuba and Brazil, not only with reference to the law of obligations, but also with reference to all the legal provisions contained in those codes.

This is obviously an opinion based only on legislative data, since the doctrinal or jurisprudential formants underline a kind of permanence of the *bonus pater familias*, not so much as an expression in itself, as for its broader paradigmatic content in terms of a prescriptive framework. Indeed, this figure operates as a reference to a system of rules and values, and above all to diligence and good faith, that provides an answer as to the concrete intentions of the parties and corresponds to an ideal of fair and honest conduct.

From the point of view of the statutory provision, the PLACL appear to be in line with the approach adopted by the new Latin American civil codes, since both references to diligence call on the legal operator to review the diligence expected by the parties involved in each obligation of the contractual performance, or rather, the 'diligence' exercised by the obligor (Article 93(1)) and the 'proper diligence' exercised by the party that terminated the contract (Article 93(2)).[45]

[42] See JM Iturraspe, 'La buena fe contractual' [IJ-LXXVIII] *Revista Iberoamericana de Derecho Privado* 123.

[43] See Arts 101, 102(2).

[44] Referring to Bolivia, we should not forget, among other things, the strong influence of the Italian Civil Code of 1942.

[45] Similar considerations may come into play in relation to the evaluation of the time and place of the single obligation; these are explicitly referred to in Art 73 ('Place of performance') and Art 74 ('Time of performance') of the PLACL.

Apparently, this choice of the PLACL is in line with the preliminary work on the *Código tipo de obligaciones para América Latina*, where there is no reference, technically speaking, to the *bonus pater familias*; however, scholarly opinion, in order to limit the various 'hypotheses' when the grounds for damages are linked to a performance attributable to the obligor and, therefore, in order to define the concept of 'non-performance', highlights the current use of the concept by legal practitioners.[46]

The reference to the *bonus pater familias* parameter of diligence, even if it is not made explicit, may be regarded as an operational rule in the Latin American legal systems. One could speak of a cryptotype, or a part of the wider 'mute law', ie that successful formula by which an eminent Italian jurist wished to underline not only Australopithecus law, but also the everyday legal norm, which has faded in the classical structures inherited from the twentieth century under the pressure of globalisation, which is inevitably a legal phenomenon, not just an economic one.[47] In other words, the standard of the *bonus pater familias*—in a law of obligations strongly influenced by the value of good faith such as emerges in the Latin American context—refers to the behaviour of a person who could be defined as: diligent, reliable, fair and watchful in weighing his actions; careful in the management of his interests; and careful not to abuse his rights to the detriment of others.

What emerges is a draft that refers not so much to the fault of the *bonus pater familias* to characterise failures and injustices, but rather to the non-observance of specific rules and principles, and particularly the principles of diligence and good faith, which refer, conceptually speaking, to the same notion. They have a specific role, ie, to help the lawyer in defining *a posteriori* the exact content of the obligation and also of the duty of care implied in the same, as well as the extent of the non-performance.

The evaluation of the diligence exercised by the contractual parties obviously affects the foreseeability of the harm. The PLACL pay particular attention to this issue, with reference to the compensation of contractual damage. Article 100(1) provides that 'the non-performing party shall be liable for harm it could have foreseen at the time of the conclusion of the contract and that results from its non-performance'.

Damages recoverable for contractual liability correspond to the foreseeable damage at the time of the conclusion of the contract: this is a rule already accepted by the PECL (Article 9:502(3)), the DCFR (Articles III-3:702 and III-3:703) and the Common European Sales Law (CESL) (Articles 160 and 162). The inclusion of the rule itself is intended to delimit the hypothesis of contractual liability, by referring to the evaluation of the probability of the risk, which in turn requires further evaluation that is not always easy to achieve.

46 See San Martín Neira (n 26) 321ff.

47 On this point, see R Sacco, *Il diritto muto* (Bologna, Il Mulino, 2015), which provides a detailed study of the latency of the expression in the field of law.

What is the parameter of foreseeability? That of the good man of business? That of the diligent man or that of the extra-diligent man? The doctrine suggests that the starting point is a general assumption, namely the use by the debtor of 'normal diligence', and hence the adoption of the precautions fitting to the nature of the obligation, in order to facilitate its fulfilment.[48]

Seen in this light, the rule of the 'foreseeability of the harm' may have a dark side as part of its applicability in the Latin American legal system, where diligence requires skill, attention and the duty of care in performing the contract. The Latin American legal systems require a positive effort in fulfilling the obligation, which would be tantamount to the *bonus pater familias* of the Roman legal sources.[49]

In conclusion, the assessment of diligence required by the PLACL raises a number of hermeneutic issues for the legal practitioner, and underlines the role which that practitioner can play in establishing an accurate yardstick for non-performance. This is especially true given the lack in the legal text of a general criterion to determine compensatory damages in contractual liability,[50] and with a view to identifying the exact type of care required, which will obviously affect the extent of the debtor's liability for the foreseeable damage at the time of the conclusion of the contract.

IV. Prevalence of Good Faith and Diligence Over Reasonableness: An Outsider Standard in Latin America

The development of new civil codes, the harmonisation of private law and the formulation of supranational principles of contract law underscore the strength of the historical legal rules of the Latin American system and, in relation to the issue here addressed, of its provisions on non-performance of the contract.

In this connection, the PLACL suggest that observers of that legal system make a comparison between the provisions linked to the Latin American legal tradition and those introduced by the circulation of foreign legal models. *Quid iuris* on reasonableness? The question arises in relation to the spate of references to reasonableness by legal scholars following the harmonisation of European

[48] See MC Gianfelici, 'Caso fortuito e impedimento ajeno a la voluntad del deudor' in AJ Bueres and A Kemelmajer de Carlucci (eds), *Responsabilidad por daños en el tercer milenio* (Madrid, Abeledo Perrot, 1997) 180, underlining that the reference to *diligencia normal* is in itself an exemption from debtor's liability, but also that the same occurred in the reception of the old Law no 24.032, which provided an additional paragraph to Art 514 for non-culpable infringement, allowing the debtor to discharge himself of his liability showing that 'para cumplir habría sido menester emplear una diligencia mayor que la exigible por la índole de la obligación'.

[49] See Lanni (n 9).

[50] This comment is by Morales Moreno (n 12) 238.

private law.[51] The question arises again bearing in mind that the PLACL pay less attention to diligence, intended as the contrary of fault, than to good faith.[52]

References to 'fault' and 'diligence' go hand in hand. They are affected by the 'objectifying' trend that is part of the assessment of fault in harmonised private law; this effect is particularly evident in the field of civil liability, in which fault represents a central aspect of the institute itself. By way of example: in the PETL, the term 'fault', intended as the verbal synthesis of behaviour that is both negligent and fraudulent, even if still considered as a symptom of wrongful conduct in view of civil liability,[53] is connected with the change of predetermination of the required standard of conduct, which basically draws on specific factors operating in each individual case, such as the duty to protect others from harm (Article 4:103),[54] or corporate liability (Article 4:202).[55]

Not only the new Latin American civil codes, such as that of Argentina, which was referred to in the previous section, but also the preliminary drafts of new civil codes show a definite penchant for 'objectifying' the assessment of the debtor's fault, as determined in the compilation of the Latin American legal system according to Vélez Sársfield's code. Among these, it is worth mentioning that of Puerto Rico, which has sparked a lively debate among legal scholars.[56]

Article 105 of the draft new Civil Code of Puerto Rico, referring specifically to *culpa*, establishes that 'fault or negligence of the debtor is the omission of that kind of diligence required by the nature of the obligation; it is related to circumstances of people, time and place. If the obligation does not underline the diligence to be

[51] The growing trend to make use of the category of 'reasonableness' reached its apex in the DCFR: C von Bar, E Clive and H Schulte-Nölke (eds), *Principles, Definitions and Model Rules of European Private Law* (Munich, Kluwer Law International, 2009) developed by the Study Group on an European Civil Code and the Research Group on EC Private Law (Acquis Group), in which there is a veritable explosion of references to reasonableness: there are about 500 references to this criterion in this text alone.

[52] See above para 3.

[53] Certainly, the legacy received in the EU context in matters of liability focuses on the 'qualification of the action of the subject as an individual' and the idea of responsibility is mostly intended as 'fault liability'. However, in Europe the line between fault liability and strict liability appears to be a mobile one, which, as pointed out by legal scholars, is subject to change in connection with the decisive influences of the Vienna Convention, the Directive on the sale of consumer goods, and the reform of the BGB, as well as the ideas developed by the French and Italian doctrines; see C Castronovo and S Mazzamuto, *Manuale di diritto privato europeo* II (Milan, Giuffrè, 2007) especially 224, 240, 602ff.

[54] See Art 4:103 PETL: 'a duty to act positively to protect others from damage may exist if law so provides, or if the actor creates or controls a dangerous situation, or when there is a special relationship between parties or when the seriousness of the harm on the one side and the ease of avoiding the damage on the other side point towards such a duty'.

[55] See Art 4:202(1) PETL: 'a person pursuing a lasting enterprise for economic or professional purposes who uses auxiliaries or technical equipment is liable for any harm caused by a defect of such enterprise or of its output unless he proves that he has conformed to the required standard of conduct'.

[56] For a short survey, see M Figueroa Torres, *Recodification of Civil Law in Puerto Rico, a Quixotic Pursuit of the Civil Code for the New Millennium* [2008] *Electronic Journal of Comparative Law*, http://www.ejcl.org/121/art121-21.pdf.

provided for the performance, the action required corresponds to the one of a reasonable and prudent person …'.

Legal experts note in this provision, first, its complete adherence to the spirit and letter of Article 512 of the Vélez Code, and thus the vitality of a rule of the law system from a diachronic-comparative perspective; secondly, they may also notice the presence of a 'safeguard' article: the Puerto Rican legislator has added a reference to a standard of diligence set by a 'prudent' and 'reasonable' person.

The call for prudence is related to a widely known concept, recurrent in the Latin American legal tradition, concerning the evaluation of the debtor's fault. It has been correctly put before the reasonableness criterion, as that is a concept definitely unrelated to the traditions of the Roman law system, however fashionable it may currently be in the draft recodifications of civil law, particularly in those of European private law unification.

The Puerto Rican draft Code suggests a consideration of the role of reasonableness in contemporary Latin American civil law and particularly in the final version of the PLACL. It is indeed true that parameters for assessing the non-performance of the contract impose on the legal practitioner a comparison between the actual conduct of the parties and their expected behaviour; it is also true that the omission from the Principles themselves of an explicit reference to diligence could inadvertently open the door to reasonableness.

This is a risk that is confirmed by the experiences of European private law harmonisation. There, resistance is taking shape to the prefiguration of the *bonus pater familias* as a model of general diligence for the performance of obligations.[57] There is a slant towards the concepts of 'fault' and 'diligence', which have both to be intended in relation to the specific obligation, even if conceived in light of a common assumption: the correct behaviour of the debtor corresponds to that of a 'reasonable person'.[58]

This approach clearly emerges from Article 4:102(1) PETL, where there is an assumption that a person can cause damage due to negligence if his conduct does not match that of a 'reasonable person'.[59] It is clearly evident in the light of

[57] For a development of this theme, see C van Dam, *European Tort Law* (Oxford, Oxford University Press, 2006) 805.

[58] This reference appears at first to be the result of the influence of the common Law system, and specifically of the 'reasonable man' of English law. The expression 'reasonable man' or more often, 'reasonable person', is currently the most significant expression of the reasonableness criterion which has established itself in the Anglo-American legal systems, where statute law, as is well known, plays a subsidiary role to judicial law. For a discussion of the topic, see S Troiano, *La 'ragionevolezza' nel diritto dei contratti* (Padua, Cedam, 2005) 82, where the author underlines this figure with detailed attention to the debate concerning this subject in the common law.

[59] Art 4:102(1): 'The required standard of conduct is that of the reasonable person in the circumstances, and depends, in particular, on the nature and value of the protected interest involved, the dangerousness of the activity, the expertise to be expected of a person carrying it on, the foreseeability of the damage, the relationship of proximity or special reliance between those involved, as well as the availability and the costs of precautionary or alternative methods'.

Article 1:302 PECL, in which the person acting in good faith and in accordance with the conditions required of a reasonable person is assumed to be reasonable.[60] After analysing them with a view to their possible incorporation into the Latin American legal system, these references seem unable to improve the work of legal practitioners. Beyond the need for harmonisation between the civil and common law systems—a typical requirement of the European legal experience—it can be said that the reference to the reasonable person rather than to the *bonus pater familias* surreptitiously changes the approach, tending towards what in fact appears as a mainly abstract model of conduct, or rather to a model of conduct the identification of which is left to legal practitioners to interpret.[61]

Actually, in Europe as well as in Latin America, the problem consists in evaluating the options for selecting a criterion founded on a long-standing civil law tradition (expressed by the referral to the diligence of a *bonus pater familias*), against the options related to the adoption of a new standard of conduct (corresponding to the behaviour of a reasonable person). In other words, rather than discarding the reference to the 'reasonable person' out of hand, it seems more appropriate to balance its use.

Indeed, if we consider the idea of a reasonable person in accordance with the criterion of relationality, and assume for the sake of comparison an index or frame of reference, it seems impossible to establish what is 'reasonable' and what is 'unreasonable'; furthermore, it seems impossible to predict the minimum standard of reasonable conduct. This inevitably affects the complex setting of the unitary vision of principles and rules that characterise civil law relations.

Unlike good faith and diligence, reasonableness lacks definiteness. Although it is a notion that can be adapted to any single case, it represents both the 'goal' and the 'way to reach it',[62] thus remaining a notion with undefined outlines and limits.[63]

[60] The word 'reasonable' is used by the Principles to express various requirements (on this subject, see C Castronovo (ed), *Principi di diritto europeo dei contratti*, I–II (Milan, Giuffrè, 2001) 131), as provided for by Art 1:302 in the context of the systematic division into 'terminology and other rules'. Indeed, Art 1:302 expresses a rule: 'reasonableness is to be judged by what persons acting in good faith and in the same situation as the parties would consider to be reasonable'. This 'vagueness' was toned down in another part of the article by a further clarification: 'in assessing what is reasonable the nature and purpose of the contract, the circumstances of the case and the usages and practices of the trades or professions involved should be taken into account'. This sets limits on the interpretation of legal practitioners, by referring to 'particular circumstances'.

[61] In this regard, it is worth asking whether the practical definition of the wording 'reasonable person' imposes on legal practitioners a more or less intense commitment than does 'diligent person'. Doubts also emerge with reference to the choices made in other legal environments where, in determining the requirements of reasonableness and fairness, it was considered appropriate to refer to the general principles of law (as in Art 3:12 of the new Dutch Civil Code).

[62] In this sense, A Ruggeri, 'Ragionevolezza e valori attraverso il prisma della giustizia costituzionale' in M La Torre and A Spadaro (eds), *La ragionevolezza del diritto* (Turin, Giappichelli, 2002) 99.

[63] In this sense, A Ricci, *Il criterio della ragionevolezza nel diritto privato* (Padua, Cedam, 2007) *passim* and 188, which affirms that from a substantive point of view, the concept is translated into some basic standards, such as the proportionality of the standards of collective consciousness, or even that of the appropriateness of the means to the goal, or that of the non-contradiction of facts and legal situations *lato sensu*.

Reasonableness entitles the legal interpreter to exert a judicial power which is greater than that deriving from good faith, and at the same time obscures the clarity of the rules of conduct of private citizens.

Furthermore, the reference to reasonableness in evaluating the conduct of the contractual performance gives rise to considerations founded on 'utilitarianism' and 'economic efficiency', while in the Latin American experience, good faith is mainly oriented towards moral considerations.[64] One of the merits of the PLACL is their avoidance of any reference to the standard conduct of the 'reasonable person'. In this way, they prevent the loss of specificity of several categories already in use in different Latin American law systems, such as diligence, fairness and good faith.[65] In other words, they avoid the harmful effects of a transplant, responding to legal developments outside Latin America, as reference to a specific criterion in that area is inherently limited and confined to a specific context.[66]

The acceptance of an undefined concept, which is also apparently 'interchangeable' with the idea of good faith and diligence, represents a strong risk for Latin America, even if in this context the reference to 'reasonable person' does not have the same impact as in Europe. Its adoption is strongly linked to the harmonisation of private law, in which legal categories and patterns of thought are accepted that are considered 'prestigious'—especially those hailing from Europe, by reason of the dialogue between the Latin American and European doctrines.[67]

Clearly, this is not a mere lexical problem. There is the risk of adopting vague and uncertain concepts, especially when these are apparently more suitable for the economic than the social sciences.[68] From a broader point of view, a further

[64] See A Di Majo, 'L'osservanza della buona fede nei principi Unidroit sui contratti commerciali internazionali' in J Bonell and F Bonelli (eds), *I Contratti commerciali internazionali e Principi Unidroit* (Milan, Giuffrè, 1997) 157.

[65] A real warning is issued by FD Busnelli, 'Note in tema di buona fede ed equità' [2001] *Rivista di diritto civile* 555ff (= [2002] *Roma e America* 99–121): '... there is the danger of vagueness, which occurs mainly in the perspective of an alignment between the concept of good faith and the concept of reasonableness ... a notion so nuanced ... can seem a kind of passepartout, ... which therefore lends itself to be used now in one direction, now in the exactly opposite'. Much in the same vein: Troiano (n 58) 446; the author recognises in reasonableness a neutral criterion of assessment, tied to a personal and pragmatic conception of justice, which requires, because of its neutrality, reference to a standard of conduct by which to operate.

[66] References to reasonableness appear in the new Civil Codes of Peru (Arts 195, 252, 1987, 2104), Brazil (Arts 562, 1530, 1807), but also in the historical Civil Codes, and especially that of Chile (Arts 779, 1276, 1935, 1977, 2125 etc), where it does not rise to the rank of 'principle' but rather to 'canon' of interpretation (in reference to the 'reasonable time' or 'reasonable performance', or the quantification of a 'reasonable refund' and 'reasonable compensation', or even the identification of 'reasonable cause').

[67] On this subject, see E Cortés Moncayo, *La culpa contractual en el sistema jurídico latinoamerican*, 2nd edn (Bogotá, Universidad Externado, 2009) 208–09, which makes reference to the main examples of 'innovation' introduced by the reform projects of the law of obligations, which carry the risk of 'improper' export to different law experiences in Latin America.

[68] In this sense, RL Lorenzetti, *Las normas fundamentales de derecho privado* (Santa Fe, Rubinzal, 1995) 350, with reference to the relation between *hombre racional* and *hombre razonable*.

hazard appears, stemming from the potentially distorting effects of the varying relations between language and law.[69]

Stating that in the Roman law system, the behaviour of the debtor in the performance of the contract conforms to the diligence of the *bonus pater familias* indirectly refers to a conceptual expertise capable not only of describing the legal phenomenon inherent in the performance, but also of interfering with it.

In the civil law systems, the legal proposition not only describes facts and conduct: it also makes them happen. As a consequence, the circulation of words, ideas, propositions and, more widely, foreign legal models could determine the circulation of legal concepts not in keeping with the systematic approach of the civil law system.[70]

Even if globalisation inevitably leads to the circulation of legal models, it is not possible to postulate a lack of communication among the national legal experiences; likewise, it is reasonable and unavoidable to consider the existence of a communicating system between the national systems themselves. The duty to forestall decisions made under the duty to forstall the decisions that were made imitating the 'Old World', as well as those conditioned by pseudo-colonial influences, represents a timeless warning to the Latin American countries.

For these reasons, the choices made by the PLACL can be considered commendable, as they do not compromise the heritage of thought and experience that has until now been widely shared by the Latin American legal doctrine: the standard of

[69] In comparative research, significant developments in the analysis of the problem occurred both from an international perspective, in the discussions held in Sydney in 1986 at the Académie Internationale de Droit Comparé (see *Rapports Nationaux Italiens au XIIe Congrès International de Droit Comparé—Italian National Reports to the XIIth International Congress of Comparative Law* (Milan, Giuffrè, 1986), and from the national point of view, in the pioneering research carried out by R Sacco, 'Lingua e diritto' [2000] *Ars interpretandi. Annuario di ermeneutica giuridica* 117–34; id, 'Traduzione giuridica' in *Digesto delle discipline privatistiche*, Civil Law section (Torino, Utet, 2000) 722ff. This topic has been widely developed by Italian scholarship, at least in the second half of the twentieth century. All scholars involved in the issue of legal interpretation have approached this matter: among others, N Bobbio, 'Scienza del diritto e analisi del linguaggio' [1950] *Rivista trimestrale di diritto processuale civile* 342ff and id, *Contributi ad un dizionario giuridico* (Turin, Giappichelli, 1994), concerning the problems of language related to the technical provisions; U Scarpelli, *Semantica, morale, diritto* (Turin, Giappichelli, 1969), with relevance to the joint consideration of the 'linguistic', 'logic' and 'therapeutic' semantics for proper use of the language; R Orestano, *'Diritto' incontri e scontri* (Bologna, Mulino, 1981) 395ff and id, '"Realtà", "parole", "valori" nella scienza del diritto' [1985] *Rivista di diritto civile* 461ff, with reference to the concept of legal order and the implications of common language in the juridical discourse; L Lantella, *Pratiche definitorie e proiezioni ideologiche nel discorso giuridico* (Milan, Giuffrè, 1979); L Lantella, E Stolfi and M Deganello, *Operazioni elementari di discorso e sapere giuridico* (Turin, Giappichelli, 2004), with reference to the historical development of the language of private law.

[70] This is a consequence of the circulation of the legal model, for various reasons, including the prestige of a model or a legal system, the combination of national and supranational courts, the existence of bilateral economic relations between two or more different legal systems and, consequently, the adoption of models of compromise (on these and other causes of circulation of legal models, see R Sacco, 'Introduzione al diritto comparato' in *Trattato di diritto comparato* (Turin, Utet, 1992) 132ff, and, in respect of European civil law, see GA Benacchio, *Diritto privato dell'Unione Europea* (Milan, Giuffrè, 2010) *passim* and especially 149–68.

reasonableness can represent at most a combination of good faith and diligence,[71] in order to enhance the actual circumstances used in assessing the conduct of the parties in the performance of the contract.

V. Gross Disparity Due to an Impediment Beyond the Control of the Debtor

In civil law systems, even though the *pacta sunt servanda* principle, with its various specifications and its referral to the principle of good faith, commits the parties to the performance of their obligations according to the contractual terms negotiated at the time of the agreement, that commitment to perform is considered not to satisfy a principle of 'contractual justice' when, due to a change in circumstances, it can lead to the failure of one of the parties or, more generally, to an imbalance of the original contract synallagma.

This theme is to some extent traditional in the civil codes of the Roman law system, where it is variously described as *onerosità sopravvenuta, imprevisión, force majeure, bouleversement, Störung der Geschäftsgrundlage.*[72] By way of example, Article 1091 of the new Argentinean Civil Code provides that a debtor likely to suffer harm by the performance of the contract if it has become prohibitively

[71] This is the perspective taken by the PECL, ie, that defining the concept of reasonableness connects it directly with good faith and fairness, considering the specific situation in which the contracting parties interact, in the framework of the nature and purpose of the contract. Otherwise, the 'links' are not further elucidated by the DCFR, as evidenced in the definition of reasonableness (see Art I.-1:104 DCFR), where the drafters' intent was clearly not to 'confuse' the criterion of good faith with that of reasonableness. On this subject, see C von Bar and E Clive, *Principles, Definitions and Model Rules of European Private Law. Draft Common Frame of Reference (DCFR)*, Full Edition, I, (Munich, European Law Publishers, 2009) 90ff.

[72] In addition, there is the 'hardship clause' that highlights the growing flow of ideas between the common law and the civil law. The responses of the various national legal experiences to changes in contractual circumstances present several distinctive features; all of them, however, espouse a common principle, that of equitable *reductio-remissio* of the contract in case of excessively imbalanced performance, that is to say, the need to adapt the contract in accordance with the principles of good faith and fairness; for a diachronic-comparative reconstruction of the Euro/Latin-American dialogue on this subject, see the interesting work of JF Chamie Gandur, *La adaptación del contrato por eventos sobrevenidos. De la* vis cui resisti non potest *a la clausola de* hardship (Bogotá, Universidad Externado de Colombia, 2014). Approaching the subject from a comparative perspective reveals a basic distinction between conventional instruments, which favour the automatic adjustment of the contract (as in the 'indexation clauses' of Italian law), and instruments that look at the effects of the changing circumstances (such as 'hardship clauses'); for a systematic approach to the topic, see F Macario, 'Adeguamento del contratto e obbligo di rinegoziazione nel diritto italiano e tedesco. Contributo di diritto comparato alla luce del diritto europeo dei contratti' [2006] *Atti Convegno Italo-Tedesco*, http://www.lex.unict.it/congressoitalotedesco/macario_it.pdf.

expensive due to extraordinary and unpredictable events may request termination of all or part of the contract, or its adaptation.[73]

There is no doubt that the current legal framework for gross disparity also derives from special legislation in civil matters, especially that dealing with consumer protection; in some Latin American countries, such as Brazil, this is actually the main vector for the recognition of the gross disparity rule in the Civil Code; it is applied to all contracts based on the persistence of the legal relationship in time.[74]

Of course, this chapter is not the proper platform for a more in-depth examination of this subject, but it is safe to affirm that, in the light of a diachronic comparison, the aforementioned examples suggest to the reader how civil codes and consumer law taken together have neatly marked the borders of a shared regulatory framework: non-performance due to gross disparity responds to the principle of contractual equity, which appears as a common principle of Latin American law contract law.

These 'borders' have been recognised by the PLACL, which address the topic of gross disparity in Article 37. A clearly delineated rule emerges, whose core provision seems to be founded on the identification of the 'requirements of good faith' and, more specifically, on the evaluation of 'the relationship of trust existing between the parties as well as the nature and purpose of the contract'. Both represent two specific instruments that can be used to assess liability for non-performance; furthermore, the provision raises various interesting issues for the legal practitioner, two of which will be debated here.

The first issue is related to the detection or, even better, to the neat definition of the notion of 'extraordinary and unforeseeable' events. These appear to be mostly related to the specific contractual obligation;[75] furthermore, in relation to the provisions of Article 37 PLACL, scholars dealing with the harmonisation of European private law will immediately note that Article 3:104 DCFR and, even more, Article 8:108 PECL provide further support in suggesting that it is unreasonable to expect the promisor to avoid or overcome such an impediment or its

[73] The new rule strengthens the institution of *imprevisión* (already present in Art 1198 of the recently abrogated Civil Code), according to the interpretation given by Argentinean legal scholars and the courts, especially in relation to the absence, in the new legal text, of any reference to the default situation in which a debtor had to find itself in the old Code.

[74] In Brazil, the rule of gross disparity became a full part of civil law with the Civil Code of 2002 (Arts 478–80), which accorded general value to a rule already established in the *Código de defesa e proteção do consumidor* of 1990, according to which, if new circumstances arise that render the contractual clauses excessively onerous, the consumer has a fundamental right to obtain their adjustment (Art 6, V).

[75] Inevitably, the type of contract concluded by the parties and, a fortiori, the amount of information available to them or to which they have access, affect the delimitation and characterisation of foreseeable events. As emphasised by way of example in JM Iturraspe and MA Piedecasas, *La revisión del contrato* (Buenos Aires, Rubinzal Culzoni, 2008) 32, in international contracts the possibility of foreseeing a certain event can be almost non-existent for one of the parties, but not for the other, who may be aware of phenomena occurring in his country or in the economic/legal system in which the contract will operate. The duty of information thus appears instrumental to the fulfilment not only of the main performance, but also of the secondary duties deriving from good faith.

consequences. This would be similar to the assertion that non-performance is not excused if the debtor could reasonably be expected to foresee the impediment at the time the obligation was incurred.[76] In comparison with the DCFR and the PECL, it is important to note that in the PLACL, the concept of diligent contracting is implicit.

The second issue is related to the general need to identify criteria to determine whether or not a form of gross disparity is developing. The PLACL do not consider the mathematical model in the Peruvian Civil Code of 1984 (Articles 1447 and 1449);[77] nevertheless, they do make some progress compared with systems in which the criteria themselves had to be identified by the supplementary work of legal scholars and courts.[78] The choice of spelling out principles such as 'the existence of an advantage' as well as 'the urgent needs, ignorance or lack of experiences of one party' may well point the legal practitioner to a stepwise assessment of the conditions of the contract that need to be complied with in good faith and, prior to that, of what was actually agreed by the parties.

The different options provided for by Article 37 PLACL call on the legal practitioner to consider a common need: to strengthen the principle of good faith in contract law.[79] The PLACL clearly stated from the outset that parties must act in accordance with the requirements of good faith and that agreements limiting good faith will have no effect whatsoever (Article 7); thus, even readers without any in-depth legal knowledge can see that good faith represents the basic principle of the gross disparity theory.

A very close connection emerges between infringement of good faith and application of the gross disparity rule: the PLACL, in facts decided to forestall the powerful response elicited in Argentinean legal circles by the theory of *imprevisión*

[76] See C de Geest, 'Specific Performance. Damages and Unforeseen Contingencies in the Draft Common Frame of Reference' in P Larouche and F Chirico (eds), *Economic Analysis of the DCFR: The Work of the Economic Impact Group within the CoPECL Network of Excellence* (Munich, Sellier, 2010) 128, who, questioning the usefulness of gross disparity, uses the economic analysis of law and, in particular, the so-called incomplete contracts theory, believing that the goal of this instrument is to make contractual relations more flexible and stabilise long-term relationships.

[77] The combination of Articles 1447 and 1449 shows that the right to termination of the contract must take into account the value that the performance had when the contractual terms were negotiated: the action itself can be proposed when at the moment of its fulfilment the value of the performance is more than two-fifths greater than the value which the performance itself had at the time of the conclusion of the contract.

[78] This occurred in the Argentinean legal experience. Before the new Civil Code, besides unforeseeable and exceptional changes of circumstances, legal scholars identified three criteria for the evaluation of gross disparity of performance: an increase in the sacrifice compared to an unchanged interest; the stability of the sacrifice in relation to an interest which conversely decreased; the joint alteration of sacrifice and interest. Even if not recent, a valid reference is still found in FJ López de Zavalía, *Teoria de los contratos. Parte general* (Buenos Aires, Rubinzal Culzoni, 1975) 410. Of course, in this matter a significant role is played by the autonomy of the parties negotiating contractual terms, as is clear from the significantly wider use of the hardship clause identified in the Argentinean courts, as reported in AA Alterini, 'Teoría de la imprevisión y cláusula de hardship' [2002] *Roma e America. Diritto romano comune* 62.

[79] This point of view is not isolated, but common to different Latin American countries, as stated in the effective synthesis offered by Alterini (n 78) 55.

and the related imbalance in contractual relationships. Indeed, according to the recently abrogated Article 1198 of the Argentinean Civil Code, in the event of *imprévision*, the debtor could request dissolution of the contract due to difficulties in fulfilling the obligation because of excessive cost; in this way, unfulfilled performances were no longer due and those already carried out had to be returned, having become without cause, in application of the 'unjustified enrichment' principle.[80]

Conversely, in Article 37(3) PLACL the 'adaptation of the contract' is established as a rule, in order to make it consistent with the agreement. In accordance with this option, renegotiation proposes itself as a real institution of Latin American contract law, and at the same time commits the courts to making that law more solid. This means that, with regard to the 'general rules' of the Latin American civil codes based on the principle of *pacta sunt servanda*, the *reductio ad equitatem* either for a lesion *ab initio* or for a lesion *superveniens* loses its status of 'exceptional operative rule'.[81]

These rules, which were already part of the common Roman law tradition of the Latin American countries, now assume an official role and formally become two sides of the same coin. We could say that the principle of corrective equity requires the judge to decide on the balance of interests throughout the life of the contract.[82] This consideration retains a certain value, particularly in those cases, such as the recently enacted CESL, in which there is no role for renegotiation and, more generally, for the adaptive adjustment of the contract.

[80] On this subject, it should be borne in mind that the termination of a contract is an extreme choice, frequently not approved by legal scholars and jurisprudence, which stress that termination itself is an incomplete resolution, since it does not allow for renegotiation or adaptation of the contract (see Iturraspe and Piedecasas (n 75) 449). Thus, in line with legal scholarship, the Argentinean courts give the aggrieved party the possibility not only of termination, but also of adaptation of the contract to changes in circumstances. For a reconstruction of the thinking of the Argentinean courts, see JL Amadeo, 'La teoría de la imprevisión en la jurisprudencia de la Corte Suprema' [1982] *La Ley* 521ff.

[81] These rules are exceptional because they are provided by special legislation or linked to the interpretation of the courts, according to the principle of good faith. The use of the *pacta sunt servanda* principle as a general rule (see Art 1545 Civil Code Chile; Art 1796 Civil Code Mexico; Art 519 Civil Code/Bolivia; Art 1361 Civil Code./Peru; Art 1602 Civil Code Colombia; Art 1291 Civil Code Uruguay; Art 1416 Civil Code Salvador), is strengthened by the example of the French Civil Code (see Art 1134), but there are currently numerous exceptions in those civil codes that have been reformed in the last 50 years (on this subject, see Chamie Gandur (n 72) 269ff, containing specific references to the reform of civil codes).

[82] This principle has been extensively applied by the courts. Over the past several decades, this has happened in different legal experiences. See A Kemelmajer de Carlucci, 'Art 1109', in AC Belluscio and EA Zannoni (eds), *Codigo civil y leyes complementarias. Comentado, anotado y concordado* V (Buenos Aires, Astrea, 1994) 326 (with reference to Argentina); F Criscuolo, 'Equità e buona fede come fonti di integrazione del contratto. Potere di adeguamento delle prestazioni contrattuali da parte dell'arbitro [o del giudice] di equità' [1999] *Rivista dell'arbitrato* 71ff (with reference to Italy); U Perfetti, 'La giustizia contrattuale nel Draft Common Frame of Reference del diritto privato europeo' [2009] *Rivista di diritto civile* 669–88 (with reference to the harmonisation of European private law).

VI. Final Remarks

The PLACL represent a significant expression of Latin American legal scholarship, which is often deeply involved in the development of supranational principles, model laws and model codes, in an effort to enhance the process of harmonisation of Latin American law. The PLACL are a key project, drawing the attention of comparative lawyers involved in the analysis of the Latin American legal system, in the search for a new balance between tradition and innovation in the framework of globalisation-led legal interaction. Indeed, these Principles are anchored in the common environment represented by legal scholarship, as well as in the ability of Latin American lawyers to place individual national experiences in Latin America in the overall context of a more general Latin American common law.[83]

This is why I believe that the creation by the drafters of the PLACL of a comparative commentary on these Principles will help in clarifying several critical issues, among which: Can the various provisions on non-performance of the contract be interpreted as deriving from a peculiarly Latin American legal outlook? Might the extensive reference to good faith mislead legal practitioners in interpreting the logic of the legal system? Could a more explicit mention of *culpa* and *diligencia* help to recover not only the tradition of the Latin American civil codes, but also certain principles and core values of the legal system? Can the Principles play a role in the harmonisation of national consumer laws and thus in redefining the limits inherent in the logic of division between B2B and B2C contracts?

[83] This reflection derives from the awareness of the supra-national role of the Latin American legal doctrine, as well as of the particular strength of its formants, and thus of its ability to create continuous comparisons with other legal experiences in the same area, especially in order to find solutions applicable to specific cases; see Lanni (n 19) 9, on the line of investigation of S Schipani, *La codificazione del diritto romano comune* (Turin, Giappichelli, 1999) 119ff. In this respect, it seems particularly significant to recall that in Latin America, the civil code projects and the new civil codes were drafted by legal scholars, using their ability to compare the different national legal experiences on the continent, as part of a more general Latin American 'common law' (see S Schipani, 'I codici latino-americani della "*transfusion*" del diritto romano e dell'indipendenza. Verso codici della "*mezcla*" e "codici tipo"' in S Schipani (ed), *Dalmacio Vélez Sársfield e il diritto latinoamericano* (Padua, Cedam, 1992) 645ff; JL de Los Mozos, 'Codificación y recodificación: reflexiones con motivo de la reforma del código civil peruano' [2001] *Revista general de legislación y jurisprudencia* 91–116; A Guzmán Brito, 'La sistemática de los códigos civiles de la época clásica de la codificación Iberoamericana' [2005] *Roma e America. Diritto romano comune* 283–355. The same might have been said in the past of, among others, the codes of Vélez Sársfield, of Andrés Bello, of Clóvis Beviláqua and of Tristán Narvaja; see JC Palmero, 'Unidad del derecho privado latinoamericano' [1986] *Revista del derecho comercial y de las obligaciones* 381, and id, 'Aportes del derecho argentino al sistema latinoamericano en materia de la teoría general de las obligaciones' [2008] *Roma e America. Diritto romano comune* 79 and 88.

12

The Principles of Latin American Contract Law: A Response from an Outsider

HUGH BEALE

I. Introduction

I wish to begin by congratulating all those who have taken part in producing the Principles of Latin American Contract Law. From simply reading the Principles (even only in the English translation), it is obvious that an enormous amount of work and care has gone into their preparation. It is also evident from the quality of the draft that the project is very fortunate to have lawyers of great skill working on it.

It would be presumptuous for an outsider who has read only the Principles, and none of the background papers or *travaux préparatoires*, to offer criticism or evaluation of the Principles and their contents. It would be particularly inappropriate for the criticisms to come from someone with limited knowledge of civil law systems in general and almost no knowledge of contract law in Latin America. For example, there has been some discussion of whether the Principles contain any specifically Latin American features. I would be quite unable to identify a specifically Latin American feature. I do not know which, if any, Latin American jurisdictions have separate commercial codes or extensive consumer protection legislation.

So instead, in this short paper I shall pose a series of questions about the purposes of the Principles, how they are intended to function and their underlying philosophy. There may well be answers to my questions in the background papers or at least in the minds of the participants in the project. Asking the questions may encourage the participants to articulate their assumptions and the organisers to find a way of making the material available, hopefully in English as well as Spanish. My hope is that the questions and the answers to them, first, can provide criteria by which those with more knowledge than I have can evaluate the Principles; and, secondly, can indicate what may still need to be done, how the project may be taken forward.

II. Seven Questions

After reading the Principles, I was left with essentially seven questions, though there is some overlap between them.

(1) What purpose or purposes are the Principles to serve? Are they intended as themselves law, or merely as a model which can be copied or which can inspire reform or development of the law in the various jurisdictions?

(2) The aim of Principles of Latin American Contract Law is presumably to achieve a degree of commonality. If this is correct, what is the purpose? Is it merely to suggest ways in which the different national laws could be improved, a kind of law reform project that is shared in order to avoid duplication of effort? Or is the aim to achieve a degree of harmonisation of the laws in order to make trade between the various states in Latin America easier?[1] Or is the aim to help to open up markets in Latin America to traders from outside, to make Latin American countries 'more attractive places to do business', as part of the general move towards globalisation?[2]

(3) If we assume that the principal purpose is to facilitate interstate trade, whether on a purely regional or a global basis, how are the Principles to be used? Is the aim to unify the laws of contract across Latin America? Or is it to provide an alternative law for cross-border trade, along the lines of the United Nations Convention on the International Sale of Goods (CISG)[3] or the optional Common European Sales Law (CESL) that at one stage was proposed by the European Commission?[4] Or is the idea to provide 'soft law' of the kind epitomised by the Principles of European Contract Law[5] (PECL) and the UNIDROIT Principles of International Contracts?[6]

[1] cf the aims of much of the contract legislation emanating from the European Union. Even though many of the directives appear to be consumer protection measures, their legal basis is promotion of the Internal Market: see S Weatherill, 'Reflections on the EC's Competence to Develop a "European Contract Law"' (2005) 13 *European Review of Private Law* 405. The initial aim was to give consumers confidence to 'shop abroad' by ensuring that whatever the applicable law, they would have minimum rights. Subsequently, the principal aim has become to encourage traders to sell across borders by reducing the differences between the laws, either by full harmonisation or via an optional 'European' law (see n 4). For a brief account of this change in aim and the development of European contract law since 2001 see H Beale, 'The Story of EU Contract Law—From 2001 to 2014' in C Twigg-Flesner (ed), *Research Handbook on EU Consumer and Contract Law* (Cheltenham, Edward Elgar, 2016) 431.

[2] cf the aims apparently underlying the World Bank's *Doing Business* reports. For the 2016 report see http://www.doingbusiness.org/~/media/GIAWB/Doing%20Business/Documents/Annual-Reports/English/DB16-Full-Report.pdf.

[3] Vienna, 1980.

[4] Proposal for a Regulation on a Common European Sales Law, 11 October 2011 COM(2011) 635 final, withdrawn by Commission Work Programme 2015: A New Start, COM(2014) 910 final (16 December 2014), Annex II item 60, 12.

[5] See O Lando and H Beale (eds), *Principles of European Contract Law, Parts I and II* (Alphen aan den Rijn, Kluwer Law International, 2000); O Lando, E Clive, A Prüm and R Zimmermann (eds), *Principles of European Contract Law, Part III* (Alphen aan den Rijn, Kluwer Law International, 2003).

[6] 4th edn, 2016.

(4) Who are the intended users of this law, whether it be hard or soft? Is it for all business-to-business contracts? Or is it aimed specifically at the needs of smaller enterprises, who are generally thought to find differences between national legal systems more problematic than do larger businesses? Is it intended that the Principles should apply also to consumer contracts and, if so, with what supplementation, if any?

(5) If the target is cross-border contracts, are the Principles to apply to cross-border contracts of all types, or only to contracts made in a specific manner (such as distance contracts) or certain types of contract (for example, contracts for the sale of goods)?

(6) What is the 'guiding philosophy' of the Principles? Are the parties expected to be able to look after their own interests, so that the law should take a relatively individualistic stance, or is the philosophy more communitarian, so that the law is intended to encourage each party to behave in a generally fair and reasonable manner and to have reasonable regard to the other party's interests?

(7) My last question is a purely factual one to which I should be able to find the answer, though I suspect my lack of Spanish would be a major handicap. It is: what other law is out there? Do most of the Latin American jurisdictions have a commercial code or consumer protection legislation that will supplement the Principles?

Asking questions is one thing; providing answers is quite another. Certainly, it would be wrong to suggest that the organisers should be able to provide definite answers to all these questions, let alone answers that are unanimous among all the participants in the project. In the two major European projects in which I was privileged to take part, the Commission on European Contract Law, which produced the PECL, and the Study Group on a European Civil Code,[7] the participants held a wide range of views as to the purpose of the exercise, from laying the groundwork for a unified law, through providing a soft law instrument that could be chosen by parties to cross-border contracts, to just an interesting academic exercise. Nor do I recollect the Commission on European Contract Law deciding on the philosophy that should inform the PECL or even holding any sustained discussion on possible philosophies. The discussion was usually much more pragmatic, around finding a solution that everyone could accept and how to capture it in words.

Moreover, it is evident that principles of contract law can serve more than one purpose at the same time. Article 1:101 of the PECL provides:

> Article 1:101: Application of the Principles
>
> (1) These Principles are intended to be applied as general rules of contract law in the European Union.

[7] See the series, Study Group on a European Civil Code, *Principles of European Law* (Munich, Sellier European Law Publishers, various dates). The Study Group was chaired by Professor C von Bar. Much of its work was later incorporated into the Draft Common Frame of Reference, see C von Bar, E Clive and H Schulte-Nölke (eds), *Principles, Definitions and Model Rules of European Private Law: Draft Common Frame of Reference* (Munich, Sellier European Law Publishers, 2009).

(2) These Principles will apply when the parties have agreed to incorporate them into their contract or that their contract is to be governed by them.
(3) These Principles may be applied when the parties:
 (a) have agreed that their contract is to be governed by 'general principles of law', the 'lex mercatoria' or the like; or
 (b) have not chosen any system or rules of law to govern their contract.
(4) These Principles may provide a solution to the issue raised where the system or rules of law applicable do not do so.

The first paragraph of this article may be read as purely aspirational, an expression of hope on the part of the members of the Commission who would like the PECL to form the basis of a unified law of contract.[8] But it also refers to a second function: to help the institutions of what is now the EU to draft and to apply EU measures. Clearly, the second aim is not directly relevant to the Principles of Latin American Contract Law given that, at present, there is no supranational organisation with relevant legislative powers. Ultimate unification may well be a goal in Latin America also, though it must be a distant goal.

PECL Article 1:101 paragraph (2) and paragraph (3)(b) refer to the parties choosing to have their contract governed by the PECL, or the PECL being applied when the parties have not chosen a law to govern the contract. At present, this is not possible. At least in European private international law, any contract must be governed by a national law and any court deciding a dispute must apply the mandatory rules of the applicable law, subject only to the overriding mandatory provisions of the law of the forum.[9] Had the CESL been adopted, in practice this would have changed: though every contract would remain subject to a national law, if the parties had agreed to use the CESL for their contract, the contract would have been governed by 'the CESL provisions', which would have formed a part of the law of each Member State, rather in the same way as parties using the law of a country that has adopted the CISG may choose to use the CISG for international sale contracts (or, to be precise, the CISG will apply unless the parties opt out of it). The mandatory rules of the CESL would have applied in place of the mandatory rules of the otherwise applicable law.[10]

Meanwhile, however, the PECL can perform other useful functions. Many countries allow contractual disputes to be arbitrated according to non-national principles. Thus in the United Kingdom, the Arbitration Act 1996 provides that

[8] See PECL, Introduction, xxiii.

[9] See Regulation (EC) No 593/2008 of 17 June 2008 on the law applicable to contractual obligations (the 'Rome I Regulation'), Art 9. At one stage during the discussions that preceded its adoption, the European Commission suggested that the Rome I Regulation should permit contracts to be governed by 'rules of the substantive law of contract recognised internationally or in the Community': COM(2005) 650 final (2005/0261 (COD)), 5. However, the suggestion was dropped, in part because of the uncertainty over which rules should count as 'internationally recognised'.

[10] CESL Reg Art 11. This would again be subject to the overriding mandatory provisions of the law of the forum: Rome I Reg Art 9.

the arbitral tribunal shall decide the dispute in accordance with the chosen law or, 'if the parties so agree, in accordance with such other considerations as are agreed by them or determined by the tribunal'.[11] So the parties may agree to arbitration according to the PECL,[12] and an arbitrator who is required to decide the case 'in accordance with internationally accepted principles of contract law' or the like can treat the PECL as a statement of internationally accepted principles.

Even in jurisdictions that do not have a provision of this kind, it is possible for the parties to adopt the PECL as part of their contract. The contract will remain subject to the mandatory rules of the applicable governing law, but if there are few relevant mandatory rules, the effect will not be very different from having the dispute decided according to the PECL.

Last, but by no means least, is the use envisaged by PECL Article 1:101(4) as a model for legislative reform or judge-led development of the law. This has been possibly the most significant use of the PECL to date. For example, the PECL were an influential model in some of the newer democracies in Central Europe and the Baltic states, many of which have revised or are in the process of revising their laws of contract or their civil codes.[13] The Principles and/or the DCFR have been relied upon by the Advocates-General in the European Court of Justice (ECJ) for interpretive purposes[14] and the PECL have even been referred to in English courts as a key reference point from which any departure needs to be justified.[15]

Most of these functions could be performed by the Latin American Principles of Contract Law. However, which functions are to be the primary focus of the Principles, in other words the answers to my questions, may be relevant to both their content and their form.

III. The Content of the Principles

The points that I have mentioned may be important to any evaluation of the contents of the Principles for a number of overlapping reasons.

[11] s 46(1), reflecting Art 28(l) of the United Nations (UNCITRAL) Model Law on International Commercial Arbitration 1985.

[12] Whether this has happened in practice I do not know.

[13] See 'European Initiatives (CFR) and Reform of Civil Law in New Member States' in (2008) XIV *Juridica International*, especially I Kull, 'Reform of Contract Law in Estonia: Influences of Harmonisation of European Private Law' (2008) XIV *Juridica International* 122; A Kisfaludi, 'The Influence of Harmonisation of Private Law on the Development of the Civil Law in Hungary' (2008) XIV *Juridica International* 130; J Rajski, 'European Initiatives and Reform of Civil Law in Poland' (2008) XIV *Juridica International* 151.

[14] eg, Case C-404/06) *Quelle* [2008] 2 CMLR 49, at [AG44], n 28 (citing PECL); Case C-227/08 *Martin v EDP* [2010] 2 CMLR 27, at [AG51]; Case C-445/06 *Danske Slagterier* [2009] ECR I-219 at [AG94], n 57 (both citing DCFR); Case C-618/10 *Banco Espanol de Credito SA v Camino* [2012] 3 CMLR 25, at [AG4].

[15] *Chartbrook Ltd v Persimmon Homes Ltd* [2009] UKHL 38 at [39]. See also *Yam Seng Pte Limited v International Trade Corporation Limited* [2013] EWHC 111 (QB) at [124].

A. Which Parties?

We may start with the question, to what parties are the Principles intended to apply, and to what extent? Article 1(1) states:

> These Principles set forth general rules applicable to domestic and international contracts, whether private or commercial in nature.

This suggests that the Principles are to apply to contracts of all types, including consumer contracts and business-to-business contracts.

i. Consumer Contracts

The PECL apply to consumer contracts. However, it was decided not to include specific consumer protection measures in the PECL, because it was envisaged that the PECL would be supplemented by European and national consumer protection rules.[16] In effect, the PECL would provide the general law which applies to contracts of all types but which is often supplemented by other provisions for specific types of contract like consumer contracts.

In this respect, there was a major change in approach when, at the behest of the European Commission, the PECL were incorporated into the Draft Common Frame of Reference[17] (DCFR). In 2001, the European Commission had published a consultation paper[18] that provisionally proposed, among other things, to 'improve the quality of legislation already in place'.[19] Subsequently, the Commission published an *Action Plan on Contract Law*, which proposed the creation of a Common Frame of Reference (CFR).[20] The European Commission then funded a 'Network of Excellence' to draft the CFR, basing it largely on existing research—namely, the PECL, the work of the Study Group on a European Civil Code and the Principles of Existing EC Private Law produced by the 'Acquis Group'.[21] The purposes of the CFR were twofold.[22] First, it should provide 'fundamental principles, definitions and model rules' that could assist in the improvement of the existing *acquis communautaire*, particularly in a parallel review of eight consumer Directives that was to be carried out.[23] Secondly, the CFR might form the basis of an Optional

[16] PECL, Introduction, xxv.

[17] See n 7 above.

[18] Communication on European contract law COM(2001) 398 final.

[19] See COM(2001) 398 final at paras 57–60, which refer to various earlier initiatives to simplify European legislation.

[20] See *Action Plan on A More Coherent European Contract Law* COM(2003) final, OJ C63/1 (referred to below as *Action Plan*) and *European Contract Law and the Revision of the Acquis: The Way Forward* COM(2004) 651 final, 11 October 2004 (referred to below as *Way Forward*).

[21] Research Group on the Existing EC Private Law (Acquis Group) (eds), *Principles of the Existing EC Contract Law (Acquis Principles)* (Munich, Sellier European Law Publishers, 2007).

[22] For a fuller discussion of the purposes of the CFR, see H Beale, 'The Future of the Common Frame of Reference' (2007) 3 *European Review of Contract Law* 257.

[23] *Way Forward* (n 21) 3. The Directives to be reviewed were 85/577 ('Door-step Selling'), 90/314 ('Package Travel'), 93/13 ('Unfair Terms'), 94/47 ('Timeshare'), 97/7 ('Distance selling'), 98/6 ('Unit

Instrument if it was decided to create one.[24] For either purpose the CFR had to include consumer protection rules.

The Principles of Latin American Contract Law do not contain any specific references to consumers. To what extent are the general rules of contract law supplemented by consumer protection in the Latin American jurisdictions? If they are, are the consumer protection rules broadly similar in the different jurisdictions? If they are significantly different, the differences may constitute a trap for either the consumer buying or the trader selling 'across the borders', depending on which law will govern the contract.[25] If there are no such rules, are they not wanted or needed?

ii. Business-to-business Contracts

For business-to-business contracts, whether the Latin American jurisdictions have commercial codes or legislation on specific types of contract matters when we look at possible lacunae in the Principles. For example, there is relatively little dealing with what I would call 'gaps in the parties' agreement'. What if there is no explicit agreement on an issue that seems essential in the kind of contract that the parties seem to be making, such as the price to be paid for goods, yet it is clear that the parties consider themselves bound so that this is not a case in which they have yet to complete their negotiations? Compare the PECL:

> Article 6:104: Determination of Price
>
> Where the contract does not fix the price or the method of determining it, the parties are to be treated as having agreed on a reasonable price.[26]

To an outsider like myself, there is a variety of possible explanations for the omission. One might be that many Latin American jurisdictions have commercial

prices'); 98/27 ('Injunctions') and 99/44 ('Consumer sales'). This review led to the Proposal for a Directive of the European Parliament and of the Council on consumer rights, COM(2008) 614. The version of the directive that was ultimately adopted, Directive 2011/83/EU of 25 October 2011 on consumer rights, was much narrower, in particular leaving the directives on Unfair Terms in Consumer Contracts (93/13/EEC) and Consumer Sales (1999/44/EC) almost untouched. The influence of the CFR on the drafting of the Consumer Rights Directive is questionable: see M Hesselink, 'The Consumer Rights Directive and the CFR: Two Worlds Apart?' (2009) 5 *European Review of Contract Law* 290.

[24] *Action Plan* (n 20) 2, 23–24; *Way Forward* (n 20) 8–9. This purpose would have been fulfilled if the CESL had been adopted.

[25] This will depend on the relevant rules of private international law, of which I am again ignorant. In Europe, under Art 6 of the Rome I Regulation (Regulation (EC) No 593/2008 of 17 June 2008 on the law applicable to contractual obligations), the parties to a consumer contract may choose which law is to apply to the contract but the consumer cannot be deprived of the protection of the mandatory rules of the state in which the consumer is habitually resident if the contract resulted from the trader doing business with or directing its activities to consumers in that state. This means that a trader who is seeking to sell across borders may need to know the mandatory rules of each country towards which it directs its activities.

[26] Other examples of 'gap-filling' rules of this kind in the PECL are Arts 6:102: Implied Terms and 6:108: Quality of Performance.

codes or provisions on specific contracts which lay down rules which will provide a solution.[27] Another, of course, might be that the drafters were not able to agree that there may be a binding contract in the absence of agreement on such an essential element of the price—an issue that was long controversial in some European jurisdictions, for example in France until the *Alcatel* case in 1995.[28]

iii. Small Businesses

In relation to business-to-business contracts I also raised the question whether the Principles are aiming at all businesses or principally at smaller businesses. It is normally thought that differences between the laws of contract in different states pose more of a problem for small businesses than for large businesses. A large business may have sufficient expertise in-house to be able to identify any risks it would encounter by using a foreign law to govern its contract. Even if the business would have to employ a law firm to give advice on foreign law, if the business is large, the contract or series of contracts in question is likely to be more valuable than when the business is a small one, so that the cost of obtaining legal advice for a large firm will be relatively lower than for a small firm.

This suggests that small businesses might be a principal target, or at least principal beneficiaries, of the Principles. If that is the case, however, it seems appropriate to consider the particular needs of smaller businesses. The problems are not only that smaller businesses are unlikely all to be able to afford expertise on foreign law. They have other needs as well.

Particularly when a small business is dealing with a larger business, it is the small business that may have to deal on the other party's standard terms. It is also unlikely to have the expertise to analyse these, particularly when they are in a foreign language. So this is a reason for including controls over unfair terms that have not been negotiated. Indeed, one of the main arguments for adopting the CESL for business-to-business sales when the CISG is already available in most Member States is that the CISG does not deal with unfair terms, leaving the matter to the law that otherwise applies. That law may or may not provide protection against unfair non-negotiated terms.

B. The Type of Contract Negotiation Envisaged

If we assume that the Principles are aimed at least in part at cross-border contracts, it is also pertinent to ask how the drafters envisage such contracts being made—through face-to-face meetings between the parties or entirely 'at a distance', whether by letter, phone, email or clicking on one party's website? The same

[27] cf Art 1448 of the Spanish Civil Code, which seems to allow the price to be left open when there is a contract for the sale of goods that are fungible and for which there is a market.

[28] Ass Plén 1 Dec 1995, JCP 1995 II 22 565, n J Ghestin; see, Note 2 to PECL Art 6:104.

issue arises in purely domestic transactions as more and more contracts are made without face-to-face contact but via the Internet.

In Europe we have developed the notion of the distance contract:

> 'distance contract' means any contract concluded between the trader and the consumer under an organised distance sales or service-provision scheme without the simultaneous physical presence of the trader and the consumer, with the exclusive use of one or more means of distance communication up to and including the time at which the contract is concluded.[29]

However, to date the response to distance contracts has, to my mind, been inadequate. A consumer who enters a distance contract with a trader is quite well protected: under the Consumer Rights Directive,[30] the trader is obliged to provide a wide range of information to the consumer before the contract is concluded,[31] including the information that, in many cases and particularly when the consumer is buying goods, the consumer has a right to withdraw from the contract without giving any reason and in most cases without cost.[32] However, there is no equivalent provision when goods are bought under a distance contract by a business, however small. That was true even in the proposed CESL. I now think that was a mistake and that a business buyer, buying at a distance, should have a right to withdraw from the contract (at least as a default rule) and should be provided with the same pre-contractual information as a consumer.

i. Withdrawal Rights

The rationale for allowing a consumer to withdraw from a distance contract, or to withdraw an offer to buy, is that the consumer will not have had the chance to examine the goods before buying them. This will often also be the case with a business buyer. Moreover, I suspect that traders find it very difficult to distinguish between consumers and business buyers. So in practice many distance sellers must allow the buyer to cancel the order whether or not the buyer is a consumer. However, I do not think that a business distance buyer should have to check the trader's terms to see whether the trader extends this right to business buyers, nor have to rely on the trader's goodwill. It would actively encourage business-to-business sales over the internet and by other distance means if there were normally a right of cancellation.

It is true that not everyone needs a right of cancellation, because they are buying goods which they have bought before. This is particularly likely when the buyers are businesses, as they are more likely to have bought the same goods on a previous occasion. Nonetheless, I would give a right of cancellation, at least as the default

[29] Consumer Rights Directive (2011/83/EU), Art 2(7).

[30] See above. This directive replaces the earlier directives on doorstep selling (85/577/EEC) and distance selling (97/7/EC).

[31] See Art 6 of the directive.

[32] See Arts 9–16.

rule. First, if buyers do not need the right to cancel, they will seldom exercise it and therefore it will cost the trader very little. Secondly, it would be possible to allow the business buyer to waive their right of cancellation, perhaps in exchange for a small discount in order to encourage them to do so. With website sales the magic of information technology can easily be used to ensure that a business buyer can waive the right to cancel by having to click on a separate pop-up acknowledgement, perhaps at the time that they choose the delivery method. The pop-up box might also require the buyer to 'self certify' that they are a trader, with a warning that trying to obtain a discount when you are not a trader amounts to fraud.

ii. Pre-contract Information

Similarly, it seems sensible to require a trader who offers to sell to both consumers and business buyers by distance means to provide the same information for both types of buyer. Whatever is required, the seller is likely to emphasise the positive aspects of the product as a way of encouraging sales. It is the negative aspects—for example, whether digital content is compatible with the buyer's hardware or other software—which are less likely to be revealed and which therefore should have to be disclosed. It is of course true that a business buyer is likely to be better informed and more sophisticated than a consumer and therefore might ask more questions before concluding the contract. However, it would encourage business-to-business distance sales if business buyers could have the same confidence that they have been given the information they need, and that the information is correct, as would be the case with a consumer buyer. Moreover, in practice the trader will be providing the required information anyway for consumer buyers—so there would be no extra cost in providing it for business buyers also.

C. An Optional Instrument or Unification?

The Principles may be conceived as a set of rules that the parties may choose, and as we saw earlier, this option encompasses several possibilities. The parties might be allowed to choose these rules to govern their contract, or at least to choose them as rules by which any dispute should be arbitrated; or they may merely incorporate the Principles into the contract. Alternatively, the Principles may be envisaged as the basis for a unification of contract law throughout Latin America. The precise purpose that is intended has tricky implications for some of the contents and how the Principles are to relate to the rest of the law of the relevant jurisdiction.

As we saw earlier, in Europe any contract must be governed by a national law and any court deciding a dispute must apply the mandatory rules of the applicable law, subject only to the overriding mandatory provisions of the law of the forum;[33] but some laws allow more choice in arbitration. If the parties merely adopt the

[33] See Rome I Regulation, Art 9.

Principles as part of their contract, the Principles so incorporated will necessarily remain subject to the mandatory rules of the applicable law, just like any other term that the parties may have agreed. In this case, there is no particular problem.

If it is envisaged that an arbitrator or a court should treat the Principles as displacing the otherwise applicable law, however, it becomes important to know what is to be displaced and what is not—in other words, what topics are within the scope of the Principles and what are not, so they remain governed by the otherwise applicable law. To some extent this can be gathered from a simple list of contents. Thus it is evident that the CISG and the proposed CESL both contain rules on offer and acceptance intended to displace the national rules on formation. Likewise, it is obvious that the CISG does not deal with issues of validity of contracts and so questions of validity are left to the relevant national law. Equally, the proposed CESL did not deal with representation (ie the power of an agent to bind a principal) or with assignment.[34] But the fact that an instrument does not contain a rule that is found in national law does not necessarily mean that the matter is outside the scope of the instrument so that the national rule will continue to apply despite the parties' choice of the instrument to govern the contract.

This issue arose with the proposed CESL. Some issues would have been within the scope of application of the CESL even though it contained no provision directly on the issue and dealt with it in some other way. For example, some Member States have implemented the Directive on Unfair Terms in Consumer Contracts[35] in such a way that the fairness test applies to any term supplied by the trader, whether or not the term was individually negotiated—or have left in place pre-existing legislation to that effect.[36] In the CESL, the controls over unfair terms applied only to terms that were not individually negotiated; there were no controls over individually negotiated terms in consumer contracts other than under general articles such as Article 51, Unfair exploitation.[37] Control over unfair contract terms was within the scope of application of the CESL.[38] The broader rule in the relevant Member States, even if it is regarded as mandatory for contracts that are governed by the pre-existing national rules, would not have applied when the parties had chosen to use the CESL for their contract.

[34] An omission that might have led to very difficult questions if the CESL had been adopted and claims arising under contracts governed by it had been assigned. See H Beale and G Ringe, 'Transfer of Rights and Obligations' in G Dannemann and S Vogenauer (eds), *The Common European Sales Law in Context: Interactions with English and German Law* (Oxford, Oxford University Press, 2013) 521.

[35] 1993/13/EEC.

[36] See H Schulte-Nölke, C Twigg-Flesner and M Ebers, *EC Consumer Law Compendium* (Munich, Sellier European Law Publishers, 2007) 226. The UK must now be added to the list of Member States that have a wider control: see Consumer Rights Act 2015, s 62.

[37] On the applicability of Art 2, Good faith and fair dealing, to negotiated clauses, see below, text after n 47.

[38] Thus Recital (26) listed 'the assessment and consequences of unfairness of contract terms' as a topic covered by the CESL. The European Parliament adopted an amendment that would have brought this into the text itself: European Parliament legislative resolution of 26 February 2014 on the proposal for a regulation of the European Parliament and of the Council on a Common European Sales Law (COM(2011)0635—C7-0329/2011—2011/0284(COD)), Amendment 76.

Were the Principles to be used as the basis for complete harmonisation of the laws of contract in Latin America, at first sight this issue might not arise. Presumably, the existing law of contract in each state would be repealed, so there would be no question of which law would apply. The harmonised law of contract would be exhaustive and self-sufficient. Take, for example, the article on contracts contrary to public policy:

> Article 41. Absolute and relative nullity
>
> Contracts that violate the law, public policy, or good morals incur absolute nullity. Contracts deemed null to protect the interests of certain people incur relative nullity.

As the Principles do not state the rules of public policy, a court asked to apply this article would presumably have to decide for itself what public policy should be as well as whether the contract violated it. In contrast, if the Principles are to be an optional system that parties may adopt to govern their contract or which arbitrators may apply, it no longer seems right to assume that the Principles are exhaustive and self-sufficient. Rather, the reference to public policy would presumably then be taken as a reference to rules of public policy that are outside the Principles and that remain a matter for the law of each state. In that case, it would be useful to indicate which law is relevant: for example, to add that the relevant public policy is both the public policy of the otherwise applicable law and the public policy of the country in which the contract is to be performed. The same applies to Article 39, which requires that a contract's cause must be lawful.[39] Lawful according to which law?

In fact, even if contract law were to be harmonised on the model of the Principles, issues of scope would still arise. Unless and until the whole of the law of obligations were unified, there would still be questions about whether a particular topic was within the harmonised area or outside it. Let me take an example that was discussed when we were drafting the CESL: the rule, found for example in French law, that the original seller of property that has a hidden defect (*vice cachée*) may be liable to a subsequent purchaser of the property with whom the original seller has no direct contract. Is that to be treated as a matter of contract law governed by the CESL, so that the rule would not apply if the CESL were used, or a rule of delict (or a *sui generis* rule) that would apply despite use of the CESL if the law otherwise applicable to the relevant contracts were French law? (To the best of my knowledge, the issue was never resolved!)

A last difference between a unified law and an optional instrument follows from their different natures. Fully harmonised contract law will simply apply as part of the law that is applicable under the rules of private international law. An optional law may need rules as to what amounts to an effective choice to use the system,[40] and rules to the effect that the decision whether the optional law is to apply, and

[39] Art 39(2). On Art 39 see further below.

[40] cf CESL Reg Arts 8 (Agreement on the use of the CESL) and 9 (Standard Information Notice in contracts between a trader and a consumer).

also issues relating to pre-contractual negotiations (such as whether a contract has been formed or may be avoided on some ground relating to pre-contractual behaviour), may be dealt with by the tribunal in the same way as if a valid contract had been formed.[41]

i. Cross-border Contracts

Whether the primary aim of the Principles is to make it easier to contract across borders, rather than the improvement of the various domestic laws, may be relevant to the substance of the articles. The additional costs to cross-border contracting caused by differences in the applicable laws will not be reduced by having a uniform set of rules on paper if the rules are applied very differently in the various jurisdictions. This makes me worry about two types of provision: first, provisions that may be intended to have a relatively narrow application but that might be applied expansively in some jurisdictions but not in others; and, secondly, provisions that are very 'open-textured' and so might be applied very differently in different jurisdictions.

An example of the first type of provision is the article on cause. Article 9 provides that cause, along with consent and subject matter, is an essential element of a contract. Cause is then defined:

> Article 39. Cause of the contract and obligation
>
> (1) All obligations require a cause. A cause is presumed to exist as long as it is not proven otherwise, even if it is not expressed.
> (2) The cause of the contract must be lawful.

I have no difficulty with the requirement that the contract's cause must be lawful; but does cause in Article 39 have any other function and, if it does, what is that function? In France, the doctrine of cause has been used in relatively recent times[42] to deal with two problems that do not seem to me to be obvious candidates for its application: the problem of exclusion and limitation of liability clauses in one party's standard terms when the court thinks the clause may undermine the other party's reasonable expectations, as in the *Chronopost* case[43] and subsequent decisions;[44] and cases that look very much like exploitation by one party of the

[41] ie *Kompetenz-Kompetenz*: cf CESL Art 8(1): '... The existence of such an agreement and its validity shall be determined on the basis of paragraphs 2 and 3 of this Article and Article 9, as well as the relevant provisions in the Common European Sales Law'.

[42] See generally J Rochfeld, 'A Future for la cause? Observations of a French Jurist' in J Cartwright, S Vogenauer and S Whittaker (eds), *Reforming the French Law of Obligations* (Oxford, Hart Publishing, 2009) 73.

[43] Cass com 22 October 1996, H Capitant, F Terré, Y Lequette and F Chénedé, *Les Grands Arrêts de la Jurisprudence Civile*, vol 2, Obligations, Contrats spéciaux, Sûretés (Paris, Dalloz, 2008) no 157.

[44] These are described in H Beale, B Fauvarque-Cosson, J Rutgers, D Tallon and S Vogenauer, *Ius Commune Casebooks for the Common Law of Europe: Cases, Materials and Text on Contract Law*, 2nd edn (Oxford, Hart Publishing, 2010) 179–82.

other's inexperience and ignorance. An example is the so-called 'video rental case'[45] in which a company leased to a husband and wife 200 video cassettes for eight months with a view to the couple setting up a video club in the village where they lived. The community was far too small to support such a venture. As the couple's plan was impossible, the Cour de cassation held that the contract lacked cause. Would it be expected or legitimate for a court faced with a similar case under the Principles to decide in the same way? Or should it give relief if the facts bring the case within one of the specific provision on invalid contracts, such as the article on gross disparity?

Article 37. Gross disparity

(1) A party may seek the adaptation of a contract or any of its clauses, or to annul the contract, if it or they give the other party an excessive advantage in contravention of the requirements of good faith.

...

Provisions that do not have a closely defined scope of application may end up subverting more precisely targeted and limited provisions.

No one who recalls that I am an English common lawyer will be surprised by my choice of an example of the second type of potential problem, the article that is open textured. It is the provision on good faith:

Article 7. Good faith

(1) The parties must act in accordance with the requirements of good faith.
(2) Agreements limiting good faith shall have no effect whatsoever.

I am not seeking to argue that the Principles of Latin American Contract Law should not include this article. The PECL, the DCFR and the CESL have all contained a similar article, though they have all referred to 'good faith and fair dealing', rather than to good faith alone, in order to make it clear that the parties are not merely required to abstain from deliberately harming each other—ie to abstain from bad faith—but that they are required to meet an objective standard. As the CESL put it:

> 'good faith and fair dealing' means a standard of conduct characterised by honesty, openness and consideration for the interests of the other party to the transaction or relationship in question.[46]

However, in Europe we have been concerned that judges from different backgrounds may interpret and apply the good faith and fair dealing requirement in very different ways. Of course I am aware that good faith and fair dealing is a familiar concept in most, if not all, Latin American laws, but that does not mean that its application is predictable. I was attending a conference with French lawyers

[45] Cass civ (1) 3 July 1996, Bull civ 1996 I no 286; D 1997, 499, note P Reigne; for a translation see the *Ius Commune Casebook* (n 44) 183.

[46] CESL Reg Art 2(b).

at which the role of good faith was being discussed. The French lawyer on my left remarked that every French lawyer knows what is required by good faith; to which the French lawyer on my right replied: 'Correct; but every lawyer gives a different answer'. Even if this riposte was a gross exaggeration, it is unlikely that lawyers from different jurisdictions will always give the same answer.

For this reason, the role of good faith and fair dealing in the European instruments has been limited in a number of ways. First, to take care of the problem discussed earlier, it was indicated that the general article should not subvert specific, more restricted provisions. Thus in the CESL the Recitals stated:

> The principle of good faith and fair dealing should provide guidance on the way parties have to cooperate. As some rules constitute specific manifestations of the general principle of good faith and fair dealing, they should take precedent [*sic*] over the general principle. The general principle should therefore not be used as a tool to amend the specific rights and obligations of parties as set out in the specific rules ...[47]

Thus the CESL provided for controls over unfair terms only when the terms had not been individually negotiated, and the good faith and fair dealing requirement should not be used as a 'back door' way of controlling terms that had been negotiated but nonetheless the court thought to be unfair.

Secondly, some sets of principles have sought to limit the effect of conduct that is contrary to good faith and fair dealing. The DCFR provided:

> III.–1:103: Good faith and fair dealing
>
> ...
>
> (3) Breach of the duty does not give rise directly to the remedies for non-performance of an obligation but may preclude the person in breach from exercising or relying on a right, remedy or defence which that person would otherwise have.

However, in the CESL this was abandoned. Article 2 (Good faith and fair dealing) provided:

> ...
>
> (2) Breach of this duty may preclude the party in breach from exercising or relying on a right, remedy or defence which that party would otherwise have, or may make the party liable for any loss thereby caused to the other party.

Thirdly, in some contexts an attempt was made to encourage uniform application by providing the court with guidelines. For example, Article 49 of the CESL (Fraud) gave guidance on when good faith and fair dealing requires a party to point out an error that the other party has been making:

> Article 49 Fraud
>
> ...

[47] Recital (31).

(3) In determining whether good faith and fair dealing require a party to disclose particular information, regard should be had to all the circumstances, including:
   (a) whether the party had special expertise;
   (b) the cost to the party of acquiring the relevant information;
   (c) the ease with which the other party could have acquired the information by other means;
   (d) the nature of the information;
   (e) the apparent importance of the information to the other party; and
   (f) in contracts between traders good commercial practice in the situation concerned.

However, the most important method of securing uniform interpretation is to provide examples of what is and is not contrary to good faith and fair dealing. I will consider this in the next section of the paper.

ii. Cross-border Contracts and non-Latin American Systems

A last point affecting the content of the Principles is that if at least part of the aim is to make it easier to contract with parties outside Latin America, it may be necessary to deal with issues or legal devices that are found in other legal systems—for example in common law jurisdictions—even if they are not found or are uncommon in Latin America. An example is the way in which common law systems tend to privilege a written record of the contract over oral agreements, sometimes applying the so-called 'parol evidence rule': a classic statement of the rule would be that 'parol evidence may not be admitted to add to, vary or contradict a deed or other written instrument'.[48] If applied, the rule has the effect that any promise or statement which is not in the written document ('parol' means informal, ie not in the deed or other document) is simply excluded from the contract. This is explained by saying that the parties intended the written agreement to be complete, and any promise or statement not included in the document was not part of the 'final deal' or was not intended to create legal obligations. At least in England and Wales, this rule now creates no more than a presumption that the written document was complete:[49] if the court is convinced that the oral statement or promise was meant to be binding they will simply say that the writing was not intended to be complete, so that the parol evidence rule does not apply.[50] But contracts drafted by common lawyers often include a 'merger clause', to the effect that the document is a complete and exhaustive statement of the terms of the contract. It is not just a question of old habits dying hard; many lawyers and judges think that such a clause is valuable:

> The purpose of an entire agreement clause is to preclude a party to a written agreement from threshing through the undergrowth and finding in the course of negotiations some

[48] *Jacobs v Batavia and General Plantations Trust Ltd* [1924] 1 Ch 287, 295.
[49] *See Gillespie Bros & Co v Cheney, Eggar & Co* [1896] 2 QB 59, 62.
[50] eg, *J Evans & Son (Portsmouth) Ltd v Andrea Merzario Ltd* [1976] 1 WLR 1078, 1083.

(chance) remark or statement (often long forgotten or difficult to recall or explain) on which to found a claim such as the present to the existence of a collateral warranty. The entire agreement clause obviates the occasion for any such search and the peril to the contracting parties posed by the need which may arise in its absence to conduct such a search. For such a clause constitutes a binding agreement between the parties that the full contractual terms are to be found in the document containing the clause and not elsewhere, and that accordingly any promises or assurances made in the course of the negotiations (which in the absence of such a clause might have effect as a collateral warranty) shall have no contractual force, save insofar as they are reflected and given effect in that document.[51]

A merger clause, in effect, forces the parties to put the whole of their agreement down on paper. When both parties are aware of the clause and its likely effect, that is no doubt a good thing; but a clause which is in one party's standard contract terms and was not known to the other party may take the other party unfairly by surprise. So the European restatements all contain a provision on merger clauses, such as this from the CESL:[52]

Article 72 Merger clauses

1. Where a contract in writing includes a term stating that the document contains all contract terms (a merger clause), any prior statements, undertakings or agreements which are not contained in the document do not form part of the contract.
2. Unless the contract otherwise provides, a merger clause does not prevent the parties' prior statements from being used to interpret the contract.
3. In a contract between a trader and a consumer, the consumer is not bound by a merger clause.
4. The parties may not, to the detriment of the consumer, exclude the application of this Article or derogate from or vary its effects.

IV. The Form of the Principles

The purposes to which the Principles of Latin American Contract Law are to be put should also have an impact on their form. The present draft contains only articles. I understand that Comments of the kind found in the PECL and the DCFR, and comparative notes such as are also in those instruments, have not yet been prepared.

[51] Lightman J in *Inntrepreneur Pub Co Ltd v East Crown Ltd* [2002] 2 Lloyds Rep 611, at [7].

[52] cf PECL Art 2:105 (under which a merger clause that has not been individually negotiated only creates a presumption that the written contract contains all the terms agreed) and DCFR Art II.-4:104. Under the CESL, a merger clause that had not been individually negotiated might be invalid as an unfair term under Ch 8 of the CESL.

A. Comments

To my mind, preparing Comments to the articles is vitally important, for a number of reasons.

First, Comments have an important role to play in giving guidance to courts and practitioners as to how the Principles are to apply. I argued earlier that if an international instrument is to succeed in reducing the costs of cross-border trade, it is not enough that the words of the instrument are the same in each jurisdiction; the articles must also be applied in a reasonably uniform manner. This is a particular problem with provisions that may have been intended to be narrow but may be interpreted very broadly, for example the requirement for cause,[53] and with open-textured norms such as good faith and fair dealing.[54] The articles themselves may give some guidance, as does the CESL Article 49 (Fraud), but it is often easier and more informative to provide the guidance through the Comments. For instance, it would be very helpful to provide examples of the type of problem that the drafters envisage will fall to be dealt with by PLACL Article 7 (Good faith) and of the type of conduct that will or will not meet the standard of behaviour required.

Secondly, Comments will be very helpful if there is a move to get the Principles adopted as legislation, whether by way of unification or as an optional instrument. However well drafted the articles, it is hard for legislators to understand what is intended from a set of articles alone. This was demonstrated by the European Commission's experience with the CESL proposal. Because of the tight time scale (the Expert Group that produced the first draft[55] had only 12 months in which to work), the CESL was initially published without Comments. The Commission very soon found it had to ask for Comments to be prepared in order to help it in the discussions in the Council working group. In particular, it asked for Comments that gave examples of how the CESL would apply and that explained the relationships between the various articles. Draft Comments on many of the chapters were prepared and though they have never been published, Commission officials reported using the draft Comments extensively in the discussions. If the original CESL proposal had contained Comments giving a fuller explanation of how it was to work, it might not have encountered such opposition in the Council.

Comments and examples have another, equally important, function: to test the articles. I am sure that the CESL would have been a better proposal if the Comments had been prepared at the same time as the articles. In preparing the Comments and creating examples of how the articles would apply, we found a significant number of cases in which articles could have been improved in either drafting or substance, and a few outright mistakes and omissions.

[53] See above, text at n 42.

[54] See above, text at n 46.

[55] See *A European contract law for consumers and businesses: Publication of the results of the feasibility study carried out by the Expert Group on European contract law for stakeholders' and legal practitioners' feedback* (May 2011).

It may not be enough, however, for the Comments to explain and illustrate how the Principles are to operate. Particularly if one of the aims of the Principles is to be a model for law reform, it is important to explain how the drafters arrived at this text for the Principles of Latin American Contract Law. To what extent does each article represent a rule or solution to a problem that is common to all the jurisdictions involved? Presumably the project was worthwhile only because there are some significant differences between the systems; so some of the articles must represent a choice between one or more possible solutions. A legislator considering whether or not to replace her domestic law of contract with provisions from the Principles will need to know why she should do so. In other words, what were the possible solutions on each issue and why did the drafters choose one solution rather than another? It must be admitted that the Comments to the PECL did not explain these choices in a consistent fashion. The Commission's *Action Plan* called for the CFR 'to identify best solutions, taking into account national contract laws (both case law and established practice), the EC *acquis* and relevant international instruments'.[56] What was not stated in the original *Action Plan*, but was soon proposed by the researchers and accepted by the Commission, is that where a 'policy decision' has been made, to choose one rule or definition in preference to another, the policy decision should be clearly explained with the reasons for the choice.[57] The DCFR tried to explain the choices, even in the case of articles that had been taken over from the PECL, though it was not always easy to recall the reasoning behind choices that had been made some time ago.

B. Comparative Notes

I hope that sooner or later the Principles will be supplemented by Notes, in order to explain the sources from which the Principles are derived and to compare their similarities to and differences from the national laws. Notes of this kind are very helpful to anyone who wants to know how the Principles differ from a national law, be they a legislator who is considering whether the Principles should be adopted or a lawyer who is seeking to advise a client what difference it would make if a contract were to be subject to the Principles rather than to one of the existing national laws.

Comparative Notes would also make the Principles available as a kind of tool for translation from one system to another, or a search engine to enable one to find out whether a rule in one system has an equivalent in another system. As one of my Dutch colleagues involved in the DCFR project put it, we can envisage a day when the DCFR will make it possible for a lawyer sitting at her computer terminal to find out what is the relevant answer to a point on private law in every legal

[56] *Way Forward* (n 20) para 3.1.3, 11.

[57] See First Annual Progress Report on European Contract Law and the Acquis Review, COM(2005) 456 final, para 2.6.3.

system in the European Union. She will be able to identify how the DCFR deals with the particular point in which she is interested and then, through the Notes to the relevant article, to find the equivalent rule in each system listed. The same could be true of the Principles of Latin American Contract Law.

Further, if one purpose is really to open up Latin American markets to traders from outside the region, by making Latin American contract law more accessible and easy to use, it would be useful to include in the Notes comparisons to other major legal systems, such as Chinese law or a common law system such as that of the United States.

V. Conclusion

The many people who have contributed to the Principles of Latin American Contract Law are to be congratulated on what they have achieved. The Principles presented in this volume are a very good beginning. However, to make the Principles really useful for almost any of their possible purposes, a lot of work remains to be done, in particular on Comments and Comparative Notes. But first it seems that some decision will have to be made about the intended purposes of the Principles, as these may affect both the final substance and the form of the final product. Some of the work—particularly producing Comparative Notes—will necessarily be painstaking and sometimes tedious. I very much hope that it will be carried forward with as much enthusiasm as must have gone into the version presented in this volume. I wish everyone involved the best of luck with the work.

APPENDIX: *PRINCIPIOS LATINOAMERICANOS DE DERECHO DE LOS CONTRATOS*— PRINCIPLES OF LATIN AMERICAN CONTRACT LAW*

Capítulo 1. Capítulo preliminar

Sección 1. Ámbito de aplicación

Artículo 1. Ámbito de aplicación

(1) Estos principios establecen reglas generales aplicables a los contratos civiles y comerciales, internos e internacionales.
(2) Estos principios se aplican con preferencia a cualquier otro cuerpo de principios en materia de contratos, a contratos conectados a los países de América del Sur, del Caribe y a las jurisdicciones del Continente Americano regidos por el sistema de derecho continental.
(3) Estos principios se aplicarán cuando las partes sometan su contrato, en todo o en parte, a estos principios, pudiendo referirse a ellos de manera genérica o específica a algunas de sus disposiciones.
(4) Estos principios se aplican también en cualquiera de los siguientes casos:
   (a) Cuando las partes hayan acordado que su contrato se rija por los principios generales del Derecho, la Lex mercatoria o expresiones semejantes.

Chapter 1. Preamble

Section 1. Scope of application

Article 1. Scope of application

(1) These Principles set forth general rules applicable to domestic and international contracts, whether private or commercial in nature.
(2) These Principles apply preferentially over any other principles of contracts to contracts connected to countries located in South America, the Caribbean, and jurisdictions of the Americas governed by the civil law system.
(3) These Principles shall be applied when the parties agree that their contract be governed by them, either in whole or in part, and the parties can refer to these Principles in general or to specific provisions of them.
(4) These Principles also apply in any of the following cases:
   (a) When the parties have agreed that their contract be governed by general principles of law, the *lex mercatoria*, or the like.

* This text corresponds to the text approved by the drafting committee in October 2014. The translation was provided by Adriana Maestas and Manuel Alcalde of Linklaters LLP New York, and reworked by Rodrigo Momberg and Stefan Vogenauer, then at the Institute of European and Comparative Law, Oxford.

(b) Cuando las partes no han elegido en forma expresa un Derecho estatal aplicable al contrato, ni resulta de las circunstancias del caso concreto, que el contrato está más estrechamente vinculado con otro ordenamiento jurídico estatal.
(c) Para interpretar y complementar instrumentos internacionales de Derecho uniforme.
(d) Para interpretar y complementar el Derecho estatal que rige el contrato.
(e) Para interpretar, complementar e integrar contratos sometidos al Derecho o instrumentos internacionales de Derecho uniforme.
(f) Como modelo para los legisladores estatales o internacionales.

Artículo 2. Orden público y normas imperativas

Estos Principios no restringen la aplicación de las normas imperativas y la actuación de los principios protegidos por el orden público, sean de origen nacional, internacional o supranacional, que resulten aplicables conforme a las normas de Derecho internacional privado.

Artículo 3. Usos y prácticas

(1) Las partes quedan obligadas por los usos que hayan aceptado y por las prácticas que hayan establecido entre ellas.
(2) Igualmente, quedan obligadas por los usos ampliamente conocidos y generalmente observados en ámbito de su actividad, salvo que su aplicación no produzca resultados razonables, o que las partes los hayan excluido expresamente.

(b) When the parties have not expressly chosen the laws of a specific State to govern their contract or when the contract is not more closely connected with another State's laws based on the circumstances of the case.
(c) To interpret and supplement international uniform law instruments.
(d) To interpret and supplement the domestic law governing the contract.
(e) To interpret and supplement contracts governed by international uniform law.
(f) As a model for national or international legislators.

Article 2. Public policy and mandatory rules

Nothing in these Principles shall restrict the application of mandatory rules or the operation of principles that are protected by public policy, whether of national, international, or supranational origin, which are applicable in accordance with the rules of private international law.

Article 3. Usages and practices

(1) The parties are bound by the usages to which they have agreed and by the practices which they have established between themselves.
(2) Moreover, they are bound by the usages that are widely known and regularly observed in the sphere of activities concerned, except where the application of such usages would produce unreasonable results or the parties have expressly excluded them.

Artículo 4. Aplicación, interpretación e integración de los Principios

(1) Las partes pueden modificar, derogar o excluir la aplicación de estos Principios o de algunas de sus disposiciones, salvo que se indique lo contrario.
(2) En la interpretación de estos Principios se tendrá en cuenta su carácter internacional así como sus propósitos, incluyendo la necesidad de promover la uniformidad en su aplicación.
(3) Las cuestiones que se encuentren comprendidas en el ámbito de aplicación de estos Principios, aunque no resueltas expresamente por ellos, se resolverán en lo posible según sus principios generales subyacentes.

Sección 2. Principios generales

Artículo 5. Libertad de contratación

Las partes son libres para celebrar contratos y para determinar su contenido, no siendo contrario a derecho o al orden público.

Artículo 6. Fuerza obligatoria del contrato

Todo contrato válidamente celebrado es obligatorio para las partes.

Artículo 7. Buena fe

(1) Las partes deben comportarse conforme a las exigencias de la buena fe.
(2) Las limitaciones convencionales contrarias a la buena fe no producen efecto alguno.

Capítulo 2: Formación del contrato

Sección 1. Definición y elementos del contrato

Artículo 8. Definición del contrato

El contrato es un acuerdo por el cual dos o más partes crean, transfieren, modifican o extinguen un vínculo jurídico de contenido económico.

Article 4. Application, interpretation, and supplementation of the Principles

(1) The parties may vary, derogate from, or exclude the application of these Principles or any of their provisions, except as otherwise provided.
(2) In the interpretation of these Principles, regard is to be had to their international character and to their purposes, including the need to promote uniformity in their application.
(3) Issues within the scope of these Principles but not expressly settled by them are as far as possible to be settled in accordance with their underlying general principles.

Section 2. General Principles

Article 5. Freedom of contract

The parties are free to enter into contracts and to determine their content, so long as this does not violate the law or public policy.

Article 6. Binding force of contract

A contract validly entered into is binding upon the parties.

Article 7. Good faith

(1) The parties must act in accordance with the requirements of good faith.
(2) Agreements limiting good faith shall have no effect whatsoever.

Chapter 2. Formation of the contract

Section 1. Definition and elements of the contract

Article 8. Definition of contract

A contract is an agreement by means of which two or more parties create, transfer, modify, or extinguish a legal relationship of an economic nature.

Artículo 9. Elementos del contrato

Son elementos esenciales para la formación del contrato el consentimiento, el objeto y la causa.

Article 9. Elements of a contract

Consent, subject-matter, and cause are the essential elements required to form a contract.

Sección 2. De la negociación del contrato

Section 2. Contract negotiation

Artículo 10. Libertad y retiro en las negociaciones

(1) Las partes deben negociar conforme a la buena fe los términos del contrato.
(2) Las partes son libres de negociar los términos del contrato y de retirarse de dichas negociaciones en cualquier momento.

Article 10. Freedom of and withdrawal from negotiation

(1) The parties must negotiate the contractual terms in accordance with good faith.
(2) The parties are free to negotiate the contractual terms and to withdraw from the negotiations at any time.

Artículo 11. Del retiro contrario a la buena fe

(1) El daño causado por el retiro de las negociaciones contrario a las exigencias de la buena fe debe ser indemnizado.
(2) En ningún caso se indemnizará la pérdida de los beneficios esperados del contrato no celebrado.
(3) Está especialmente obligado a esta reparación el que inicia una negociación o se mantiene en ella sin ánimo o posibilidad de contratar.

Article 11. Withdrawal against good faith

(1) Compensation must be provided for the loss caused by withdrawing from negotiations in bad faith.
(2) In no event shall compensation be provided for the loss of expected benefits under a contract that is not concluded.
(3) A party that initiates or continues negotiations when not able or not intending to reach an agreement is specifically required to provide this compensation.

Artículo 12. Deber de confidencialidad

(1) La información confidencial que se haya obtenido en virtud de las negociaciones del contrato no podrá usarse o ser revelada por quien la recibe.
(2) El incumplimiento de este deber obliga a indemnizar los daños y a restituir los beneficios obtenidos.

Article 12. Duty of confidentiality

(1) A party receiving confidential information in the course of negotiating a contract may not use or disclose such confidential information.
(2) Remedy for breach of this duty will include compensation for the losses and restitution of benefits received.

Sección 3. La formación del consentimiento

Section 3. Formation of consent

Artículo 13. Perfeccionamiento del contrato

El contrato se entiende perfeccionado en el momento en que la aceptación produce sus efectos, salvo acuerdo de las partes o ley en contrario.

Article 13. Conclusion of the contract

Contracts are concluded at the time of valid acceptance, unless the parties agree otherwise or unless otherwise provided by law.

Artículo 14. El consentimiento de las partes

El consentimiento de las partes se manifiesta por declaraciones o conductas.

Article 14. Consent of the parties

The consent of the parties is demonstrated by their statements or conduct.

Artículo 15. Definición de oferta

(1) La propuesta de celebrar un contrato constituye oferta si revela la intención del proponente de quedar obligado en caso de aceptación y resulta suficientemente precisa.
(2) La oferta puede ser dirigida a una o más personas determinadas, o al público en general.

Article 15. Definition of offer

(1) A proposal for the conclusion of a contract constitutes an offer if it indicates the intention of the offeror to be bound in case of acceptance and if it is sufficiently definite.
(2) An offer may be made to one or more specific persons or to the public at large.

Artículo 16. Efecto y retiro de la oferta

(1) La oferta produce efectos desde que llega a su destinatario.
(2) La oferta puede retirarse hasta antes de que llegue al destinatario.

Article 16. Effect and withdrawal of offer

(1) An offer becomes effective when it reaches the offeree.
(2) An offer may be withdrawn before it reaches the offeree.

Artículo 17. Revocación de la oferta

(1) La oferta puede revocarse hasta que el destinatario haya enviado su aceptación.
(2) En los casos en que la aceptación consista en una conducta diversa de la declaración, puede revocarse hasta el perfeccionamiento del contrato.

Article 17. Revocation of offer

(1) An offer may be revoked before the offeree has dispatched an acceptance.
(2) If acceptance consists of conduct differing from a declaration of acceptance, it may be revoked until the contract is concluded.

Artículo 18. Oferta irrevocable

(1) La oferta es irrevocable si el oferente le ha atribuido ese carácter, o ha fijado un plazo para la aceptación y el oferente no se reserva expresamente la facultad de revocarla.
(2) Tampoco puede revocarse la oferta si el destinatario ha podido confiar, conforme a la buena fe, en que la oferta era irrevocable.

Article 18. Irrevocable offer

(1) An offer is irrevocable if the offeror has indicated that it is irrevocable or has fixed a time for its acceptance and the offeror does not expressly reserve the power to revoke it.
(2) An offer may not be revoked if the offeree has been able to rely, in good faith, on the offer being irrevocable.

Artículo 19. Caducidad de la oferta

La oferta caduca, aun si es irrevocable, en los siguientes casos:

(1) Si fue rechazada por el destinatario, en el momento en que el rechazo llega al oferente.
(2) Si la respuesta del destinatario contiene adiciones, limitaciones u otras modificaciones que alteran sustancialmente los términos de la oferta.
(3) Si el oferente fallece o se incapacita antes de la recepción de la aceptación.
(4) Si no es aceptada dentro del plazo fijado por el oferente o, en ausencia de plazo, dentro de aquel esperable conforme a la buena fe.

Artículo 20. La aceptación

(1) Constituye aceptación toda declaración u otra conducta del destinatario que indique conformidad con la oferta.
(2) Las modificaciones a la oferta hechas por el destinatario comportan la propuesta de un nuevo contrato.

Artículo 21. El silencio como aceptación

El silencio o la inacción por sí solos no constituyen aceptación, excepto en los casos en que la ley, la voluntad de las partes, los usos y prácticas, o los comportamientos precedentes de las partes, le otorguen tal carácter.

Artículo 22. Efectos de la aceptación

(1) El contrato se perfecciona en el momento en que la aceptación llega al oferente.
(2) Si la aceptación consiste en una conducta, el perfeccionamiento tendrá lugar desde el momento en que el oferente la conoce.

Article 19. Expiration of the offer

The offer will expire in the following cases, even if it is irrevocable:

(1) When rejected by the offeree, at the time the rejection reaches the offeror.
(2) When the offeree's reply contains additions, limitations, or other modifications that materially alter the terms of the offer.
(3) When the offeror dies or is incapacitated prior to receiving the acceptance.
(4) When it is not accepted within the time fixed by the offeror or, if no time is fixed, within a time that may be expected in good faith.

Article 20. Acceptance

(1) Any statement made by or other conduct of the offeree indicating assent to an offer constitutes acceptance.
(2) Modifications to an offer by the offeree constitute the proposal of a new contract.

Article 21. Silence as acceptance

Silence or inactivity does not in itself amount to acceptance, except when it is considered to be an acceptance by operation of law, the intention of the parties, customs and usages, or the prior conduct of the parties.

Article 22. Effects of acceptance

(1) A contract is concluded at the time the acceptance reaches the offeror.
(2) When acceptance consists of conduct, conclusion of the contract will take place at the time the offeror becomes aware of such conduct.

(3) Si en virtud de la oferta, o de las prácticas que las partes hayan establecido entre ellas, el destinatario puede indicar su asentimiento ejecutando un acto sin notificación al oferente, la aceptación surte efectos desde que dicho acto se ejecuta.

(3) If by virtue of the offer or as a result of practices that the parties have established between themselves, the offeree may indicate assent by performing an act without notice to the offeror, acceptance will be effective at the moment the act is performed.

Artículo 23. La oportunidad de la aceptación

(1) La aceptación, cualquiera sea su forma, produce efectos si llega al oferente dentro del término fijado; a falta de plazo, dentro de aquel que resulte conforme a la buena fe, atendidas las circunstancias de la negociación y los medios de comunicación empleados por el oferente.
(2) La aceptación de las ofertas verbales deberá ser inmediata, a menos que de las circunstancias resulte otra cosa.

Article 23. Time of acceptance

(1) Any form of acceptance is effective when it reaches the offeror within the fixed time or, if no time is fixed, within a time period that is in accordance with good faith, having regard to the circumstances of the negotiation and to the means of communication employed by the offeror.
(2) An oral offer must be accepted immediately, unless the circumstances indicate otherwise.

Artículo 24. La aceptación tardía

(1) La aceptación tardía produce efectos cuando el oferente, sin demora, hace llegar su conformidad al destinatario.
(2) Asimismo, produce efectos si de la comunicación escrita que contiene la aceptación tardía se desprende que debería haber llegado al oferente dentro del plazo.

Article 24. Late acceptance

(1) A late acceptance is effective if the offeror immediately notifies the offeree to that effect.
(2) In addition, it is effective if the written communication containing the late acceptance shows that it should have reached the offeror within the fixed time.

Artículo 25. La conformidad con los términos de la oferta

(1) La respuesta a una oferta que contenga adiciones, limitaciones o modificaciones constituye una contraoferta.
(2) Sin embargo, si no alteran sustancialmente los términos de la oferta, la respuesta constituirá una aceptación y el contrato se entenderá perfeccionado con dichas adiciones, limitaciones o modificaciones.

Article 25. Agreement with the terms of the offer

(1) A reply to an offer that contains additions, limitations, or modifications constitutes a counteroffer.
(2) However, if the terms of the offer are not materially altered, the reply constitutes an acceptance, and the contract will be concluded with such additions, limitations, or modifications.

(3) Aunque las limitaciones o modificaciones no alteran sustancialmente los términos de la oferta, la respuesta se entenderá como un rechazo en los siguientes casos:
   (a) Si la oferta expresamente exige la conformidad total o parcial con los términos propuestos.
   (b) Si el oferente, sin demora, informa al destinatario su disconformidad con los cambios.

Artículo 26. El retiro de la aceptación

La aceptación puede ser retirada hasta el momento en que produce efectos.

Sección 4. De los vicios del contrato

Artículo 27. Ámbito de aplicación

Esta sección de los Principios se ocupa de los vicios del contrato por error, dolo, intimidación y excesiva desproporción.

Artículo 28. El error

El error consiste en la ignorancia o falso concepto de los hechos o del derecho, de tal magnitud que una persona razonable y en la misma situación no habría contratado o lo habría hecho en términos sustancialmente distintos.

Artículo 29. Causales de error

(1) El error vicia el contrato:
   (a) Cuando es provocado por información suministrada por la otra parte.
   (b) Cuando la otra parte lo conoció o debió conocerlo y no lo informó, contrariando la buena fe.
   (c) Cuando ambas partes han padecido el mismo error.

(3) Even when the limitations or modifications do not materially alter the terms of the offer, the reply will be understood as a rejection in the following cases:
   (a) When the offer expressly demands full or partial acceptance of the proposed terms.
   (b) When the offeror without delay informs the offeree of its objection to the changes.

Article 26. Withdrawal of acceptance

Acceptance may be withdrawn until the time at which it becomes effective.

Section 4. Defects of the contract

Article 27. Scope of application

This Section of the Principles addresses the defects of contract that arise from mistake, fraud, threat, and gross disparity.

Article 28. Mistake

Mistake means ignorance or an erroneous assumption relating to facts or to law when of such importance that a reasonable person in the same situation would not have concluded the contract or would have done so on significantly different terms.

Article 29. Grounds for mistake

(1) Mistake vitiates a contract when:
   (a) It is caused by information supplied by the other party.
   (b) The other party knew or should have known of the mistake and did not disclose it, against good faith.
   (c) Both parties made the same mistake.

(2) En estos casos hay nulidad si el error es excusable o el riesgo de su existencia no fue o debió ser asumido por quien lo padece.

(2) In these cases, the contract is null if the mistake can be excused or the risk of its existence was not or ought not to have been assumed by the person who made it.

Artículo 30. Impedimento para alegar el error

La parte que incurre en error no puede demandar la nulidad del contrato si la otra ofrece ejecutarlo con las modalidades y el contenido que aquélla entendió celebrarlo.

Article 30. Impediment to invoking mistake

A mistaken party may not claim nullity of the contract if the counterparty offers to perform it in the manner and with the content according to which the mistaken party had intended to form the contract.

Artículo 31. Error en la declaración o en la transmisión

Las disposiciones de los artículos anteriores son aplicables al error en la declaración de voluntad y en su transmisión.

Article 31. Mistake in expression or transmission

The provisions of the foregoing articles apply to mistakes in expressing and transmitting intention.

Artículo 32. El dolo

(1) El dolo es la inducción fraudulenta a la celebración del contrato, por acción u omisión de una de las partes o un tercero.
(2) El dolo vicia el contrato cuando aparece claramente que sin él las partes no habrían contratado y no ha habido dolo recíproco.

Article 32. Fraud

(1) Fraud is the deceitful inducement to conclude a contract by means of an act or omission of a party thereto or of a third party.
(2) Fraud vitiates the contract when it is clear that in its absence the parties would not have concluded the contract and there has been no reciprocal fraud.

Artículo 33. Efectos indemnizatorios del dolo

(1) El autor del dolo debe indemnizar los perjuicios causados.
(2) La parte que al tiempo de la celebración del contrato tuvo conocimiento del dolo de un tercero responde solidariamente.

Article 33. Compensation for fraud

(1) The defrauding party is liable for damages.
(2) The party that was, at the time the contract was concluded, aware of the fraud committed by a third person is jointly and severally liable.

Artículo 34. Intimidación

El contrato puede anularse si una parte fue inducida a celebrarlo mediante la amenaza ilícita de un mal inminente y grave.

Article 34. Threat

A contract may be annulled if a party has been led to conclude it by an unlawful threat of an imminent and serious harm.

Artículo 35. Calificación de la intimidación

Para calificar la intimidación debe atenderse a la edad, al género, a la condición de la persona y a las demás circunstancias que puedan influir sobre su gravedad.

Article 35. Determination of threat

Consideration must be given to the age, gender, personal condition, and other circumstances of the party in question that might have a bearing on the seriousness of the threat.

Artículo 36. Casos que no constituyen intimidación

La amenaza del ejercicio regular de un derecho y el simple temor reverencial no anulan el contrato.

Article 36. Events not constituting threat

Threatening the regular exercise of a right and simple reverential fear are not grounds for annulling a contract.

Artículo 37. Excesiva desproporción

(1) Una parte puede demandar la adaptación del contrato o de cualquiera de sus cláusulas, o su nulidad si otorgan a la otra una ventaja excesiva contraria a las exigencias de la buena fe.
(2) Para calificar esa ventaja se deben tomar en cuenta todas las circunstancias, especialmente la dependencia de la parte que sufre el perjuicio, las extraordinarias dificultades económicas que la aquejan, la apremiante urgencia de sus necesidades, su ignorancia o falta de experiencia.
Igualmente, deberá considerarse la relación de confianza existente entre las partes y la naturaleza y finalidad del contrato.
(3) A solicitud de la parte agraviada, el juez puede adaptar el contrato a fin de ajustarlo al acuerdo que habrían alcanzado las partes conforme a la buena fe.
(4) La parte contra quien se demanda la nulidad puede, igualmente, solicitar su adaptación en los términos del inciso precedente, siempre y cuando haga saber inmediatamente esta decisión a la otra parte.

Article 37. Gross disparity

(1) A party may seek the adaptation of a contract or any of its clauses, or to annul the contract, if it or they give the other party an excessive advantage in contravention of the requirements of good faith.
(2) All circumstances must be taken into account when considering the existence of an advantage, in particular the dependence of the aggrieved party and its extraordinary economic distress, urgent needs, ignorance, or lack of experience.
Likewise, the relationship of trust existing between the parties as well as the nature and purpose of the contract must be taken into consideration.
(3) Upon request of the aggrieved party, the judge may adapt the contract in order to make it consistent with the agreement that would have been reached by the parties in accordance with good faith.
(4) The party against which an action of nullity is brought may also request adaptation in accordance with the previous paragraph, provided it promptly informs the other party of this decision.

Sección 5. Objeto, causa y solemnidades del contrato

Artículo 38. Objeto del contrato

(1) El objeto del contrato debe ser determinado o determinable, posible y lícito.
(2) Es ilícito el prohibido por la ley, contrario a las buenas costumbres o al orden público.

Artículo 39. Causa del contrato y de la obligación

(1) Toda obligación requiere una causa. Aunque no se exprese, se presume que existe mientras no se pruebe lo contrario.
(2) La causa del contrato debe ser lícita.

Artículo 40. Forma y solemnidad

(1) Un contrato será válido, en cuanto a la forma, si cumple con los requisitos establecidos en el derecho que lo rige o con los fijados en el derecho del Estado en que se celebre o con el derecho del lugar de su ejecución.
(2) Si las personas se encuentran en Estados distintos al momento de la celebración del contrato, el lugar de celebración se entenderá como aquel en el cual el contrato se perfecciona, de conformidad con estos Principios.

Capítulo 3. Nulidad del contrato

Artículo 41. Nulidad absoluta y relativa

Los contratos que contravienen la ley, el orden público o las buenas costumbres adolecen de nulidad absoluta. Son de nulidad relativa los contratos a los cuales la ley impone esta sanción sólo en protección del interés de ciertas personas.

Section 5. Subject-matter, cause, and formal requirements of the contract

Article 38. Subject-matter of the contract

(1) The subject-matter of a contract must be ascertained or ascertainable, possible, and lawful.
(2) It is unlawful when it is prohibited by law or when it is contrary to good morals or to public policy.

Article 39. Cause of the contract and obligation

(1) All obligations require a cause. A cause is presumed to exist as long as it is not proven otherwise, even if it is not expressed.
(2) The cause of the contract must be lawful.

Article 40. Form and formal requirements

(1) As to form, a contract is valid when it complies with the requirements of the law that govern it, or the legal requirements of the State in which it is concluded, or the law of the place where it is to be performed.
(2) When persons are located in different States at the time a contract is concluded, the place of conclusion shall be understood as the place where the contract is concluded in accordance with these Principles.

Chapter 3. Nullity of contract

Article 41. Absolute and relative nullity

Contracts that violate the law, public policy, or good morals incur absolute nullity. Contracts deemed null to protect the interests of certain people incur relative nullity.

Artículo 42. Forma de alegar la nulidad

La nulidad puede alegarse por vía de acción o excepción.

Sección 1: Nulidad absoluta

Artículo 43. Legitimación

La nulidad absoluta debe ser pronunciada por el juez, aun sin mediar petición de parte. Puede también ser alegada por cualquier interesado, aunque no haya sido parte en el contrato.

Artículo 44. Imposibilidad de restitución

No habrá lugar a restituciones a favor de quien sabía o debía saber el vicio de nulidad absoluta.

Artículo 45. Imposibilidad de convalidación de la nulidad absoluta

El contrato nulo de nulidad absoluta no puede ser convalidado.

Sección 2: De la nulidad relativa

Artículo 46. Legitimación

La nulidad relativa sólo puede ser alegada por las personas en cuyo beneficio se establece. Puede ser saneada por convalidación del contrato y por la prescripción de la acción.

Artículo 47. Nulidad total o parcial

(1) Si se pronuncia la nulidad de una o varias cláusulas de un contrato, éste subsistirá con las restantes, a menos que por la naturaleza misma del contrato, o la intención original de los contratantes, ello no fuere posible. En este último caso, el juez debe pronunciar la nulidad íntegra del contrato.

(2) En la nulidad parcial, en caso de ser necesario, el tribunal podrá adaptar el contrato observando las exigencias de la buena fe.

Article 42. Invoking nullity

Nullity may be invoked through an action or a defence.

Section 1. Absolute nullity

Article 43. Standing

Absolute nullity must be determined by a court, and may be undertaken at the court's own initiative. It may also be invoked by any interested party, even when such party is not party to the contract.

Article 44. Restitution not possible

There is no restitution for the party who knew or should have known of the contractual defect of absolute nullity.

Article 45. Confirmation under absolute nullity not possible

An absolutely-null contract cannot be confirmed.

Section 2. Relative nullity

Article 46. Standing

Relative nullity may only be invoked by the person for whose benefit it is established. It may be cured by confirming the contract and by prescription of the action.

Article 47. Total or partial nullity

(1) Where one or more individual terms of a contract are found to be null, the remaining terms of the contract will continue in effect, unless this is not possible due to the nature of the contract or the original intention of the parties. In the event of the latter, a court must rule on the nullity of the entire contract.

(2) As to partial nullity, if necessary, a court may adapt the contract in accordance with the requirements of good faith.

Artículo 48. Convalidación

(1) Hay convalidación cuando el contratante que puede demandar la nulidad relativa manifiesta expresa o tácitamente su voluntad de tener al contrato por válido. El acto de convalidación no requiere la conformidad de la otra parte.
(2) El contrato convalidado se entiende válido desde su celebración y, en ningún caso perjudica a terceros de buena fe.

Article 48. Confirmation

(1) The party with the right to invoke relative nullity may confirm the contract by expressly or implicitly expressing its intention to uphold the contract as valid. The act of validation does not require the consent of the other party.
(2) The confirmed contract will be understood as valid as of its formation and in no way will it impair third parties in good faith.

Artículo 49. Opción con los medios de tutela

La parte que tenga derecho a demandar la nulidad del contrato y, al mismo tiempo, pueda ejercer alguno de los medios de tutela por incumplimiento, podrá optar entre aquella y éstos.

Article 49. Option with the means of relief

The party with the right to invoke the nullity of the contract or exercise one of the means of relief for non-performance may choose between these options.

Sección 3. De los efectos de la nulidad

Section 3. Effects of nullity

Artículo 50. Efectos de la nulidad

(1) La nulidad producirá la extinción del contrato.
(2) Anulado el contrato, los contratantes deberán restituirse recíprocamente las prestaciones que hubieran recibido en virtud del mismo. Si la devolución en especie no es posible deberá restituirse su valor.

Article 50. Effects of nullity

(1) The nullity results in the extinction of the contract.
(2) Once a contract has been nullified, the parties must reciprocally make restitution of that which they would have received under the contract. If restitution in kind is not possible, restitution of the value thereof must be made.

Artículo 51. Suspensión de las restituciones

Mientras uno de los contratantes no cumpla con la restitución a la que está obligado, no puede el otro ser compelido a cumplir por su parte lo que le incumba.

Article 51. Suspension of restitution

A party shall not be compelled to comply with its restitutionary obligations whilst the other party does not comply with its own restitutionary obligations.

Artículo 52. Efecto respecto de terceros

La nulidad es oponible a los terceros, salvo cuando hayan adquirido a título oneroso y se encuentren de buena fe.

Article 52. Effect on third persons

Nullity may be upheld against third persons, except when they have acquired rights through the payment of valuable consideration and in good faith.

Capítulo 4. De la simulación

Artículo 53. La simulación entre las partes

La declaración privada de los contratantes disconforme con lo convenido en forma ostensible podrá hacerse valer por cualquiera de ellas.

Artículo 54. Los terceros y la simulación

(1) Los terceros de buena fe podrán hacer valer la declaración privada o lo convenido en forma ostensible según su conveniencia.
(2) Los terceros podrán pedir la declaración de simulación en la medida en que la declaración simulada afecte sus intereses.
(3) En caso de conflicto entre terceros serán preferidos aquellos de buena fe que hagan valer el acto ostensible.

Capítulo 5: Efectos del contrato frente a terceros.

Sección 1. Representación (pendiente)

Sección 2. Estipulación a favor de otro

Artículo 60. Ámbito de aplicación

(1) Cualquiera puede estipular a favor de una tercera persona y tanto el estipulante como el beneficiario pueden demandar lo estipulado.
(2) Si el tercero rechaza el beneficio, se considera que nunca adquirió el derecho.

Artículo 61. Derecho de revocación

(1) El estipulante puede revocar la estipulación o sustituir al tercero mientras éste no haya aceptado. La aceptación del beneficiario hace irrevocable la prestación.

Chapter 4. Simulation

Article 53. Simulation between the parties

A private declaration by the parties that is inconsistent with that which they have overtly contracted for may be enforced by either party.

Article 54. Simulation and third persons

(1) Third persons in good faith may enforce the private declaration or that which they have apparently contracted for, at their discretion.
(2) Third persons may seek a declaration of simulation to the extent the declaration affects their interests.
(3) In the event of a dispute between third persons, preference will be given to the third persons in good faith that enforce the overt act.

Chapter 5. Effects of a contract on third persons

Section 1. Agency (pending)

Section 2. Contracts in favour of third parties

Article 60. Scope of application

(1) Any party may contract in favour of a third party, and both the promisee and the beneficiary may demand what has been contracted.
(2) If the third party renounces the benefit, it will be considered as having never acquired the right.

Article 61. Right of revocation

(1) The promisee may revoke the contract or substitute the third party as long as the third party has not accepted it. The acceptance of the beneficiary renders the right conferred irrevocable.

(2) En caso de revocación o de falta de aceptación, la prestación quedará a favor del estipulante a no ser que del contrato resulte otra cosa.

Artículo 62. Excepciones

El promitente puede oponer al tercero todas las excepciones que se funden en el contrato celebrado con el estipulante.

Sección 3. Promesa del hecho ajeno

Artículo 63. Promesa del hecho ajeno

El que ha prometido la obligación o el hecho de un tercero, está obligado a indemnizar al otro contratante si el tercero rehúsa obligarse o no cumple el hecho prometido.

Capítulo 6. Interpretación

Artículo 64. Intención común de las partes

Conocida claramente la intención de las partes se estará más a ella que a lo literal de las palabras.

Artículo 65. Criterios para la determinación de la intención común de las partes

Para determinar la común intención de las partes se tendrán en cuenta, entre otros criterios:

(a) Las reglas de interpretación acordadas por las partes.
(b) La conducta de las partes durante la etapa de formación del contrato.
(c) La ejecución del contrato por las partes o de una de ellas con aprobación de la otra.
(d) Los comportamientos anteriores, concomitantes o posteriores de las mismas partes en otros contratos sobre la misma materia.

(2) In the event of revocation or of lack of acceptance, the right will remain with the promisee, unless the contract indicates otherwise.

Article 62. Defences

The promisor may assert against the third party all defences arising out of the contract concluded with the promisee.

Section 3. Promise that the third party will do something

Article 63. Promise that the third party will do something

A party that has promised that a third party will assume an obligation or do something will be liable for compensating the counterparty if the third party refuses to be bound or does not comply with the promised obligation.

Chapter 6. Interpretation

Article 64. Common intention of the parties

Once the intention of the parties is clearly known, it will prevail over the literal meaning of their words.

Article 65. Criteria for determining the common intention of the parties

When determining the common intention of the parties, regard shall be had, among others, to the following criteria:

(a) The rules of interpretation agreed upon by the parties.
(b) The conduct of the parties during the formation of the contract.
(c) The performance of the contract by the parties or performance by one party with the approval of the other party.
(d) Prior, concurrent, or subsequent conduct of the same parties in other contracts of the same nature.

(e) La naturaleza y el objeto del contrato.
(f) Los usos del lugar de la celebración del contrato.

(e) The nature and subject-matter of the contract.
(f) The usages of the place where the contract is concluded.

Artículo 66. Significado de las palabras

Las palabras técnicas de toda ciencia o arte se tomarán en el sentido que les den los que profesan la misma ciencia o arte; a menos que aparezca claramente que se han tomado en sentido diverso.

Article 66. Meaning of words

Technical words and terms of art shall have the meaning assigned to them by those practising in the respective field, unless it is evident they have been assigned a different meaning.

Artículo 67. Interpretación sistemática

Las cláusulas del contrato se interpretarán las unas por las otras, de forma de darles el sentido que más convenga al contrato en su totalidad.

Article 67. Systematic interpretation

The clauses of a contract shall be interpreted one by another, so as to give them the meaning that most conforms to the contract in its entirety.

Artículo 68. Conservación del contrato

El sentido en que una cláusula puede producir algún efecto, deberá preferirse a aquel en que no sea capaz de producir efecto alguno.

Article 68. Upholding the contract

The interpretation of a clause that is able to produce some effect shall be preferred to the interpretation of a clause that is not capable of producing any effect.

Artículo 69. Cláusulas ambiguas

(1) Las cláusulas ambiguas se interpretan a favor de la parte que contrató bajo la influencia dominante de la otra, teniendo en consideración para esta calificación la dependencia de la parte que sufre el perjuicio, las extraordinarias dificultades económicas que la aquejan, la apremiante urgencia de sus necesidades, su ignorancia, falta de experiencia o de habilidad en la negociación.
(2) En los demás casos, las cláusulas se interpretarán en el sentido que favorezca el equilibrio contractual.

Article 69. Ambiguous clauses

(1) Ambiguous clauses shall be interpreted in favour of the party that has contracted under the dominant influence of the other party, taking into consideration the dependence of the affected party, its extraordinary economic distress, its imperative urgent needs, its ignorance, its lack of experience, or its lack of bargaining skill.
(2) In all other cases, clauses shall be interpreted in favour of contractual equilibrium.

Artículo 70. Cláusulas no bilateralmente negociadas

Las cláusulas no bilateralmente negociadas deberán interpretarse contra la parte que las hubiera propuesto.

Article 70. Clauses not negotiated bilaterally

Clauses not negotiated bilaterally shall be interpreted against the party that proposed them.

Artículo 71. Interpretación conforme a la buena fe

En todo caso el contrato deberá ser interpretado de acuerdo con la buena fe.

Capítulo 7. Cumplimiento de las obligaciones contractuales

Artículo 72. Concepto de Cumplimiento

Cumplimiento es la ejecución de la prestación en los términos en que fue acordada.

Artículo 73. Lugar del cumplimiento

(1) La obligación debe cumplirse en el lugar determinado en el contrato o que sea determinable conforme a éste.
(2) El lugar de cumplimiento puede ser establecido por acuerdo de las partes, de manera expresa o tácita.
(3) Si la regla precedente no resulta aplicable, lugar de cumplimiento es:
  (a) El domicilio del acreedor, para las obligaciones dinerarias.
  (b) El lugar en que se encontraba la cosa al tiempo de constituirse la obligación, para las obligaciones cuyo objeto es una especie o cuerpo cierto.
  (c) El domicilio del deudor, para los demás casos.

Si el deudor se muda, el acreedor tiene derecho a exigir el pago en el domicilio actual o en el anterior. Igual opción corresponde al deudor, cuando el lugar de pago sea el domicilio del acreedor.

Artículo 74. Momento del cumplimiento

(1) La obligación debe cumplirse en el momento determinado en el contrato o que resulte de éste, de su naturaleza, los usos o la buena fe.

Article 71. Interpretation in accordance with good faith

Contracts shall always be interpreted in accordance with good faith.

Chapter 7. Performance of contractual obligations

Article 72. Performance defined

Performance is the fulfilment of an obligation according to its terms.

Article 73. Place of performance

(1) An obligation must be performed at the place fixed by or determinable from the contract.
(2) The place of performance may be expressly or implicitly agreed upon by the parties.
(3) If the previous rule does not apply, the place of performance shall be:
  (a) For monetary obligations, at the address of the obligee.
  (b) For obligations, the subject-matter of which are specific goods, at the place where the goods were located when the obligation was concluded.
  (c) For all other obligations, at the address of the obligor.

If the obligor moves, the obligee has the right to demand payment at the current or previous address. The obligor has the same option when the place of payment is the address of the obligee.

Article 74. Time of performance

(1) An obligation must be performed at the time fixed by or resulting from the contract, its nature, usages, or good faith.

(2) Si no fuere posible establecer el momento de cumplimiento de acuerdo con esas pautas, se estará a las siguientes reglas:
   (a) Si puede ejecutarse inmediatamente, su cumplimiento tendrá lugar en el más breve plazo posible desde que se contrajo.
   (b) Si por su naturaleza supone necesariamente un lapso para su ejecución, su cumplimiento tendrá lugar en el más breve plazo posible desde que se contrajo.

(2) If it is not possible to fix the time of performance in accordance with these rules, the following rules shall apply:
   (a) If performance can take place immediately, it shall take place within the shortest time possible after the conclusion of the contract.
   (b) If a lapse of time is required due to the nature of the performance, it shall be performed within the shortest time possible after the conclusion of the contract.

Artículo 75. Cumplimiento anticipado

(1) El deudor puede anticipar el cumplimiento, a menos que perjudique gravemente los intereses de la otra parte. El cumplimiento anticipado de una obligación no afecta la ejecución de la obligación recíproca.
(2) El acreedor puede renunciar al plazo establecido en su favor.

Article 75. Earlier performance

(1) The obligor may perform early, unless this seriously harms the interests of the other party. Earlier performance of an obligation does not affect the performance of the reciprocal obligation.
(2) The obligee may waive the lapse of time established in its favour.

Artículo 76. Exigibilidad anticipada de la obligación

El cumplimiento de la obligación no puede exigirse antes de expirar el plazo, excepto:

(a) Al deudor constituido en quiebra o que se halla en notoria insolvencia.
(b) Al deudor que no ha constituido las garantías prometidas o que disminuye por hecho imputable las seguridades otorgadas.
(c) Cuando el plazo esté establecido sólo en favor del acreedor.

Article 76. Early enforceability of an obligation

Performance of an obligation may not be demanded prior to the lapse of the time agreed, except:

(a) Of an obligor declared bankrupt or insolvent.
(b) Of an obligor that has not established the promised guarantees or that effects a reduction in the security granted due to a cause attributable to the obligor.
(c) When the time period is only fixed in favour of the obligee.

Artículo 77. Cumplimiento por un tercero

La prestación también puede ser ejecutada por un tercero, excepto que se hayan tenido en cuenta las condiciones especiales del deudor, o hubiere oposición conjunta del acreedor y del deudor. Tercer interesado es la persona a quien el incumplimiento del deudor puede causar un menoscabo patrimonial y puede pagar contra la oposición individual o conjunta del acreedor y del deudor.

Article 77. Performance by third person

Performance may also be carried out by a third person, except when special conditions of the obligor have been considered or the obligee and obligor both oppose this. An interested third party is a person for whom the failure of the obligor to perform may cause monetary damage and who may pay even if either the obligee or the obligor, or both oppose it.

Artículo 78. Gastos

(1) Salvo acuerdo en contrario, cada parte debe soportar los gastos del cumplimiento de su obligación.
(2) Si el acreedor ha incurrido en mora corresponde a éste soportar los gastos que deriven de ella.

Article 78. Costs

(1) Unless otherwise agreed, each party shall bear the costs of performing its obligation.
(2) An obligee is liable for the costs arising out of a default attributable to it.

Capítulo 8. Incumplimiento de las obligaciones contractuales

Chapter 8. Non-performance of contractual obligations

Sección 1. Del Incumplimiento en general

Section 1. Non-performance in general

Artículo 79. Concepto de incumplimiento

(1) Incumplimiento es la falta de ejecución de la prestación en la forma pactada.
(2) El cumplimiento imperfecto comprende toda disconformidad entre lo acordado y lo ejecutado por el deudor.
(3) El incumplimiento del deudor comprende el hecho de las personas que emplee para ejecutar su prestación.
(4) Si el incumplimiento no es imputable al deudor no habrá lugar a indemnización

Article 79. Non-performance defined

(1) Non-performance is a failure to perform in the agreed manner.
(2) Defective performance includes all forms of non-conformity between that which was agreed and that which was performed by the obligor.
(3) Non-performance by the obligor includes the persons it employs to perform the obligation.
(4) There shall be no grounds for damages if non-performance is not attributable to the obligor.

Artículo 80. Carácter esencial del incumplimiento

Se entiende que el incumplimiento es esencial cuando:

(a) Las partes así lo han acordado respecto de obligaciones determinadas o de supuestos específicos de incumplimiento.

Article 80. Fundamental non-performance

Non-performance shall be understood as fundamental when:

(a) The parties have agreed that it is with respect to specific obligations or specific events of non-performance.

(b) El incumplimiento es doloso.
(c) La conducta del deudor incumplidor, hace perder razonablemente al acreedor la confianza en el cumplimiento posterior del contrato.
(d) Prive sustancialmente al acreedor de aquello que podía esperar de acuerdo con lo que era previsible para las partes, al momento de celebrarse el contrato.

(b) The non-performance is intentional.
(c) The conduct of the non-performing party gives the obligee reason to believe that it cannot rely on the other party's future performance.
(d) It substantially deprives the obligee of what it was entitled to expect according to that which was foreseeable for the parties at the time the contract was concluded.

Artículo 81. Acción u omisión del acreedor

El acreedor no puede invocar el incumplimiento causado por su propia acción u omisión

Article 81. Acts or omissions of the obligee

The obligee may not invoke non-performance due to its own acts or omissions.

Artículo 82. Fuerza mayor o caso fortuito

Fuerza mayor o caso fortuito es un hecho ajeno al control del deudor que, sin ser un riesgo a su cargo, le impide cumplir la obligación, temporal o definitivamente, y cuyo acaecimiento y efectos no ha podido resistir.

Article 82. *Force majeure* or acts of God

Force majeure or an act of God is an event beyond the control of the obligor whose risk has not been assumed by the obligor, that temporarily or permanently impedes it from performing an obligation, and the occurrence and effects of which it could not have avoided.

Artículo 83. Imposibilidad total o parcial de cumplimiento

(1) La imposibilidad sobreviniente total y definitiva para cumplir una obligación contractual, causada por caso fortuito, extingue la obligación y libera al deudor. En tal caso, el acreedor podrá optar por resolver el contrato o reclamar la cesión de los derechos y acciones que, a raíz de la imposibilidad, el deudor tenía contra un tercero.

Article 83. Total or partial impossibility of performance

(1) The total and final supervening impossibility of performing a contractual obligation due to an act of God extinguishes the obligation and releases the obligor. In this event, the obligee may choose to terminate the contract or require the assignment of the rights and actions that, due to the impossibility, the obligor held against a third party.

(2) Si la imposibilidad es parcial o temporal, el acreedor puede, respectivamente, suspender la contraprestación o reducirla en una proporción equivalente, salvo si, como consecuencia de la imposibilidad, se ve privado de aquello que podía sustancialmente esperar de acuerdo con lo que era previsible para las partes, al momento de celebrarse el contrato. En este último supuesto, regirá la opción prevista en el punto (1).

(2) When the impossibility is partial or temporary, the obligee may suspend performance or reduce it by an equal proportion, respectively, unless, as a result of the impossibility, the obligee is substantially deprived of what it was entitled to expect according to that which was foreseeable for the parties at the time the contract was concluded. In the event of the latter, the option set forth in paragraph (1) shall apply.

Sección 2. Medios de tutela del acreedor

Section 2. Means of relief for the obligee

Artículo 84. De los medios de tutela

(1) En caso de incumplimiento, el acreedor podrá ejercer, a su elección y según proceda, alguno de los siguientes medios de tutela:
- (a) cumplimiento específico;
- (b) reducción del precio;
- (c) resolución del contrato;
- (d) excepción de contrato no cumplido; e
- (e) indemnización de daños

(2) La indemnización de los daños podrá ejercerse de manera autónoma, o en conjunto con los demás medios de tutela.

Article 84. Means of relief

(1) In the event of non-performance, the obligee may, at its discretion and as appropriate, exercise one of the following means of relief for the non-performance:
- (a) specific performance;
- (b) price reduction;
- (c) termination of the contract;
- (d) defence of the unperformed contract; and
- (e) damages.

(2) Damages may be claimed separately or in conjunction with the remaining means of relief.

Artículo 85. Comunicación en los cumplimientos imperfectos

(1) En caso de cumplimiento imperfecto, el acreedor deberá comunicar la disconformidad en un plazo razonable contado desde el momento en que debió tener conocimiento.

(2) A falta de comunicación, el acreedor no podrá exigir el cumplimiento, ni resolver el contrato.

Article 85. Notice of defective performance

(1) In the event of defective performance, the obligee shall give notice of the non-conforming performance within a reasonable time after it should have become aware of it.

(2) If notice is not given, the obligee may not demand performance or terminate the contract.

Artículo 86. Cumplimiento específico

(1) El cumplimiento específico procede siempre en las obligaciones dinerarias.
(2) Tratándose de obligaciones no dinerarias, el cumplimiento específico se sujeta a las limitaciones siguientes:
  (a) No procede cuando el cumplimiento sea imposible. Sin embargo, el acreedor puede exigir al deudor la cesión de las acciones y derechos que tuviere contra terceros;
  (b) Aun siendo posible el cumplimiento específico, éste no procede cuando resultare extremadamente gravoso para el deudor, teniendo en cuenta que el acreedor puede satisfacer su interés con otro medio de tutela.
  (c) No procede tampoco cuando su ejecución signifique una afectación a la dignidad de la persona.

Article 86. Specific performance

(1) Specific performance can always be demanded for monetary obligations.
(2) In the case of non-monetary obligations, specific performance is subject to the following limitations:
  (a) It may not be demanded when performance is impossible. However, the obligee may require that the non-performing party assign its rights and actions against third parties.
  (b) Even though it is possible, specific performance may not be demanded when it is extremely burdensome for the obligor, taking into consideration that the obligee may satisfy its interest by choosing another means of relief.
  (c) Further, it may not be demanded when it represents an injury to personal dignity.

Artículo 87. Reparación y sustitución en los cumplimientos imperfectos

(1) Tratándose de cumplimientos imperfectos, el cumplimiento específico comprende, con las mismas limitaciones del artículo anterior, la reparación o la corrección de la falta de conformidad o la sustitución.
(2) La sustitución requiere siempre el incumplimiento esencial.

Article 87. Repair and replacement of defective performance

(1) Regarding defective performance, specific performance includes the repair or cure of the non-conformity or replacement, subject to the limitations contained in the previous article.
(2) Replacement always requires fundamental non-performance.

Artículo 88. Reducción del precio

(1) En caso de cumplimiento imperfecto, el acreedor puede aceptarlo y reducir el precio en proporción a la diferencia entre el valor que la prestación ejecutada tenía al tiempo en que se realizó y el que habría tenido en ese mismo momento, si hubiere existido cumplimiento.

Article 88. Price reduction

(1) In the event of defective performance, the obligee may accept this and reduce the price in proportion with the difference between the value of the performance at the time it was carried out and the value it would have had at that same time if the performance had occurred.

(2) La reducción del precio es incompatible con la indemnización del menor valor de la prestación.
(3) En todo caso, el acreedor puede demandar la indemnización de cualquier otro daño.

(2) Reduction in price is not compatible with compensation for reduction in the value of performance.
(3) In any event, the obligee may demand compensation for any other damages.

Artículo 89. Resolución por incumplimiento

(1) Cualquiera de las partes de un contrato puede resolverlo cuando la otra haya incurrido en un incumplimiento esencial.
(2) El incumplimiento recíproco no obsta a la resolución del contrato.
(3) La resolución puede ser judicial o por comunicación.

Article 89. Termination due to non-performance

(1) Any party to a contract may terminate it when the other party incurs fundamental non-performance.
(2) Reciprocal non-performance shall not prevent the termination of the contract.
(3) A contract may be terminated by a court or by notice.

Artículo 90. Resolución por comunicación.

La resolución opera mediante comunicación escrita a la otra parte, la que producirá efectos desde su recepción.

Article 90. Termination by notice

Termination exercised by written notice to the other party shall be effective upon receipt.

Artículo 91. De los efectos de la resolución

La resolución extingue los efectos del contrato. Así y todo, no afecta las cláusulas que las partes hayan previsto para la resolución de controversias o las relativas al incumplimiento mismo, tales como cláusulas penales, exonerativas o limitativas de responsabilidad.

Article 91. Effects of termination

Termination extinguishes the effects of a contract. Notwithstanding, it does not affect the clauses agreed to by the parties for the settlement of disputes or those related to non-performance itself, such as penalty clauses, exemption clauses, or clauses limiting liability.

Artículo 92. Efectos restitutorios

(1) Resuelto el contrato, deberán restituirse, de manera simultánea, las prestaciones ya ejecutadas, junto con los frutos percibidos.
(2) No proceden las restituciones respecto de prestaciones divisibles que han sido cumplidas recíprocamente con anterioridad a la resolución.

Article 92. Effects of restitution

(1) On termination of the contract, concurrent restitution shall be made for performance that has taken place and any fruits received.
(2) Restitutions of divisible performance reciprocally carried out prior to termination cannot take place.

Artículo 93. Imposibilidad de restitución

(1) Para el caso que no sea posible la restitución, pese a la diligencia del obligado a restituir, tendrá derecho al valor de la prestación, fijado al momento de la imposibilidad. Si por el contrario, tal imposibilidad es imputable al deudor de restitución, el acreedor tendrá derecho a que el primero le deje indemne.
(2) Ambas partes podrán optar por exigir a la otra la cesión de derechos o acciones que tuviere en contra de terceros respecto de la destrucción o pérdida del objeto.
(3) No habrá lugar a la restitución del valor si la parte que resolvió el contrato prueba que la pérdida de la prestación se produjo a pesar de haber actuado con la debida diligencia.

Article 93. Restitution not possible

(1) When restitution is not possible, in spite of the diligence exercised by the obligor, the obligee shall be entitled to the value of the performance fixed at the time of impossibility. However, when such impossibility is attributed to the obligor, the obligee shall first be entitled to full compensation.
(2) Each party may choose to demand that the other assign its rights or actions against third parties regarding the destruction or loss of the subject-matter.
(3) Restitution of value shall not take place if the party that terminated the contract proves that the loss of performance took place in spite of having acted with proper diligence.

Artículo 94. Cláusulas resolutorias

(1) Las partes podrán incorporar al contrato cláusulas que confieran al acreedor la facultad de resolverlo, siempre y cuando especifiquen los incumplimientos que darían lugar a esta resolución.
(2) Estas cláusulas no privan al acreedor de la posibilidad de optar por cualesquiera de los otros medios de tutela.

Article 94. Termination clauses

(1) The parties may incorporate into the contract clauses that provide the aggrieved party with the power to terminate it, provided they specify which non-performances give rise to termination.
(2) These clauses shall not deprive the aggrieved party of the possibility to choose any other means of relief.

Artículo 95. Excepción de contrato no cumplido

Cada parte puede negarse a ejecutar su prestación si la otra no ejecuta la suya, a menos que por la naturaleza del contrato o por acuerdo de las partes el cumplimiento de una deba anteceder al de la otra.

Article 95. Defence of the unperformed contract

Each party may refuse to perform if the other does not perform, unless performance by one must take place prior to performance by the other due to the nature of the contract or an agreement between the parties.

Artículo 96. Suspensión del cumplimiento

Asimismo, puede negarse cuando, antes de la fecha de cumplimiento, el deudor ha sufrido un menoscabo significativo en su aptitud para cumplir, o en su solvencia. La suspensión cesa si el deudor cumple o da seguridades suficientes para el cumplimiento.

Article 96. Suspension of performance

In addition, it may be refused when, prior to the date of performance, the non-performing party suffers a significant impairment to its ability to perform or to its solvency. Suspension shall cease if the non-performing party performs or adequately guarantees performance.

Artículo 97. Indemnización de daños

(1) En todos los casos en que el incumplimiento cause daños, y siempre que no haya fuerza mayor el acreedor podrá pedir su indemnización.
(2) Son causa de exoneración las circunstancias que constituyen caso fortuito, sean sus efectos permanentes o temporales.

Article 97. Damages

(1) For all events in which non-performance results in damages, excepting *force majeure*, the obligee may request compensation.
(2) Acts of God are grounds for exemption, whether their effects are temporary or permanent.

Artículo 98. Daños indemnizables

La indemnización de daños comprende el daño patrimonial y extrapatrimonial.

Article 98. Damages subject to compensation

The recovery of damages covers monetary and non-monetary harm.

Artículo 99. Intereses e indemnización de perjuicios

El incumplimiento de una obligación dineraria obliga el deudor al pago de los intereses, sin perjuicio de la indemnización de otros daños.

Article 99. Interest and damages

Non-performance of a monetary obligation requires the obligor to pay interest, notwithstanding compensation for other harm.

Artículo 100. De la previsibilidad del daño indemnizable

(1) El deudor responderá de los daños previsibles al tiempo de celebración del contrato y que provengan del incumplimiento.
(2) En caso de dolo o culpa grave, el deudor responderá de todos los daños que sean consecuencia del incumplimiento.

Article 100. Foreseeability of harm

(1) The non-performing party shall be liable for harm it could have foreseen at the time of the conclusion of the contract and that results from its non-performance.
(2) In the event of fraud or gross negligence, the obligor shall be liable for all harm that results from its non-performance.

Artículo 101. Contribución del acreedor a su daño

La indemnización queda sujeta a reducción si el acreedor, con su acción u omisión, contribuyó al incumplimiento.

Article 101. Contribution of the obligee to its harm

Compensation is subject to reduction when the obligee has contributed to the non-performance by way of its acts or omissions.

Artículo 102. Mitigación de las pérdidas

(1) La indemnización queda sujeta a reducción si el acreedor omitió adoptar las medidas que, de acuerdo con la buena fe, eran razonables para mitigar las pérdidas. La reducción corresponderá a la cuantía en que hubiere podido mitigarse el daño.
(2) El acreedor, en todo caso, tendrá derecho a la indemnización de lo que haya invertido en la mitigación de las pérdidas.

Article 102. Mitigation of loss

(1) Compensation is subject to reduction when the obligee has failed to take reasonable measures to mitigate loss in good faith. Reduction shall correspond to the amount by which the loss could have been mitigated.
(2) In any event, the aggrieved party will be entitled to compensation for what it has allocated towards mitigating the loss.

Artículo 103. Resolución e indemnización de perjuicios.

Si el acreedor opta por la resolución y celebra en términos razonables con un tercero un contrato de reemplazo sobre el mismo objeto, tiene derecho a la indemnización de la diferencia de precio entre ambos contratos, sin perjuicio de la indemnización de otros daños según las reglas precedentes.

Article 103. Termination and damages

If the aggrieved party terminates the contract and concludes in reasonable terms a substitute contract on the same subject-matter with a third person, the aggrieved party may claim compensation for the price difference between both contracts, without regard to compensation of any other harm according to the preceding rules.

Sección 3. Pactos relativos a la responsabilidad por incumplimiento

Section 3. Agreements regarding liability for non-performance

Artículo 104. Cláusula penal

Las partes pueden incorporar al contrato una cláusula penal, la cual libera al acreedor de la prueba del daño.

Article 104. Penalty clause

The parties may incorporate a penalty clause into the contract that will release the aggrieved party from proof of harm.

Artículo 105. Opción entre cláusula penal e indemnización

El acreedor no podrá escoger entre demandar la pena o la indemnización de los daños, salvo pacto en contrario.

Article 105. Choice between penalty clause and compensation

The obligee may not choose between claiming a penalty and damages, unless otherwise agreed.

Artículo 106. Cumplimiento específico y pena.

El acreedor no puede pedir el cumplimiento de la obligación y la pena, sino una de las dos cosas, a su arbitrio, a menos que se haya estipulado la pena por el simple retardo, o que se haya estipulado que por el pago de la pena no se entienda extinguida la obligación.

Article 106. Specific performance and penalties

The obligee may not request both the performance of the obligation and the penalty. It may only request one of these, at its discretion, unless a penalty is provided for simple delay or it is agreed that the obligation will not be understood as extinguished for payment of the penalty.

Artículo 107. Modificación de la pena

A petición de parte o de oficio, el juez podrá alterar el monto de la pena, cuando éste resulte manifiestamente excesivo o irrisorio.

Article 107. Modification of the penalty

A court may, upon request by a party or on its own initiative, modify the amount of the penalty when it is manifestly excessive or derisory.

Artículo 108. Rebaja por cumplimiento parcial

Si el deudor cumple solamente una parte de la obligación y el acreedor acepta esa parte, tendrá derecho para que se rebaje proporcionalmente la pena estipulada por la falta de cumplimiento de la obligación.

Article 108. Reduction due to partial performance

If the obligor only performs part of an obligation and the obligee accepts such part, it will be entitled to proportionally reduce the agreed penalty for non-performance of the obligation.

Artículo 109. Compatibilidad de la pena y los medios de tutela

La pena será compatible con los medios de tutela establecidos para el incumplimiento.

Article 109. Compatibility between penalties and means of relief

The penalty shall be compatible with the means of relief established for the non-performance.

Artículo 110. De las arras

(1) Cualquiera de las partes pueden, al tiempo del contrato, entregar una cosa para asegurar el cumplimiento de sus obligaciones.
(2) Mediante este pacto se estiman anticipadamente los perjuicios que se puedan derivar del incumplimiento y se libera al acreedor de la carga de probar el daño.
(3) El acreedor tendrá derecho a conservar las arras en caso de incumplimiento. Si quien incumple es quien las recibió, deberá restituirlas dobladas.

Article 110. Earnest money

(1) Any of the parties may, at the time the contract is concluded, deliver something to guarantee the performance of its obligations.
(2) Through this agreement, the harm that might result from non-performance is estimated and the obligee is released from proof of harm.
(3) The obligee will be entitled to keep the earnest money in the event of non-performance. If the obligor is the party that received the earnest money, it shall repay the amount multiplied by two.

(4) En caso de cumplimiento, las arras se imputarán al precio si la naturaleza de la prestación lo permite y, en caso contrario, se restituirán.
(5) El acreedor no puede demandar al mismo tiempo las arras, la indemnización de los daños y la cláusula penal, sino cualquiera de las tres.

(4) In the event of performance, the earnest money shall be applied to the price if permissible in accordance with the nature of the performance; otherwise, it shall be returned.
(5) The aggrieved party may not concurrently invoke earnest money, damages, and a penalty clause; it must choose one of the three.

Artículo 111. Cláusulas que limitan o excluyen la responsabilidad

Pueden las partes incorporar al contrato cláusulas que limiten o excluyan su responsabilidad, con las siguientes excepciones:

(a) que se trate de un incumplimiento por dolo o culpa grave;
(b) no puede exonerarse de responsabilidad por los daños derivados de la lesión a la persona del acreedor;
(c) no puede excluirse o limitarse el derecho a reclamar la prestación, ni su valor; y
(d) no serán válidas las cláusulas que contraríen la buena fe, considerando para ello especialmente el precio y la naturaleza del objeto del contrato en que se incorporan.

Article 111. Limitation and exemption clauses

The parties may incorporate into the contract clauses that limit or exclude their liability, except in the following cases:

(a) with regard to non-performance due to fraud or gross negligence;
(b) with regard to liability for harm derived from injury to the aggrieved party's person;
(c) with regard to the right to require performance or the value thereof that cannot be limited or excluded; and
(d) clauses contrary to good faith shall not be valid, having regard in particular to the price and nature of the subject-matter of the contract into which they are being incorporated.

INDEX